T0110841

House of Versace

the untold
story
of genius,
murder,
and survival

House of Versace

Deborah Ball

Three Rivers Press • New York

Photo credits in order of appearance: Luca Bruno/Associated Press;
Dave Benett/Getty Images; Astrid Stawiarz/Getty Images; Luca Bruno/
Associated Press; Associated Press; Alessandra Tarantino/Associated Press;
Gill Allen/Associated Press; Vittoriano Rastelli/Corbis; Dave Benett/Getty
Images; Luca Bruno/Associated Press; Andrew Savulich/Associated Press;
Seth Wenig/Associated Press; Fantini Mosiaci (last three photos).

Library of Congress Cataloging-in-Publication Data
Ball, Deborah.
House of Versace / Deborah Ball.
p.   cm.
Includes index.
1. Fashion design—Italy—History.   2. Gianni Versace S.p.A.—History.
3. Fashion designers—Italy.   4. Versace, Gianni.   5. Clothing trade—Italy—
History.   I. Title.
TT504.6.I8B35 2009
746.9'2092—dc22   2009032748

ISBN 978-0-307-40652-1
eISBN 978-0-307-46240-4

Cover design by Laura Duffy
Cover photograph © Toni Thorimbert/SYGMA/CORBIS

First Paperback Edition

146122990

For my parents, Georgina and Lawrence
For my brothers and their families
For Fabrizio

Contents

Contents

one

"They've Shot Gianni"

*i*T WAS MIDAFTERNOON ON JULY 15, 1997, AND A BREATHLESS heat had settled on Rome, making the Eternal City so hot that stiletto heels sank slightly into the melting asphalt, leaving pockmarks on the sidewalk. Piazza di Spagna, with its undulating, double-helix staircase, was a hive of activity. Early that morning, police had cleared the cream-colored marble steps, shooing away the penny-ante artists and the slick Romeos who chatted up pretty tourists, so that television crews could mount bulky cameras and lights onto two makeshift towers.

The crews were setting up for the next evening's broadcast of *Donna sotto le stelle,* or *Woman Under the Stars.* *Donna sotto le stelle* was the sort of eye candy that had become a staple of Italian television in the 1980s. Eighteen fashion houses, including Valentino and Fendi, would send their most fabulous evening gowns sashaying down the floodlit Spanish Steps, with the balmy backdrop of Rome adding to the festive air. To add a pinch of drama, the organizers of the show always chose one designer to honor. This year, they'd picked Gianni Versace.

Gianni's sister, Donatella, had arrived the evening before at the Hotel De La Ville, a seventeenth-century palazzo turned hotel perched at the top of the steps. As usual, she stayed in the best room—a deluxe eighth-floor penthouse with a wraparound terrace that offered postcard views stretching from the cupola of the Vatican to the Colosseum. The suite boasted a white baby grand piano, bequeathed to the hotel by composer Leonard Bernstein, who had once lived there for six months. Santo, the elder brother of Donatella and Gianni, hated fancy suites and had unpacked his bags in a more modest room at the same hotel.

That morning, each house had had an hour-long slot to rehearse its models on the Spanish Steps, the trickiest of catwalks, with 135 marble stairs, many worn slippery smooth from centuries of tourist traffic. Dozens of models gingerly tested their descents in the stilettos they would wear the next day. Donatella had the first slot for the rehearsal that morning. The producers knew the ratings dropped soon after the start of the show, as a marathon of pretty models in pretty clothes tired viewers quickly, so they had scheduled the most important designers first. This year, Versace was to open the show. Due to the unwieldy number of designers, the show's organizers had set a limit of no more than fifteen dresses each. Donatella had ignored the quota and brought thirty-five, confident that the house's signature glitz would be irresistible to the show's producers and that no one would complain.

Moreover, she was bringing Naomi Campbell, the star of supermodels, famous for her perfect body, her showmanship, and her ability to work a dress with grace and swagger. Naomi was too important to attend that morning's run-through, so another girl had stood in for her. Naomi had arrived in Italy a few days before to take in a quick holiday on the Amalfi coast, and a chauffeured car was ferrying her to Rome for the evening dress rehearsal. Even in a world crowded with million-dollar egos, Naomi was the ultimate diva, thanks as much to her personal antics as to her lithe body. The twenty-seven-year-old superstar's appetite for gorgeous men, fast cars, and copious amounts of cocaine provided endless fodder for gossip columns. Naomi's tantrums were legendary: She would throw such a violent fit over lost luggage in London that police officers had to drag her kicking and screaming from the plane. Another time, she threw a cell phone at her maid, leaving a gash that required stitches.

But with Gianni, Naomi was a different, more tractable creature. She had long been his favorite model—the woman he often had in mind when he designed his gowns. She showed off his frocks in their full glamour, her feline grace a perfect foil for his lissome dresses. Versace had brought her fame as one of the original supermodels, the group of exquisite girls Gianni had launched. He also played the role of the protective big brother, a salve to her skittish, high-strung character. Cementing her bond with the clan, Naomi had become fast friends with Donatella, who often invited her for weekends at the Versace mansion on Lake Como.

As Naomi made her way to Rome, two conference rooms on the first floor of the Hotel De La Ville had been transformed into a makeshift backstage, overflowing with pre-fashion-show detritus, as makeup artists, hairdressers, and seamstresses wrangled the girls into the highly polished, über-sexy Versace look for the dress rehearsal. Dressed in skinny jeans and devoid of makeup, the girls sat giggling and gossiping, sipping on cans of Diet Coke and chatting as they waited their turns. Some were as young as fourteen and still had prepubescent, almost boyish figures. Indeed, aside from the supermodels, many models are surprisingly plain without makeup. They are chameleons that designers can transform into the type of women they want to project that season.

Against one wall stood a line of vanity tables, outfitted with bright klieg lights and littered with bottles, tubes, and hairpieces. Makeup artists held the girls' chins firmly, turning their heads left and right to get a good look at their work. The room grew stifling with the sickly smell of hair spray, cigarette smoke, and espresso vapors. Because the show was just a one-night stand and not part of a fashion marathon, the hair and makeup people had a relatively easy time of it. During fashion week, when the girls scurry from show to show, the hair and makeup artists have to rush to remove the fake nails, elaborate hairdos, or full-body bronzing gel that the last designer demanded. A model who works the whole five-week runway season will find her skin, hair, and nails wrecked by the relentless grooming.

Once made up, the bare-breasted models stripped down to just heels and tiny G-strings, their Brazilian bikini waxes on full display, and waited for dressers to help them wiggle into the clothes without smudging their makeup or leaving stains on the dresses from the greasy lotion they'd applied to their legs to make them shine under the lights. Models often crash-dieted or downed laxatives before a big show, so Versace's motherly seamstresses, pins hanging from their mouths, stood ready to nip and tuck dresses to make them fit again. Double-sided tape was strapped to the models' breasts to keep them from popping out of Versace's signature plunging necklines on stage. Trays of food sat untouched.

Donatella's assistants then took Polaroid shots of each woman in her assigned dress, complete with any jewelry and handbags she would wear for the show. The photos were then taped to a rack holding the entire outfit, so that the models wouldn't forget anything. Donatella was watching a seamstress fit a model into a dress, mulling some last-minute changes to the lineup, when her cell phone rang. Of course, it was Gianni, calling from Miami Beach to pepper her with questions.

Since the 1970s, Gianni had staged scores of fashion shows and had long since mastered the kind of catwalk orchestration that Donatella was attempting now. He knew that a runway show—with as many as sixty outfits flying by in fifteen minutes—had to be as tightly choreographed as a ballet, with weeks going into choosing just the right music, lights, and girls. The music must set the tone and establish the pace for the models; the designer must decide which model shows off a particular outfit in its best light; and the order in which the outfits are shown will determine the overall impact of a collection, with the opening and closing pieces being the most important choices. A model normally shows at least two outfits per show, and may have as little as thirty seconds to change, further complicating the task of matching the right girl with the right dress in the right sequence.

Gianni, hyperaware that a miscalculation of any of these variables can mean the difference between a hit show and a flop, grilled Donatella on what dresses she had decided to show and how each one looked on certain girls. The Rome show, strictly television entertainment, was less critical than the Milan and Paris catwalks, since buyers and the top fashion editors didn't attend it. Nonetheless, Gianni was still obsessed with the show being perfect and was nervous about how Donatella would handle the event. While Gianni loved his sister profoundly, he didn't fully trust her judgment.

When Gianni was diagnosed with a rare type of inner-ear cancer in the summer of 1994, he'd been forced to entrust Donatella with more of the day-to-day responsibility of running the house as he underwent chemotherapy treatments. Donatella and Gianni's relationship had a tenor that some likened to that of twins, and she had long played the role of Gianni's sounding board and alter ego in what became one of the greatest collaborations in fashion. Several years earlier, he'd agreed to let her design a new line, Versus, despite the fact that Donatella had no formal design training and couldn't even sketch. Versus—with rock-chick pieces heavy on the leather and studs that echoed the aesthetic of its designer and prices that were a quarter that of Gianni's signature line—had gotten reasonably positive reviews. But it was when Gianni fell ill that Donatella—at age forty-two, nine years younger than her brother—truly stepped out of his shadow for the first time. She reveled in the limelight, happily directing Gianni's team, most of whom had been with him since the birth of his empire. She gave interviews for fawning magazine profiles, including a ten-page spread titled "La Bella Donatella" that had appeared in *Vanity Fair*. But after Gianni recovered from his cancer treatments, the pair started to clash. Gianni sensed his team was still looking to Donatella for direction, and he resented it. For months, their relationship was prickly.

By 1997, tensions still simmered. A week before the Rome television show, Donatella and Gianni had been together in Paris for the Versace couture show, which Gianni had spent tens of thousands of francs to stage at the frescoed pool bar at the Ritz, the opulent hotel that sits in Place Vendôme. Several years earlier, when Gianni decided to start presenting a couture show at the Ritz, some in the French establishment were miffed. The Ritz was an institution in Paris, hosting luminaries such as Ernest Hemingway, for whom a bar in the hotel is named, and Coco Chanel, who made a duplex suite in the hotel her home for more than thirty years and who represented the very institution of French fashion that Versace, the brash upstart from southern Italy, was intent on supplanting.

For Gianni's July 1997 show at the Ritz, he intended for the models to descend a double staircase to a glass walkway he'd had built over the turquoise pool. Donatella had urged Gianni to use Karen Elson as the final model, the one who wears couture's traditional pièce de résistance, the wedding dress. Elson was the girl of the moment, her fame ignited earlier that year when photographer Steven Meisel convinced her to shave off her eyebrows and dye her hair bright red for her first cover for Italian *Vogue*. But the day before the show, Donatella sat in an empty front row, watching Gianni, dressed in a simple pullover sweater and pleated pants, pace up and down over the clear plastic tarp that had been laid over the glass runway to keep it perfectly clean. He bristled as he watched Elson nervously descend the stairs and walk the runway. Gianni didn't like her lopey, horselike gait, and he raged at Donatella for having suggested the girl in the first place. So he substituted Naomi, who did him proud as she sauntered by in the wedding dress—a baby-doll-like slip of slinky metal mesh adorned with oversized silver crosses. Elson burst into a fit of tears, while Donatella wore a stony look on her face. Gianni's ruling showed he didn't trust her with key decisions.

After the contretemps in Paris, Donatella was determined to retain some degree of autonomy. She was happy to see Gianni skip the Rome show and get an early start on his summer holiday. Gianni had long since stopped coming to *Donna sotto le stelle* anyway. He hated how he and his rival designers were crammed together into one mind-numbing production, where petty jealousies inevitably erupted. The designers had to share the models hired for the show, and some tried to hog the prettiest women by taking too long to dress them. Giorgio Armani and Valentino had once gotten into a screaming match when Valentino took more than his allocated time to rehearse his models.[1] The heat was also a constant problem. The designers showed their latest collections—clothes for fall and winter—and the girls wilted under heavy dresses and fur coats, their elaborate makeup melting. But mostly Gianni didn't come because he was just plain exhausted. The show at the Ritz had demanded a week of eighteen-hour days as Gianni readied more than one hundred handmade gowns. Much to everyone's relief, Gianni and Antonio D'Amico, his companion of fifteen years, had flown off to spend a few days in Gianni's thirty-five-room Miami Beach mansion.

With Versace as the show's featured house, it would be Donatella who would close the broadcast, descending the Spanish Steps hand in hand with Naomi—a triumphant moment for a woman who as her brother's muse had thrived even as she felt confined to his shadow. Donatella recognized that Gianni was the strongest link of the Versace trio, his genius providing the spark that had brought success and its spoils to them all. His presence was the ballast that steadied the lives of all three siblings. And, despite his recent illness, creatively and commercially he was still at the top of his game. By the late 1990s, Gianni had refined and honed his look, eliminating the garishness that had marred some of his earliest designs. He had come to define the have-it-all ethos of the millennium's final decade. He was now counted among Yves Saint Laurent, Coco Chanel, and Giorgio Armani as one of fashion's greatest designers.

It was barely after lunchtime in Rome—and dawn in Miami—when Donatella got Gianni's first call. He bugged her with questions about how the rehearsal was going, and she grew more and more annoyed. Finally she snapped, "Gianni, you can't help me from there," and hung up.[2] When he called again a half hour later, she ignored the phone and continued to fit the models.

A short time later, Santo, the oldest and most businesslike of the Versace siblings, got a call on his cell phone. He figured it was his brother, but instead it was a Versace assistant calling from Milan. "They've shot Gianni," she told him. That was all she knew.

In that horrible moment, Santo felt a flash of practical anger. Why had his brother gone to Miami, a city notorious for its violence? How many times had he urged Gianni to hire bodyguards? Ever the problem solver in the family, Santo began thinking of how he would get Gianni back to Italy and into a hospital to recover.

His face grim, he ran to find Donatella, pulling her away from a fitting with a model. "Donatella, *vieni qua subito*! Come with me!" he shouted in a panicked voice that jolted the models and assistants, who knew Santo to have the coolest head of the three siblings. Donatella, alarmed, trailed behind him. When they were alone, Santo told her, "A lunatic has shot Gianni. But don't worry. He's already on the way to the hospital, and they'll take care of him."

Donatella didn't believe her brother. Immediately she began making calls to Miami. When she reached a Versace assistant who was in touch with the hospital, she screamed hysterically with her premonition that her brother Gianni was dead.

"Yes, Donatella," said the grim voice on the other end. "Gianni's dead."

Donatella let out a cry that reached the models still rehearsing on the steps outside. Then she fainted. Santo, standing next to her, blanched and began to shake. After a few minutes, he and Emanuela Schmeidler, Versace's longtime PR chief, managed to carry Donatella up to her suite.

In her room, she came to and sat slumped on the bed, sobbing with Santo. Suddenly, she shot upright, alarmed with concern that the children would hear the news on the television. An aide ran to the bedroom next door, where Donatella's children, eleven-year-old Allegra and six-year-old Daniel, had been watching cartoons. It was too late. Italian television was running bulletins with news of Gianni's death and the kids had seen it. Distraught, they ran to their mother.

The events that followed would be a blur for Santo and Donatella; both of them were overcome with shock, pain, and grief. It took thirty bodyguards to hustle them through the scrum of photographers outside the Hotel De La Ville; one of them had even tried to climb down the side of the building to steal a photo of the pair in their suite. A paparazzo got a shot of Donatella, hunched in the backseat of a black Mercedes, the pain on her face visible behind giant black sunglasses. The car drove them to Ciampino, Rome's military airport. Italy's richest man, Silvio Berlusconi, who would later become the country's prime minister, had offered to lend the family his private jet to fly them to Miami, but an Italian construction magnate beat him to it, making his private plane immediately available.

After a ten-hour flight, Donatella and Santo landed at Miami's airport at 3:30 a.m. and drove straight to Gianni's mansion on Ocean Drive, in the heart of the South Beach district that the Versace lifestyle had done so much to popularize.[3] Madonna had offered to let them stay at her house if they didn't want to stay at Gianni's home, but they declined. They would spend the next day and a half at the palazzo Gianni had spent millions to renovate and had loved so much—and which was now the scene of the crime.

The house was under siege from the media. Television helicopters circled overhead, while dozens of photographers and cameramen camped out on the street, snapping photos of the impromptu shrine of flowers and candles that had sprung up on the front steps where Gianni's blood had just been washed away. When word spread that Donatella and Santo had arrived, part of the pack shifted to the back door in the alley behind the mansion. Later, when Donatella and Santo prepared to leave for the funeral home, Gianni's staff dispatched several extra limos as decoys to try to clear the area of paparazzi, but it didn't work. Bodyguards had to surround them, holding oversized umbrellas to shield them, and a shoving match ensued as the bereaved pair struggled to get into a limo.

At 5 p.m., Santo, Donatella, and Gianni's partner, Antonio, arrived at the funeral home, a run-down place in a dreary Miami suburb, to see Gianni for the last time. His face was partially disfigured from the bullets, despite the efforts of the mortician to cover the damage.[4] Donatella insisted on dressing Gianni personally, overcoming Santo's protests. With a dozen bodyguards and police officers standing sentry outside, they conducted a small ceremony in the funeral home's chapel and then cremated Gianni's body.

That evening, the family sat down to dinner. Santo and Donatella had expressed little emotion all day, surrounded as they were with lawyers, PR people, and friends who had filled the house. Gianni's chef made a simple pasta dish. Afterward he served vanilla *budino*, an Italian version of flan, which had been Gianni's favorite dessert. Seeing it, Donatella and Santo broke down and cried.[5] In the middle of the night, when the media siege had ebbed, Donatella sneaked outside to kiss the spot where Gianni had been shot.

The next day, Donatella, Santo, and Antonio boarded a flight back to Milan. Santo held the bronze box containing Gianni's ashes cradled in his lap. The trio spoke little during the long flight home. In Miami, they left behind one of the biggest manhunts ever undertaken in the United States.

✤ V ✤

While Donatella and Santo flew back home, the Versace PR office got busy preparing for the funeral. They decided to hold it on Tuesday, July 22, 1997, exactly one week after Gianni's murder. From Miami, Donatella, reeling in a mix of searing grief and anger over Gianni's violent death, had decided she wanted to stage a funeral the world would never forget. "Gianni was killed like a stray dog," she spat at her public relations chief. "I want him to have a funeral fit for a prince." She directed her assistant to look over films of royal funerals for ideas on how to stage it. She decided that only one site was fitting for her beloved brother's commemoration: the Duomo, Milan's magnificent cathedral. Santo initially appeared shocked at his sister's decision, but he acquiesced.

While the fashion house was based in Milan, none of the Versaces had particularly liked the city. They had come from Italy's deep south, a languid, backward, mafia-ridden region that was the antithesis of the ascetic, hardworking north, where *meridionali*, or southerners, were regarded with suspicion and prejudice. Gianni had always found Milan a sad city, with its brown and gray palette and pinched, conservative people. Like many southerners who moved north in search of opportunity, Gianni respected the Milanese's Calvinist work ethic, but he nonetheless escaped the city every Thursday evening to spend the weekends on Lake Como. Donatella, with her bleached blond hair and loud clothing, felt that the snobby Milanese looked down on her. Santo also appreciated the opportunity Milan offered him but resented the antisouthern sentiment so common in the city.

Indeed, Milan's old-line families had never entirely welcomed the Versaces, with their rough manners, southern accents, and flashy lifestyles. From the time of the postwar economic boom, many Milanese harbored a deep antipathy for southerners like the Versaces, regarding them as corrupt wastrels who lived off the industriousness of the north. By the time of Gianni's death, this sentiment had found a powerful outlet in the Northern League, a new political party that advocated outright secession from the rest of Italy. To blue-blood Milanese, Gianni's designs, so popular with the nouveau riche that had emerged with the Milan stock market booms of the 1980s and 1990s, were vulgar and in poor taste. Giorgio Armani, with his cerebral suits, northern heritage, and more discreet homosexuality, was far more acceptable. So, too, was Miuccia Prada, who came from an upstanding Milanese family that had made leather traveling trunks for the city's upper crust since before the war. But the city's haute bourgeoisie, with their double-barreled names and their preference for the restrained elegance of French couture, couldn't fathom the popularity of Gianni's clothes. Who would dare buy those outfits? All that money the company made, they whispered, could only have come from the mafia.

So when Donatella demanded that Gianni's funeral be held in the Duomo, some Milanese found the request outrageous. In recent years, even the cream of the city's society were no longer afforded a funeral in the Duomo. The church, with a capacity of more than four thousand, was just too big. It was the site of only civic funerals, such as the one for the victims of a mafia bombing in Milan in 1993.

The world's third largest Catholic church, the Duomo di Milano is a great, hulking triangle that seems to sink into the square. Erected over the course of six centuries but never fully completed, Milan's cathedral was originally meant to evoke the airy grace of French Gothic landmarks such as Notre Dame. Instead, it had morphed into a jumble of styles, as one architect after another tried to impose his vision on it. Though impressive in terms of pure size, the church is rather gloomy; it's so large that even the brightest sunlight doesn't pierce the stained glass windows enough to lift the penumbra inside. Three rows of Sequoia-sized columns, their pink Candoglia marble gone grayish-yellow with age, make it even more oppressive. But for all its gloominess, the Duomo represents the nostalgic heart of the city for the Milanese. Soaring above the roof is the Madonnina, a four-meter-high gold-plated statue of Mary that is the symbol of Milan. Donatella was demanding nothing short of a state funeral for her brother—a celebration of the truncated life of her sexy, iconoclastic, modern, and subversive brother to be held in the heart of the Italian establishment.

When Versace's PR office asked the mayor to forward the Versaces' request to the city's cardinal, ecclesiastical authorities worried that the Mass would become a sort of fashion show–cum–gay pride spectacle for a man who had publicly repudiated the Church. Eventually Don Angelo Mayo, the Duomo's head priest, relented, acceding to the reality that the Duomo was the only site big and grand enough to accommodate the celebrities expected at the funeral.

The house of Versace produced the funeral as if it were the ultimate fashion show—which it *was*. Staffers sent invitations to the house's favorite stars, who were then booked at the Four Seasons, the five-star hotel next door to Versace's headquarters in the heart of the Via Montenapoleone neighborhood. In the top-floor atelier of Versace headquarters, Gianni's couture seamstresses pulled out the detailed measurements that recorded the sizes of the house's favored VIPs. Around the clock, they churned out sober outfits for the female members of the Versace family, as well as for VIPs such as Princess Diana and Naomi Campbell. Assistants then laid out the outfits—complete with handbags, black lace veils, and shoes—in their hotel suites. Seating charts were done and redone as the guests confirmed their attendance.

Once Don Mayo had agreed to the Mass, the press office managed to secure a series of allowances from the Duomo and the city authorities that surprised many in Milan. They convinced the city to close off the whole length of Via dell'Arcivescovado, the broad avenue that runs along the south side of the cathedral, a concession not even granted to Pope John Paul II during his visit to the city several years earlier. The Duomo canceled two of its eleven daily masses and arranged to clear the church of tourists an hour before the 6 p.m. service. To manage the crowds and protect the luminaries, the city deployed hundreds of extra police officers around the Duomo and in front of Versace headquarters, supplementing the scores of private security personnel hired by the family. The Duomo agreed to set off about twenty pews in the central nave with wood barriers, to block off access to the VIPs. Rumors instantly circulated that Santo had greased the path with a $500,000 payment to convince the church to hold the Mass; he vehemently denied having paid so much and said that he gave the usual small sum the family would have donated to the church for a funeral.

By the day of the funeral, the world's media had descended on Milan. The American networks sent crews from New York, paying thousands of dollars to secure satellite time to transmit live feeds via television trucks parked outside the cathedral. Crews from the BBC, CNN, and Japanese and French television stations had taken rooms in hotels around the Duomo. In an effort to impose a modicum of sobriety to the media melee, the cathedral's press office told journalists seeking accreditation to dress appropriately: Men had to wear dark suits, and women couldn't wear dresses exposing their shoulders or too much leg. Inside the church, Versace aides cordoned off an area immediately inside the VIP entrance for the press, so that they would have the best shots of the star-filled front rows. By the time the first guests started to arrive, the journalists had been in place for hours, jostling for the best vantage points.

In the summer, the Duomo offers refuge from the heat, and guests entering the church for Gianni's funeral were grateful to step into the dark coolness. The local citizenry entered through the main bronze doors from Piazza del Duomo and quickly filled the entire rear half of the church. Some used plastic bags and purses as placeholders hours before the Mass was to start. Others stood on pews to get a glimpse of the luminaries entering in the front.

At about 5:30 p.m., a cortege of dark Mercedes pulled up to the designated VIP entrance on Via dell'Arcivescovado. Each VIP held a white embossed invitation. Just like at red-carpet events, photographers and reporters were lined up on the far side of a barrier outside the entrance. A phalanx of gawkers stood under the blazing sun, some wolf-whistling at the prettier models, others reaching out toward celebrities for an autograph, which was nearly always refused. Handsome young men dressed in black Versace suits were deployed just inside the entrance to escort the notables to their pews in front of the altar. To reach the VIP section, attendees had to pass in front of one of the cathedral's most curious statues: a skeletal St. Bartholomew, his loose skin slung over his back like an empty sack after being flayed alive.

The press office had made sure the Duomo's insistence on a sober ritual was respected. (They had instructed friends to make donations to a cancer charity rather than send flowers; Tom Cruise and Nicole Kidman gave $25,000.) Several simple arrangements, heavy on the white roses that were among Gianni's favorite, sat at the base of the pillars on either side of the altar, but the church was otherwise unadorned. The press office had arranged for the family and their closest celebrity guests to dress in black or midnight blue, to avoid any hint of ostentation. Despite the heat, Donatella and Allegra wore black lace veils and long black gloves.

In the front row, the family was a tableau of grief. Santo, looking drawn and tired, wore a loosely cut black jacket over a dark mock turtleneck and pleated trousers. With his arms crossed and his face stony, he followed the Mass distractedly, occasionally turning to the pew behind him to comfort his distraught eldest child, Francesca. On his right sat his wife, Cristiana. At the far end of the pew, separated by a few significant feet from the other family members, was Antonio D'Amico, clad in a dark suit, black tie, and the white shirt that was worn principally for formal occasions in Italy. D'Amico had been inconsolable over the last week and had found himself almost unable to attend the Mass. His relations with his lover's family had been strained since the moment he met Gianni at a dinner fifteen years earlier, particularly with Donatella, who resented anyone who competed for her brother's affection. Now with Gianni gone, neither Santo nor Donatella had to maintain the pretense of getting along with Antonio, and his relationship with them deteriorated quickly. Glassy-eyed, Antonio stared at the floor, clutching his arms in front of him.

On Santo's left sat Donatella, shorn of her usual tumble of jewelry, her loose hair covered with a black mantilla and her face only lightly made up, gazing disconsolately into the middle distance, barely following the service. Next to her was Allegra, squirming in the heat under her Empire-style black dress. Allegra was on the cusp of adolescence, still displaying the chipmunk cheeks, baby fat, and polished skin of a healthy child, yet showing the first signs of young womanhood in the self-possessed way she moved. She occasionally struggled to pull her veil back over her sun-flecked chestnut hair, which was held in place by a simple headband. She cried frequently into the white handkerchief an assistant had given her, looking fretfully across to the press photographers snapping pictures of her. She periodically raised her face to her mother for comfort, tilting her head to lay it on Donatella's shoulder, but her mother stared blank-eyed at the floor. When Allegra broke out in heavy sobs during the reading of the gospel, Donatella stirred, curving her arm around her daughter to pull her close.

Paul Beck, Donatella's husband, sat in the pew behind his wife and Santo, clutching his squirming son, Daniel, in his lap, occasionally nuzzling the boy to quiet him. Paul, with his carefully trimmed goatee and highlighted blond hair swept back from a neat middle part, towered over the whole group. His height was rivaled only by that of Naomi, who stood next to him, nearly six feet tall in her heels.

The supermodel hung her head low, a dark veil falling to her shoulders. She wore a simple black sheath the Versace seamstresses had made for her, topped by a long-sleeved jacket with no lapels, and a large silver cross at her throat. Her long hair hung straight down to her waist, her legs were bare, and she wore unadorned low black pumps. Since Gianni's death, she'd been inconsolable. After the murder, her London agent had barely been able to convince Naomi to keep an assignment in South Africa for an appearance at a special event with Nelson Mandela. (Mandela personally called the model to talk her out of canceling the trip.) The morning of the funeral, as she ran the gauntlet of the press to reach the Versace palazzo, she'd broken down in tears, clutching her purse to her face to block the flashbulbs.

By the time of Gianni's death, Naomi was as close to Donatella as a sister would be—Donatella once flew in a star hairdresser from New York to give them both hair extensions while they ate spaghetti in Donatella's marble bathroom. Naomi also played the role of an unlikely aunt to Allegra. During the Mass, when Don Mayo invited the congregation to exchange gestures of peace, Allegra embraced her mother first and then stood on tiptoe to receive a hug from Naomi.

Across the aisle, in the adjacent front row, sat as unlikely a group as one would see in a church. Front and center was Elton John, his pudgy frame swathed in a dark Versace jacket with a Chinese-style high collar. With his single earring and pageboy haircut, he resembled an aging schoolboy. He and his partner, David Furnish, had flown in on his private jet that morning from St. Tropez, where the singer had recently bought a new home. David, fresh-faced in an open-necked white shirt and dark jacket, sat alongside Elton, protectively patting the arm of his lover.

Elton was one of Gianni's closest friends and a fierce admirer. They first met in the mid-1980s, when Elton, who already wore Gianni's designs, was shopping in Versace's flagship store on Via Montenapoleone in Milan and asked to meet the designer. The two clicked instantly, sharing an artist's restlessness, and the pair often hit the antiques galleries and auction houses together. At Gianni's Manhattan townhouse, Elton had his own suite, complete with a bed that Gianni had specially commissioned from the hot New York artist Julian Schnabel. The longtime rock star dressed almost exclusively in Versace. "Elton practically has a museum of my creations in his house," Gianni once said. "He's got more pieces in his closet than I have in my archives."

Next to Elton sat Gianni Versace's most famous client, Princess Diana. Elton, who had helped Gianni cultivate a friendship with Diana, had sent his private jet to pick her up from the south of France, where for the last week, she had been making waves with her first much-publicized holiday with new boyfriend Dodi al-Fayed, the forty-one-year-old son of the billionaire Mohamed al-Fayed, owner of Harrods. About five years earlier, Diana had become arguably Gianni's biggest trophy when she came to him, newly separated from her husband, Charles, the Prince of Wales, and looking for a sleek new style. Gianni came up with a series of outfits that were classic but possessed a dash of glamour—sheaths that fit like gloves, slim gowns in bold colors, and form-fitting suits. After Diana's separation, Elton had started inviting her to his spread in Windsor, where she often saw Gianni. Always savvy at cultivating his celebrity clients, Gianni charmed Diana, personally handling some of her fittings. When she heard of Gianni's murder, Diana had immediately agreed to come to the funeral. She and Gianni had not been close friends, but she was genuinely traumatized by his death. Moreover, Diana loved a good funeral; the pathos appealed to her self-image as comforter of the afflicted, the elegant dark clothing feeding her sense of drama. "Don't worry," Diana told Donatella before the funeral. "Gianni is in a better place now."

Diana was, of course, wearing a Versace outfit designed for the occasion. Gianni's seamstresses had whipped up a midnight blue sleeveless sheath topped by a dark jacket. A string of marble-sized pearls set off her summer tan and complemented her sober, doe-eyed gaze and glossy pink lipstick. Despite the heat outside, she wore black stockings. Halfway through the Mass, she shed the dark jacket, unaware of the church's proscription against uncovered skin. At her feet sat a shiny crocodile purse, embellished with large gilt medusas, the Versace logo. Unable to follow the Mass in Italian, she grew more distracted as the service went on, her hands flitting from the cream-colored missal to her pearls. Gianni's service would be one of the last public appearances of Diana's life. Just six weeks later, she would die in a grisly car crash in Paris, and many of the same VIPs would gather once again to commemorate the young princess.

On the other side of Diana sat Sting and his wife, Trudie Styler, who was covered in an oversized peasant-style black veil that wrapped over each shoulder. Arrayed behind them was the royalty of fashion. Her signature sunglasses firmly in place despite the gloom of the cathedral, Anna Wintour, powerful editor in chief of American *Vogue*, sat next to André Leon Talley, *Vogue*'s influential editor at large, who stole curious glances at Diana throughout the Mass. On the other side of her, Karl Lagerfeld, the imperious designer of Chanel and a close friend of Gianni's, stared straight ahead, his chalk-white hair tucked back into his signature ponytail. Behind them sat the editors of French, British, and Italian *Vogue*.

Also behind Diana was Giorgio Armani, dressed in his usual uniform of a long-sleeved, dark stretch sweater, dark pleated pants, and white tennis shoes. Armani and Versace were the yin and yang of Italian fashion, setting out two distinct looks that would come to define the two extremes of Milanese style. For more than two decades they had embraced different aesthetics and succeeded equally at them. Both had broken from the pack of aspiring designers at virtually the same time in the mid-1970s. In their different ways, they each created a fresh style of dressing for a new generation of independent, professional women who didn't want to be trussed up in the stuffy French designs their mothers wore. In later years, when they'd both reached global fame, it was said that Armani dressed the wife, and Versace the mistress.

Armani and Versace shared a prodigious work ethic and hunger for success; both men lived in apartments above their studios in order to devote as much time to work as possible. But otherwise, the two could hardly have been more different. If Versace's shows were exuberant, Armani's shows were ostentatiously muted. Gianni Versace's homes were overflowing baroque containers for all manner of art, furniture, and homoerotic sculptures; Armani's were spare in their elegance, the walls bare of paintings, the occasional orchid a rare adornment. While Gianni spun an elaborate tale of his childhood as the son of a provincial seamstress, Armani scrupulously refused to embellish his own modest origins.

Armani may have been grieving the violent death of his rival at the funeral Mass, but by no measure were the men friends. Milan would never have become a fashion mecca without the both of them, yet the pair nonetheless loathed each other. To Armani, Versace, with his sadomasochistic flourishes, punk collections, and general garishness, was an abomination, an insult to women. Armani had been public in his criticism, declaring that Versace presents women "as bait for men, the incarnation of vulgar sex fantasies, a sort of nightclub where they do strip teases for local hoods."[6]

Versace, in turn, found Armani tedious and lacking in passion. "I dress a woman who is more beautiful, more glamorous," Gianni told the *New Yorker* shortly before his death. "He, on the other hand, has a type of woman who is always a little somber, a little dull. They call it chic. I've never seen it as chic, but everyone has his own opinion."[7]

The funeral audience fumbled with their programs as Don Mayo read his sermon. "Today's service isn't something driven by opportunism, or, worse still, a spectacle," he said, with perhaps more cautionary hopefulness than accuracy. "It is a gesture of faith, rich with meaning. . . . We share in the sorrow of Donatella and Santo with discretion and respect."

Next came the testaments, musical and otherwise, from Gianni's spectacular friends. A Versace assistant gave Sting and Elton John the signal, and the pair slipped out of the pew. They crossed in front of the altar, Sting kneeling quickly to make the sign of the cross, Elton giving a curt bow. They climbed the three steps to the spot where a microphone stood. Don Mayo had warned against anything except religious music at the service, so the press office had chosen "The Lord Is My Shepherd." Despite the simplicity of the psalm, the seventy-eight-year-old priest who directed the cathedral's choir had demanded that Sting and Elton John audition before he gave permission for them to sing.

Clutching the lyrics, the pair sang unaccompanied. For an instant, Elton choked up, and Sting put a hand on his back to steady him. Donatella broke down in tears. Santo, for the first time during the Mass, buried his face in his hands, sobbing. As the last strains of the psalm faded, a line slowly formed for those taking Communion, many of them gawkers grabbing the chance to approach the altar and steal a look at the stars.

After hours penned behind the wooden barricades, the press at last got the money shot they'd been waiting for when, during Communion, Elton broke down in heaving sobs. Diana quickly turned to embrace him. Flashes popped as the paparazzi snapped the photo that would make the front pages of the next day's newspapers around the world.

As the men's choir sang the last psalm, Don Mayo made his way over to the Versace family. Donatella roused herself, giving the priest a piteous look as she murmured her thanks. Santo bent on one knee to kiss the elderly priest's hand. Allegra began to cry again. A bevy of Versace assistants sprang into action, shepherding the mourners, many with tears streaming down their faces, into a sort of receiving line in front of the family. A posse of six bodyguards stepped forward to escort Diana out of the church, setting off an explosion of flashbulbs. The more minor luminaries followed. Valentino, his hair slicked back in a frozen bouffant that framed his sun-baked face, exited alone. A gaggle of supermodels, looking modestly pretty, with little makeup and loose hair, stopped to speak with the family. Carla Bruni, her eyes rimmed red and her hair parted simply in the middle and hanging loose around her shoulders, lingered a moment with Antonio, who clutched his arms across his chest to control himself. Carolyn Bessette Kennedy, clad in a slim black trousers suit, her long blond hair streaming down her back, mixed with the Aga Khan, Rupert Everett, Carla Fendi, and Eva Herzigova, as the photographers scrambled to get shots of the stream of VIPs.

As the celebrities drifted away and the photographers began to pack away their gear, Donatella and Santo clung to each other and made their way to the black chauffeured car waiting outside.

❖ V ❖

With any death, the trying times truly begin after the funeral, when the family struggles with the vacuum left by the absence of the loved one and begins the painful task of constructing a new life. But in the following months and years, the death of Gianni Versace would bring his family to the brink of professional and personal ruin. Gianni had provided the center of gravity for the entire clan, his genius the animating force that steadied their lives. His murder would send them spinning out of orbit. Without him, the deep dysfunction that had remained hidden for two decades bubbled over quickly, threatening to overwhelm the entire Versace clan.

Even as they mourned their brother that hot July day in Milan's Duomo, Donatella and Santo knew the whole world was already wondering whether they were up to the task of sustaining Gianni's legacy. Gianni had died at his peak; the Versace name had achieved the status of icon, becoming shorthand for the exuberantly sexy style that helped define the 1990s. More than any other designer, Gianni Versace satisfied the public's hunger for sex, fame, and money that characterized the burgeoning global prosperity of that decade.

A restless son of a provincial seamstress, Gianni had achieved his breakthrough by marrying the raw energy of the street to the finely cut elegance of couture, plundering for inspiration everything from Pop Art to ancient Greece. For him, clothes were meant to be fun, fabulous, and fast. He chose as his muse the prostitute; he raised vulgarity to an art form. Sometimes he stepped over the line, and his detractors dubbed his vision "hooker's haute couture." His clothes never evoked indifference. His S&M collection, with leather dog collars and studded harnesslike bodices, offended even fashion sophisticates. But his clothes sold and were worn. By the late 1990s, he had changed the vocabulary of fashion.

Gianni also bridged the gap between fashion and celebrity, melding two currents of pop culture and harnessing the growing power of the media. A master at public relations, he conjured up lush, flamboyant images that compelled the gaze: Elizabeth Hurley in a black dress held precariously together with gold safety pins; Madonna clad in a Versace bathing suit while painting the nails of a poodle; Claudia Schiffer nude except for a carefully positioned Versace dinner plate. He turned fashion models into full-fledged stars. His clothes and celebrity friends reflected his carefree ethos, a determination to devour everything life offered.

His designs, for all their sexual sport, their antic sampling of history and art, and their brass, appealed to a human need for freedom that ran deeper than fashion—an urge bursting to the surface of society in the sexualized, globalized, postreligious late twentieth century. Gianni "was the great post-Freudian designer—one who had no guilt whatsoever," said Richard Martin, the curator of the Costume Institute at the Metropolitan Museum of Art.[8] For Gianni, sex was a celebration of life itself, and by the 1990s, Western society had caught up with him. His blend of high and low culture, his fierce individuality, and his impatience with decorum and class strictures also spoke to the new moneyed class that was springing up in Miami, Rio de Janeiro, and Moscow, who loved his *épater la bourgeoisie* creed. At the same time, his designs appealed to baby boomers' daughters who were coming of age and felt freer than ever to brandish their sexuality and independence without fear of losing their power.

Yet Gianni's death came just as the world itself was changing. Such sexually loaded designs and images were beginning to run their course, having lost the initial frisson of excitement and novelty. Fashion was turning toward a more restrained, knowing style, and minimalist designers such as Miuccia Prada, with her prim, retro designs and love of high-tech materials, were ascendant.

HOUSE OF VERSACE

Moreover, enormous changes in the global fashion business were already emerging, forces that would challenge family-owned companies such as Versace. Globalization, the easy money of the 1990s, the media's mounting obsession with fashion and its celebrity clients—changes wrought or harnessed in part by Versace himself—forever altered the game for fashion companies. Successful luxury brands needed a worldwide network of opulent stores, a constant stream of new products, and thousands of pages of advertising a year just to compete. Top fashion companies were now big corporations that had the budgets and management depth to sustain and supply the sprawling machine that was the new worldwide business of selling style.

Gianni had fed and unleashed a beast that threatened, in turn, to devour his surviving siblings. As long as Gianni was alive, Donatella and Santo could count on the bedrock of his talent to hide the cracks in the house's glittering façade. Now, as Donatella stepped into Gianni's place as creative director and Santo had to make crucial business decisions alone, his absence opened a Pandora's box of troubles.

His death would throw a harsh spotlight on Donatella, the flighty kid sister whose meager talents and self-destructive personality would, over the next decade, come close to sinking the company, destroying her family, and killing the woman herself. Santo, the diligent eldest sibling, would struggle to salvage two decades of hard work. But it was Allegra, Donatella's delicate eleven-year-old daughter, whose life would change the most. Just months before his death, in one angry, resentful, rash decision, Gianni had unknowingly condemned his beloved niece—his *principessa*—to many years of woe. The Versaces had risen far and fast from the rocky poverty of Calabria, to conquer all of Italy and the world. The near-fall of their empire, and its tentative salvation, would come even more quickly.

two

The Black Sheep

*G*IANNI VERSACE, FETED AT THE END OF HIS LIFE BY ROCK AND royalty, could hardly have come from more humble origins. He was a son of Italy's deep south, a forlorn region perennially trapped in a cycle of poverty, corruption, and relentless emigration. Calabria, the region of his birth, covers the tip of the toe of the Italian boot; it is a territory overrun for centuries by foreign invaders and buffeted by torrential rains, deadly droughts, and earthquakes. Malaria was a constant scourge; shopkeepers regularly stocked antimalaria tablets until the 1940s. In the isolated villages high in the Aspromonte mountains, the final surge of the Apennine chain that runs down the spine of the Italian peninsula, a system of sharecropping survived until the 1960s. Poor, illiterate families worked vast tracts of clay-tinged land owned by a few wealthy clans, and starting at age six children were sent into the hills to herd animals. They didn't speak proper Italian but a dialect gleaned from the Greek, Spanish, and Arab tongues of Calabria's invaders, a linguistic distinction that would further isolate them from the rest of Italy throughout the twentieth century.

In such hopeless conditions, emigration spread like a plague. In the late 1800s, a third of Calabrians emigrated, many to America, a flow that continued well into the 1980s. The region's hardscrabble frontier air forged a Calabrian character that is dogged, rough, and tinged with melancholy, while family ties are fierce even by southern Italian standards. Those characteristics would also define the Versace clan, contributing to both their success and their tribulation.

Reggio di Calabria, the area's largest city, is a port town jammed into a narrow crystalline coastline that runs like a ribbon around the foot of the Aspromonte mountains. The northeast tip of Sicily almost touches Calabria, and the strait in front of Reggio is often as still as a lake, affording a clear view of Mount Etna, its peak blanketed in snow in the winter. Despite its natural beauty, Reggio's isolated position—the highway to the nearest large city wasn't built until 1963—made it an exceedingly provincial town, lacking the noble history of its southern sister cities, Palermo and Naples. Gianni Versace would chafe at his isolation almost as soon as he was old enough to walk.

Reggio bore the forbidding weight of natural tragedy: An earthquake in 1908 killed two-thirds of the population and collapsed the city. By the 1930s, city planners had rebuilt Reggio from scratch in a bland Liberty style punctuated with a few intimidating, Fascist-era buildings and had laid the streets in a tidy crosshatch style. Lining the boardwalk were magnolia bushes, palms, and jasmine flowers, which gave off an intoxicating perfume that is characteristic of the Mediterranean spring.

The Versaces were not originally from Reggio; their provenance was even more remote than that of the region's city. Antonio Versace, known to everyone as Nino, was born in 1915, the youngest of five children, in a family that hailed from Santo Stefano, a tiny farming town high in the Aspromonte. Nino's family were the poor relatives of a wealthy clan—a distant relative was later kidnapped for ransom in the 1950s—and his father was forced to sell firewood to scrape out a living. Lean and fair skinned, with blondish hair and angular features, Nino was a serious, solitary young man. He was, however, a gifted and passionate athlete. He played semiprofessional soccer, where he earned the nickname U Carro Armato, or "The Tank," and was also an avid bicyclist, competing often in races in Calabria and Sicily, where he bested professional racers who competed in the Tour de France.

In 1938, after his obligatory two years of military service with Mussolini's Fascist army, he fell in love with a local girl—much to the consternation of his family: The young woman's family had a poor reputation in Reggio. "Don't you know a nice girl for Nino?" his brother asked his wife, hoping to derail the romance. She thought of a serious, hardworking young woman who had just begun working as a seamstress and arranged for Nino to have a garment made by her. Her name was Francesca Olandese.[1]

Francesca, known as Franca, was born in 1920 in Reggio to a family of higher social standing than the Versaces. Her father, Giovanni, a shoemaker, had an iconoclastic streak. As a young man, he had joined the Anarchist Party, a hard-left group that was a precursor of the Italian Socialist Party, and he mixed with anti-Fascist activists. According to Versace family legend, the local police would throw Giovanni in jail whenever a leader of the Fascist Party from Rome came to Reggio for a visit.

Franca, the youngest of five children, had the most forceful character among her siblings, and, despite her youth, became a natural leader in the family. Possessed of her father's determination and stubbornness, she dreamed of becoming a doctor, possibly a gynecologist. However, Calabrian mores were so oppressive that women could hardly dream of getting a university education, much less having a profession. They weren't allowed to walk through town unaccompanied. The morning after a wedding, the bride's family would flourish bloody sheets from their window to prove to neighbors that their daughter had been a virgin. Police even turned a blind eye to *il delitto d'onore*, or honor killing, whereby a husband could kill an adulterous wife. When Franca told her father she hoped to be a doctor, he would hear none of it.

"Franca, you're a girl, a signorina," her father told her one day. "You can't go to school with boys. You can't work in a place where there are men. Go learn a trade."[2] She was allowed to attend school only until her early teens.

One of the few respectable trades for a woman in prewar Italy was sewing, and at the age of thirteen girls went to the local seamstress to learn how to sew as part of their preparation to manage a household. Before the war, one of the leading seamstresses of Reggio was a woman known as La Parigina, or the Parisian, because legend had it she had trained in a couture house in Paris. Franca convinced her to take her on as a trainee. The teenager's meager income from her work with La Parigina helped support her family. But Franca soon exhibited the entrepreneurial spirit she would pass on to her children. By 1940, when Franca was twenty, she had opened her own shop.

Soon after she met Nino, war broke out in Italy, and he was drafted for a second time by the Fascist regime to fight. But because he was one of the few young men in the city who could read, he spent the war in a desk job in Reggio and never saw combat, which allowed him to court the ambitious young woman. Franca and Nino fell in love despite their contrasting personalities—she was extroverted and curious, while he was quiet and withdrawn to the point of coolness. However, they shared a prodigious work ethic. In late 1942, Nino and Franca married in a spare wartime ceremony. In November 1943, the young couple's first child arrived and, following tradition, they named her Fortunata, after Nino's mother. Because Nino's brother had also named his first daughter Fortunata, Franca and Nino nicknamed their daughter Tinuccia.[3]

Wartime deprivation, coming on the heels of the Great Depression, fell particularly hard on Calabria, already one of Italy's poorest regions. The area had scarcely recovered from the 1908 earthquake, and new buildings were often shabby and dilapidated. Some residents were so poor that, when they wore out their clothes, they turned them inside out to get as much use as possible from them. Work was extremely scarce, the economy having ground to a standstill under Mussolini's autarky—his attempt to render Italy completely self-sufficient by cutting off nearly all trade with the outside world. Families subsisted on fishing, agriculture, and small crafts.

On December 16, 1944, Santo was born, named after his paternal grandfather. His birth came about four months before Allied troops reached Milan, marking the liberation of Italy. After the war, the Versaces could finally settle into family life during a time of peace. On December 2, 1946, Franca and Nino welcomed a second son, Giovanni Maria—Giovanni for his maternal grandfather the anarchist, and Maria for Nino's sister. Gianni, as they called him, would inherit his grandfather's iconoclastic streak.

When the war ended, Italy was on its knees, emerging from the conflict as one of Europe's most backward countries. The long land war and frequent Allied bombing had destroyed Italy's meager industrial base. In Reggio, life was exceedingly simple. Refrigerators hadn't arrived yet, so the ice man made the rounds in a miniature three-wheeled truck, with large blocks of ice in the back covered in thick wool to keep them from melting. He broke off blocks for five lire, or about two cents, each.

Few families had cars, and those that did reluctantly traversed the treacherous, single-lane provincial highways that connected Reggio to the rest of Calabria. But by the early 1950s, Italy saw the first signs of the postwar boom that brought living standards a bit closer to those of the United States or the United Kingdom. By the end of the decade, northern companies such as Fiat and Pirelli were churning out cars, tires, and machine tools at full tilt. This sparked a massive new wave of emigration—ever the scourge and the salvation of Italy's south—as millions of poor southerners flocked to Milan and Turin in search of work in the hulking new factories there. As always, prosperity would not come to Reggio; the Reggini would have to go to it.

Stories quickly spread through Reggio, not only about the opportunities in the north but also about how northerners mocked these newcomers, who often couldn't read and who arrived from the countryside with their belongings packed in battered cardboard boxes bound with rough twine. Settling in the north, Calabrians squeezed alongside their brethren from Naples, Sicily, and Puglia into ugly tenement blocks that had been thrown up in the cold, foggy periphery around Milan and Turin. Others moved to Germany, Belgium, or Switzerland to work in coal mines or on construction sites. Very few returned.

But, even as many abandoned Calabria in the early 1950s, the Versaces managed through hard work to capture a slice of the new economic boom. After the war, Nino had taken over his brother's coal business, using a scooter to haul the ore up the hill to clients' homes. When Italians switched from coal heating to gas, Nino started delivering canisters of gas. Then he began to sell the city's first refrigerators and simple washing machines. The first Cinquecentos, the tiny cars that Fiat sold at just 500,000 lire, or about $250, began to replace scooters and bicycles in Reggio, and Nino and Franca could afford the family's first car. In 1958, Nino brought home a television, one of the very first in the city. That year, forty friends and relatives crowded into the family's living room to watch the Sanremo music festival, when Domenico Modugno, a little-known Pugliese performer, sang "Volare" for the first time, a sweet ballad that instilled a sunny new image of Italy the world over. Nino and Franca left the windows open so that the neighbors could listen to the music.[4]

During the 1950s, the young family could afford some modest middle-class comforts. They moved into a spacious apartment near the city's resplendent, cream-colored cathedral, or duomo, with its glittering rose-shaped window. Tinuccia, Santo, and Gianni grew up steeped in the indolent rhythm of Italy's deep south. After Mass on Sundays, children accompanied their fathers to the Bar Malavenda, an elegant fin de siècle–style café with dark wood and brass fittings, to buy trays of pastries, while old men whiled away the afternoon at the bar, reading *La Gazzetta dello Sport* or playing cards. During the week, women stopped to chat and gossip under the colorful umbrellas in the open market near the Versace home, where wooden crates overflowed with eggplants, tomatoes, and lemons cut in half to show off their bright yellow pulp. The citrus smell, together with the aroma of fresh fish piled on mountains of chipped ice, mingled with the smell of freshly baked bread, rich espressos, and salty sea air to make for a heady Proustian aroma that Gianni would recall with affection years later. A weekday lunch was a three-hour affair, and Nino came home to eat with the entire family before returning to work.

"Life in Calabria was poetry then," Santo Versace would recall five decades later. "Everything was a victory. People had survived the war, hunger, desperation, so they were happy."[5]

Franca's shop prospered. Large-scale production of clothes was common in the United States by the mid-nineteenth century, but in Italy, what little ready-made clothes were available in the shops were ugly. For most, a woman's postwar-era wardrobe evoked misery: cork wedge heels, skirts split in the back to make for easier pedaling on a bike, and harsh, square-cut jackets. Franca could offer them something better, even beautiful. While an elite few went to Paris to buy their wardrobes at the French couture houses, most of Italy's upper crust had their wardrobes made by local dressmakers. A few top dressmakers bought the patterns made in plain cotton from the Paris couture houses to make exact copies of their latest designs. But the fees that houses such as Christian Dior and Balenciaga charged for their patterns were too expensive for most seamstresses, particularly in the provinces. Instead, tailors such as Franca bought patterns from the emerging couture houses in Rome. From the start, even in this modest way, the Versaces would forgo French fashion and embrace the possibility of Italy.

Gianni Versace had an exceptional mentor in his mother. Franca soon became known as Reggio's best dressmaker, and the city's most elegant ladies came to her when they needed a wedding dress for a daughter or a new outfit for an evening at the city's theater. Although she bought patterns from the couture houses in Rome, she often added her own touches, such as a collar of intricately beaded pearls. She was so skilled that she could cut cloth for a new dress without following a pattern, using just pins to mark the edges—a rare ability. She loved her work and devoted long hours to it—sometimes working through the night to finish a dress.

Franca particularly loved to make wedding gowns, and indeed a Versace bridal gown was a dream for many Reggio brides, a rare burst of glamour for families of modest means. In turn, weddings were a boon for Franca. In the 1950s, a bride would require not just a wedding dress, but an entire *corredo*, or the day clothes, evening clothes, overcoats, and even the underwear that a new signora required. Franca sat patiently with excited brides and their mothers, paging through heavy books with photos and sketches to help them choose, telling them what shoes and gloves to buy. On the morning of a wedding she went to the bride's house to attend to the final details.

Franca's children were among the best dressed of the city. For her First Communion, Tinuccia wore a full-length white dress with tiny buttons down the front and a skirt that was a cascade of ruffles. For Santo's and Gianni's, Franca made perfectly cut white three-piece morning suits, complete with bow ties and white gloves. A photo from the era shows a prim young Gianni in his pristine white suit, with a shy but determined smile on his face. For *carnevale* celebrations, the Italian Mardi Gras festival, Franca made the children elaborate costumes—and Gianni was her best model. One year, she dressed him as an eighteenth-century nobleman with knee-length breeches, a rich silk embroidered cape, and cream-colored shoes festooned with large bows. Even as a very young boy, Gianni absorbed his mother's sense of style; when he was in middle school, he would sometimes point out when his friends' socks clashed with the rest of their clothes.[6]

In Reggio, with its ten months of sunshine a year, mild winters slipped into balmy springs; the heat of the summers was relieved by a frequent breeze from the strait. On warm evenings, the Versaces often walked down Corso Garibaldi, where whole families went for postdinner strolls, stopping for dishes of gelato or fruit cocktail. Occasionally, Nino would take Franca dancing on one of the dance floors that were laid down during the summer on the gravelly beach on the lido, where bands played mambos or the sweet hits of a newly carefree Italy. Gianni would sit licking an ice cream, entranced as he watched his parents dance to songs such as "Parlami d'amore Mariù" ("Speak to Me of Love, Mariù").[7] Sunday was dedicated to the extended family, when Versace cousins, aunts, uncles, and grandparents ate together, joking and chatting in Calabrian dialect. After lunch, Nino gathered the children to solemnly hand out their allowances. Later, he would do the week's accounts, papers spread out in front of him, as he listened to the city's soccer team, La Reggina, play its weekly soccer match.

Nora Macheda, a young relative of Franca's who was orphaned

as a girl, came to live with the family when the children were young. Zia Nora, as she was known to everyone, helped Franca run the house and care for the children. Gianni, Santo, and Tinuccia adored Nora, who was about fifteen years younger than Franca and something of a peer and confidante for the children. A small, wiry woman with black hair cropped short, Nora, who never married, bustled around the kitchen preparing meals for the brood. During the summers, Nora took the children to a rented three-bedroom house high in the hills above Reggio. They joined cousins on Nino's side of the family, riding their bikes along the dirt paths. Sometimes they went to an American military base nearby, where Gianni and his siblings would watch films in English, understanding not a word but soaking up the glamour of Hollywood.

But the hard-earned postwar idyll of the Versace family would be cruelly shattered in a way that would affect Gianni profoundly. In May 1953, Tinuccia, then nine, fell ill with peritonitis. Franca sent Gianni and Santo to stay at an uncle's house while she sat distraught by the girl's bedside. Gianni, frenetic with worry, soon ran away from his uncle's house and came home—entering the house to see his sister in a white casket, dressed in her First Communion dress and surrounded by white flowers, in the room where his mother usually sewed. He felt like he couldn't breathe.[8]

Franca, kneeling in front of the casket, convulsed in sobs, motioned for Gianni to come over.

"Gianni, your sister has gone to heaven," she said. "You and Santo are all I have now."

For the funeral Mass, white horses drew a carriage bearing the casket, a kindle of schoolgirls dressed in First Communion dresses trailing behind it.[9]

For months, Franca was inconsolable and unable to work. She spent most of her time closed up in her bedroom crying or at the cemetery, visiting her daughter's grave. Within a year's time, however, she grew calmer. One day, she took her younger son aside.

"Gianni, you're going to have a little brother or sister," she told him.

Donatella was born on May 2, 1955.

❖ V ❖

From the time Gianni was a small boy, Franca's workshop was heaven for him. After school, he stopped at home for a snack prepared by Nora, and headed straight for Franca's shop, where he would finger the fabrics and gaze fascinated at the patterns that Franca brought back from her trips to the couture houses in Rome. He hid behind the deep red curtain that closed off the bright room where Franca received clients. In the next room were Franca's seamstresses, surrounded by bolts of cloth and baskets full of pins, buttons, and beads. He watched enthralled during fittings as his mother and an assistant pinned dresses, and garments slowly took shape. He sat on the workshop floor as Franca's seamstresses laid the fabric out on sheets of paper where the patterns had been traced in white chalk. Pins held the cloth down as the women deftly cut into the fabric. Others in the shop would sew hundreds of tiny multicolored pearls to create the beaded bodice of a wedding gown.

"Why don't you go out and play with your friends?" Franca asked Gianni, worried about all the time he spent in the shop.

"I don't want to," Gianni responded. "I want you to show me how you make the clothes."[10]

Before long, he started to use what he was learning. When he was about nine, Gianni started gathering the scraps of silk and wool that fell to the floor and stitching them into puppets, holding his own private shows afterward. At age eleven, he made dresses for a friend's dolls, staging a play baptism for them. The workshop not only inspired him; its women nurtured him. The dozen seamstresses Franca employed, many of whom traveled each day from the poor, small towns in the hills above Reggio, often had to sleep in the shop during the long days and nights of preparation for a wedding.[11] The women fussed endlessly over Gianni. "*Vieni qua, Giannino!*" they would call to him. "Come here, Giannino!" Gianni loved the attention, looking for any excuse to run errands, buying pins or zippers for the matronly ladies. On hot days in the summer, he went to buy them shaved ice *granite*.

"My life was like a Fellini film," he later told an interviewer. "I grew up surrounded by all women. I was spoiled. I had twenty girl-friends and twenty mothers."[12]

But the main woman in Gianni's life remained his mother. He was devoted to Franca, in a way surpassing even the maternal adoration typical in Italian boys. He resembled her physically, with his round face, deep-set eyes, and small frame. Franca was an affectionate mother who clearly adored her children, although she could be stern and demanding of them. Willful and determined, Franca had a strong creative streak that might have blossomed more richly in a different time and place. Despite her constrained upbringing in provincial Italy and her limited education, she was remarkably open-minded for her time, having inherited her father's iconoclastic bent. She had absorbed her family's socialist ideas—a relative rarity in a region known for strong Fascist sympathies.

"She wasn't at all one of those old-fashioned mothers," recalled a childhood friend of Donatella's. "You could talk to her about everything."[13]

Franca's bond with all three of her children was fierce. It is hard to overstate the role of the mother in Italian families; she is a venerated figure even in modern times, particularly in the more traditional south. Italian mothers lavish care and attention on their kids in measures that seem excessive by the standards of northern Europe or America; they constantly cook their children's favorite meals, ensure their clothes are perfectly laundered and ironed, and fuss over even minor ailments. Sons are an object of particular attention, even when they are grown. Children usually live at home right up until they marry, and even when they move out, they typically see or speak with their mothers every day. And, of course, sometimes such relentless loving attention can turn into undue maternal control of sons and daughters, even as adults.

By contrast, Gianni struggled in his relationship with his father. While Nino was diligent in providing for his children, he was a solitary, taciturn man, largely leaving it to Franca to bring up the kids. For the young Gianni, whose imagination was already bubbling over with ideas and ambition, Nino lacked verve and flair. His clothing—plain, gray pants, with a shirt that had big pockets for him to hold his pens and notes—appalled his son.

"His shirt was like his office," Gianni said later.[14]

Nino spent his little free time absorbed in books, particularly classics such as Homer's *Odyssey* and *Iliad*, and Dante's *Divine Comedy*. He loved to gather his children in the living room to listen to him recite passages from memory. Though his father was clearly a man possessed of his own classical imagination, Gianni found such sessions unbearably boring. The man himself was intimidating to his younger son.

"He used to scare me, even when he took me by the hand in the afternoon to go for a walk," Gianni would recall.[15]

Moreover, Nino clearly favored Santo, who closely resembled his father. The eldest son occupies a place of honor in Italian families; he bears the weight of his parents' highest expectations. In those straitened and more traditional postwar days, the oldest son shared in the responsibility for caring for the whole family. In this, Santo never disappointed. He became Franca and Nino's pride and joy. With a long face, dirty-blond hair, and a leaner, more athletic body than Gianni, he was the best-looking of the Versace siblings as well as the most accomplished. He brought home top grades, shared Nino's love of sport, and enthusiastically assisted his father in business. When Santo turned just six years old, Nino started taking him to his shop to help shovel coal and fill orders for customers. A kilo of coal cost thirty-six lire (about twenty cents) then, and Nino drilled Santo until the boy could multiply any number by thirty-six in his head to tally the price for a customer. Santo loved it; he basked in his father's approval. On Sunday mornings, when his workers were off, Nino took Santo along to clients' homes to help him unscrew empty canisters of gas and install full ones. If Santo, a gifted basketball player, had a game and couldn't go to the shop, Nino drafted Gianni to help instead. But Gianni hated it, grumbling and complaining the whole time. Sometimes he simply defied his father.

"Nino sometimes told Gianni he had to come help, but there was no way," Zia Nora remembered. "He would just say no."

The constant comparisons to Santo embittered Gianni. His teachers often pointed out the differences between the two brothers. Nino and Franca badly wanted to see their children earn university degrees, which few families in Reggio could yet afford. They were pleased to see Santo grow into a serious young man. Gianni, however, was directionless, a dreamer and a slacker. His parents made their displeasure known.

"My parents adored Santo because he was the perfect child, the one who studied and always did what he was told, while I was the black sheep," Gianni said much later. "I was the one who answered back, the one who didn't study. It weighed on me."[16]

Santo's athletic prowess, a source of great pride for Nino, also embarrassed Gianni, a skinny kid with little interest in sports. One winter, the family went skiing in the Aspromonte, when Gianni took a violent fall and badly broke his tibia. Emergency surgery left an ugly nine-inch scar that marred his leg so badly that as an adult he would try unsuccessfully to have a plastic surgeon erase it. Worse still, Gianni brought home abysmal grades, frequently failing subjects such as Latin, geography, and math, and scarcely passing the rest of his courses, even art. He constantly cut classes to go to the beach. Franca sometimes drafted her seamstresses to corral her unruly son and get him to school.

"I can still picture him with two of the seamstresses, dragging Gianni under his arms, his hands covered in chocolate," said Anna Candela, a close family friend. "They were literally lifting him off the ground."[17]

When he made it to school, he sat in the back of the drab classroom, paying little attention, instead filling notebook after notebook with sketches. Once, his teacher summoned Franca to the school. She showed her Gianni's notebooks, filled with drawings of women with huge busts and tiny wasplike waists. "Signora, your son is some sort of sex maniac," the teacher said. The truth was far different, of course. Gianni had a boyish fascination not with women as sex objects but as the divas of the day—namely, the sultry actresses Gina Lollobrigida and Sophia Loren, who starred in the films he avidly watched at the local cinema.

"Those sketches were a sign of what I would become," he would say decades later. "But how could I explain that to a teacher in Reggio Calabria in 1956?"

While Santo was protective of Gianni, he scolded him for wasting his allowance, usually on clothes, magazines, and later, tickets to concerts and the theater. In turn, Gianni tried to squeeze more money out of his older brother.

One of the few occasions that brought father and son together was the opera. Nino loved opera and often took Gianni with him. Once when his mother dressed him in a gray velvet jacket and black pants to go to the Teatro Cilea in Reggio to see Giuseppe Verdi's *Un ballo in maschera*, Gianni, sitting next to his father, who was dressed in black, felt like a prince. He found the costumes and the sets dazzling, touching a creative chord that would resonate later.[18]

But Gianni did not dream then of being a clothing designer. Instead, he wanted to become a musician—he idolized the American composer George Gershwin—and he pestered his parents to send him to a local high school for the arts. Nino wouldn't hear of it. He wanted Gianni to earn a surveying degree at a technical high school. As rural areas poured their population into the cities in the south, a building boom was sweeping Reggio, and Nino reckoned that a degree in surveying was a ticket to a secure job. He insisted Gianni enroll at the city's technical high school, housed in an ugly gray Fascist-era building that was as forbidding as a prison.

Although the teenage Gianni languished at school, he blossomed in Franca's atelier. He spent more and more time in his mother's shop, passing the afternoons sketching or cutting photos out of fashion magazines. During the family's summer retreats to the mountains, he would disappear for hours, a sketchbook tucked under his arm. When he was about fifteen, his mother started sending him to Messina to deliver garments to be embroidered by a particularly skilled craftswoman there, and to buy fabrics for the shop. He loved rummaging through dozens of thick spools of fabrics, looking for something unique. These short trips across the strait gave him the first taste of life beyond Reggio. The standards of Reggio society and achievement soon felt suffocating. When the time came for Gianni to take the state exam necessary to receive a high school diploma, he simply skipped it and never received the degree, bitterly disappointing his father.

Moreover, as Gianni advanced through his teenage years, Nino must have also worried about Gianni's lack of interest in girls, especially as Santo was gaining a reputation as a young lothario. The skinny, shy Gianni seemed a *mammone*, a mama's boy, forever tied to Franca's apron strings. Classmates began to notice that Gianni was different, and some began to avoid him. That only made him more reluctant to attend school.

According to Angelo Bernabo, a former classmate, "He was certainly a very sensitive person. He had this falsetto voice, a very high-pitched voice, so he was classified as 'different' immediately. Some people were afraid that, if they hung out with him, others would jump to the wrong conclusions."[19]

Once, Gianni dressed up as a woman for *carnevale*. "He was the spitting image of a woman," a close friend recalled. "We had to go pick him up and I saw him walking down the street in this outfit. I thought, *O mio Dio*, what if someone sees us!"

As a teenager, his growing awareness of being gay was a heavy burden for Gianni. In the early 1960s, homosexuality was still deeply taboo in Calabria, where sexual mores remained suffocatingly strict. It was shameful for a family, particularly a Calabrian father, to have a gay son. Italian mothers of the era sometimes protected their gay offspring, but in Calabria they often took the side of the father in ostracizing a homosexual child. Gay men were the target of taunts—they were called *ricchiuni*, Calabrian dialect for "queer"—and, occasionally, violence. Gianni hid his sexuality, never speaking about it to his parents, or even Santo, who, according to some friends, found his brother's emerging sexual orientation embarrassing. Nora was the only one to whom he confided his secret, and she, in turn, was extremely protective of the teenager, defending him when Franca or Nino lost their patience with Gianni.

But any anguish over his sexuality, and his concealment of it, did not stop Gianni from exploring his desires. He started to hang out on an isolated beach just north of Reggio, where a tiny alternative scene bustled. Teenagers smoked pot, women bathed topless, and gay men met up. After high school, Gianni went to Taormina and Catania, two cities on Sicily's eastern coast that had some gay nightclubs and saunas. When he was alone with one of the few gay friends he'd found in Reggio, he could allow himself some freedom, joking about his sexuality.

"A gay man in Reggio had problems," said Bruno De Robertis,

who was one of Gianni's few close gay friends in Calabria. "In Reggio, gay life didn't exist—there were no bars or clubs. But I could talk with Gianni about everything—about traveling, about sex, about leaving Reggio. It was a subject that brought us together."[20]

By the time he was eighteen, Gianni began to dream of escaping his native city.

"Reggio was very, very provincial then," said another close friend. "And there was Gianni, with his 'problem.'"

Gianni found refuge in the form of his baby sister. From the start, Donatella was the *cocca*, or coddled baby, of the family. Nine years younger than Gianni and eleven years younger than Santo, she was the much-cherished replacement for her dead sister, Tinuccia, a living gift to compensate for the great loss of the family's first daughter. Following Donatella's birth, Franca and Nino broke with the Calabrian tradition of bestowing family names on their children, instead giving her a name that was derived from *dono*, or "gift" in Italian. Donatella would benefit not only from her parents' love for Tina but from the Versaces' increasing prosperity. By the time Donatella was born, the family had a relatively affluent lifestyle that included three cars and a small beach-side vacation cottage. As a result, everyone spoiled little Donatella. Her cousin Tita Versace has said that "anything Donatella wanted, they made sure she got it."[21]

Franca was extremely attached to Donatella. The loss of her first daughter had shaken Franca deeply, despite her solid, optimistic character. When she gave birth to Donatella, she poured her grief for her eldest child into her love and affection for her youngest one. While she loved her sons, she had yearned for a little girl, and she spoiled Donatella without reserve, taking her shopping and having her seamstresses make her elaborate dresses. In her shop, Franca sometimes emptied the big baskets she used to hold bolts of cloth and plopped Donatella in one, rocking her gently as she worked. As she grew older, Donatella would remain much closer to her mother than to Nino, who would always be a remote figure for the little girl.

Surrounded as she was by adults, Donatella grew up fast, and Gianni soon made her his accomplice in his teenage rebellion. He would send her to steal the keys to their parents' car from Nino's nightstand so that he could go dancing or to a concert, or have her pilfer money from their parents' wallets when he had spent his entire allowance. She eagerly went along, relishing the attention given her by her big brother.

"Everything he asked me to do for him was fun for me," Donatella would recall. "I've never found anyone who was as exciting and fun."[22]

Gianni sometimes loaded Donatella into his baby blue Cinquecento to take her with him to the beach, where they spent hours with Gianni's friends at the Bagno Milea, popular for its three hundred wooden changing rooms, lounge chairs, and purple and white umbrellas. Other times, they headed to the beaches on the Ionic coast, which afforded more hours of sunlight and where young people soaked up the sun from as early as April.

As she grew up, Donatella played by the rules of Reggio, displaying more focus and ambition than her errant brother. Unlike Gianni, Donatella was a diligent student, particularly in English. But otherwise, the siblings shared similar characteristics. While Santo was more exuberant and garrulous, neither Gianni nor Donatella was very expansive or open to outsiders. Both shy and taciturn by nature, they had a small clutch of close friends and would often shoot strangers a wary, steely look. As one childhood friend described it, "Donatella hated it when there were new people around, or someone she didn't know, because she couldn't be herself."

Meanwhile, Santo, ever the diligent elder brother, fulfilled his parents' dreams for their children. He played for Reggio's semiprofessional basketball team and excelled in high school, where he studied accounting. Around the same time, he began to help with the family's finances, negotiating the terms of loans and investments with the bank managers.

"When we were kids, Gianni and I were the clubbers and he was the one who finished his homework and then went to help our mother close the shop," Donatella once said of her oldest brother. "Gianni and I used to say, Santo is so boring! But we knew we could count on him."[23]

In 1963, after high school, Santo enrolled in the University of Messina—Reggio wouldn't have its own university until years later—shuttling back and forth across the strait from Sicily to attend classes. At school, he became one of the top leaders of a large left-leaning political group, displaying natural organizational skill at a time when student politics in Italy was stirring with fresh radical ferment. While many students in Italy take seven or eight years to finish their degrees, Santo, ever the methodical student, rushed through in four. In 1968, he became the first in the family to finish college, earning an economics degree with top honors, having produced a 410-page thesis entitled "The Economic Effects of Public Spending on Gross National Product."

"There was always Santo, the calm one, Gianni, the *enfant terrible* and me, Gianni's accomplice," Donatella later recalled.[24] "Santo was a sort of father figure. Instead, Gianni was my friend."[25] The youthful dynamic among the three siblings would mark their adult relationships with one another, fostering their success in the years ahead—and, thanks to the inevitable dysfunction among them, ultimately leading them close to ruin.

three

Breaking Free

*a*S GIANNI FLIPPED THROUGH FASHION MAGAZINES IN HIS mother's workshop and began to dream of a future far from Reggio, he learned that there was just one place in the world where style was determined: Paris. In the 1950s, the entire world of couture was governed by a small group of French designers. Tradition dictated that hopeful young couturiers leave their homeland behind and come to the French capital. But the Parisians were hardly going to admit a brash and un-tutored young man from the provinces of Italy. The world would have to change before that happened—and it did.

Though he could not have realized it as a teenager sketching in his mother's dress shop, Gianni would, through-out his life, contend with a fashion establishment casually intent on keeping out upstarts such as himself. Ultimately, he would be a leader of a movement that would upend the ruling class—and challenge the primacy of Paris itself.

From the vantage point of the early twenty-first century, it is hard to imagine how thoroughly the fashion burghers of Paris dictated what the civilized world wore. Starting in the late nineteenth century, Paris had been the world's undisputed fashion capital, home to Coco Chanel, Madeleine Vionnet, and Jean Patou. World War II temporarily shut down the industry, but when the Nazi occupation of France ended in 1944, Paris reasserted itself as the ultimate arbiter of fashion, as Christian Dior, Givenchy, and Balenciaga dictated trends that rippled throughout Europe and the United States. For a well-dressed American or European woman, French high fashion was the *only* choice. But Parisian haute couture was an expensive, time-consuming process that only idle, rich women could afford—about as far from the vibrant, homey workshop of Franca Versace as a lady could get.

In practice as well as in principle—from the cutting of the first pattern to the sewing of the final button—French haute couture was the most elite enterprise that existed in twentieth-century business. To gain admittance to a designer's salon, a woman had to secure an introduction to the house's vendeuse, or saleswoman, through a friend or relative. In wealthy families, mothers would present their daughters to their vendeuses when the girls came of age. Once a woman became a client, she had to submit to at least three fittings for each outfit. In the workrooms, seamstresses known as *petites mains*, or little hands, assembled the finished garment, every buttonhole, seam, and pleat finished by hand. If the garment was an evening gown or a particularly elaborate jacket or cocktail dress, it might then be sent out for hand embroidering with precious stones, sequins, feathers, or crystals. A day dress could take a few weeks to make, while an embroidered gown could require months. When the dress was finally ready, men in livery delivered the clothes, packed in enormous cardboard boxes and buried in layers and layers of crinkly tissue paper. Even the most jaded ladies felt a shudder of excitement when a new couture outfit arrived.

Couture clothes suited that exclusive and exclusionary class of women who closely followed the strict rules for dressing of the 1950s, when a proper lady had different outfits for morning, lunch, and evening. Unsurprisingly, the styles of that decade excelled in their extravagance and, very often, discomfort—as was the case with apparel from Christian Dior. His New Look was the dominant style of the decade, and it featured a fierce, doll-like shape, lavish ballerina skirts, tightly fitted bodices, and molded jackets that required an armature of tight corsets and padding to smooth a woman's figure into a perfect, wasplike shape. But while undeniably elegant, French couture was anything but youthful—or sexy. In the 1950s, "women didn't care about looking young," said Karl Lagerfeld. "An eighteen-year-old wanted to look like a woman with jewellery and a mink coat because this was the fashion."[1] Two decades later, Gianni Versace would be part of a vanguard that would challenge these ingrained notions of the presentation of the body—replacing them with a glorification of youth and sexuality that would transform fashion and force Paris itself into its embrace.

Even though French fashion reigned supreme during Gianni's youth, Italian style was beginning to blossom at the time. Italy's clothing design sprang from the country's tradition of producing beautiful, high-quality fabrics. Centuries ago, Venetian merchants traded silk in Byzantium and Persia. Como's first silk looms were established in the 1500s, while weavers in Biella were spinning whisper-soft wool by the 1800s. Parisian couture houses had always bought some of their textiles from Italy, but after the war, Italian fabrics became even more popular because they were relatively cheap but of fine quality. Moreover, the Parisian couturiers employed Italian artisans to do skilled handwork, such as embroidery, and bought accessories such as shoes and lingerie from them.

In the years preceding World War II, Mussolini's autarky policy crippled the Italian fashion industry, as designers struggled to buy raw materials and cut off exports, particularly to the lucrative American market. But when the conflict ended, Rome-based couture houses flourished. Italy's upper class had become more accustomed to patronizing the Roman couturiers during the war. When Paris was liberated, the Romans resumed buying French couture patterns, but they increasingly balked at paying the high fees the Parisians charged. By 1955, Paris couture prices had risen about 3,000 percent over prewar levels.[2] With their rich fabrics, lower labor costs, and skilled craftsmen, the Roman couturiers quickly discovered they could compete with the French houses, and regional dressmakers like

HOUSE OF VERSACE

Franca Versace began buying couture patterns there. Italian couturiers soon settled on a style that was much less fussy than the Parisian look, with its abundant flounces, flourishes, and bows. Italian clothes were simpler in line, and used good-quality, soft materials, elegant draping, and vibrant colors to create a fresh, more easygoing look. And the prices—as little as $100 for a day dress—were half those of French frocks, a price that was affordable for Franca's local clientele.

The world started taking notice. American fashion magazines began to promote Italy as charming, sunny, and unstuffy. "The Italian woman of breeding has a certain quality of relaxation which endows her clothes with an easy grace, a free, uninhibited movement," wrote *Vogue* in January 1947. "Her thonged sandals help too, for her legs and feet are possibly the best in Europe."[3] The young Gianni Versace soaked up this praise for the less-restrained Italian style. In his mother's studio, he pored over the movie magazines featuring the Italian and American films that celebrated the sensual pleasures of Italian life.

About four hundred miles up the coast from Reggio, Rome's film industry was burgeoning. So many international stars were flocking to Cinecittà, Rome's fabled studios, that it was dubbed "Hollywood on the Tiber." The couturiers began to make costumes for the films and got to know the stars, who loved the easy elegance of Roman designs. For a time, Ava Gardner's contract with her studio required that she wear only clothes made by Sorelle Fontana, an atelier owned by three sisters in Piazza di Spagna. Where the stars went, the press followed. In 1955, *Life* magazine ran a cover feature entitled "Gina Lollobrigida: A Star's Wardrobe," featuring 250 sketches of her clothes, mostly made by Roman couturier Emilio Schuberth. One was a strapless evening gown in delicately pleated silk chiffon that morphed from a soft cream at the bust to a rich moss green at the waist. The play on colors as well as the snug, simple cut emphasized the star's renowned twenty-two-inch waist. The young Gianni surely saw these designs and was influenced by them—and by the overall glamour of the Italian look that emerged during the 1950s, just in time to shape his nascent fashion sensibility.

In 1951, the Roman couturiers gained an important new ally in Giovanni Battista Giorgini, a Florentine with a noble hawklike face and an aristocratic pedigree. For nearly thirty years Giorgini had been the leading buyer of Italian craft goods such as linens and fine ceramics for American department stores. Spying an opportunity, he convinced ten Roman designers to hold a runway show in his magnificent home, Villa Torrigiani, in Florence, where they displayed 180 outfits before eight American department store buyers and a host of Florentine aristocrats, who were ordered to wear only Italian designs to the event. The show was a success: *Women's Wear Daily* published a front-page article headlined "Italian Style Gains Approval of U.S. Buyers."

Within a couple of years, Giorgini moved the shows to a larger space, the Sala Bianca in Palazzo Pitti, a vast, Renaissance-era palace on the south side of the River Arno that was once the seat of the Medici dynasty. After the shows, Giorgini threw sumptuous parties in Renaissance palazzi guaranteed to dazzle, with their coffered ceilings and sumptuous frescoes. The Americans, suitably impressed, soon became the biggest fans of the new Italian look, drawn to the lower prices and cleaner, simpler looks that better suited U.S. tastes than their French counterparts. The Italian couturiers, many of aristocratic birth, also seemed to embody the carefree lifestyle of Italy's blossoming dolce vita.

"One season we would all be in Capri or Sardinia, and the next Saint Moritz—with trips to New York wedged in between," recalled Irene Galitzine, a Russian émigré who set up her own fashion house, threw grand parties in her apartment in Rome,[4] and created the famous palazzo pajamas, a wide-legged jumpsuit made of soft silk.

More important, the regular shows prodded the couture houses into producing more clothes in the factory that were ready-to-wear, rather than painstakingly made by hand. (In 1954, one Italian clothing manufacturer took the measurements of twenty-five thousand women to produce an accurate sizing system for ready-to-wear clothes.[5]) Giorgini had invited to Palazzo Pitti a small number of so-called boutique labels, or designers who made very high-quality ready-to-wear clothes. The best known of these couturiers was Emilio Pucci.

Pucci, a Florentine nobleman, had created chic ski and resort wear that was soft and unstructured. His brightly colored prints and tight stretchy trousers were an instant hit, done in exuberant blues and pinks and swirly patterns that looked great with the sandals and tanned bare legs beloved by *Vogue*. Made with a new synthetic silk-and-nylon material, his superlight jersey dresses were slinky, comfortable, and—perfect for the jet set—didn't wrinkle. At $39.95 for ski pants and $190 for a dress, Pucci's designs were very expensive ready-to-wear that was chic enough to compete with couture.[6]

By the 1960s, when Versace was a teenager traveling with his mother on her buying trips to Rome and Florence, the first ripples of a youthquake began to wash over fashion. Women worldwide yearned for a new wardrobe to match their growing social freedom. They were no longer willing to spend hours in fittings, and their social calendars didn't require such formal wardrobes. Initially, the revolution came from London, which spawned a flock of designers catering not to society ladies but girls on the street. These designers launched some of the first collections of ready-to-wear clothes that were fashionable and offered the instant gratification that made-to-measure clothes didn't—a lesson the young Versace would quickly absorb. He certainly followed the work of the first and most successful of these London designers, Mary Quant, renowned as the "inventor" of the miniskirt, whose pleated dresses and hot pants in wild, pyrotechnic colors defined the Swinging London look. The clothes were photographed on Lolita-like models such as Twiggy, with their long legs and über-slim figures, and were a huge break from the corseted, glove-and-hat style of the 1950s. Better yet, the prices were low enough that a broad swath of young women could now aspire to dress fashionably. The London look was an inspiration to Gianni, who would soon try out the modern new designs on his kid sister.

The older French couture designers haughtily resisted the new ready-to-wear tsunami. Since France had very few department stores—women bought their clothes in small boutiques—they had never felt the pressure to make clothes for the mass market.

"Coco Chanel vowed she'd never do ready-to-wear because she didn't want to dress everybody," said Gerry Dryansky, a *Women's Wear Daily* reporter in the 1960s. "The couturiers' ambitions weren't so high. They were rich and lived well, but they never intended to build colossal businesses. Their snobbism was greater than their greed."[7]

Christian Dior famously refused to provide a wedding dress for

Brigitte Bardot, considering her too vulgar for his confections. "Couture is for grannies," retorted Bardot. And many agreed. In 1964, a UK magazine announced the death of couture with fictional obituaries for Balenciaga and Givenchy.

At the same time, a sharp increase in the cost of skilled seamstresses forced couture prices ever higher. By the 1970s, legend had it that only one hundred women in the world still regularly commissioned haute couture clothes. As Gianni Versace would soon see firsthand, his fellow Italians were quickly stepping into the breach. The change in the fashion business would open the door for his radical talents.

Franca Versace understood, in a way that her husband did not, that Gianni could succeed on his own terms. So when her son flunked out of high school in 1965, Franca, anxious to see him settled into a profession, decided to open a freestanding boutique next to her atelier. Taking the name from the French fashion magazine, Gianni called it Elle di Francesca Versace.

The shop was Gianni's diploma—and his ticket to freedom. Twice a year, he went with Franca to Palazzo Pitti to watch the shows and place orders for the shop. He bought soft knits from Missoni and pleated dresses from Krizia. As the shop grew, he began going to Paris as well, where he fell in love with Chloé, a line that made gauzy blouses, long skirts, and evening dresses that were light as a cloud. He found a kindred spirit in the brand's young German designer, Karl Lagerfeld, starting what would become a lifelong friendship. Lagerfeld had made a name for himself at storied couture houses such as Balmain and Jean Patou, but by the early 1960s, finding couture out of touch, he began hiring himself out to the new ready-to-wear houses in France and Italy.

Franca—who had let Gianni tend her clients and had taught him how to make clothes to flatter a woman who didn't have a perfect figure, cutting a skirt or a dress in such a way as to hide saddlebags or slim a waist—despaired when she saw some of the trendy clothes that Gianni brought back. She preferred the more traditional designers who served up the sort of mother-of-the-bride outfits—ruffled blouses and staid *tailleurs,* or tailored suits and dresses—that would appeal to a provincial lady. When Gianni came home with more daring designs, Franca scolded him testily for buying clothes that she thought would be hard to sell.[8]

HOUSE OF VERSACE

Gradually, however, the new designs attracted Reggio's younger women. "They were beautiful women, maybe thirty-two or thirty-five years old, already married and with kids, but they had wonderful figures," said a former shop girl at the Versace boutique in Reggio. "The boutique sold the sort of clothes that Reggio didn't have until then, because in the past, ladies like them would have worn couture."

The boutique catered to Reggio's *alta borghesia* (upper crust), including the wives of bankers in search of new cocktail dresses or mothers looking to buy their daughters special dresses for university graduation. Its ground floor had white tables with glass tops and an antique glass and wood case that held small evening purses. Long steel-blue curtains set off creamy white wallpaper. Unlike in the United States, where impersonal department stores dominated and one-on-one service was rare, shopping in Italy was a leisurely affair. Ladies lingered in the Versace shop, browsing through the racks in the air-conditioned coolness, then a rarity in Reggio. Shopgirls fetched drinks, while Franca or her son conferred with the signora to understand what she needed. As a modern touch, Gianni had a stereo system installed, which played the latest songs by Frank Sinatra or Mina, a soulful Italian singer popular in the 1960s.

Gianni proved to be a skilled salesman with a sharp eye for what best suited a woman, suggesting the accessory or finishing touch that would make her stand out, such as tying a scarf around her waist or fastening a shawl of fluttering voile at her neck with a jeweled brooch. He learned how women saw themselves and how to make them feel attractive.

"When he dressed you, people would tell you how great you looked and ask you where you shopped," said Santo Versace.[9] The word spread and the boutique grew.

Encouraged by the success of the shop, Gianni decided to try his hand at designing clothes himself. At first, he commissioned a small clothing manufacturer to make up some relatively staid suits and dresses. He also started making suggestions when he met with clothing manufacturers on his buying trips.

"Gianni used to come with his mother to buy clothes for his shop," recalled Laura Biagiotti, a Rome-based clothing manufacturer who later became a prominent designer. "I remember him as a sweet, shy young man. He used to sit at my drawing table and make sketches of what he wanted us to make for him."[10]

Already fiercely determined, he started bringing a folder full of his sketches to the shows at Pitti, hoping to attract the interest of one of the clothing manufacturers that showed there. "I remember this young man, very thin and wide-eyed, armed with a huge desire to succeed and with this big folder full of sketches, trying to sell them," recalled Beppe Modenese, head of Italy's fashion trade group. "I've rarely seen someone so determined."[11]

At one trip to Pitti in early 1972, Gianni's sketches attracted the attention of Ezio Nicosia and Salvatore Chiodini, owners of Florentine Flowers, a knitwear company based in Lucca, a small medieval town near the coast in Tuscany. Nicosia's wife was the line's designer, but the company had faltered when her clothes failed to appeal to contemporary shoppers. Gianni gave Nicosia and Chiodini some advice as to what might appeal to young people. The two Tuscan businessmen liked his ideas and, desperate for some fresh blood to revive Florentine Flowers, asked Gianni to join the company.

The offer had to have been a shock to the budding designer. It was the opportunity Gianni had always hoped for, but it meant leaving his home behind, forsaking the familiar and the possibility of modest prosperity for a far more uncertain future. His dream would separate him from Franca and from the local legacy of the Versaces, and give him a foothold in a world he had only dreamed of until then.

In a move that would determine his professional relationships for the rest of his life, Gianni turned for advice to the man he trusted most: Santo Versace. His brother had just returned from two years of military service and was about to open an accountancy practice on the block next to the family's home. In what would be the first of innumerable negotiations on Gianni's behalf, Santo helped broker his brother's first contract. Gianni, displaying a confidence he didn't entirely possess, told Santo to ask for the same amount received by the hot new designer Walter Albini. Nicosia agreed.[12]

Gianni flew to Tuscany on February 5, 1972. He was twenty-five years old and happy to finally break free from Reggio. He went straight to Florentine Flowers's yarn supplier to choose the materials for a "flash" spring-summer collection that could prop up sales of the items that were currently in the stores. Gianni was already getting in deeper than he realized, taking a risk that showed his reflexive ingenuity. He knew little about how to work with knitwear; he designed as if he were working with fabric. He asked the factory to weave knits with intricate woven and braided patterns, something they had never done before, and then he cut the knits as if he were working with wool or silk, by, for instance, slicing it on the bias. The minicollection was a hit. Nicosia was so pleased that he bought Gianni a black Volkswagen convertible with a white top.

"I felt this pressure to show them I could do it immediately," Gianni would say later. "I wanted a new type of knit, one that was like fabric. It was very difficult, but, when I was discouraged, I thought of my mother, and how she used to stay up all night just to finish a dress."[13]

After just a few months in Tuscany, Gianni left Florentine Flowers to move to Milan, drawn by the rising buzz of the fashion scene there as well as the possibility of winning bigger jobs. That very year, several hot design houses—Krizia, Missoni, and Walter Albini—had abandoned Florence to stage their shows in Milan. The new ready-to-wear designers had grown increasingly unhappy with the Pitti shows. The explosion of new brands meant they had to share a runway and show only sixteen garments in a production so drab that it drained the zest from the designs. Department store buyers and journalists lobbied the designers to show in Milan, which had many more direct flights from the United States and other European capitals. Milan, the birthplace of the Futurist movement in 1909, had become the publishing capital of Italy by then, and was home to the biggest magazines and newspapers. Condé Nast established its Italian headquarters in Milan in the mid-1960s, when it launched Italian *Vogue*. International ad agencies set up their Italian headquarters in the city. Furthermore, Milan's proximity to Italy's textile producers in the north was a huge advantage, not just to manufacturing but to the design process itself.

By the early 1970s, Italian designers had gained an invaluable edge over their American and French rivals by working directly with the textile producers to create entirely new fabrics that draped differently than simple silk, cotton, or wool, and even had a different touch and sheen. A clutch of designers were staging their first shows in Milan, often using the ballrooms of big hotels. The early shows were little more than amateur hours, where designers drafted family and friends to build the backdrops, dress the models, and help with the lighting. Local hairdressers agreed to do the models' hair for free in exchange for a mention in a show's program. At the time, models were so cheap that dozens were hired per show. Gianni attended these shows and watched how they were put together; they would become the model for his own extravaganzas in the years ahead.

In Milan, the young designer moved into the Principessa Clotilde residence on the east side of the city, in Porta Nuova. His neighbors were penniless aspiring male and female models sent by their agencies, which had secured discounts on the spartan apartments. The residence was soon dubbed Principessa Clitoris, because of the high concentration of beautiful young flesh staying there and the horde of Italian playboys they attracted.

"Girls, guys—that residence was a place of perdition," Santo recalled.[14] Gianni loved the energy and sexuality of it, which would infuse his own life and influence his designs.

Gianni was becoming a player in a nascent Milanese fashion scene that was something of a Wild West, drawing neophyte models who hadn't yet managed to break through in New York or Paris, home of the major agencies. New modeling firms were mushrooming in Milan, sometimes established by men looking only to meet pretty girls, encouraging them to attend parties and dinners to generate buzz for their new businesses. These model hounds picked them up at the airport, sent them roses, and brought them to new nightclubs where they were feted with champagne—and, more and more often, cocaine. The young women were often paid little—sometimes just fifty dollars for a fitting and a show.

"The flower children, the new culture, were coming forward," said Polly Mellen, a major magazine editor in the 1960s. "It was all parties, drugs and madness, and the girls who chose to be part of it were the girls who were booked."[15]

Gianni was participating in a social revolution in Italy amid violent political unrest, as the nation's postwar dolce vita mentality burned away in a blaze of bombings, kidnappings, and violent demonstrations. In the first half of the 1970s, more than four thousand acts of political violence occurred in Italy, most of them in Rome, Turin, and Milan, including sixty-three murders, culminating in the killing of Aldo Moro, former prime minister, by the Red Brigades, a Marxist guerrilla group. Along with this upheaval came social changes at warp speed, which transformed how women dressed. Couture became a symbol of the hated bourgeoisie.

Around the world, the 1970s were a contrarian decade in fashion, as rules of taste were deliberately broken, and outrageous looks— hot pants, platform shoes, maxicoats, and polyester shirts open to the waist—reigned supreme. In Italy, however, such tastelessness was less popular. Certainly, young women shed their twinsets, black leather pumps, and pleated skirts in favor of jeans, Eskimo coats, and tie-dyed shirts. Young people who wore the old styles were suspected of harboring Fascist sympathies and could find themselves the target of bullying. But the zany aspects of 1970s style never really took root in Italy. As the decade wore on, shoppers everywhere looked for more toned-down clothes, particularly for the office, and the Italians were quick to meld the urge for casual dressing with the polish and elegance that had gone missing in the early part of the decade.

American department stores were enthusiastic buyers of the new Italian designers. They loved the clean lines of the Italian clothes, particularly the jerseys and the prints, which were feminine and elegant without the stuffiness of the French designers' works. The new jersey fabrics that skimmed and flattered a woman's body and came in fun, colorful patterns were easy to sell to American women, who wanted relaxed clothes that still looked good.

In Milan, Gianni drank up the new volatile, cosmopolitan atmosphere, bringing it into his life and his designs. With its concerts, films, and theater, the city represented everything that was new and free for Gianni, a place where his ambitions were welcomed, not squelched as they had been in the south. He drank up everything the city had to offer, spending his evenings listening to jazz at the Osteria dei Binari, a club frequented by the young Milanese intellectuals, and going to lunch on Saturdays at Bice, a homey trattoria on a side street off Via Montenapoleone.

Reggio felt far away, and Gianni kept it at a distance. He made a clean break with Calabria, cutting off old friends and embracing his new life in Milan. Nonetheless, he suffered from the city's rampant antisouthern prejudice, flinching when he heard the Milanese disparage the *terroni,* an insulting term for southerners that roughly translates as "peasant." He soon shed his Calabrian accent. After his success at Florentine Flowers, Gianni was looking for other contracts and, fighting a natural shyness, he latched on to anyone who could help him.

"He really wanted to meet people," said one textile designer who was an early supporter of his work. "I tried to introduce him to the Milan scene, but there was a certain amount of jealousy among the fashion crowd then. And the fact that he came from Reggio Calabria didn't help in Milan in those days. But he was willing to sell a piece of himself in order to be successful."[16]

In 1973, Gianni received another new opportunity: The owner of Genny, a clothing line that largely consisted of *abiti da cerimonia,* or matronly dresses and tailored jackets and skirts for occasions such as baptisms and weddings, approached him to revamp the company to appeal to a younger audience.

"I saw this young man who had this dark beard and fair skin," the owner's wife, Donatella Girombelli, recalled. "He seemed so terribly shy, almost scared." She and her husband, Arnaldo, offered him a contract to design for Genny. Gianni hesitated before accepting. He found Genny very provincial, and he had offers from more established houses. But Arnaldo Girombelli, who rode around in a chauffeured Bentley, offered him a high salary and a budget for everything from costly fabrics to special finishings, something he could only have dreamed of at most other companies.

Working for a large enterprise for the first time was a new challenge for Gianni—one that revealed his lack of professional design training. Unlike many other working designers of the era, Gianni didn't know how to sketch in a formal way. At Genny he scratched out boxy silhouettes and worked with a group of assistants who fleshed them out into finished sketches that pattern cutters then turned into garment models rendered in cheap fabric. Gianni found inspiration once he had a real sample garment in his hands. He pinned and snipped at it, adding details such as beading or changing the cut of a skirt. Often—in a method that would become his distinctive way of working—he draped the fabric on a mannequin and pinned, trimmed, and arranged it until a dress took shape, almost as if it were a sculpture.

At Genny, Gianni displayed the first flashes of inspiration that would later become his signature looks. He was a man of mixtures, combining masculine with feminine, sportswear with dressier items, leather with silk—and thus breaking long-standing rules of fashion. In one early collection, he made a brown and white jacket of Prince of Wales fabric, a check fabric used for men's suits, to wear over a silk shirt printed with roses. He had lace embroidered into *pied-de-poule* fabric, that staple of ladylike suits. His clothes were sweet—clean, but with "a touch of poetry," according to Girombelli—displaying little of the aggressively sexy look he would later become famous for.

Department stores, particularly in the United States, snapped the collections up. Between 1973 and 1980, Genny's sales tripled to ten billion lire ($6 million). Gianni soon took on another contract, with the manufacturer that produced Callaghan, a rather bland ready-to-wear line. Recognition now came swiftly. In 1975, Italian *Vogue* featured his clothes in a spread dubbed "Versace Versatile." The next year, French *Vogue* highlighted several of his Callaghan designs, saying, "With its youthful stamp, Versace's style is beginning to represent Italian fashion at the cutting edge. Unknown just three years ago, he is one of the designers that people are talking most about."[17]

Gianni worked tirelessly, as if he had to grasp his sudden opportunities before they vanished. He often woke in the middle of the night, struck by an idea, and started throwing down rough sketches. He rose at dawn to visit fabric suppliers and check on the samples at Callaghan's factory in Novara. Always a reluctant driver, he frequently rear-ended cars in front of him because his mind was on work. During the week before a fashion show, he would work as late as 4 a.m., obsessing about which clothes to show and making last-minute alterations. He was so nervous then that his voice trembled when he spoke.[18]

"He was a Stakhanovist, an overflowing river," recalled the owner of Callaghan. "He could work for hours and hours, until something was perfect."[19]

Gianni constantly observed how women dressed, trying to work out what they wanted and how he could improve on it. One August while on vacation in Capri, he took a walk with a friend around the legendary Piazzetta. He had recently designed a jersey dress—the sort popularized in the film *Saturday Night Fever*—with lace at the cuffs and the neckline. He'd shown the dress in silk on the runway but had it produced in jersey, so that it didn't wrinkle when tucked into a suitcase. He counted the number of women he saw wearing the dress.

"Ten, eleven, twelve!" he said to his friend. "Look, it's selling."[20]

But while the early collections were wearable and sold well, they hardly heralded the arrival of the revolutionary designer Gianni would become—the man who would invent new fabrics and new ways of dressing that would shock and surprise, and go on to redefine fashion's vocabulary. While he came up with some inspired ideas, he still made mistakes in color and his cut, and his collections varied greatly in quality and theme from season to season.

Gianni's early designs "were always sort of skittish and sexy and immediately comprehensible," said Joan Juliet Buck, the editor of *Women's Wear Daily* in the 1970s and later the editor of French *Vogue*. "There was nothing intellectual about them—they were like candy."[21]

❖ V ❖

Franca Versace was immensely proud of the son she had nurtured and encouraged to strike out on his own, leaving behind the refuge of family and the comfortable bourgeois achievement of Elle di Francesca Versace. Yet a worsening health problem tempered her ability to enjoy her son's success.

By the mid-1970s, Franca had been chronically ill for nearly a decade. In 1965, she had had an operation that sparked an infection that lingered in her liver and developed into cirrhosis, a condition that arose despite the fact that Franca had been a teetotaler. Over the years she grew sicker and sicker, and the doctors in Reggio didn't know how to treat her. Soon after Gianni left for Milan, Santo took Franca to a clinic in Modena, near Bologna, that specialized in liver disease. There, the doctors told him his mother was gravely ill. Franca began to shuttle between Reggio and the Modena clinic, where she submitted to debilitating treatments. Gianni, devastated, visited often, bringing her packs of newspapers and magazines to distract her from her misery. She loved to play cards, keeping a deck in her nightshirt, and she and her younger son played for hours in her hospital room.

Whenever she felt well enough, Franca visited Milan, spending weeks at a time with Gianni, who took her to meetings with business partners. She sat in the audience at his shows and eavesdropped on what other people said about her son's collection, then relayed it all—both positive and negative—to Gianni.[22] (To Gianni's disappointment, Nino felt entirely out of place in his son's new world and refused to attend any of his shows.)

Though pale and clearly very ill, she insisted on helping during the stressful days before her son's runway shows. A woman accustomed to the quality and care of handmade garments, she grew agitated during her visits to the Genny and Callaghan factories, pointing out imperfections, insisting that the workers redo garments. "How can you send this thing onto the runway?" she would ask Gianni. "Just look at this hem!"

When Gianni's best pattern cutter fell ill and an assistant botched a series of skirts, "she repinned them and had me hold up an edge," recalled Franco Lussana, one of Gianni's first employees. "She took a pair of scissors and sliced off an edge. They were perfect."[23] At the end of some of Gianni's first shows, Franca would burst into tears as she rushed backstage, immensely proud of her son. Gianni, exhausted, would hug her hard, cracking jokes to keep from crying himself.[24]

"I don't even know where to begin to describe what Gianni is becoming!" Franca, shaking her head, told friends when she went home to Reggio. "There were so many people there! Who knows what he could become one day?"

four

Sister, Playmate, Confidante

*b*Y HIS THIRTIETH BIRTHDAY IN 1976, GIANNI VERSACE HAD achieved a level of success that Franca—or Nino—had never expected for him. His contracts paid him the equivalent of hundreds of thousands of dollars a year—an impressive sum at the time for the fashion industry. Yet, he was still just one of many Italian designers creating for commercial houses. Moreover, little in the style of his clothes made him hugely distinctive. Still a journeyman, one of the many fashion folk thriving in the fast, mercurial, and uncharted territory of Milanese fashion—which itself was still an outlying province in the world of fashion—Gianni had to find his own vision if he wanted to become a designing force.

Early on, Gianni's search for a stylish new ideal settled on his little sister. Even when she was a little girl, Gianni saw her as his emerging muse. By the time Donatella was about eleven and Gianni was twenty, he had already started to make her over in his image of a modern, free-spirited woman. Gianni convinced the pre-teen to have highlights put in her light brown hair. He brought her to a young hairdresser who was a close friend of Gianni's. As Donatella got older, her brother kept pushing her to go lighter and lighter. "At 14, I was a little blonde," she recalled. "At 16, I was platinum. Gianni was delighted. My mother was not."[1]

Growing up, Donatella wasn't the prettiest young woman in Reggio; her best feature was a smooth alabaster complexion that tanned easily. Like most Calabrian women, Donatella was petite—no more than five foot three—but she had the thick hands and chunky legs characteristic of many southerners. Starting in her girl-hood and continuing through the rest of her life, she hated her stubby legs, and as a teenager she took to wearing towering heels. Egged on by Gianni, Donatella got up at 6 a.m. to style her hair and apply heavy makeup before going to school. Her big brother then helped sneak her out of the house to avoid Franca's wrath should she see her adolescent daughter made up like Cleopatra.[2]

"I was terrified of my mother—much more than my father," Donatella would relate years later. "She was the one who would say something about what I was wearing, not my father. She could give me this look. But at the same time, she was a very open-minded person."[3]

Like most Calabrian teenagers, she lived at the beach. Starting in the spring, she and her girlfriends spent hours on the wide, sandy shores on the Ionic coast, roasting under the southern sun without even an umbrella or lounge chair. Sometimes, just hours before head-ing to the beach, she would buy fabric at a shop, take it to her mother's seamstresses, and ask them to whip up a bikini for her. The seam-stresses would, of course, comply; from her parents to their employees to her two brothers, everyone in young Donatella's life would spoil her straight through her adolescence. For instance, as a teenager, Donatella developed a love for face and body creams that would nearly become an obsession as an adult. She often stopped at a local *profumeria* near her house and stocked up on the latest potions, with little regard for the cost. "Santo will come by to pay the bill," she told the shop owner. Without fail, her older brother duly complied.

For his part, when he still lived in Reggio, Gianni treated Donatella like an adult, taking her to discos and concerts on the beach when she was not yet a teen. While Donatella's girlfriends were rarely allowed to go to nightclubs as young women, Franca gave in because she knew Gianni would be with her. On many evenings, Donatella and Gianni would stay up late talking in the living room, and then go out, not to return until nearly dawn.

"They would go out for a walk after dinner and wouldn't come home until 4 a.m.," Zia Nora remembered. "I was so worried. I used to stay up and wait for them."[4] Franca, too, would worry, concerned about the risks involved in growing up too fast—risks that Gianni made real.

"He had me do things that were impossible at my age," Donatella recalled. "By the time I was twelve or thirteen, I was already an adult. My mother was furious."[5]

For Gianni, Donatella was not just an inspiring and vivacious female but a useful companion around town. His growing bond with his little sister helped ease the problem of being gay in Reggio. While he never spoke of his homosexuality with Santo, he confided most things to Donatella, and his emergent sexual orientation was obvious to her. He was happy to take her with him everywhere because the presence of a girl helped draw attention away from the fact that he was always hanging out with other young men. He was feeling more and more suffocated in Reggio, and Donatella, who was maturing into a hip teenager, was like oxygen to him. As confidante, muse, and alter ego, Donatella would flourish in her brother's company for more than a decade before she would start to chafe at the confines of that intimacy. During those early years in Reggio, it was as if Donatella "had come from Gianni, like a rib taken from his side," according to one journalist. "She was the gay man's version of a trophy wife—a trophy sister."[6]

From its beginning, their bond left little space for outsiders; the intimacy between them came at a cost to their relationships with others. That pattern was established early. At fifteen, Donatella started dating Enzo Crupi, a local boy with black curly hair and a short, compact physique who was five years her senior. Gianni took an instant dislike to Enzo, who was from a modest family background and was sometimes churlish with Donatella, and he nagged his sister to dump him. He found an ally in Franca, who cared little for Enzo herself. Franca began to push Donatella to consider going to college far away from Reggio, to free her daughter not just from Enzo but from Gianni's fast-living influence.

"My mother couldn't wait until Gianni moved away because she thought he was ruining me," Donatella said. "I didn't get along with kids my own age, because I was so used to hanging out with people older than me."[7]

Like Gianni, Donatella found delight and meaning in the Elle di Francesca Versace—not because she wanted to design, but because the boutique was her personal treasure trove. The shop sat right across from the family's new home, on Via Tommaso Gulli, a side street that ran between the Piazza del Duomo and the boardwalk. The airy eight-room apartment had ten-foot ceilings and thick walls that kept out the noise and the heat. After finishing her studies in a small room off the kitchen, Donatella often went down to the shop, which became a natural hangout for her and her friends. She spent hours there, trying on the new clothes, fixing her makeup in the mirrors, and chatting with the shopgirls and her mother's clients.

But thanks to Gianni, Donatella was not limited to sporting the sort of clothes favored by the ladies of Reggio. On his buying trips to Rome and Milan—and later London and Paris—Gianni picked out clothes that he thought would suit his little sister. While she wasn't tall, she was very thin—an Italian size thirty-eight, or an American size four—and could pull off daring outfits. He filled his suitcases with clothes for Donatella that were far more fashionable—long knit skirts that fell to the ankle or high leather boots—than anything other teenage girls in Reggio could dream of wearing. By the time she was about twenty, Donatella was already wearing clothes by Kenzo, a Japanese designer working in Paris who was known for his avant-garde styles. Once, Gianni bought the two of them full-length leather coats that made them stand out like Manhattanites in their one-horse town.

Even by the more liberal standards of the 1970s, Donatella drew stares in Reggio for the outré look that Gianni molded for her. He sometimes sketched outfits for her and brought them to his mother's seamstresses to make.

Sister, Playmate, Confidante

"Gianni always treated me like an adult, never my age," Donatella told one journalist. "He once made me a miniskirt in patent leather, black, and a bright-yellow top, with patent-leather boots and blond hair to here. I was so young. We were lying about my age, telling everyone I was older."[8]

While Donatella was shy and wary around outsiders, she was warm and generous with people close to her. She grew close to some of the girls who worked in her mother's shop, who confided their personal problems to her. Donatella was also remarkably generous. If a shopgirl admired something Donatella was wearing, she often gave it to her. When one of the employees got engaged, Franca always let her choose any bridal gown from the boutique, including dresses by couturiers such as Yves Saint Laurent. Donatella would happily fuss over the girls for weeks, helping them choose their bridal outfits, shoes, and jewelry, and like her mother with her clients, she would come to their homes the morning of the wedding to help with makeup and button them into their gowns.

Gianni also transmuted to his sister his own yearning for a life beyond the confines of Reggio. Franca, too, was eager that her daughter not suffer under the same constraints that had choked off her own options a generation earlier. Donatella was clearly not designed or inclined to be a wild child of Calabria who would later settle down into matrimony and domesticity. She felt—and her mother and brother agreed—that she was destined for greater things. Unlike her brother, though, Donatella had no clear idea of what those greater things might entail.

❖ V ❖

A year after Gianni left for the north, Donatella also left Reggio, going to the University of Florence to study languages, focusing on Spanish and English. She settled on Tuscany because two girlfriends planned to enroll in school there—and possibly because it offered the chance to be close to her big brother. One girl, Mariella, lasted only a month before returning to Reggio. The other girl was also named Donatella, but had long, jet-black hair and dark, sensual looks.

Donatella's student days in Florence would be the happiest time of her life, free as she was of the confines and mores of Reggio. She had responsibility for nothing but her own fun, and she took advantage of her freedom. In the mid-1970s, Italian campuses were erupting in riots and demonstrations over workers' rights, the war in Vietnam, and America's nuclear politics, and it was a time of enormous change for women, as divorce and abortion were legalized and more women began to work outside the home—wrenching changes for a still-traditional Catholic country. While at the university, Donatella took little interest in politics, preferring a carefree life of discos, concerts, and hanging out with friends in one of the many student bars and *birrerie* (pubs) the city offered. She hated the Beatles, finding them too commercial, preferring instead the Rolling Stones; Mick Jagger was her favorite singer. She wore her blond hair parted simply in the middle, falling straight to just above her shoulders. Already a heavy smoker, she dressed like a gypsy, wore heavy eye makeup, and hung out with the trendiest students on campus. "My friends were very, very avant-garde at that time," she recalled proudly.[9]

She and her friend Donatella Benedetto shared a room in a stately apartment on a side street between the covered market at San Lorenzo and Florence's Duomo, the green, pink, and cream cathedral with its distinctive brick dome designed by Filippo Brunelleschi. The two girls spent little time studying, managing to cram successfully for their exams in just a few days. Otherwise, they were happily footloose. They called their parents once a week from public phone booths, feeding the machine with *gettoni*, rough-hewn, bronze-colored tokens that cost two hundred lire (about ten cents) each.

"The food at the university cafeteria was terrible, so as soon as our parents sent us money, we went to a restaurant," Benedetto recalled. "We found this wonderful place that made these thick Florentine steaks. Whenever the parents of any of our friends came, we immediately got them to take us out to eat." The two young women loved to visit the Officina Profumo Farmaceutica di Santa Maria Novella, a thirteenth-century pharmacy-turned-beauty-shop, to buy jar after jar of face creams.

The roommates often swapped tops and sweaters, but not pants, because Donatella Versace had a tiny waist, much smaller than her friend's. She never forgot the style tips her brother had taught her;

while her friends dressed in jeans and casual shoes, Donatella always wore stilettos, deftly navigating the cobblestone streets of Florence. Even the slippers she wore at home had high heels.

Even though Donatella was nearly twenty by this time, Franca fretted about her daughter's distance from home and often made the long trip north to check on her, sleeping on a cot in the girls' room. She always arrived bearing a gift for each girl, often a sweater or a scarf from her boutique. To Franca, Donatella remained the precious daughter she had been since the day she was born, conceived to replace the one so tragically taken from her. She spoiled her adult child just as she had when she was a girl, bustling around their small room, picking up the clothes that were left strewn around and doing her daughter's laundry. "Look at what a mess your clothes are!" she scolded Donatella. But then she took the girls and their friends out for dinner.

The students spent several months at a time in Florence, when classes were in session, but then returned to Reggio for long stretches when they didn't have to attend classes, in order to save money. Donatella's parents had bought her a car, but the girls often took the overnight train to shuttle back and forth to Florence, a twelve-hour trip. Absentminded, they usually forgot to book a sleeping berth and often spent the night on the floor of the grimy trains, elbow to elbow with other Calabrian émigrés returning home from the industrial Italian north for a holiday.

"We didn't care," Benedetto would say more than thirty years later. "We spent the whole night laughing and talking. Donatella had this wonderful sense of humor. I remember the two of us laughing together all the time. We had just so much fun."

Fun was their main area of concentration while attending university. Neither girl gave much thought to what they would do after graduating. Most Italian students who gain a degree in languages go on to teach high school, but Donatella never intended to follow such a dull path. Given her passion for concerts and music, she dreamed of finding work in public relations or even show business. At the worst, she could always help run her mother's boutique.

She held on to one important link to her life in Calabria: She continued to date Enzo, even as she shuttled back and forth to

Florence. But Enzo had made it clear that he wouldn't leave Reggio. And Gianni, always jealous of Donatella's attentions toward Enzo and ever eager for a companion and muse, was steadily pulling her into his buzzing new world of international fashion, with all its lures and promises.

❖ V ❖

Despite his early success, Gianni was still unsure of himself. He was juggling several contracts and longed for a sounding board. Donatella was just twenty, whereas Gianni was near thirty, and he needed her youthful, female perspective. She would be his one-person research department, or the sort of blithe, vibrant woman Gianni ached to dress. Most important, he knew that if he was to achieve his dream of becoming an independent designer, he had to capture the energy that Donatella represented—and spin it into truly original clothing.

As soon as Donatella moved to Florence in 1973, Gianni began pestering her to make the three-hour train ride to Milan so that he could show her his designs. Whenever he had to go to Ancona to make the final changes for the Genny collection at the factory there, he had her meet him in Bologna to take the train together to the factory. (On the train, Gianni often ran into Gianfranco Ferré, another rising star who was shuttling to a factory in Bologna. The two men would become friends.) When Gianni staged his shows, the two Donatellas went to Milan to help prepare, bunking together in his apartment.

"I began coming every weekend," Donatella Versace remembered. "And then the weekends got longer and longer. Gianni used to say, 'Stay another day!' Even if Gianni was very talented, he could be very insecure. He wanted my opinion."

Franca was not pleased. She worried that Gianni was hijacking Donatella's future, and she pestered her daughter not to go to Milan to see her brother so often. She wanted Donatella to choose her own path—whatever that might be—instead of blindly following her big brother.

"Have you done that exam yet? Have you finished that paper?" she asked Donatella. "You're living Gianni's life! You should be living your own life." She scolded Gianni for monopolizing Donatella and distracting her from her studies, and warned him to leave her alone. But Gianni thought Donatella was wasting her time in school. "Why do you study so much?" Gianni asked her, annoyed. He saw his sister's future in Milan, at his side.

Donatella had a different angel on each shoulder, each one entreating her to choose a life that contradicted the other's urging. "I had my mother on one side, and then I had Gianni saying, 'Come on, stay one more day!'" Donatella remembered. "Sometimes I wouldn't tell her that I'd gone to see Gianni. I was between a rock and a hard place."[10]

Her path would, in a sense, be chosen for her when one of those two angels went silent. In June 1978, Donatella was just weeks away from completing her degree, busy finishing the thesis that is required at Italian universities. The evening before she was to defend her thesis, she called her mother, who had been admitted to the clinic in Modena the week before to undergo a new treatment. Zia Nora had come to keep the young student company and tidy up after her. Donatella was distraught to hear how weak Franca sounded on the phone.

"Mama, I'm coming to see you tomorrow," she told her.

"No, you have to stay and defend your thesis," Franca said weakly. "I don't want you to come."

Even as she urged Donatella to stay in Florence, Franca knew that she had little time left. She worried about Donatella, who remained a *bambina* in Franca's eyes. A week earlier, when Santo was driving Franca to the clinic, she gravely made her son pledge that, in case she died, he would take care of a particular matter.

"Santo, everything that I have must go to the baby," she told him. "I want you to promise me that you'll take care of it." Franca worried that her daughter, who had both the blithe spirit and the vulnerability of a spoiled child, would be adrift without a steady hand to guide her.

After speaking with her mother, Donatella rescheduled her thesis defense and rushed to Modena. But she was too late. Franca died on June 27, 1978, at the age of fifty-eight. None of her children had made it to the clinic in time to say good-bye.

Donatella never returned to Florence. "At that point, I hated university," she said. "I felt that it was the thing that had kept me from her."[11]

Franca died without a will, which under Italian law meant that her estate would automatically be divided among all three of her children and Nino. Santo went to Gianni and his father and told them of the conversation with Franca. They immediately acceded to their mother's bidding, and Santo hired a lawyer to draw up papers whereby he and Gianni would renounce their portion of Franca's inheritance. As a result, Donatella, ever the baby of the family, inherited the boutique that Gianni and his mother had worked so hard to establish.[12]

For Gianni, Franca's death was devastating. "I had learned to love her with absolute abandon once I was an adult, when I could truly appreciate her strength," he said later.[13] Having lost his staunchest support, he channeled that devotion to Donatella.

For some time, Gianni had been urging Donatella to join him permanently in Milan, arguing that to return to Reggio—and Enzo—would smother her. Donatella was more attached to Reggio than to Gianni, but losing her mother at twenty-three left her devastated and adrift—just as Franca had feared. The young woman had never been close to her father, and Gianni offered a ready refuge while she grieved.

"Donatella still needed her mother at that age," said cousin Tita Versace. "It was very difficult for her."[14]

She was, however, motivated not just by grief but by glamour. Years of hearing the stories of Gianni's travels, and the small bit of high life she'd already tasted when tagging along with him, were now irresistible to her. Gianni had taken her with him to New York occasionally, and the city had entranced her. (Both siblings had to overcome an early fear of flying.) On his trips there, he had gone with friends to Studio 54, the legendary disco that was the symbol of 1970s debauchery. Later, in the early 1980s, he would also take her to the Saint, the dazzling gay disco on the site of the 1960s concert hall the Fillmore East, complete with a ceiling on which lights revealed a universe of constellations.

"Gianni used to drag Donatella with us and she was a kid then," a friend recalled. "The mix of Studio 54 and the Saint was like visiting either hell or paradise, depending on how you saw it."

To Gianni's delight, Donatella finally decided to move to Milan, settling into her brother's spare bedroom on Via Melegari. The apartment sat in Milan's toniest neighborhood, home to the city's old industrial families. Around the corner lived the Invernizzi family, a wealthy Milan clan whose home was a miniature Versailles, with its lush gardens, lily pad ponds, and strutting pink flamingos. Even though his apartment was a rental, Gianni spent a fortune refitting it in lavish Art Deco style. His expansive lifestyle was already expensive, the young designer showing the penchant for heavy spending that would split the three siblings in the decades ahead—and nearly prove to be the undoing of their family business. But in 1978, the apartment was for Gianni and Donatella both refuge and stage set.

Donatella arrived on Gianni's doorstep, reeling from her mother's death. The loss of Franca had shaken both of them deeply and brought them even closer. Gianni felt enormously protective of his baby sister, as if he replaced the presence of a wife and his mother with Donatella. Moreover, having Donatella by his side in Milan was like an anchor for Gianni, particularly amid the stress and strain of racing to snap up the opportunities that were coming to him. He was ever the Calabrian son, needing his family close by to feel grounded.

Donatella, in turn, found comfort in Gianni's new world, a place where she could continue to be the flighty kid sister for many years to come. Their bond became inextricable and codependent. Each was instantly able to read the other's moods and thoughts. Over the next few years, they happily spent virtually every waking hour together, living together, working together, taking their meals together. But Gianni's impulse to protect and indulge Donatella meant that she never had to grow up. As Gianni grew richer and more successful, Donatella acquired the brittleness of a spoiled child, one who was wholly unprepared to face the responsibilities and hard choices of adulthood.

The apartment on Via Melegari was relatively spacious, with two bedrooms and about 1,400 square feet of living space. The decision to live together was more than a matter of sharing living quarters, a city, or even the profession of fashion. The fates of brother and sister would be irrevocably linked for the remainder of their lives.

Yet, even as they settled into life in Milan, Calabria kept pulling the Versaces home. Soon after Franca's death, Gianni made a return visit. One day, Nino didn't turn up for lunch. Santo and Gianni grew more and more worried as the afternoon wore on without any word from their father. Then Gianni understood. "You know where we'll find him?" Gianni said to his brother. "At the cemetery."

The brothers drove up to the cemetery, which sat on a hill behind the city. It was a hot day, but a breeze was drifting in from the sea. They found Nino sitting disconsolately on a stool in front of the family's gray marble tomb.

"He looked lost, abandoned, as if he had aged a hundred years," recalled Gianni later. Gianni, in tears, embraced his father. In one gesture, years of tensions between father and son melted away. Without the buffer of Franca, the pair would have to form a new bond. After a while, they returned home together. Over a coffee *granita*, Gianni managed to make his father laugh a little. They spent the afternoon in the cool of their darkened living room, saying little. As Gianni would say years later, "In the end, I realized that the little that he was able to give me was actually enough."

five

A New Era

O<small>N MARCH 28, 1978, ON THE TOP FLOOR OF THE PALAZZO</small> della Permanente, the lights went up on the first Gianni Versace collection. The Permanente, a contemporary art museum close to Milan's Giardini Pubblici, had become the hot place among new designers because Krizia, Fendi, and Missoni were showing there. Launching a solo collection was risky and expensive, and Gianni was happy that the Permanente was cheaper than showing in one of the city's big hotels. All the designers shared the same lights and runway at the museum, which helped keep costs to a minimum. He could also bask in the reflected glory of his bigger rivals.

Over the previous year, Gianni had grown restless. He was tired of being a hired gun and was ready to break out on his own. He had five years under his belt and had proved that he was a bona fide commercial success, dressing not just a tiny slice of fashionistas but real women as well, a skill he'd honed during his years at his mother's boutique in Reggio. Gianni's bosses were thrilled with his work, and they paid him accordingly. By the mid-1970s, Santo was flying to Milan every month or two, negotiating richer and richer contracts for his brother with the brand owners he was toiling for.

"In those years, he was selling so much that if he had asked for one hundred million [lire] [$60,000] more, they would have given it to him," Santo said. "It was an incredible machine. We felt like we were minting money."[1]

But working for hire was limiting for a designer who ached to do his own thing without having to answer to others. Like the other young talents who were juggling contracts and making owners rich, he was handcuffed to brands that catered to women whose tastes ran toward twinsets, pearls, and neat, pleated skirts. Frustrated, he began bickering more and more with his bosses over new ideas he wanted to realize. He watched jealously as a few designers broke free of the pack. One inspired particular envy. In 1974, Giorgio Armani, a forty-year-old newcomer from the small northern city of Piacenza, had burst onto the scene with a new look of slouchy jackets and pants that were the talk of the fashion press. By 1977, Gianni, yearning to have his own brand, turned to Santo for help. Santo started spending half of each month in Milan to work out a business plan that would make his brother's dream come true.

In his March debut at the Permanente, Gianni showed a handful of designs created under his own name, slipping them into a show of his Genny and Callaghan collections. He staged the show on a shoe-string; the models, sprawled on the floor with mirrors in hand, did their own makeup, and Donatella and some girlfriends pitched in as dressers, helping the women into their outfits. Gianni, the tension etched on his face, darted from model to model, adjusting a sash, fixing the drape of a skirt, and making frantic, last-minute adjustments before the show.

The lights went up on a show that had little of the polish or strut of the big time. To break with the sleepy routine typical of the era, Gianni sent his models out in groups of four or five. Striding casually, the girls bumped into one another on the crowded runway, twirling willy-nilly and tapping their toes distractedly to the blaring disco music. The collection had a floral, romantic theme, with skirts resembling upside-down flowers, their large overlapping petals done in soft wool lined with silk or chiffon. Inspired by the military look that was popular then—in keeping with Italy's tense political scene that year—Gianni also showed leather trench coats, their masculine aura softened by fuchsia, emerald green, and mustard yellow linings. Backstage, friends and fans mobbed Gianni, who looked tired and slightly stunned. But, despite all his effort, the press largely hated the collection, finding the clothes gimmicky and confused. Privately, Gianni had to agree that it wasn't his best work. Nonetheless, he was on the map. A few months later, both Italian *Vogue* and French *Vogue* picked his trench coats to show in their fashion spreads.

Santo had moved to Milan by the time of Gianni's first show, giving up an accounting practice he was just getting off the ground in Reggio. After finishing his military service in 1972, Santo had briefly considered going into academics, but instead got a job in a local bank in Reggio. He soon grew bored, however, and quit after just six months to become an accountant. By then, Gianni's star had begun to rise, and Santo decided to take a leap and ally with his brother. He had another reason to go north. He had met a pretty, dark-haired woman named Cristiana Ragazzi, the daughter of the owners of Il Torchietto, a homey trattoria in Milan's Navigli neighborhood, an area known for its nightclubs, bars, and restaurants. Instead of living with Gianni, as would be typical with Italian siblings, Santo, perhaps put off by his brother's sexuality and his high-living ways, rented a 650-square-foot apartment in a quiet residential neighborhood.

"We went out a bit together, but Gianni worked a great deal," Santo would say more than thirty-five years later. "Plus, he had his tastes and I had mine."[2] He spent evenings instead with the fledgling company's accounts spread out on a table at Il Torchietto, while Cristiana's parents brought him dinner. The trattoria soon became a hangout for the fashion crowd.

Gianni found the legal and financial side of his work stultifying;

he was happy to leave such tedious details to his brother. Santo convinced a friend from the military to keep the books while he handled business strategy and sales. "That way, Gianni was free to do anything he liked," Santo recalled.[3]

He had great faith in his brother's talent. When a friend of Gianni's asked Santo, "Why do you want Gianni to go out on his own? He's already earning a ton with all of these other contracts," Santo replied, "Because, if we have any luck at all, we're going to be bigger than Yves Saint Laurent." Later, when the friend told Gianni what his brother had said, Gianni said, "If Santo said that, he must be right."[4]

Along with his siblings, there was a new member of the Versace inner circle for the early shows. Paul Beck was twenty-three years old. Gianni had met him at a casting call for male models the year he showed his first collection. Paul was among the passel of apple-pie Americans who were streaming into Milan as the number of runway shows and advertising shoots soared. He was a child of the American suburbs, having grown up in a spacious single-family home in Lynbrook, a sleepy bedroom town on Long Island, a forty-minute train ride from Manhattan. After earning a degree in environmental biology, he had moved to Italy, where he found modest success as a model—and where his life could hardly be more different from his suburban upbringing. Tall and strapping, with blond hair swept back in a feathery cut, he had the slightly guileless, flat look of an Ivy League jock. A few years later, after he'd lost the blush of youth, Paul would become a dead ringer for television host and soft-rock songster John Tesh.

Gianni loved Paul's wholesome look and featured him in one of his very first ad campaigns. In one shot, Paul lay sprawled on his back, dressed in a white evening jacket, with a model swathed in a white fox coat straddling him. When Gianni staged a presentation of the men's collection for buyers in his new showroom, he hired Paul, among other models. The next season, Gianni moved on to men better and more distinctive-looking than Paul, but he retained Paul as his fit model, the one who tries on the samples in the atelier. Paul was at his side during his earliest runway shows and became a fixture among Gianni's group of friends. Soon, he was practically living at Gianni's apartment on Via Melegari.

❖ V ❖

At the cusp of a new decade, fashion was in limbo, caught between the hedonistic, antiestablishment ethos of the 1970s and the glamorous, body-conscious look that would be popularized by the hit television program *Dynasty*. As the political upheaval of the 1970s ebbed, newly minted young professionals in the United States and Europe wanted a more polished wardrobe. Women were entering the workplace in force; they needed a professional look that was neither frilly nor overly masculine. Italian designers offered clothes that were elegant and crisp yet feminine.

As fashion lurched toward a new era, Gianni also searched for his own idiom. His collections veered from theme to theme—sweet Renaissance-inspired dresses one season, followed by black catsuits covered in Escher-like optical designs the next. Sometimes, the cut of a dress was clumsy or the print on a shirt was slightly askew. But Gianni gradually began to show the flashes of inspiration that set him apart. More and more he dealt in the startling contrasts—the mix of masculine and feminine, hard-edged fabrics and softer materials—that would become his signature. He combined materials that would ordinarily clash—leather and silk, suede and linen, denim and satin—using clever cuts and color to meld the dissonant elements. He paired leather jodhpurs with a wool double-breasted checked jacket and a soft crepe de chine blouse. In another collection, he wrapped a wide floral-patterned belt around a silk pinstriped jacket, the contrast making for an unorthodox but elegant look.

Gianni's years in his mother's atelier showed in the way he cut dresses to flatter a woman's figure. For instance, when making Grecian-style dresses, he draped the soft fabric so that it skimmed the body and concealed extra bulges at the hips or waist. A ruche would smooth the waist and bust into a neat silhouette. He often cut on the bias, creating a flattering shape that flowed off the body and hid a multitude of figure flaws.

Season by season, his clothes grew in definition and popularity. When he made a flouncy skirt and cape in georgette silk in a gray and white Prince of Wales check, Roberto Devorik, an Argentine-born retailer who sold Gianni's clothes in the United Kingdom, had an idea.

Devorik was friendly with Diana, the Princess of Wales, who had recently announced her first pregnancy. The news had set off a frenzy of coverage of the blushing young royal, who was looking for a dress style less stuffy than the Laura Ashley–inspired wardrobe common to the British aristocracy. If Devorik could put Diana in a stylish take on the Prince of Wales theme, it was bound to end up in the newspapers.

"Why don't you adapt the collection for the princess while she's pregnant?" Devorik asked Gianni on a visit to Milan. "It would be great publicity."

"Absolutely not!" Gianni said. He found pregnant women's bulging bellies grotesque. "I would never dress a pregnant woman. You must be mad."[5]

❖ V ❖

As Gianni developed his style, Santo struggled with the business side of the fledgling brand. He had none of his younger brother's verve or creative nous, with little interest in, for example, art or architecture. Exuberant yet pragmatic, with an innate love of order and precision, Santo loved being the fixer in the family. He didn't envy Gianni's role in the spotlight at all and was happy to know he was the steady hand on the family rudder. He shared his younger brother's volcanic energy—he slept little, ate quickly, and spoke in a lightning-fast patter. But he was by far the most expansive of the trio and the most charismatic, fixing a guest with his steely blue eyes and proffering a warm handshake or kiss on both cheeks. Unlike Gianni and Donatella, he reveled in his Calabrian heritage, enjoyed telling family stories and extolling the virtues of the deep south.

Although he was a born salesman, with a head for numbers and the sharp negotiation skills that Gianni lacked entirely, he got off to a rocky start. Soon after his arrival in Milan, he signed production contracts with the manufacturers who were already making Gianni's other lines, Genny and Callaghan. But the arrangement was an instant flop. One order for one million dollars' worth of clothes went unfilled because the factories weren't ready. Other deliveries didn't reach the boutiques in time. Crates of Gianni's designs piled up in warehouses, only to be discarded the following season. Some stores, left in the lurch, refused to buy Gianni's clothes for years afterward.

Within several months, Santo set about revamping his business model. Even as he was venturing out on his own, Gianni was still designing the other lines, collecting the rich fees that Santo had negotiated for him. Soon he insisted that Gianni receive royalties on them as well, and Gianni's contract work started earning him millions of dollars annually.

"It wasn't that they were writing blank checks for him, but it wasn't far off," Santo recalled. "The companies that Gianni was working for had to make money, but when things went well, we made money as well. Gianni started to earn the sort of money that had been unheard of until then."[6]

Santo used part of the cash to assemble a small sales force dedicated to Gianni's own line, opening an 8,500-square-foot showroom on Via San Primo, a cozy side street off Via Montenapoleone, where buyers from department stores and independent boutiques could look at Versace clothes. He invested in a joint venture for production so that Versace could keep a close eye on the factories.

Most important, however, he set up a network of boutiques that sold only Gianni's clothes. At the time, there were virtually no single-brand boutiques; most shops sold an array of French and Italian brands. But that left a designer at the mercy of the boutique owner, who decided how much to buy and how to display the clothes. Santo understood that Versace-exclusive boutiques on the best streets in Italy would offer Gianni priceless publicity and control over how to show and sell the clothes. He imported the model of franchise stores, which then existed largely in the United States. (There wasn't even a word in Italian for franchising.) Under this system, owners of boutiques agreed to open a Versace shop and pay the company a slice of the sales of the clothes. The boutiques shouldered the risk of outfitting a store; Santo required them to use Versace-approved architects, who dictated a specific look for the shops. In order to create more buzz, the boutique owners pledged to run Versace advertising in local newspapers and magazines and stage mini runway shows in their city. Santo traveled tirelessly up and down Italy, looking for entrepreneurs willing to open shops on the best corners. To help potential franchisees, he extended them credit so that they could buy the first collections or gave them more time to pay for the clothes.

HOUSE OF VERSACE

He aimed high. "We have to be next to Chanel," he told his team over and over. He pushed them to ferret out a space on Rue du Faubourg Saint-Honoré, Paris's classiest shopping street, convincing skeptical French boutique owners of the potential of this tiny Italian brand. Soon they had shops on Via Condotti in Rome and in Porto Cervo in Sardinia, the latest playground in Italy for Europe's aristocrats and trust-fund babies. The strategy was extremely risky for an unproven brand. If Gianni's collections flopped repeatedly, the boutiques would quickly sink.

As he hustled to build up his brother's brand, Santo grew into a natural, even evangelical, leader, hiring a clutch of young managers who venerated their boss. Santo, who slept less than six hours a night, had a hyperactive energy that galvanized his team. During meetings, he rarely sat still, jumping up and pacing the room excitedly as he spoke. "Versace is a religion," he repeatedly told his team. He walked up and down the main shopping thoroughfares in Europe and the United States until he knew each corner by heart. With his high energy and willingness to take big gambles, Santo managed to channel his brother's ideas and create a dynamic young business.

As Gianni's popularity grew, Santo was juggling more and more—lunching with buyers who visited the showroom quarterly during the selling season, discussing sales targets with new franchisees, and courting bankers who would loan Versace the money to grow. In 1982, he made an around-the-world trip to open shops in Sydney, Los Angeles, New York, and Paris. While Gianni worked frantically backstage before a show, Santo coolly greeted the buyers and magazine editors seated in the front of the house, talking up his brother's latest collection. He was an ideal ambassador for Gianni, with his distinguished looks and slim, athletic frame and wearing his uniform of a perfectly cut black jacket over a collarless shirt.

This didn't mean he always approved of his brother's designs. When Gianni began creating clothes for men—silk shirts, loose trousers with exaggerated folds and pleats, and elaborate knit sweaters—the straitlaced Santo blanched. "Look, Gianni, you should be designing for someone like me!" he admonished his brother. "Look at what I wear—a basic jacket, a polo shirt." Gianni scoffed at him. The clothes turned out to be a hit, offering men the sort of fashionable wardrobes that women had always enjoyed. Santo thereafter steered clear of the creative side of the business.

But Santo's charisma and evident passion for Gianni's work won over many who might otherwise have been wary of supporting such a young brand. In his big brother, Gianni found the figure that was often filled by a designer's lover at other design houses; Pierre Bergé provided the protection and succor that a neurotic Yves Saint Laurent needed to thrive, while Sergio Galeotti was supporting Giorgio Armani in his new venture across town.

"Gianni's great fortune was to have Santo as his partner," said one executive who worked for the Versaces early in their careers.[7]

❖ V ❖

By the mid-1980s, Santo's business model had clicked. As Gianni's clothing sales took off, Santo signed a few licenses, or contracts with outside companies, to make other Versace products such as shoes, purses, and ties. Licenses were a quick way to boost a brand's image, allowing shoppers who couldn't afford a one-thousand-dollar dress to buy a little slice of high fashion in the form of a scarf or perfume. The licensees made the items and sold them to boutiques, paying a percentage of sales—usually about 8 percent—to Versace. (A license can backfire for a brand, however, if the owner of the brand doesn't closely monitor the quality of the product, as would eventually be true for Pierre Cardin, Yves Saint Laurent, and later, Gucci.)

But with profit came profligacy. One of Santo's early tasks was to rein in Gianni's spendthrift habits. When they were kids, Santo scolded Gianni for wasting his entire allowance on candy or magazines. But now, Gianni, no longer the black sheep of the family, had the upper hand. Gianni wanted to use the fabrics he liked, stage the extravagant shows he wanted, and use the priciest photographers for his ad campaigns. By 1986, Gianni would be spending more than 7 billion lire—or $4 million at the time—in advertising. He scoffed at his big brother's pleas for restraint, and in part, Gianni was right. The company was growing fast. The house's overall sales rose from 250 billion lire (about $150 million) in 1983 to 380 million lire (about $220 million) in 1986.[8] But Santo, thrifty by nature, thought the money was wasted.

HOUSE OF VERSACE

"Gianni didn't want to hear it when Santo told him how much something cost," said Anna Cernuschi, one of Gianni's top seamstresses in the 1980s. "He hated being told how much he was spending. He wanted to be totally free."[9]

During the 1980s, the Versaces plowed some of their profits into real estate, buying properties for investments or indulgence. Santo, predicting that Milan's housing and office market was about to explode, bought a clutch of apartments around the city—but the biggest deal was also the one that raised the most eyebrows in the Versaces' adopted city. In 1981, they bought a 19,000-square-foot apartment on Via Gesù, a small street running between Via Montenapoleone and Via della Spiga. The palazzo was three stories high, covered about 45,000 square feet, and boasted one of the most beautiful courtyards in Milan, featuring a large compass composed of tiny black and white pebbles, with a second courtyard complete with a bubbling fountain flanked by flower beds. In the rear was a large garden with rose trellises, weeping willows, magnolias, and cedars. One wing of the mansion housed a winter garden and a greenhouse.

The palazzo had been the home of some of Milan's most important families, including the Bonomi clan, who were prominent real estate tycoons. Much of the southwest corner of the building had been damaged by Allied bombs during the war. In 1946, the Rizzoli family, a wealthy publishing clan, bought the building and began to restore it. The family members were leading lights of the city's postwar leftist intellectual movement. In the basement of one wing, they installed a projection room, where they held one of the first showings of Federico Fellini's neorealist masterpiece *La Dolce Vita*.

When the Rizzolis were split by internal feuds and the downturn in the Italian economy, they began selling parts of the family home to the Versaces. Many Milanese were horrified to see such arrivistes supplant one of the most prestigious names of the city. Gianni would justify their dismay, bringing notoriety to the palazzo with his parade of rock stars, Hollywood actors, and royalty, all dazzled by the nouveau riche opulence. The home would become literally emblematic of his burgeoning brand. On the knocker of its main double door, Gianni noticed an odd, if ominous, mythological figure: the head of a medusa, the legendary demon that turns any human being she lays eyes on to stone. He had been looking for a logo for his growing brand and found the medusa fitting, a reference to a childhood spent playing among the Greek relics in Calabria. The medusa was an apt symbol of the Versace brand's sensibility, at once classical, alluring, theatrical, garish, and dangerous.

In all, the Versaces spent 14 billion lire ($8 million) to buy the building. Gianni sank another 6.3 billion lire ($3.7 million) to restore it to its original high-classical style. In his private apartment, which occupied one entire floor, Gianni tried to re-create the look of a Renaissance piazza, complete with antique pillars, trompe l'oeil columns, Greek vases in terra-cotta, and Roman busts. In his bedroom was a canopy bed dating from Renaissance Florence, and his bathroom featured an enormous beige marble sunken tub and murals of neoclassic figures. He turned the Rizzolis' old theater in the basement into a pool and gym. In 1987, after restoring the rest of the building, he moved his team to one wing, making Via Gesù his official new headquarters.

The purchase of the Rizzoli mansion sparked the first questions about the finances of the fledgling business—questions that would dog the Versaces for years. How could the company have found the money for such an extravagant acquisition? And how was it possible that Santo had paid for the palazzo in cash? As the Versaces and their company extended their reach, opening new shops and new factory space and buying lots of advertising, the speculation only rose.

The acquisition of the Via Gesù mansion, as well as the sharp growth in Versace's business, fueled rumors of mafia involvement in the company. By the 1980s, it was practically a given that organized crime would seek to insinuate itself into any decent-sized business in southern Italy. In Calabria, it was virtually impossible for companies to operate without encountering pressure from the 'Ndrangheta, the local mafia. While the 'Ndrangheta is less famous abroad than the Sicilian Cosa Nostra and the Neapolitan Camorra, by the 1980s it was becoming one of the most powerful crime syndicates in Italy. Born shortly after the unification of Italy in 1861, it sprang from gangs of bandits who robbed the rich, and it flourished in the face of government corruption and indifference in the south. Until the mid-1970s, it operated mainly in Calabria and was involved in petty extortion and kidnapping.

HOUSE OF VERSACE

But with the arrival of the international drug trade, the 'Ndrangheta exploded, spreading its influence first to northern Italy and then abroad. It became one of the largest importers of cocaine to Europe, channeling much of it through the Calabrian port of Gioia Tauro. The group also skimmed money off public works projects and ran money-laundering operations. In Calabria, by the 1980s, the threat of extortion by 'Ndranghetisti became a constant fear for local businessmen, who were increasingly frightened by the group's reputation for ruthlessness and violence. Since the 1970s, Italian authorities have succeeded in infiltrating parts of Cosa Nostra and the Camorra by recruiting *pentiti,* or turncoats, but the strength of the bonds among Calabrian family members has made the 'Ndrangheta among the most difficult of Italy's criminal organizations to crack. The group recruits members on the basis of blood relations; sons of 'Ndranghetisti are expected to follow in their fathers' footsteps.

With recurring wars among 'Ndrangheta families making the front pages of Italian newspapers, some observers suspected the Versaces' sudden good fortune to be a front for mafia activity. In addition to their rich investments in prime Milan real estate, they were opening stores all over the country and buying ads in Italy's leading magazines—giving the impression that they were spending more than they could possibly be taking in. Such whispers enraged Santo, who felt they sprang from the heavy antisouthern prejudice in Milan and jealousy at the clan's purchase of Via Gesù, a symbol of the city's blue-blooded class. He and his siblings worked hard to establish the house, and insinuations that it was the fruit of dirty money infuriated him. He vehemently denied any connection between Versace and organized crime.

Santo's indignation was justified. In fact, the company began making a profit shortly after its inception. A close examination of Versace's first balance sheets shows that sales of Gianni's early collections took off quickly, providing enough profits to fund the capital increases. (The Versaces also bought the Via Gesù mansion at a relatively cheap price, acquiring part of it at a foreclosure auction.) For the first decade of its existence, sales of Gianni's collections grew by double digits each year. Retailers who had easily sold Genny, Callaghan, and Complice, another popular outside collection that Gianni designed, were quick to place orders for the new Versace line.

Moreover, Gianni was earning millions of dollars from his outside contract work, which Santo invested in factories, advertising, and a sales force. The new house was riding a wave of demand by baby boomers for fashionable clothing. As young women shunned their mothers' seamstresses, new ready-to-wear designers such as Gianni found themselves in the midst of a sea change in tastes and habits. Moreover, in a market that was far less crowded with designer brands, it was relatively easy to open new shops, while licenses also offered a quick way for a new brand to grow. At the same time, Gianni's designs had struck a chord. So by the end of the 1980s, Versace's sales would double.

The rumors have persisted over the years, despite a dearth of evidence of corruption at Versace. From the house's inception, Italy's tax police, who also investigate financial fraud and money laundering, audited Versace's accounts year after year, spending weeks at a time with Santo's team sifting through the house's books, but they never found any evidence of foul play. In thirty years of antimafia investigations, magistrates in both Milan and Reggio have never discovered a connection between organized crime and the Versace family. White-shoe banks in Milan such as Banca Commerciale Italiana, who would have shied away from working with suspect companies, financed the house's growth from the start. Starting in 1986, Santo hired outside auditors from KPMG to certify the accounts each year. But a decade later, Gianni's death would reignite the spurious talk of mafia involvement, undoing years of effort by Santo to prove the house was clean.

❖ V ❖

Even as Milan's old-line families turned up their noses at the Versace trio, their city was speeding into a period of wholesale change. An industrial metropolis long before it became a fashion capital, Milan, with its flat light and paucity of world-class monuments, has never been a typical Italian city. Unlike Rome and its palette of burnt orange, warm pink, and deep yellow, or Naples, with its bracing blue sky, Milan is a city of grays and browns, the monochrome skyline relieved only by the rose marble of the Duomo. Even its most beautiful buildings are smudged with smog from nearby factories, and heavy bombing during the war left it pockmarked. During the frenzy of building to accommodate the influx of southerners in the postwar boom, the city replaced its wartime rubble with ugly concrete apartment blocks that grew grimmer with age, as graffiti and car fumes took their toll.

In the midst of all this grimness, Milan's fashion quarter is an oasis. Largely spared the pounding of wartime bombs, its eighteenth-century architecture remained intact. The main byway is Via Montenapoleone. The street was once the home of the food shops, stationery stores, and leather craftsmen that served Milan's wealthiest families, as well as the city's best seamstresses, such as Biki, the granddaughter of Puccini, who, in the 1950s, turned the great soprano Maria Callas from an ugly duckling into a poised swan. Via Montenapoleone was so elegant that delivery boys coming from other neighborhoods changed into their best clothes to drop their goods there. At the edge of the area sat La Scala, the eighteenth-century opera house that hosted the debut of a young Giuseppe Verdi and for decades served as the artistic home to Callas. From its birth, the opera house was a favorite for Italian aristocracy, who owned the private boxes and paid for them to be elaborately decorated, passing them down from generation to generation. Largely destroyed during the war, its reconstruction symbolized the rebirth of Italy, culminating in a 1946 concert under the direction of Arturo Toscanini. In modern times, it became famous for its pre–Christmas season opening, when international celebrities mix with well-heeled Milanese ladies, draped in their finest furs, diamond jewelry, and couture outfits ordered specially for the evening.

The Milanese—the country's bankers, industrialists, and entrepreneurs—have long prided themselves on their role as the Calvinists of Italy, with a pinched restraint that has far more in common with their Swiss neighbors just to the north than their sunny compatriots in Naples or Rome. Yet in the 1980s, Milan changed radically. More than any other part of Italy, the city, home to Italy's stock market, embraced the new greed-is-good ethos that was sweeping other Western countries and made a rapid and wholehearted transition from an industrial metropolis to one based on services. It became the capital of Italy's second economic miracle. For the new yuppie class in

Milan, inspiration came not from old-line families but from Silvio Berlusconi, a Milan native, who became Italy's richest man during the decade by introducing commercial television to the country. With his soap operas, quiz shows, and imports of American fare such as *Dynasty*—all with copious amounts of commercial advertising—he wrought a cultural revolution. The Italians, sick of the ideological conflict of the 1970s, were happy to plunge into a new prosperity, snapping up the refrigerators, cars, and televisions they saw advertised on Berlusconi's networks. The change was felt nowhere more than in Milan, as the city's publishing, newspaper, and advertising industries thrived. A triumphant ad slogan became shorthand for the decadence and exuberance of the city in the 1980s: *Milano da Bere*, which roughly translates to "Milan is good enough to drink."

In this heady new commercial era, Versace and the other new fashion designers, having paid their dues in the 1970s, now took off. Boutiques pushed out the old-line shops on Via Montenapoleone, and the street became known as the Quadrilatero d'Oro, or Block of Gold. The sidewalks were immaculately kept, with carpets and plants, and the buildings were free of the graffiti that marred so many structures in Milan. The designers became local stars. Restaurants frequented by the fashion pack, such as El Toulà, a Veneto restaurant near La Scala; Bagutta, a Tuscan restaurant off Via Montenapoleone; and La Torre di Pisa, all buzzed.

When they first arrived in Milan, Gianni and Donatella loved to make fun of the Milanese, with their nasal, clipped accents and heavy fur coats, ladylike gloves, and patent-leather purses. But by the 1980s, Versace had helped to create an entire nouveau riche social milieu that had redefined Milan itself. His clothes—with their bright colors, bold patterns, close fit, and unconventional new fabrics—were right for a growing class of women who wanted to show off more.

"When I came to Milan, I found the sense of style here extremely boring," Donatella said in 2008. "Everyone was dressed the same, in this very bourgeoisie style, without any sense of fashion."[10] Now that the Versaces had remade the style of Milan, they would settle into relationships that would bring tumult into the family—even as they were growing a business that could dominate the world.

SIX

Rivals and Lovers

b Y THE EARLY 1980S, GIANNI'S NEW BRAND WAS A SUCCESS IN Italy, with dozens of shops dotting the peninsula, and was breaking through in a handful of other European countries as well. But while Gianni was an emerging force at home, he was failing to romance the critical U.S. market. The editors of the European editions of *Vogue* and *Harper's Bazaar* liked the theatricality and variety of his collections, but the powerful women who ran the fashion magazines in the United States found his clothes flashy and trashy. Twice a year when buyers from Neiman Marcus, Saks Fifth Avenue, and Bergdorf Goodman came to the Milan shows, Gianni and Santo courted them assiduously. Santo tirelessly chatted them up in the showroom, taking them through the collection piece by piece. Meanwhile, Gianni invited them to sumptuous dinners in his apartment and sent bouquets of flowers to their hotels. But the Americans were unmoved. They felt that American women, just entering the workplace in force, wanted to be taken seriously; they wouldn't want to sport black leather biker jackets, peekaboo black lace gowns with beading applied like clusters of caviar, and skirts so short they were little more than belts. Some of Gianni's publicity stunts didn't help his cause. For a fashion show in New York, he once chose a song featuring a woman faking an orgasm. "I'm coming, I'm coming, I'm coming," she sang breathily. The runway show was supposed to have traveled to Chicago, but the organizers there heard about the music and canceled it.[1]

"It was very, very difficult for us in the U.S.," a former Versace executive recalled. "We had boutiques in important cities, but in the U.S., if you weren't in the department stores, you were no one. They saw Versace as something extravagant that would appeal to a limited number of shoppers." And if the fashion professionals didn't embrace the clothes, then American customers would spurn them. Years later, when the Metropolitan Museum of Art assembled a collection of Gianni's work, the curators struggled to find New York society ladies who had early Versace pieces to lend.

While Gianni attempted to woo America, Giorgio Armani's courtship of the U.S. market was heating up, his clothes appealing to a generation of professional women. From the start, Gianni had sensed that Armani would be his main rival. Anna Zegna, the scion of a prominent textiles family, had worked in Gianni's press office between 1979 and 1982. "Gianni used to have me count the number of [magazine] covers Armani had and how many he had," she remembered. "It was a nightmare. There was this constant race to see who had more."[2]

Armani and Versace could hardly have been more different. Armani, twelve years older than Gianni, had a rigid, chilly character forged in a deprived childhood in Piacenza, a northern industrial city heavily bombed during the war. Like Gianni, Armani had a sister who had died in childhood, and he had a cool relationship with a distant father. And while Gianni, born right after the war, enjoyed a largely carefree childhood, Armani's early years were marked by wartime hardship and fear. His father, a petty bureaucrat in the local

Fascist Party, was imprisoned after the war; when Armani was badly burned in an accident with gunpowder, other children stole his crutches, as punishment for his father's Fascist past.

"I dragged myself home by clinging to the walls and crying because of the pain," Armani recalled later.[3] After Armani's father was released, the family moved to a working-class neighborhood in Milan. For the young Armani, the blue bloods who strolled leisurely down Via Montenapoleone on Sunday afternoons were as distant as a dream. Gianni found his calling early in his mother's atelier, but Armani's aesthetic sense bubbled up in fits and spurts. An avid photographer, he developed a fascination with the human body that led him to study medicine after high school but he ended up dropping out. Working in La Rinascente, a middle-class Milan department store, he grew frustrated by the men's suits on offer, their stiff structure dictated by London's Savile Row tailors. Starting in 1962, he worked with Nino Cerruti, a prominent textile manufacturer in Biella, a region renowned for its fine wool, and he soon came up with a new vision of men's clothing.

Armani would ride a wave of social change in fashion. By the 1970s, men were looking for a new, more relaxed style, while women needed temperate, elegant clothes. Searching for a tailored yet sensual look, Armani experimented with lighter fabrics from the Cerruti mills and took the padding out of jackets. Sergio Galeotti, Armani's exuberant, much-younger lover, nagged him for two years to start his own company. Legend has it they hocked their Volkswagen to help raise the money needed to rent a two-room office on Corso Venezia for a year. When Armani presented his first collection at a Milan hotel in 1974, his new concept of the jacket instantly revolutionized fashion by blurring the distinction between sportswear and business wear for both men and women. He tore out the lining, shoulder pads, and body-sculpting darts from jackets and erased the creases from trousers; he changed the proportions of the collar, lapels, and shoulders and moved the buttons. Fine wools, linens, and cashmeres allowed the slouchy jackets to skim the body. The cut was slightly oversized, which flattered the heavy-set and made thin people look charmingly waifish. The clothes came in painterly shades of grays, sandy beiges, and eggshell.

Thus was born the Armani power suit, destined to become an iconic uniform of the 1980s, with its air of nonchalance, entitlement, and sexy cool. It gave women office wear that didn't drain them of their femininity; men felt graceful and sexy in suits that also conveyed a sense of bodily mass and power. The success of Armani suits would transfer the locus of tailored fashion southward from London to Milan.

"Before Armani, people thought of England as the epitome of tailoring, and then Armani stole the spotlight," said Richard James, a prominent Savile Row tailor. "Suddenly, Italian was glamorous and English was fuddy-duddy."[4]

Americans immediately fell for Armani, charmed by his unstuffy designs that had more vitality than those of U.S. designers. By the time Gianni launched his own line in 1978, Armani's clothes were already selling in Barneys, Saks Fifth Avenue, and Bloomingdale's.[5]

"Armani was always going to be a bigger business," said Ellin Saltzman, who was head of fashion buying for Saks Fifth Avenue in the 1980s. "In those days, Armani was perfect, tailored classic day wear."[6]

Then came a piece of good fortune that would prove the power of mass media to transform fashion—and launch Armani irrevocably. It was the kind of pioneering product placement that Gianni later copied with enormous success. In 1980, Armani's clothes played a starring role in director Paul Schrader's film *American Gigolo*. John Travolta, who was originally cast as the lead, had chosen forty Armani outfits to wear in the film. After Travolta was replaced by Richard Gere, the producers stuck with Armani (and Travolta remained an Armani client as well). When Gere, naked to the waist and swaying to rock music, lovingly packed his luggage with Armani shirts and ties, millions of fashion fans were born. Thus did Armani hitch his young brand to Hollywood's star power. His company sales grew from $90,000 in 1976 to $135 million five years later.

Bankers and businesspeople joined the artists, ad executives, and movie types who originally cottoned to Armani's clothes. (Jackie Onassis, reincarnated in a new persona as editor at a Manhattan publishing house, wore his clothes to work.) In April 1982, *Time* magazine put Armani on the cover, dubbing his clothes "Giorgio's

Gorgeous Style." The eight-page article thoroughly established Armani as a cultural star, with his precociously white hair and Paul Newman–blue eyes set off by an oaken tan.

For all of his clothes' public association with sexuality and glamour, Armani's natural sobriety permeated his designs, giving them an aura of asceticism and authority that also characterized the man and his business. He had a terrible fear of losing his good looks, despite the fact that he grew more handsome with age, as a few wrinkles tempered his finely sculpted face, with its high cheekbones and slim, haughty nose. His personal uniform of close-cut navy or black cashmere sweaters and flat-front pants accentuated a lean physique that never wore an extra pound. He didn't drink or smoke, and he abstained from heavy food, begrudgingly serving delicacies such as caviar and lobster only at the formal dinners he hosted. Terrified of looking foolish, he stopped dancing at the age of twenty-five and tore up photographs of himself that he didn't like.[7]

Armani's fierce discipline was an indispensable contributor to his rapid, spectacular success and inspired cultlike devotion from many of his managers. But by the early 1980s, swapping stories of Armani's obsession for control was a bitchy parlor game in Milan. His contracts with his workers decreed that merely attending another designer's runway show was a fireable offense. He eschewed the outside runway producers who typically helped designers plan shows, preferring to cast the models, choose the music, and give detailed stage directions himself.

"Something as simple as the girl putting her hands on her hips the wrong way could ruin the magic I envision," he told *W Magazine* in October 2000.[8] Once, when he staged his runway show in a storied building in the historic center, he covered the magnificent frescoes on the ceiling so that they wouldn't distract the audience from his clothes.

In 1985, Armani suffered a blow that would leave him even more autocratic and remote when Sergio Galeotti died of AIDS. Though homosexuality had ceased to be taboo in Italy by the 1980s, Armani continued to hide his sexual orientation and ordered his public relations department to tell the press that Galeotti had died of a heart problem. (When *Il Messaggero*, Rome's daily newspaper, wrote the truth, Armani threatened to pull his ads.) To manage his grief, Armani resorted to antidepressants for a time, before throwing himself full force into his work, displaying a steely determination that left little room for a personal life.

"Giorgio has no friends," his sister, Rosanna, once told a journalist. Armani agreed: "When do I have time to make myself friends?"[9]

In his relationships with people as well as in his style and temperament, he was the antithesis of the romantic Calabria-born designer striving to become his main rival in Italian fashion. By 1981, Gianni's top-floor apartment on Via Melegari was getting crowded. With Paul Beck spending much of his time there, and Donatella having moved in, it was close quarters for the three. Gianni had just one full bathroom, leaving the trio to jostle to use it in the morning. And the place had become a magnet for Gianni's entire social crowd. Donatella and Paul hit it off from the start. With Gianni working very long hours, they often found themselves alone together. Donatella, still suffering from the loss of her mother, felt somewhat out of her depth in Milan. Shy by nature, she struggled to carve out a group of friends of her own and, in the beginning, returned frequently to Reggio. To the catty fashion pack in Milan, the glamorous designer's sister came off as provincial, with her hair sometimes badly bleached or clumsily cut and with a heavy Calabrian accent that made the haughty Milanese cringe. When she became nervous in the company of strangers, her face settled into a heavy-lidded stony look, accentuating the fact that her eyes were set close together.

Although she was very slim, Donatella hated her body. Next to her brother's model friends, with their long, slim limbs like stretched smooth taffy, her own short legs and meaty hands looked stubby and inelegant. Extremely vigilant about her weight, she was constantly on a diet, sometimes getting by on little more than rice and vegetable puree. "Look at how fat I am!" she complained to friends, ignoring their protests to the contrary. Never very photogenic, Donatella hated being photographed and was often captured with a diffident, stern expression. Soon, however, she learned to turn her left side—her better one—to the camera.

Feeling so out of place, she had many reasons to cling to Paul, who was her age, and the tight circle of friends who worked for her brother. Because Paul's Italian was poor, the pair mostly spoke in English, even though Donatella's command of the language was still tenuous. But the language barrier didn't stop them from having fun. Donatella and Paul went dancing often in the evening, while Gianni, exhausted from designing several lines in addition to his signature brand, went to bed early. While Donatella's stylish way of dressing and fresh prettiness attracted men—she looked young, even passing for a teenager—she dated little. Gradually, however, she felt a spark for Paul. Paul reciprocated and the couple moved into a spartan rented apartment on the other side of Milan.

Within about a year, Gianni hired Paul to help develop the accessories for the men's line, a small job. Even after several years in Italy, Paul remained something of an outsider. His Italian improved little and he had only a faint grasp of the country's popular culture. But Gianni saw him as potentially useful to the business. Eager to expand abroad and to win over the recalcitrant American customer, he realized that Paul and his perfect English would help him. Santo, despite intensive language courses, never managed to learn English, and Gianni's command of the language was fine for party chitchat but was hardly polished at the time. Donatella spoke passable English, but, as she did in Italian, she spoke so quickly that the words tumbled out of her mouth garbled, often leaving her interlocutor perplexed.

Outsiders may have marveled at Gianni's ability to absorb Paul into the family fold, but, in its own way, the move proved how strong family ties are for southerners. Calabrians like the Versaces believe deeply that blood is always thicker than water; the family has provided the only bulwark against centuries of abuse at the hands of kings, brutal rulers, and corrupt state officials. Even when it was divided by vicious internal feuds, a Calabrian family closed ranks in the end.

With time, Paul's sweet, easygoing personality and sunny temperament made him a favorite with the Versaces' friends and employees. Once, during a hot car trip to visit Versace's factory outside Milan in the summer, he convinced other employees to play hooky for a couple of hours and go for a swim. His evident affection for Donatella and his popularity at the company helped ease tensions between Gianni and Donatella, the result of the siblings' volcanic personalities.

At the beginning of 1982, Gianni threw himself wholeheartedly into a new project—designing the costumes for a new production of Richard Strauss's *Josephs Legende* at La Scala. Gianni's debut would be one of the most important nights of his life, but not because of his work on the costumes. Santo had tried to talk Gianni out of taking on the La Scala project, worried it would distract him from his own still-emerging brand. But at times, fashion failed to sate Gianni's creative restlessness; the theater let him stretch and experiment with shapes and patterns that were unthinkable for use in a ready-to-wear line. Indeed, Gianni's proudest moment would come not after a fashion show but when he saw his costumes on stage in 1986 at the premiere of a Paris ballet staged by Maurice Béjart, the French choreographer. "I cried that night," he told a *New Yorker* journalist.[10]

By the time of the Strauss production, Gianni, now thirty-six years old, was dating a handsome forty-year-old man, whom he invited to the La Scala debut. After the show, the couple followed the stream of dancers and musicians to Biffi, the storied restaurant next to La Scala where celebratory post-opera dinners were traditionally held. Smiling broadly, Gianni soaked up kudos from the crowd. Then a friend approached with a much-younger man in tow. As the two made small talk, Gianni's gaze lingered on the stranger, a strikingly good-looking young man dressed in a white suit that showed off a lithe body, smooth olive skin, and dark green eyes. With his full lips, dark curly hair, and languid features, the man could have stepped out of ancient Rome—or out of a Versace ad. It was a look that Gianni adored. "Why don't you join me at my table?" he asked, suddenly forgetting his boyfriend's presence at the event.

Antonio D'Amico was twenty-four years old and, like Gianni, was a son of Italy's deep south, although his childhood had been far rockier than Gianni's. Born in Brindisi, on the spur of the Italian boot, Antonio had moved to Milan with his mother and little sister when he was three, soon after his parents separated. His mother, a petite, dark-haired young woman who resembled Ava Gardner, found work as a seamstress in a coat factory and sent Antonio and his sister to live with some nuns who took in children. Every two weeks, she gathered the small family for a walk in the park or a gelato. After a few years, when she remarried, the children came to live with her again, but soon the small family suffered another blow. On Christmas Day, Antonio, then fifteen, was sitting next to his fourteen-year-old sister during the long holiday lunch when the girl suddenly felt sick. She quickly collapsed, dead from a heart defect.

After high school, Antonio bounced from job to job, helping in a tailor's shop and working as a chef. With his good looks and ready smile, he also landed a bit of second-rate modeling and acting work, becoming a minor celebrity in Italian *fotoromanzi*—magazines that told love stories using photos of the actors along with dialogue boxes to explain the action. They were cheesy but enormously popular among Italian housewives in the years before American soap operas arrived on Italian television. He had relationships with both men and women.

One day in February 1982, Antonio was on a shoot when a friend, who owned a large textiles shop in Milan and knew Gianni, invited him to the ballet at La Scala. Antonio was curious to meet the designer; just a few weeks earlier, he'd bought a Versace sweater that he found terribly fashionable, with loose bat-wing sleeves and a Greek motif knit in blue and Bordeaux. When Gianni invited him to sit at his table, Antonio, swept away by the designer's charm and evident interest, assented—only to find himself sitting next to Gianni's boyfriend. Gianni continued to chat up Antonio, oblivious as his boyfriend squirmed nearby. After dinner, Gianni slyly asked for Antonio's phone number. "I'll call you," he said.

Antonio left the next day for a month-long trip to Japan for work. When he got back, his answering machine was full of messages, including four or five from Gianni. In the last one, he said, "Since you apparently don't see fit to call me back, this is the last time I'm calling you!" A few days later, Antonio made amends and went to dinner at Gianni's apartment. He was impressed by the fine Art Deco furnishings, antique sculptures, and lavish oil paintings. The designer, twelve years his senior, was the most sophisticated, charming man he'd ever met. Indeed, Gianni was a master at enchanting the people around him. When he trained his natural exuberance and enthusiasm on someone, that person came away feeling slightly starstruck. "I'm all yours," he often told journalists with a warm smile, throwing his arms open and putting them instantly at ease. He laughed easily, trading a juicy bit of gossip he knew would entertain a friend or employee. When Zia Nora arrived for a visit once, he snuck up behind her and cupped her breasts in his hands. "What big titties you have, Zia!" he teased her, as the old lady laughed and slapped his hands away.

Over dinner, Gianni admitted that his current relationship was fizzling out. Antonio, for his part, had been floating from one fling to another. They began seeing each other two or three times a week. Gianni flattered Antonio shamelessly, saying he looked like a baroque putto, the cherubic child idealized in Renaissance paintings. Antonio, dazzled by the attention, drank it up. Over the rest of 1982, the pair saw more and more of each other, spending virtually every weekend together.

After about six months, Gianni began to insist that Antonio come to work for him. (It was typical of the Versaces to absorb friends, family, and even former lovers into the company; Donatella's high school sweetheart Enzo ran the shop in Reggio, while several of Gianni's ex-boyfriends worked at the company.) He wanted to make Antonio the head of sales for Istante, a second line that was slightly cheaper than Versace's main collection, but Antonio was wary. Gianni's tight-knit staff was already tittering about their boss's latest affair; few of them thought it would last. Moreover, Donatella and Santo didn't hide their contempt for Antonio. Santo seemed skeptical about putting the inexperienced young man in charge of one of the house's collections. Donatella, ever jealous of anyone who might compete for Gianni's attentions, was cold and unfriendly with him from the start.

When Antonio agreed to work on Istante, he went to Santo's office to sign the contract. Santo, clearly annoyed, cut to the chase. "What is your relationship with my brother?" he asked sharply.

"That's none of your business," Antonio retorted. "That's between me and Gianni."

The job with Istante lasted just two months; Antonio was over his head and sensed he was unpopular with the staff. Gianni, anxious to bring his new lover into his fold, deputized him instead to work with him on his theater costumes, where he didn't have to answer to Santo. Over time, Antonio's relationship with Santo mellowed into one of mutual respect. He and Donatella, however, settled into a cold war that lasted for years.

Soon after Antonio started work at the company, his relationship with Gianni stumbled badly. Antonio was spending nearly every night at Gianni's house because Gianni complained on the rare occasions Antonio wanted to go home. Then one evening, when Antonio planned to return to his own place, Gianni didn't object. Antonio found this strange. Later that night, he slipped back into Gianni's house—to find him in a clinch with an American model on the living room sofa. Unbeknownst to Antonio, Gianni had been carrying on an affair for some time. Furious, Antonio chased the interloper out and turned on Gianni. "I don't give a shit that you're Gianni Versace!" he yelled. "You can't have everything. You can't have me and still have these flings. You have to choose!"

For a week, Gianni tried to apologize, but Antonio avoided him. Finally, they spoke. "I had no idea that our relationship was so important to you," Gianni said. Soon afterward, Antonio moved in.[11]

Despite their rough start, they made a good couple. Gianni, full of restless energy and brio, worked constantly, while Antonio, more even-tempered, was his anchor. Gianni was naturally a passionate man, and by the early 1980s, he felt an enormous excitement at the explosion of his career. As the relationship grew more serious, Gianni's friends whispered that Antonio was far too provincial for someone of Gianni's growing stature. However, Gianni found that Antonio's modest background, earthy wit, and forthright manner grounded him at a time when Gianni was being swept up in the whirlwind of his growing success.

It took a while for Antonio to get used to Gianni's intensity. The designer never switched off. It was as if he was afraid his fabulous new life would come to a halt if he let up for even a minute. Impervious to the people around him, he carried a notebook with him everywhere he went, furiously jotting down thoughts gleaned from a film he just saw, a stylish woman in the street, the color of flowers in the countryside. In the evenings, after dinner, Gianni sat on his sofa, sketching or paging through piles of newspapers and magazines, leaving a trail of paper on the floor. Whenever he was traveling, whether for vacation or for work, he sent dozens of faxes with sketches to his team, and called obsessively to see that they had followed his orders. He was so distracted that he stopped driving entirely, "for the safety of pedestrians," as he often joked. Gianni's relentlessness sometimes exhausted Antonio, who would escape to a separate room in their apartment for a break. But mostly, Gianni's kinetic energy, childlike delight in his good fortune, and insatiable curiosity provided a daily thrill for Antonio.

While he was demanding and perfectionist in his work, Gianni was disorganized and distracted in his personal life, gladly entrusting the details to Antonio. He stopped carrying money, leaving it to Antonio to manage the bills. When he changed into his silk dressing gown in the evening to relax, he left a trail of clothes on the floor behind him. A regular gym goer, Antonio nagged Gianni to join him, but Gianni stubbornly refused. "I work with my head, not my body," he told Antonio.[12] Neither fat nor slim, Gianni had the solid build typical of many Italian southerners. He had little patience for exercise, nor perhaps the need for it, as his restless energy burned up the plates of pasta he put away. If Antonio pushed him to follow a diet, Gianni refused. Antonio preened and tended to his good looks, but Gianni, who enjoyed a natural self-confidence and cared far less about his appearance, stuck to a daily uniform of slouchy black or dark blue trousers and a matching lightweight cashmere-and-silk mock turtleneck.

Despite Gianni's evident affection for Antonio, Donatella couldn't stand her brother's boyfriend. She sniped about Antonio to Gianni, criticizing his work in the atelier and pitting the staff against him.

"It was mostly about work," Antonio remembered. "She would say something against me to Gianni, but I always put her in her place. I said, listen, I don't bother you, so don't bother me. I tried never to put Gianni in a situation of having to worry about me or Donatella or of having to choose."[13] Once, when Antonio made a negative comment about an ad campaign that Donatella and Paul had just presented to Gianni, she exploded, sparking a heated argument between the two. Gianni sat in silence.[14]

Antonio found common cause with Cristiana, Santo's girlfriend. (She and Santo would marry in 1984, eight months after their first child, Francesca, was born. A son, Antonio, followed in 1986.)

Gianni had a catty, mean streak when he took a dislike to someone, and Cristiana became a target for his contempt early on. He found his sister-in-law unsophisticated, always recalling that her parents were simple restaurant owners. He also resented the fact that she never felt the need to work. "Donatella works, we all work," he complained. "Why is Cristiana the only one in the family who thinks she should be the lady of leisure?" He could be childish and petty at times. Once, he covered Cristiana's face in a family photo and announced, "Here, now that's a beautiful family!"

"The triad of Gianni, Santo, and Donatella were untouchable," Antonio declared years later. "Even if you were on the inside, it was only about those three. There were the three siblings—and then there was Paul, Cristiana, and me."[15]

❖ V ❖

Soon after Gianni and Antonio met, Paul and Donatella announced their engagement. Gianni was officially happy for the couple, but he had his doubts. One day, as his seamstresses were working on the clothes for the wedding party, he remarked, "I don't know why we're going to all this trouble. They'll split within a couple of years."

Paul and Donatella wed on the first day of spring in 1983, in a tiny church in Moltrasio, a town of just 1,700 inhabitants on the western flank of Lake Como. Versace friends and family had flown up from Reggio, while Paul's relatives arrived from the United States. Ornella Vanoni, an Italian pop star who was a fan of Gianni's clothes, was Donatella's maid of honor.

At the last minute, Gianni had designed a simple dress for Donatella. Made of ivory silk, it wrapped across in the front and tucked into a wide band at the waist, before falling into a full skirt that trailed sumptuously in the back. Donatella had pulled her hair back from her face and let it fall down her back. The only jewelry she wore, aside from her wedding band, were delicate drop earrings. Sitting across from her in the church just as the ceremony was to begin, Gianni noticed that the full skirt of the dress was bunched up and gestured frantically for her to straighten it. But when she bent down, her cleavage fell open. "No! No!" Gianni mouthed furiously, as Donatella tried to reach down without flashing her guests. After the ceremony, a beaming Donatella and Paul, who wore a white tie, white shirt, and dark suit, mixed with guests under an unseasonably warm, sunny day. "Look at how beautiful she is!" Paul kept telling friends and family during the reception.

Gianni bought the new couple a lavish apartment on Viale Majno, an exclusive neighborhood known for ornate buildings dripping with ivy. He oversaw a splashy top-to-bottom refurbishment, right down to the choice of Paul and Donatella's matrimonial bed. Over time, Gianni would buy two more apartments to add to the original one, leaving his sister with a massive twenty-one-room home spread over three floors and 4,850 square feet of living space. Now happily settled down, the Versaces looked ready to take on the world.

seven

Inspiration and Muse

b Y THE TIME DONATELLA MARRIED, SHE WAS RAPIDLY BE-
coming ever-more indispensable to her big brother. Early on,
he entrusted his hip twenty-eight-year-old sister with over-
seeing the hair and makeup for the runway shows, a task that
delighted her—and soon shaped the look of Gianni's shows.
She quickly projected onto the models her own predilection
for heavy makeup and teased hairstyles, which helped establish the defining look of 1980s fashion.

"Donatella always had this thing for hair and makeup,"
recalled Angelo Azzena, who joined the house in 1976 to
work on the ad campaigns and stage the runway shows and
would later became one of Donatella's closest assistants.
"She practically lived at the hairdresser. So when she started,
it changed. The look became one of a young, modern woman

who had the time to do her hair and makeup properly."[1] Gianni also gave her responsibility for the shoes, bags, and jewelry. Under her influence, the accessories became more and more elaborate: high heels made up in silk fabric, with a black and white baroque pattern; or elbow-length gloves with crystals sewn in geometric patterns.

But more important, Donatella filled an indefinable role of muse, sounding board, and first assistant. The position she had served in her brother's life as they grew up now became central to the expanding Versace business. Gianni found her style of dressing edgy, fresh, and glamorous: skintight leggings in bright colors, leopard-print tops, leather jackets, and stiletto heels or tall cowboy boots. She piled two or three heavy bracelets made of shining gold medallions adorned with medusa heads on her wrists; she wore sparkly, dangling earrings that resembled mini chandeliers. With access to Milan's best hairstylists and beauty salons, Donatella gradually polished her look. She wasn't yet the camp goddess she would become in later decades, but she was becoming a walking illustration of the maxim that defined the 1980s: "If you've got it, flaunt it." Her hair became sleeker and blonder, setting off her year-round, sun-baked bronze tan. Her skin was still smooth, so she could often do with little makeup. But when she did wear makeup, she favored heavy eye shadow, liner, and false eyelashes. A personal trainer helped sculpt and trim her body into the buffed look of the gym-crazed 1980s, with toned arms, a taut stomach, and sinewy legs.

From her travels with Gianni, she brought home suitcases full of skin creams and perfumes, so many that she had special shelves built in her bathroom to hold all of her toiletries. The extreme grooming, however, veiled a profound neurosis about her own appearance. Donatella was a serial self-belittler, homing in on every last physical imperfection. She charmed people by betraying a bit of her vulnerability, but her insecurities unbalanced her. She compulsively monitored her appearance in every passing mirror—even stealing glimpses in the reflection of a fork when she was at dinner.

Donatella became Gianni's shadow in the atelier, constantly trailing behind him, murmuring her opinion of his work. He sought her views on every aspect of his designs, from color schemes to dress choices for the runway. Their conversations came so thick and fast that their ideas melded into one. Donatella had a great knack for sizing up a dress or a pair of pants or a color palette and deciding whether it had that mysterious quality that would make it trendy. When show time came, she had an extraordinary eye for making Gianni's clothes arresting on the runway, adorning them with the right shoes, jewelry, and makeup.

"Donatella was extremely useful to him," said Giusy Ferrè, a leading Italian fashion journalist and a close friend of Gianni's. "She was his passport into the world of women. She was his female alter ego."[2]

Donatella was often brutal in her judgments of Gianni's work, sparking fierce arguments between the two, often in a Calabrian dialect that was indecipherable to the rest of the Versace team. Oftentimes, designers fall into a rut once they find success with a certain style. Donatella's task was to keep Gianni moving forward; she wouldn't let him repeat himself or rest on the laurels of previously successful design ideas, no matter how much combustion her nagging caused between them.

"When he raised his voice, the others were scared, but I wasn't," Donatella would say more than twenty years later. "I kept on telling him what I thought, because there wasn't anyone else who would. He risked becoming just another designer with everyone always telling him 'yes.' But I pushed him to go further. I saw what the others were doing, which I liked better, and I saw that they were more daring. I said, you're better than these other ones. If you don't risk, you won't go anywhere."[3]

She sometimes went behind his back—for instance, instructing his seamstresses to shorten his skirts, which he preferred long. When Gianni would find out, he would be furious. "You don't understand anything!" Gianni often shouted at her. "You're going to ruin me!" Another recurring battle was over shoes. Gianni preferred flats for the runway shows, but Donatella saw that they would drain his outfits of verve.

"So we agreed to do half high heels and half flats," Donatella recounted about one show. But unbeknownst to Gianni, she switched the flats for stilettos the moment before the models stepped out onto the runway. He was once so angry at seeing the girls in high heels that he threw Donatella out of the atelier. Most of the time, though, he realized she was right.

"If Gianni didn't listen to his sister and decided to go ahead with an idea she didn't like, he would come to her the next day and say, 'You were right,'" recalled Azzena. "She had great influence over him."[4]

Their fights were so fierce that it took Paul Beck several years to get used to what he described as the "Versace verbal dynamic."

"I thought somebody was going to kill someone," he later told a *Vanity Fair* journalist. "I had to leave the room. And the argument would be over something like where to put the sweaters in the new boutique on Via Montenapoleone."[5]

The bond between the siblings grew tighter as they spent long days of intense work together, speaking in such shorthand that it was impossible to say who had come up with a particular idea. Santo, working with a separate team in a different office, was largely cut out of their ménage. He just couldn't get excited about topics such as the color of a dress or a new cut for a skirt, which riveted his younger sister and brother. Donatella reveled in her role. Even as she entered her thirties, she could continue to play the flighty kid sister. She lost things frequently and stopped driving because she was so distracted. When Gianni traveled, he was always thinking of her, usually bringing back a gift for Donatella as a spontaneous token of his affection for her. Once he bought her a twenty-karat canary yellow diamond ring, the stone as big as a Chuckles jelly candy. She was always on his mind, the first person he called when he was excited about the color of a flower he'd just seen or a new city he was visiting. "If I were to marry, I would look for a girl like Donatella," he told a journalist.[6]

Even as he put his sister on a pedestal, Gianni could be terribly hard on Donatella. If he didn't care for a particular hairstyle or new outfit she wore, he was merciless in his criticism. But at the same time he wouldn't allow anyone else to speak badly of Donatella, flying into a rage if he heard a friend or employee criticize her.

In the atelier, the employees saw Donatella as a fun-loving peer, not their boss. They addressed her using the informal *tu*, instead of the formal *lei* they scrupulously employed when speaking with Gi-anni. She possessed the candid, disarming warmth common to south-erners and had little use for professional boundaries at work. She happily delved into the personal problems of female colleagues, dol-ing out tough-love advice on boyfriends and children, and celebrated their engagements and new babies. She was unhesitatingly generous. Once she lent her own large diamond earrings to a girl who was get-ting married, so that she could have "something borrowed" for her wedding day. Another employee with a seriously ill child turned up at an appointment with a doctor whom Donatella had recommended and found the bill already paid.

Donatella was fast becoming the life of the Versace party, suck-ing voluptuously on one Marlboro Red after another until her voice became a husky, smoke-cured purr. Whether in English or Italian, her rapid-fire cadences left the listener feeling a perennial half step behind. She shared the intense energy of her older brothers but had a far shorter attention span and an unnerving, feline jitteriness. She was like a tiny, tightly coiled spring. Her walk was an impatient wig-gle, slowed down by her cantilevered heels.

Gianni extolled all women, including his baby sister, treating her more like a child than a peer. He was warm and touchy, flipping the hair of a girlfriend over her shoulder in an intimate gesture or complimenting her on her lipstick. He sized up a woman instantly and had a stream of exuberant suggestions as to what would flatter her most. When he trained his sunny Mediterranean charm on a woman, she felt like a princess.

"He would always say to me, 'You're so beautiful!'" recalled An-drea Gottleib, who was a junior assistant in the buying department at B. Altman in the 1970s. "I used to think, here's this famous designer and he's telling me how beautiful I am! He used to say, 'Let me give you this shirt or dress. You would look so wonderful in it.'"[7]

"It was a wonderful period," Donatella would recall ruefully. "The 1980s in Milan were a wonderful time. We had so much fun to-gether."[8] By then, Gianni had put together a team of about two dozen young people, many in their first jobs. He often hired people on im-pulse, asking candidates what their astrological signs were before bringing them on. Santo had found office space for the small group in

Via della Spiga 25, taking the entire top floor of the building, which ringed an airy courtyard. (Donatella once proposed lining the balcony with orchids.) The space included a salon where Gianni could hold his runway shows, but it was so cramped that he had to stage as many as three shows to accommodate all the journalists and buyers. At the time, Via della Spiga was still home to a number of old-line Milanese families and small businesses. Just below Gianni's offices lived an old lady who complained about the ruckus his team made during their late nights preparing for shows and the fact that they commandeered the tiny, rickety elevator for days. Over time, Gianni charmed the lady and she put up with the noise.

In true Italian style, Gianni treated his new employees like an extended family. He loved playing the benevolent boss, giving his favorite employees affectionate nicknames; Bruno became "Brunotto" and Luca was dubbed "Lucotto." At midmorning and midafternoon, Alba, his cook, served coffee or tea in porcelain cups, with biscuits or slices of homemade cake. At 1 p.m., the entire staff sat down to a family-style lunch at a long, simple table in the dining room, with Gianni proudly presiding at the head of the table. (When an employee disappointed him, however, Gianni often turned cold, ignoring the person in the office for weeks or even months.) Very often Gianni invited a visiting journalist or department store buyer to join them, drawing him or her into convivial chatter about work, family, and gossip. Alba made Tuscan dishes such as *sformato di patate*, a baked potato dish, or oversized spinach and ricotta ravioli. Dessert was often profiterole or *torta di crema*, a cream torte.

"When you were working, this wonderful smell of Alba's cooking floated through the office," recalled Enrico Genevois, then a young employee who dealt with graphics. "You ate better there than at a restaurant. It was wonderful. There was this sense of family. We all sat around the table laughing and joking."[9]

All three Versace siblings had a sweet tooth. Gianni happily tucked in to Alba's desserts, or the cream puffs made by the sister of his top assistant. But Donatella was very disciplined. "Donatella ate, but if there were spinach ravioli, she might have just one," said Franco Lussana, a close friend of the family and a longtime Versace employee.[10]

HOUSE OF VERSACE

At Christmas, Gianni threw a holiday party, where his employees dressed up in wild costumes. One year, Lussana, who is about six feet tall, came as Tina Turner. (Donatella had Sergio Rossi, who then made shoes for Versace, whip up an enormous pair of stilettos in his size—a forty-five, or fourteen in American sizes.) Donatella's main assistant dressed up as Raffaella Carrà, a campy bleached-blond TV star who was a sort of kitsch Italian Bette Midler. Sometimes, Lussana came as Santa Claus, bearing a bag of gifts that Gianni gave to his staff, usually small pieces of jewelry or leather bags. Gianni, who didn't like to dress up, watched his employees vamp it up and doubled over in laughter with Donatella, while Paul recorded the festivities.

❖ V ❖

As the demands on Gianni's creativity rose along with the business, he became a voracious reader, devouring magazines, newspapers, and art books, and plundering them for ideas for new designs. An early favorite was *L'abbigliamento nei secoli* (*Clothing Through the Centuries*), a heavy volume with sumptuous images of dress styles around the world throughout history.[11] When he left before dawn for a trip, he insisted on stopping to buy a thick pile of publications.

"I saw him page through art books hundreds of pages long and pick out the images that interested him without interrupting our conversation for a minute," recalled Ferrè, the Italian journalist and friend.[12] When he traveled, he scanned passersby, buildings, and landscapes for ideas.

"Anything could be a source of inspiration—a flower bed, an architectural shape, the engraving on a piece of furniture, the floor of a church," said Patrizia Cucco, Gianni's personal assistant from 1985 until his death.[13]

For a single collection of about one hundred pieces, Gianni created thousands of initial sketches on reams of paper. He then talked through the thick pile of ideas with his top two assistants, who reworked the best ones into designs with proper proportions and details. In messy handwriting that exuded impatience, Gianni scribbled notes on the polished sketches with changes he wanted.

The designs then went to *modellisti,* or pattern cutters, at the factory, who made samples. Good *modellisti* were invaluable to any designer who aspired to sell large quantities. Skilled ones knew what shapes, fabrics, and sizes worked for mass production and found ways to adapt a designer's ideas without watering them down. (They also made up the detailed instructions on how the garment should be assembled at the factory, with coded marks to denote the width of seams, the placement of darts, and the size of pockets.) Sometimes, Gianni, anxious to squeeze the best out of his team, surreptitiously gave the same sketch to several *modellisti* in order to see who came up with the best sample. As his business grew, Gianni began hiring some of the seamstresses who were closing down their own shops in Milan because their older clients had died off and younger women shunned handmade wardrobes. The seamstresses made samples or modified those that came back from the factory, adding embellishments such as embroidery or lace details.

In 1982, Gianni's experimentation brought him a breakthrough that would be one of the most important innovations in postwar fashion—and a burst of originality that helped forge the quintessential Versace look. Inspired by the material used to make metal gloves that butchers wore, he created an entirely new fabric. Working with a German craftsman, he invented a mesh composed of tiny rings of metal that were interlinked to form swaths of slinky fabric.

Initially, he used the mesh to add some Excalibur-like detail to the padded shoulders of men's black leather jackets. He wanted to use it for women's clothes as well, but the fabric was far too heavy. The German supplier tried using different alloys until he came up with a fabric light enough for Gianni to make a slip dress. The garment was still heavy—about fifteen pounds—so the seamstresses had to line its skinny spaghetti straps with leather strips to bear the weight. Backstage before a show, it took two dressers to help the model into it.

But Gianni hounded the supplier until he found a way to make metal mesh fine enough to drape. The fabric gathered in gentle folds and cowls without being bulky, yet was weighty enough to slide over the body, molding to a woman's curves and glinting against bare skin. The metal mesh was a master study in the sort of contrasts that were becoming Gianni's signature, combining the alloy's cool toughness with the suppleness of traditional cloth. To make a dress, Gianni's seamstresses had to unhook the hundreds of tiny links, using tiny crochet-type hooks, and reattach them according to Gianni's pattern. The dress was also tough on the wearer: It was cold when a woman first put it on, and the links tended to scratch.

Gianni adored the new fabric, which was like putty in his hands. He used blocks of yellow, green, and silver mesh to create Picasso-inspired patterns and floating Klimt-like gold leaves. For men, he made sleeveless muscle shirts that were an instant hit at gay clubs. The mesh gowns were catnip for Italian celebrities needing red-carpet clothes that photographed well. Metal mesh dresses would feature in every collection Versace presented from 1982 until his death.

Carolyn Mahboubi, who opened a Versace franchise in Los Angeles in 1983, instantly realized how striking the dresses were: "We opened with the leather jackets and the metal mesh dresses. At the time, it was revolutionary. No one had ever done anything like that. I remember there was a Nina Ricci shop near us, and [the French designer] just looked so old compared to Versace."[14]

Gianni went on to prod his silk, cotton, and wool suppliers to make their own breakthroughs. Normally, while assembling a new collection, a designer would choose fabrics from samples already available through textile suppliers. Instead, Gianni pushed the mills to devise fabrics that were wholly original. He told silk manufacturers to finish the cloth with heat in order to create rougher textures. One year, he had the silk made in a black-and-white pattern resembling a rhinoceros hide, and then applied opaque gold patches by hand to suggest splashes of mud. Another year, the surface of a black-and-white-striped silk was corroded to create a concertina effect; on the runway, the striped pattern looked like rippling animal skin.

Years of watching his mother cut patterns for clothes gave Gianni the confidence to experiment with new shapes and cuts that would have been clumsy in less skilled hands. In 1987, he showed a bright red strapless cocktail dress, its wide, overlapping bands of silk creating tiers that resembled opulent, slightly uneven wrapped bandages. Some of the bands had an irregularly placed pleat folded into them, throwing a twist into a dress that would otherwise have been unremarkable. The next year, he showed a red wool crepe coat with its right side cut off the shoulder—as if the wearer had shrugged it halfway off. The asymmetry worked because of the immaculate cut and construction of the coat.

As he traveled more and more frequently, he trolled the world's great museums for images to appropriate for his fashions. Once, he fell in love with Art Deco design and began transposing its sharp geometric shapes to his clothes. One silk sarong had the geometric patterns of an Art Deco design lifted straight from an art book, while a little black dress had brightly colored, Kandinsky-like embroidery. Whatever his inspiration, the innovations he made were revolutionary. The kaleidoscope of new designs, colors, cuts, and fabrics he came up with were like candy for fashionable women who were looking for something new and fun, yet sophisticated.

By the mid-1980s, Gianni was working constantly, maintaining his outside contracts with Genny and Callaghan in order to subsidize the growth of his own brand. To channel all of the new ideas that came to him, he sketched in the evenings, on weekends, and during vacations, rising before dawn to visit the factories to check on samples or to meet with textile suppliers to go over new fabrics. His fashion show schedule was relentless: four shows a year for his own line plus another half a dozen for his contract brands. Despite the heavy workload, he maintained the perfectionism that is indispensable to those who have extraordinary success.

"You could never, ever say, 'It's not possible,'" recalled Cucco, his assistant. "That just made him more determined to do it."[15]

Passionate by nature, Gianni performed his work with the spirit of someone who was doing what he was born to do—and was proving hugely successful at it. When he had a new idea, he felt as impatient as a child, pestering his team to translate a sketch into a sample. Punctual to a fault, he hounded his suppliers to deliver his fabrics faster. In meetings, his words came so fast and furious that an assistant trailed behind him, taking notes on what he said so that she could explain him afterward to his guests.

He felt an almost compulsive need to check everything that went on at his new company. He stopped unannounced at the shops to check that the clothes were perfectly folded and that the windows looked right. When he arrived, he went straight to the stockroom to see that his bestselling items, such as print shirts and black cashmere sweaters, were available in every size, growing angry at the manager if anything was out of stock.[16]

Acutely conscious of his image, he sat down with his public relations person to help write press releases. He had his designers make full-color illustrations of his clothes on models complete with faces and sylphlike bodies, using them as elaborate backdrops in his office when television crews arrived for interviews. He assiduously courted fashion editors, sending them free dresses and frequently inviting them to those family-style lunches with his team. Journalists who wrote favorably about his clothes received a large bouquet of flowers the same day, along with a handwritten note of thanks. But negative press reviews stung him badly. Once, a top Italian fashion critic who typically favored Armani in her reviews came for a private look at his collection. As Gianni, keen to impress the woman, took her through the works, the journalist was full of praise. When, a few days later, Gianni opened the newspaper to find her fiercely negative article, he felt bitterly disappointed. "What a bitch!" he said, bursting into tears. "She comes in here and gives me all these compliments and then turns around to write a nasty review."[17]

Wanting desperately to break through abroad, Gianni was determined to learn English in order to communicate directly with journalists and department store buyers. He never studied formally but instead picked up phrases from American songs, films, and reviews of his designs in the English-speaking press. As a result, his English was rather picturesque and heavy on fashion-speak. "Darling" was his favorite endearment, while "Ees so booring" was the ultimate put-down for people and things that were, to him, unforgivably passé. He spoke with a thick accent, peppering his sentences with charming mistakes, but he didn't mind. Once, in 1981, an interviewer asked what had inspired a particular collection. "I tink of the life," he replied, his brow furrowed, intent on making himself understood. "Dee life today is so speedy. I tink of the woman today. Is so deeferent."

"His broken English was part of his charm," said Dawn Mello, who was buying for B. Altman, one of the first U.S. department stores to buy Versace in the 1970s. "He came up with some stock phrases for the store appearances and did this mix of Italian and English."[18] Within a few years, through pure determination, he was able to speak fluently, while still charming interlocutors with the occasional Italian phrase, most often *"Basta!"* ("Enough!")

❖ V ❖

Gianni's vision of Versace's future was so grandiose that at times it strained the people he worked with. For instance, franchisees were required to decorate the shops using designs drawn up by Versace-hired architects (who, in turn, paid a fee to the house for each shop they outfitted). Invariably, Gianni pushed for opulent designs that cost the franchisees a fortune.

"If you left it to Gianni, you would have St. Paul's Cathedral," said Roberto Devorik, who owned a London Versace franchise in the 1980s. "He wanted everything. Then Santo would be more real."[19]

Gianni could be autocratic sometimes, believing that his vision was the right one. He pushed the franchisees to buy items even if they didn't find them salable. Once Devorik refused to buy some Versace moccasins that sported garish gold medusas, reckoning they would never sell in the understated UK market. "But these shoes are a masterpiece!" Gianni protested, his high-pitched voice rising.

"Gianni, a shoe can never be a masterpiece," Devorik shot back. "I don't like them. I find them very nouveau riche. If you want the shoes in the store, you can pay for them yourself." Gianni, offended and angry, abruptly slammed down the phone.[20]

In the atelier, Gianni was an implacable perfectionist who drove his staff to their limit. Once, the night before a show, he decided to replace his suits' fitted skirts with light, diaphanous ones featuring a double layer of organza that had been printed with flower patterns. His seamstresses spent the entire night making twenty skirts—the flower patterns layered precisely to create the right look—for the show the next day.

Gianni had "an almost paranoid need for perfection," one top assistant said. "He threw his heart and soul into his work and he demanded the most from those of us who worked for him." Donatella often melted the tension caused by one of Gianni's outbursts, soothing the hurt feelings he left in his wake. Once, after Gianni brusquely criticized the work of an assistant, Donatella made up for it by buying the upset young man a plane ticket to New York to visit his boyfriend.[21]

But Gianni knew how much he needed his staff and often tried to make up for the pressure he put on them, too. During the frantic days before a show, he brought his seamstresses tea and biscuits and gave each one a small, colorful bouquet of flowers, along with a personal message of thanks. When he was on vacation, he brought back small, thoughtful gifts for his closest associates.

"He once gave me a silver tray that he found in Egypt and another time it was a caftan from India," Cucco said. "It was wonderful. It made you feel special, that he had thought of you."[22]

❖ V ❖

At the end of 1985, when the family gathered for Christmas, they had something special to celebrate. By then, the clan had established a tradition of spending the holiday together at Villa Fontanelle, the sumptuous home that Gianni had recently finished restoring. In 1977, Gianni had discovered the villa during one of his frequent trips to Lake Como, the finger-shaped lake thirty miles north of Milan, where many of Versace's silk manufacturers were located. He'd fallen in love with the lake, with its limpid light and winding one-lane roads. Since the eighteenth century, Lake Como had lured aristocratic and bourgeoisie families looking for summer homes, first from Milan, and later from England, Switzerland, and Germany. Today the cemeteries around the lake contain tombs of the many expatriates who retired to Como.

One day, on a visit to Moltrasio, a tiny town on Lake Como's western shore, Gianni discovered Villa Fontanelle. He was bewitched by the house's history. In 1865, an eccentric English nobleman, Charles Currie, built the mansion, where, legend has it, he spent entire days wandering nude in the villa's sheltered garden. Villa Fontanelle consisted of three structures: a custodian's house, a *dependance* (outbuilding), and the main villa, a three-story rectangular structure with a large terrace overlooking the lake and a small dock. Currie dubbed his twenty-seven-room home Villa Fontanelle—or "little fountains"—because of the natural springs bubbling in a grotto on the grounds.

But by the time Gianni saw Villa Fontanelle, the mansion had been largely abandoned, its walls swollen with damp and mold, their elaborate frescoes nearly destroyed, the mosaic floors in total disrepair. The newly rich found Lake Como drab and unexciting, preferring trendier vacation spots in Sardinia and Portofino. Many of the grand villas around the lake were empty husks left to deteriorate by owners who could no longer afford to keep them up.

Gianni didn't have enough money at the time to acquire Currie's entire estate, so he started out by buying one piece of it, paying eight hundred million lire ($485,000) for the first small sections. A close friend bought most of the rest. (Years later, Gianni would buy out the friend to own the entire estate.) By the time the family gathered there for Christmas in 1985, Gianni had brought the villa back to life in grand neoclassical style. He hired Queen Elizabeth's landscaper to claw the gardens back from decades of neglect. He planted yellow and red roses, citrus groves, pink begonias, and boxwoods, and built fountains with water running from the mouth of medusa heads. A swing hung from a large tree that also served as shelter for outdoor lunches. He installed marble bathrooms, restored the frescoed ceilings, and designed an all-pink bedroom for Donatella. Gianni's renovation of Villa Fontanelle opened the doors to the renaissance of Lake Como, which would once again become a favorite playground of the elite, from Russian oligarchs to Hollywood stars such as George Clooney.

By the mid-1980s, Villa Fontanelle was Gianni's escape. He and Antonio would drive out to Lake Como, often with prospective sound tracks for his next runway show playing on the car's stereo system. Gianni adored the mansion and, in turn, it was to be the site of some of the Versace family's happiest times together. Over the previous few years, on December 8, the Catholic Church's Feast of the Immaculate Conception and the traditional start of the Italian Christmas season, Gianni began having his favorite gardener erect a twelve-foot Scandinavian fir tree and decorate it with glass Christmas bulbs, ribbons, and lights. He had an eighteenth-century Neapolitan nativity scene set up in the main living room. Just before Christmas, Gianni personally helped arrange the pile of gifts under the tree. Nora and Nino flew up to join the rest of the family, where they played cards together for hours in the library.

Nino, however, never felt comfortable with his son's opulent lifestyle. Soon after the family began gathering in Como, he approached Gianni one morning. "Gianni, I didn't sleep well at all last night," he told him. Gianni, who had given his father his grand two-room bedroom suite, asked him what was wrong. "I just can't get used to that big room," his father said. "Don't you have a smaller one you can give me?" Nino came to visit only reluctantly, always accompanied by Nora. Once, he felt so ill at ease that he slipped off to the airport to fly back to Reggio without telling his children.[23]

But that Christmas would be a special one. Donatella had recently announced that she was pregnant. Gianni was thrilled at the news, although during the pregnancy, he was privately horrified at his sister's huge weight gain, her arms and neck ballooning in size. Her condition hardly slowed Donatella down. She gave up neither her Marlboros nor her stilettos, even late in the pregnancy. On June 30, 1986, at a private clinic in Milan, Donatella gave birth to a girl by Cesarean section. Gianni proudly helped choose the name of his new niece: Allegra Donata Beck.

eight

Rock and Royalty

ONE DAY IN 1986, ELTON JOHN MADE A TRIP TO MILAN ON business regarding a soccer team he owned. But while he was there, he had an important stop to make: the Versace men's shop.

For Elton John, visiting Versace's store in Milan was like going to Mecca. A compulsive shopper, he was an enormous fan of Gianni's showy clothes. In a single afternoon at the shop in London, he had bought as many as a hundred of Gianni's elaborate silk print shirts. He had been known to order Gianni's entire men's collection, sight unseen. So when Elton walked into the Versace store in Milan, the shop manager immediately called up to Gianni's office. Gianni hustled down to the store, ordering it shut for the afternoon so that he could help Elton shop undisturbed.

HOUSE OF VERSACE

That evening, over dinner, Elton found himself opening up to Gianni. It was a difficult time in Elton's life. He was battling a years-long drug problem. He was also struggling with bulimia, and the London newspapers were constantly speculating about his sexuality. In Gianni, he found a new friend—one of the closest the pop star would ever have.

"Elton totally opened up to Gianni," recalled Antonio D'Amico. "Something clicked instantly between them."[1]

Over the next few years, once Elton stopped drinking and drugging and acknowledged that he was gay, the friendship between the two men deepened. Elton found Gianni's natural exuberance a salve. For his part, Gianni loved to quiz Elton on music and pop culture, soaking up his friend's expertise in a world he knew little about. They spoke every day, playing phone pranks on each other; Elton, who normally disliked being a guest in people's homes, stayed frequently at Villa Fontanelle. They shared similar, outré sensibilities, both reveling in their status as leading lights in the gay world.

"When I'm reincarnated, I want to come back as super gay," Gianni once told Elton.

"Gianni, what do you think you are now?" Elton shot back.

Elton became a walking billboard for Versace, spending up to 250,000 pounds (about $400,000) at a time on Gianni's shirts and suits.[2] Gianni had his best illustrator make colorful sketches of a slim Elton dressed in Versace clothes, much to his friend's delight. Because of Elton's ungainly shape—narrow around the shoulders but wide at the middle—Versace seamstresses had to adapt the outfits. Elton wrote some songs for Gianni's shows ("Deep in the jungle, a story's unfolding—exotic, sexy, classic, Gee-AH-nee!"). Gianni, in turn, made the costumes for several of Elton's tours for free—embroidered, fezlike hats, vests with bold Picasso-inspired designs, and leather tuxedos.

Gianni's relationship with Elton, while driven by genuine friendship, was an early instance of the burgeoning love affair between fashion designers and celebrities that would, by the early 1990s, prove a gold mine for all involved. Gianni would lead the parade, as his clothes became must-haves for movie stars, supermodels, certain members of royalty, and even some grandees of the corporate world. This pairing came just as press coverage of the rich and famous was exploding. Finding themselves in the media's unblinking eye, celebrities quickly grasped the chance to work with designers to burnish their images. At the same time, the blanket coverage of the stars—and what they were wearing—influenced shoppers' tastes more and more. It would be a match made in heaven.

Gianni's relationship with VIPs had gotten off to a slow start, with his clothes' popularity confined largely to Italian television celebrities and pop singers. Early in his career, he had a few hits with international luminaries, virtually all men. In 1983, Versace dressed Paul McCartney and Michael Jackson for their "Say Say Say" music video. But Gianni, enormously busy with his many collections, had little time or patience to butter up stars. Indeed, with the exception of Elton (and, later, Sting), he found much of the celebrity world to be tedious. He was a happy workaholic who was content to go to bed early rather than stay out all night clubbing with the stars. Instead, Donatella was becoming a bigger part of the celebrity scene, and she quickly saw that celebrities could be a boon for her brother. While Gianni frequented the theater and ballet in his little free time, Donatella, a passionate pop music fan, was hanging out backstage with rock stars after their concerts. In the early 1980s, she approached Sting following a concert during his European tour and later charmed Bruce Springsteen, lending him the villa in Como for his 1985 honeymoon. After wearing Versace for his *Born in the USA* tour, he began talking up the Versace brand to his fellow musicians.

But winning fans among female stars was the real ticket to press coverage—and at this Gianni struggled, as Armani established himself as *the* designer to Hollywood. Armani had stepped neatly into a fashion gap in the entertainment business that had been growing for years. Until the 1970s, Hollywood studios had their costume designers make actresses' gowns for red-carpet events such as the Oscars. (MGM's chief costumer even made Grace Kelly's wedding dress.) But when the studios disbanded their costume departments, actresses were left to buy dresses on their own. The result was a series of front-page fashion flops throughout the 1970s and 1980s, with stars dressing in "oversize this, thrift-shop that," as Graydon Carter wrote in *Vogue*.[3]

HOUSE OF VERSACE

After *American Gigolo*, Armani saw gold in Hollywood's hills. In 1988, he opened a thirteen-thousand-square-foot boutique in Beverly Hills to cater to celebrities and hired as its publicist a former society columnist with a Rolodex full of the private numbers of major Hollywood celebrities. His sleek outfits were a safe option for nervous stars on an evening when millions were watching.

"When you dress in Armani, you can be sure you'll never look like a Christmas tree," said Sophia Loren. The 1990 Oscars were an Armani fashion show. He dressed Michelle Pfeiffer, Jodie Foster, Julia Roberts, and Jessica Lange, as well as six leading men, including Denzel Washington.[4] Gianni knew it would take more than friendship with Elton John to win the kind of celebrity following that could turbo-charge his business. And he thought the way to popular success might be to give the stars the sort of showstopping clothes they couldn't resist.

So, even as Armani was orchestrating his triumphant 1990 Oscar showing, Versace was more than five thousand miles away, at the Ritz in Paris, preparing for his first-ever runway show of Versace haute couture. It was a chilly January day and Gianni and Donatella had barely slept since arriving a few days before. They had worked until 3 a.m. or 4 a.m. each night, snatching a few hours of sleep before starting again at 9 a.m. (On Gianni's arrival, Karl Lagerfeld, a prolific designer and talented artist, sent over a sketch he had made of Gianni, with a note offering warm wishes for his debut.)[5] The week before, a caravan of about a dozen seamstresses and other assistants had made the trip from Milan, lugging sewing machines, irons, and large coffinlike cases full of hundreds of garments, shoes, bags, belts, and jewelry. Counting the press people, marketing executives, and Gianni's team, at least a hundred Versace employees made the trip to the Ritz.

Gianni was taking a big leap, and he knew it. It was rare for a ready-to-wear designer to launch a couture line, and only the most confident would take on the burden and expense of showing dozens of painstakingly handmade dresses twice a year. (Indeed, Santo's main lieutenant in the business quit the company in part because he felt such a young enterprise was risking too much in adding a couture line.) But with couture, everything clicked for Gianni. During the

1980s, his atelier had grown to two dozen seamstresses who started out adding hand-finishing to dresses made at the factory but were soon making one-of-a-kind outfits. Gianni had also been experimenting with his theater costumes and was eager to apply new cuts, shapes, and embellishments to his own lines. He long harbored a dream of re-creating his mother's workshop in grand style, so his new couture line was enormously gratifying to him. Moreover, his decision to launch couture would unlock the treasure chest of celebrities for him, and with them, fix a strong, bracing image of the Versace brand in the minds of millions of consumers around the world.

Gianni staged his show in the pool area of the storied Ritz Hotel, which had double spiral staircases on either end, frescoed ceilings, and a plush bar area. Days before, Ritz workers had donned scuba gear to slip poles into holes at the bottom of the pool to support a runway that would cover the turquoise water. In a kitchen area behind the pool, on the day of the show, the top makeup artist first made up Donatella, then went to work on the models, poking, combing, and painting them for as long as five hours to transform them into Versace glamour girls. The "backstage" was a tiny space just behind the staircase that the models descended to reach the runway. The space crackled with stress. Gianni's team, who normally cleared a path for their boss as he snapped orders during the intense hours before a show, struggled to get out of his way. Gianni felt enormous pressure, worried that his debut before the notoriously critical Parisians would be a bust. "Look at the creases in these dresses!" Gianni exploded. Last-minute manhandling had wrinkled the dresses, but the backstage area was too small for ironing boards.

Outside, three hundred guests descended white marble steps to the pool area. At the far end of the pool hung a large medusa logo on the landing of the double staircase that led to the backstage. When the house lights went down, a spotlight flashed onto the first model, lighting up her elaborately embroidered bodice like a blaze as she walked down the pristine white runway. A stream of models followed, dressed in pinstriped miniskirts topped with glittering bodices covered in beads, rhinestones, and pearls. Many of the girls were black or Latino, and their dark, oiled skin glowed under the spotlights. As the music morphed from Prince to Puccini's aria "Vincerò," the clothes built from miniskirted day suits to embroidered cocktail dresses, shown with voluminous silk Little Red Riding Hood capes lined in lemon yellow or neon pink.

At the end of the forty-five-minute show, Gianni emerged, visibly drained but smiling. When he heard the cascade of applause that greeted him, he knew that his collection had been a success. As he took his bow and felt the adrenaline of the previous days ebb, he reveled in the moment, knowing that he and his brand had entered a new realm—one that even his mother could never have dreamed of for him while she was alive. Indeed, with the advent of his couture collection, Gianni's great technical ability to make well-crafted dresses melded with his natural showmanship to produce clothes that were stunning in their imagery. During the early 1990s, images from his semiannual shows at the Ritz became instantly recognizable as Versace, disseminating a look that, while polarizing, was hardly boring.

Gianni's decision to launch a couture line gave a jolt to a stodgy business. The traditional Parisian couture houses were dying as women increasingly took their cues from trends bubbling up from pop music, urban teenagers, and the counterculture. Gianni's genius was to co-opt these forces and project them onto his clothes, something that earned him the envy of the French couturiers, who would struggle to compete with such bracing, exciting designs. In doing so, he pulled the curtain on fashion as an elite, rarefied enterprise and recast it as a topic of bottomless interest to the masses.

"Versace moved fashion into the public domain in the most strident way," said Hamish Bowles, former European editor-at-large for *Vogue*.[6]

He carved out a clutch of themes that he used over and over to great effect, from his "Wild Baroque" pieces with their raucous mix of leopard print and gold-leaf whorls, to second-skin bodysuits—inspired by Donatella's love of stretchy leggings—featuring clashing, gaudy colors and gold-colored chains. He created outfits that were like jewels, cramming beads, sequins, large stones, and silk embroidery into wild patterns, often using a technique applied by nineteenth-century Parisian ateliers in which craftswomen used wire supports to create layer after layer of beaded appliqués, giving bodices a rich, three-dimensional look.

In kaleidoscopic fashion, Gianni dipped into and mixed popular culture, fine arts, and couture history, making the most dissonant images look right together. Billowing eighteenth-century skirts in riotous pastel patterns were combined with cowgirl's denim shirts top-stitched in gold. He translated one of Roy Lichtenstein's most famous paintings by putting giant letters spelling "WHAAM!" on a yellow devoré evening gown. He adorned a silk halter-neck gown with Andy Warhol's celebrated images of Marilyn Monroe and James Dean.

Gianni spilled the full force of his creativity onto his prints and surpassed the work done by Emilio Pucci, considered the great postwar innovator of prints. Gianni transposed all manner of images to foulards, silk shirts, and dresses—a portrait of Elton John, postcardlike images of Miami's South Beach neighborhood, rich Byzantine Madonnas. It took great skill to know how to design and place a print so that it looked right on the cut of a shirt or the drape of a dress. His wild designs were painstaking to execute. Before computer-assisted design, prints were made by using engraved rollers or screens, one for each color. Gianni's most elaborate prints had twenty-three colors, rivaling only Hermès's legendary foulards.

"I used to go to him with five designs and I left with orders to make a dozen," recalled one Versace printmaker. "I did three hundred or four hundred designs a year for him—a tremendous amount."[7]

Gianni's evening gowns were showstoppers. He cut filmy materials such as chiffon and georgette into fine column dresses that slid easily over the body, and he used punk-inspired pins to gather up masses of light organza into ball gowns, holding up the whole confections with overalls-like suspenders. The dresses fit wonderfully.

"One had only to try on a Versace dress to find that one's tits went up, and one's ass went out, and one's waist went in," declared longtime *Vogue* writer and editor Joan Juliet Buck. "Gianni Versace's evening dresses had these zips, and so the body changed. It worked because of that kind of inner architecture."[8]

Some commentators blasted his couture collections for their cartoon glamour and happy-hooker imagery. They found his plundering of Klimt, Picasso, and Warhol facile, and branded him

"Copyace." His *horror vacui* decorations were, for some, an assault on the eyes. They found his clothes gimmicky and out of touch with real women—but Gianni himself had a different audience in mind with some of his most extravagant creations; they were intended more for the media than for sale. For instance, a series of catsuits and dresses adorned with images of *Vogue* covers were meant to be catnip for the fashion press. At times, Gianni seemed to provoke his harshest critics deliberately. In 1992, he presented a collection inspired by sadomasochism and gay leather bars, complete with black leather straps, harness bodices, and studded leather skirts. At the show, he sent as many as eight girls, hoisted in dominatrix-style leather dresses, big hair, and bold makeup, on the runway at once, a visual punch in the eye. Critics were split on whether Versace was a creative genius or a moral scandal.

"There were people who loved it, who thought it was brilliant, the greatest thing he had ever done," Holly Brubach, the fashion critic at the *New Yorker* at the time, said afterward. "And others of us, mostly women, could barely evaluate the design aspect of it because we were so offended. I have to say that I hated it."[9]

Gianni's salespeople struggled to sell the clothes, even in watered-down versions with many of the harnesses and buckles removed. But it hardly mattered. The dustup earned him reams of press coverage. The Versaces were not just dressing celebrities; they had become a media phenomenon—celebrities themselves. *Vogue* editor Anna Wintour recalled the one hundredth anniversary party for the magazine at the New York Public Library in 1992, a black-tie event with a guest list including Hollywood stars, media moguls, and the world's top designers. "I was standing at the top of the stairs and there were a lot of paparazzi and photographers," she said. "Then there was this roar that you could have heard in Washington. It was Donatella and Gianni arriving. Donatella was in one of those bondage dresses. She was absolutely *it*."[10]

Gianni's hyperbolic style appealed initially to the parvenus in cities such as Miami, Buenos Aires, and Hong Kong, who lacked a strong sense of inner style but wanted to revel in the cutting-edge cachet their new money could buy. (Rich Arab women, happy to spend as much as forty thousand dollars for an opulent Versace wedding gown, were big clients.) In the 1980s, Gianni had suffered because of his disinterest in dressing the Establishment, but during the 1990s, his exuberant, guilt-free clothes mirrored the post–Cold War economic boom spreading around the world. His clothes embraced the rampant consumerism of the decade. Meanwhile, women who had flocked to safe designers such as Armani when they first entered the workforce now wanted to cut loose. As a result, Gianni managed to channel the new yen for fun, exuberant clothes and then gave it shape with collection after collection of clothes that caught women's imaginations.

"Armani really represented the rise of the woman in the workforce," Wintour noted. "But then I think that people started saying, sure, she's in the workforce. But she can also have some fun."[11]

The 1988 ascent of Anna Wintour to the helm of *Vogue* gave Gianni an enormous boost. Until then, the American magazines virtually ignored him, even declining to attend some of his dinners and parties in Milan. Wintour set out to loosen up the venerable magazine, putting celebrities on the cover and running features on new styles and more accessible fashions. The UK-born editor found Gianni a breath of fresh air.

"My predecessor was a Geoffrey Beene and Giorgio Armani fan," she said. "I think to her eye, Gianni was a bit brash and vulgar, where as to me, it was fun."[12] When Wintour organized a benefit runway show in the early 1990s, she featured Versace, along with Chanel and Lacroix, instead of old-liners such as Valentino and Givenchy. Gianni soon became a mainstay of *Vogue*'s coverage.

"That show made him famous," Donatella recalled, the pride evident in her voice years later. "The Americans had considered him vulgar. He suffered this a lot. Then Anna arrived and realized he wasn't vulgar—he was 'glamour.'"[13]

Over time, Versace images that had originally seemed jarring became an accepted part of fashion vocabulary. Ideas that may have looked over-the-top or brash on the couture catwalk soon trickled down to more-wearable versions in his ready-to-wear collection or even licensed products that were affordable to many women. As a result, the shocking images from the runway came to influence how women dressed every day. "Try to imagine your wardrobe without the jolt of a print, the vitality of a stiletto, the glamorous bric-a-brac of chains and doodads," wrote Cathy Horyn, influential fashion critic for the *New York Times*, in 1997. "This was Versace's doing. His influence melted and spread far beyond the sexual heat of his runway."[14]

❖ V ❖

Little more than a year after his debut at the Ritz, Gianni's foray into couture paid its first huge dividend. After the couture runway in July 1991, Donatella stayed in Paris after the couture show to shoot the clothes for an ad campaign. She and the photographer were scanning the Polaroid test shots when Sam McKnight, the London-based celebrity hairdresser she'd hired to do the models' hair, pulled her aside. "Listen, Anna Harvey would like you to send her some of the Polaroids," he said. "She wants to show them to someone important. She can't tell you who it is, but, trust me, she's a very important person."

Donatella knew Harvey, a former senior editor at British *Vogue*, quite well. Perplexed, she gathered up a number of photos, including one of an eggshell blue column dress made of heavy silk and decorated with a swirly pattern of gold-tone studs and colored strass and slipped them in a FedEx package. Once Harvey received them, Donatella's assistant wheedled the name of the mysterious lady out of her: It was Diana, Princess of Wales.

Donatella instantly picked up the phone to tell Gianni. Gianni was thrilled. "What are you talking about?" he said, his voice rising in excitement. "You must be kidding!"[15]

Not long afterward, Diana appeared in British *Harper's Bazaar* in the blue-silk couture dress, in a picture by French photographer Patrick Demarchelier. The pictures showing a relaxed, sexy Diana, shorn of jewelry and wearing the sleek gown, were an instant hit—for her and for the gown's designer.

By the time she slipped on that blue dress, Diana was far from the frumpy English girl who burst onto the world's stage in 1981 with her engagement to Prince Charles. Back then, Shy Di had little sense of style beyond an English-countryside wardrobe of corduroys, flouncy dresses, and Barbour jackets. For the announcement of her engagement, she wore an off-the-rack outfit she had chosen with her mother—an unbecoming blue suit with a scalloped edge and a print blouse with a large pussy-cat bow. Her bunchy wedding gown, with its ten thousand sequins and seed pearls and twenty-five-foot train, hardly heralded the birth of a fashion star. Moreover, rigid royal protocol—hats at public events, tiaras for grand evenings, and dresses cut carefully to prevent a flash of décolleté—made her look like a schoolgirl dressed in her mother's clothes.

For the first half of the 1980s, the UK tabloids pilloried her often for her fashion faux pas: a white, majorette-style suit with gold frogging down the front, chunky velvet Laura Ashley–style dresses, buckled shoes, and too many ruffled shirts. The obligation of the future queen to dress largely in British designs kept her on a short leash. Gradually, she found her style by scrutinizing her press clippings and learning that what looked good in the mirror might not translate well to photos. She turned more and more to Anna Harvey for advice and contacts with designers. Harvey helped her find clothes that suited both her youth and stature. She pared things down, choosing sleeker, simpler outfits that were cut closer to her body, in strong colors that were visible to the crowds. (She never wore Giorgio Armani's designs publicly because she felt his muted colors didn't stand out enough.) By her late twenties, she'd made the awkward, painful transformation from a passive young girl to a dynamic and worldly, if troubled, woman.

Diana was a perfect mannequin, with her slender five-foot-ten frame, a slim neck, and broad shoulders. She wore an Italian size forty or forty-two—a size six or eight in the United States—and had the peachy skin and luminous blue eyes of a classic English rose. Designers assiduously courted her, knowing a jackpot lay in dressing the world's most photographed woman. When Diana was photographed carrying a chic Christian Dior handbag, the company soon sold one hundred thousand units, the surge in sales sending the company's revenues up 20 percent that year.

But Diana refused to take free or unsolicited clothes (although she did accept deep discounts of up to 90 percent). If a designer sent clothes to Kensington Palace without being asked, she had a dresser return them with a chilly thank-you note. Designers who dressed her were forbidden to publicize their association with her. To prevent leaks, she tended to choose outfits at the last minute, her selections depending on the weather, her mood, and whether she wanted to make a particular statement with her appearance. Her PR people were then careful to get a mention of the designer into the press.

The year after she donned Gianni's powder blue dress was the year in which she separated from Charles. Her separation gave her much more freedom to modernize her image and turn to designers such as Versace. Single, restless, and largely liberated of her royal duties, she felt free to flaunt her sexy side. Shorn of her royal title, Diana could wear French and Italian designers freely now, and Harvey contacted the houses for samples that might work. Diana began to wear higher heels and sleeveless dresses that showed off her gym-trim legs and arms, and she stopped wearing hats. She got Sam McKnight to cut her hair into a shorter, sleeker bob that looked casual but chic. Her post-Charles wardrobe was so glamorous and sensual that the UK press dubbed it her "revenge couture." On the evening in which Prince Charles admitted to his affair with Camilla Parker-Bowles on national television, she stole his thunder by wearing a form-fitting black cocktail dress cut above the knee, her nails painted poppy red. "The Thrilla He Left to Woo Camilla," read the headline in the *Sun* the next day.

Just around the time of Diana's separation, Gianni inaugurated an opulent new store on Bond Street, London's tony shopping thoroughfare. He spent more than $6 million to transform a former bank branch into a four-floor emporium. Composed of ten different types of marble shipped from Italy, each floor had a different theme—yellow stone for the ground floor, dusty pinks and apricots on the next, and deep green and turquoise for the VIP level. Brocatelle marble lined the staircase, and medusas were etched in frosted glass. At a time when spartan, Japanese-style interiors were ascendant in London fashion boutiques, the new Versace store was an extravagance.

On the opening night in May 1992, nearly a thousand guests gawked at the store, fingering pairs of mules covered with gilt seashells that cost 650 pounds ($1,000), and men's studded leather trousers, priced at 1,800 pounds ($2,700). Elton John, Joan Collins, Kylie Minogue, and Ivana Trump mixed with artists, London socialites, and magazine editors. The party was the talk of London. Gianni had invited Diana to the party, but she declined. "It will be trashy," a friend told her.[16] Instead, she agreed to a private tour.

The manager closed the store during lunch and Diana browsed, murmuring polite praise for the embroidered cashmere cardigan sweaters and tailored day suits. But she didn't buy anything. The next day, a delivery truck arrived at Kensington Palace, bearing boxes and boxes of Versace clothes. Gianni had sent her nearly the entire collection. Annoyed, she sent it all back to the shop. Gianni quickly wrote Diana a note of apology and sent her an all-white collection of soaps and candles scented of lily of the valley, her favorite flower. Diana accepted the token.

At the same time, Elton John was becoming closer with Diana, hoping to corral her patronage for his AIDS foundation. Diana had been friends with the singer since 1981, when he had played a private party for the twenty-first birthday of Charles's brother, Prince Andrew. Over the years, the two spoke privately about their struggles with bulimia, and Diana respected Elton's energetic charity work. By the 1990s, Diana was becoming more open to friendships with high-profile gay men, an association she'd avoided during her marriage. They offered her the prospect of fun and wicked conversation. Elton started inviting her to his spread in Windsor, where she got to know Gianni better.

"Diana used to keep celebrities at arm's length, but that changed later on," a close associate recalls. "She liked to commiserate on the terrible price that fame bought them."

Over the next several years, Gianni gradually became one of her favorite designers, although she often made him remove the gaudy medusas and overwrought details he piled on his clothes. He gave her first pick of his couture collection and designed pieces exclusively for her that were classic but had a pinch of glamour. His bright, clear colors and impeccable fit helped her shrug off the last vestiges of British dowdiness, giving her the sleek, international look she was known for at the end of her life. (The night she died in a car crash in Paris, in 1997, she was wearing black Versace satin sling-back shoes.)

"Diana needed fresh air," said Roberto Devorik, the owner of the London Versace franchise and a friend of Diana's. "She needed a way to show them, I'm here. She did it with Chanel, she did it with

Lacroix. But in the sexy way, she had to do it with Versace."[17] For Gianni, Diana was a wholesale vindication of charges that his designs were vulgar—that they were aimed only at arrivistes who frequented nightclubs in Miami or Arab princesses looking for ostentatious displays of their wealth.

In one outfit that emulated Diana's idol, Jackie Kennedy, Gianni designed a formfitting bubble-gum-pink suit, with a pencil skirt, a short double-breasted jacket with a round collar, and a pillbox hat. He also made her a series of slim, knee-length pastel-colored sheaths that fit her like a glove and became a sort of uniform. His evening wear was done in simple silhouettes that let her express a sexual charge at a time when she was having affairs with various men. Gianni did as many of her fittings as he could himself, but soon charged Franca Biagini, the head of the atelier, with handling the princess. (Gianni, sensing that Diana didn't care for Donatella, never sent his sister.) As she did with all top couture clients, Biagini had a mannequin made, with a wooden core and a fabric outer layer molded in Diana's size. If a client gained or lost weight, she adjusted the fabric layer.

Diana and Biagini quickly developed a rapport. The first time Biagini arrived at Kensington Palace, she found Diana waiting for her at the top of the stairs, holding a bouquet of flowers. They spent hours together in Diana's private living room, a small salon that held her old ballet shoes and photos of her sons. Diana loved going through the clothes and being fitted. Afterward, she would help the seamstress gather everything up and carry it down to the car. Every year, she sent Biagini a Christmas card with a personal note.[18]

With Elton playing matchmaker, Gianni and Diana developed the sort of obsequious friendship typical in the fashion world. Gianni reveled in his relationship with the princess. He was also quick to spot a golden PR opportunity. Years later, he told a journalist that he spoke with the princess every week. When she sent him a Christmas card, he had it framed and placed it conspicuously in his New York townhouse. But while Diana was genuinely fond of Elton, her relationship with Gianni was never as tight as he liked to claim.

"Diana and Gianni weren't really friends," said one person who was close to Diana. "They never had a one-on-one relationship. She was wary of him. With Gianni it was business. She needed a bit of glamour."

With his couture collection leading the headlines in the fashion press every six months and Diana stepping out more frequently in his clothes, Gianni took the competition for famous names to the next level. The stars were soon bewitched by Gianni's clothes, which stood out on the red carpet and photographed brilliantly. Everyone was happy: Versace showstoppers got actresses the attention they craved, and the press got strong, sexy images. It added up to priceless and profitable publicity for Gianni.

The care and feeding of celebrities fell to Donatella. When she wanted to recruit a star into the Versace camp, she began by sending her oodles of freebies, including couture dresses costing tens of thousands of dollars each. Assistants kept a file with measurements of all the house's major celebrities.

"Donatella came on after Armani, but then they became really huge pushers of the clothes," recalled Wayne Scot Lukas, a stylist who worked with many Hollywood stars. "It was, 'Darling, take the clothes.' The hugeness of Versace was this whole giving, giving, giving away of clothes. Versace gave them to celebrities, to their assistants. They bought the Versace business in America by throwing clothes at celebrities."[19]

Once Donatella had won over a star, she lavished perks and privileges upon her that lured her into the Versace lair. She flew her over to shows in either first class or in private jets and put her up in suites at the Four Seasons. The most coveted stars were given the run of the boutique on Via Montenapoleone. (If Gianni didn't like a star whom Donatella was courting, he would explode when he saw the bill from the shop.) She invited her to stay for a few days at the villa in Como, where even the most jaded celebrities were dazzled by the Versaces' opulent mode of living.

The first time Madonna came to Milan for a Versace event, Donatella went to the airport to meet her and shuttled her to Villa Fontanelle. Madonna, wanting a more sophisticated look following a no-holds-bared period highlighted by her *Sex* book, had agreed to appear in ads for Versace. Donatella had the villa filled with Madonna's favorite flowers—white gardenias and tuberoses—floating in large vases filled with water. When Madonna walked in, she was bowled over. "Look at this place!" she exclaimed as she gaped at the opulent house. "Even I wouldn't have the balls to do something like this." For the next few days, Donatella's hunky bodyguards took Madonna's dog Chiquita for long walks, while white-gloved servants waited on the star.

When, a few years later, Victoria Beckham was rehearsing in the south of France for the Spice Girls' first show, she took a break and headed to Milan for a Versace fashion show. "For six weeks, we had no social life at all—so suddenly finding myself in the front row of one of the most prestigious catwalk shows in the world felt magical," she wrote. "Donatella invited me to stay the night at Lake Como. [She] waved her wand in the direction of the Versace shop. I can still remember the thrill of being let loose and told I could choose whatever I wanted."[20]

Far more than Gianni, Donatella showed a knack for dealing with the high-strung stars: He found the celebrities tedious at times and was privately relieved to leave the care of celebrities to his kid sister. Unlike Gianni, Donatella delighted in the buzz and drama they brought. In turn, her high-camp image and plain-talking candor charmed the celebrities. Over time, she perfected her glamour-puss act, sucking voluptuously on one Marlboro Red after another and tossing off gossipy witticisms in her gravelly voice.

Donatella, now emerging as a celebrity herself, soon was appearing at the hottest parties in New York, Miami, and Los Angeles, where she befriended A-listers. She and Paul vacationed with Demi Moore and Bruce Willis in Turks and Caicos, together with their respective broods. Sting and Trudie Styler were frequent guests in Como, as were Sylvester Stallone, Prince, and Eric Clapton.

In the early 1990s, before the celebrity-fashion connection had morphed into a big business involving celebrity wranglers, publicists, and stylists, designers connected directly with stars. At Versace, Donatella's personal friendships with celebrities extended to offering them clothes for red-carpet events. She and Gianni typically chose a dress they thought would suit a particular "friend of the house" for a big event, and Donatella flew her assistant out to L.A. or New York to fit it. She would later claim her attentiveness was about camaraderie, not commerce.

"I never tried to become friends with these people because I wanted to dress them," Donatella would declare. "We were just friends. If they dressed in Versace as well, all the better. But it was different. We often had children the same age. We vacationed together."[21]

Donatella and Gianni's timing was perfect. In 1994, Time, Inc., launched *InStyle,* a sort of hybrid of *People* and *Vogue.* It featured celebrities at red-carpet events, in particular the Oscars, as well as out on the town or on vacation. The focus was always on what they were wearing. Meanwhile Joan Rivers had a hit new gig where she joshed with stars about their wardrobe choices at red-carpet appearances. The Italians were the quickest to seize on the change. The French couturiers had traditionally turned up their noses at dressing celebrities, preferring American socialites and European aristocrats, while the Americans were slow off the mark in courting Hollywood. So, as the surging appetite for celebrity news spilled over into curiosity about the clothes they were wearing, Armani and Versace became household names.

Indeed, Gianni's over-the-top courting of stars added a juicy new dimension to his rivalry with Armani. Armani's approach to celebrities was far more businesslike than Gianni's; he virtually never invited them to vacation with him and didn't lavish them with as much swag. His postshow parties were far more restrained.

"You were there, and you just knew that the Versace people were over there having fun," recalled one Armani associate. "We were having this terribly sophisticated party, but they were over there getting laid." In 1992, when Eric Clapton defected to Armani after years as a Versace client—the house had even made an embroidered strap for his guitar—Gianni, who felt stung by the defection, told journalists that the rock star now looked "like an accountant."[22] Each camp was terrified that the other would steal their prized stars. Once, when Armani had Mickey Rourke over for a show, he warned his PR team to stick close to him.

"Someone had to stay with Mickey twenty-four hours a day to make sure that none of the Versace people approached him," recalls an associate. "We had to go clubbing with him until three a.m. to make sure no one got close."

Over the next few years, the Versaces played the celebrity game to the hilt. Gianni began featuring the stars in his ads, creating wildly arresting images shot by prominent photographers such as Mario Testino and Richard Avedon: Prince in a metal mesh tank top with "SLAVE" scrawled on his face, a ripped Sylvester Stallone nude except for a strategically positioned Versace dinner plate. The Versace press office juiced the interest by giving the photos free to newspapers and magazines, who often used them on their covers.

Gianni's shows became celebrity central. He not only plunked the stars in his front row but got them to help with the sound track. Prince recorded a song called "The Versace Experience." Versace assistants left limited-edition copies of the cassettes on the seats for the audience. Guided by Donatella, Gianni embraced celebrities such as Courtney Love and Tupac Shakur at the height of controversy. He threw lavish parties for them at his house in Como and vacationed with them. Sting and his family spent weeks at the villa. Gianni's publicists coyly spilled out titillating details of the Versaces' friendships with the stars, and the media happily lapped them up. Yet, while the celebrity machine served up a relentless banquet of publicity, it came at a high cost: By the mid-1990s, Versace's promotional budget—much of it the gifts and first-class treatment for VIPs—topped $70 million. Gianni and Donatella had turned the business of dressing celebrities into an immensely costly, high-stakes new game.

nine

Supermodels, Superstar

On a chilly evening in Milan in March 1991, the audience settled into their seats under a heated tent erected in the garden behind Gianni's palazzo at Via Gesù. Right on time, the house lights went down and the strains of an operatic aria floated out. Soft spotlights fell on four women—Naomi Campbell, Cindy Crawford, Claudia Schiffer, and a platinum-haired Linda Evangelista—each clad in a black minidress and thigh-high patent leather boots. As the aria morphed into Joan Jett's "I Love Rock 'n' Roll," the models, their hair teased into voluptuous styles, strutted down the white marble runway.

For nearly thirty minutes, one stunning model after another—Helena Christensen, Carla Bruni, Stephanie Seymour, Tatjana Patitz, Dalma Callado—emerged, reveling in

HOUSE OF VERSACE

Gianni's latest hairpin-curve collection: Crayola-colored minidresses that flared at forty-five-degree angles from their waists, low-cut catsuits with yellow and blue swirls on their smooth flanks, and bejeweled bra tops combined with short skirts. Bluish lights made the models' young skin glow against the Technicolor clothes. The photographers crouching along the length of the runway let out approving wolf whistles as Gianni sent out five or six models at a time.

Then, after an imperceptible pause, the music shifted again, and George Michael's "Freedom" rose over the sound system. Naomi Campbell, Christy Turlington, Linda Evangelista, and Cindy Crawford stepped onto the runway together, wearing little Empire dresses with sweetheart necklines in black, red, and yellow. Arm in arm, the quartet strode down the stage followed by a bright spotlight, lip-synching the song and smiling broadly.

A roar went up from the audience and a hundred flashbulbs exploded as the photographers recognized the shot of the season. A few months earlier, George Michael had featured the four models in a six-minute video for his hit song. The clip, with lush images of Cindy lounging in a bathtub and Naomi dancing languidly, had become the hottest video of the year. The women's fame had been soaring over the past year. Gianni's spectacular show took the four and pushed them—and him—to a new peak. Gianni was not just dressing celebrities but also making celebrities of the models who wore his clothes.

❖ V ❖

Until about 1990, top models like Naomi, Christy, and Linda wouldn't have dreamed of walking a runway. Traditionally, modeling was divided into two separate camps. Runway models had bodies—good shoulders, small waists, boyishly slim hips, and extra long legs—that flattered designers' clothes, but their faces usually weren't pretty enough to appear in magazine ads. In turn, the models who did the magazines had gorgeous faces but were rarely thin and long enough to carry off tiny runway samples. Moreover, designers paid far too little to tempt the women onto the runway. In the late 1980s, Christy earned about $800,000 for twelve days' work selling Maybelline cosmetics.[1] A Milan fashion show paid about 1.5 million lire, the equivalent of $1,000. All the urgency and sweat of a live runway show wasn't worth the top models' time and money.

But Donatella, already busily seducing celebrities into the Versace fold, spotted an opportunity. In the late 1980s, she recognized that a trio of new women—Christy, Naomi, and Linda—were attracting media attention in a way that had never occurred for models before. Looking for new fodder, celebrity reporters turned their sights on the three new models, who were quickly dubbed "the trinity."

The first of the three to be discovered had been Christy, a California-born daughter of a pilot and a former flight attendant of Salvadoran descent. With clean, intelligent looks that exemplified an idea of sophisticated American beauty, she became a favorite of Steven Meisel, an edgy photographer who was a protégé of Anna Wintour. The second, Linda, the daughter of a General Motors auto plant worker in Ontario who had sleek catlike looks, had seen her career take off after marrying the head of a powerful modeling agency, who promoted her to the top photographers, particularly Meisel.

The third woman, the youngest by several years, would one day eclipse her sisters to become a true superstar. Born on the wrong side of the Thames River in south London, Naomi Campbell was raised by a single mother, an exotic dancer of Jamaican origin. As a teen, she aspired to become a dancer herself, and her mother scrimped to send her willowy daughter to dance school in central London. One day in 1985, when Naomi was buying tap shoes in London's West End, a model agent spotted the fifteen-year-old. When she got a glimpse of Naomi's warm, toffee-colored skin, Asian eyes, and thousand-watt smile, lightning struck. Not long after, Naomi made her debut in the British edition of *Elle*. She had turned up at the shoot with just two smudgy Polaroids, but the editor was bewitched.

Soon after, at a shoot in London, Naomi met Christy. "She was in a high school uniform," Christy recalled later. "She was really cute."[2] When Naomi moved to New York, Christy helped her meet the top magazine editors and photographers, including Meisel. By 1988, Meisel began shooting Naomi, Christy, and Linda together. It was a potent mix. Not all models look right together, but these women's different looks complemented one another. Soon magazines were booking them together.

HOUSE OF VERSACE

By then, Naomi was becoming a darling of New York's nightlife, hitting as many as five parties and clubs in an evening and drawing tabloid attention for her colorful personal life. In 1987, at just seventeen, she met heavyweight champion Mike Tyson, and they secretly began dating. When she made their relationship official by appearing ringside at one of his fights in early 1989, the media interest was tremendous. If her affair with Tyson nudged her into the media glare, her subsequent relationship with Robert De Niro put her there full-time. In September 1990, she became the first black woman to grace the cover of the September issue of *Vogue*, the most important issue of the year, with its feature on fall fashion.[3] To the paparazzi's delight, Naomi, Christy, and Linda often hit the clubs together.

Christy introduced Naomi to Donatella, who saw that the models offered a golden opportunity if she could tap the tabloids' insatiable interest in them for her own purposes. Moreover, the trio's popularity with the most influential photographers and magazine editors was the ticket to goosing editorial coverage of her brother's clothes in America.

"Gianni, we have to bring these girls over for the runway shows," she told him excitedly after returning home from one trip to New York. "They are incredibly hot. We *have* to book them for the shows."

"You must be nuts!" he told his sister. "Look at them! They don't have the bodies for the runway. How would I ever dress them?"[4] Indeed, all three women had ample breasts, hips, and bottoms— nothing like traditional catwalk models. They also had no idea how to do the quirky runway walk, where a woman slings her hips forward and keeps her buttocks tucked tightly under. Compounding the issue was their agents' resistance to Donatella's offer.

"It was nearly impossible to get the girls to come over because the pay was so low and because a lot of the girls were too big," said David Brown, a top model agent who started working in Milan in 1981. "Plus, the runway shows weren't important in terms of publicity for them."[5]

But Donatella's sixth sense was right. According to Nunzio Palamara, an early Versace employee, "Donatella was always traveling, while Gianni went to Como for the weekend. It was Donatella who brought Kate Moss," the famously waifish British model. "Gianni said, 'Who is this shrimp?' And Donatella said, 'You'll see. In two years, you'll be asking me to get her at any cost.' "[6]

Donatella began lobbying the three models' agents, promising triple and beyond the going rate for runway shows. She had by then become friendly with the trinity, hitting the clubs and parties with them in New York. She promised them perks unheard of for models: flights in the Concorde, the best suites (never a simple room) at Milan's five-star hotels, free clothes, cars, and drivers at their disposal. Once she got them to visit Milan, Donatella treated them to a few days in the luxury of Villa Fontanelle, parties and dinners at her private apartment, and nights out at Milan's hottest discotheques. The women soon acquiesced.

Their appearance in Versace's shows ushered in what would become the supermodel era, making them first-name-only famous. To this Rat Pack, Donatella added other models: Carla Bruni, Helena Christensen, Claudia Schiffer (an ethereal German blonde whose agent had refused to let her appear in George Michael's "Freedom" video), and Cindy Crawford. Not all of the women were naturals on the runway: Despite the best efforts of Versace's team, they couldn't break Schiffer of her awkward lope.

"We used to have to put Claudia in flat shoes because she didn't know how to walk," Angelo Azzena said. "She was an ugly duckling. She would get to the end of the runway, make her turn, and it was like, 'Where am I?' But Gianni didn't care. She was on the cover of American *Vogue*."[7]

Soon after the March 1991 show, Gianni and Donatella began squeezing every bit of juice out of the supermodel phenomenon. They staged bread-and-circus shows for the press in which they would send as many as six supermodels down the runway at once. Gianni hired photographers to take shots of him with the models backstage in their showstopping dresses alongside their Versace-clad famous boyfriends—images his press office fed to eager newspapers. The supermodels and celebrities would then head next door for a party at Gianni's home, where the powerful editors of magazines had an up-close-and-personal view of the couture dresses in all their glory.

"There was champagne and caviar everywhere, and the girls

were there with their celebrity boyfriends," recalled one fashion journalist. "Claudia Schiffer and David Copperfield, Stephanie Seymour and Axl Rose, Linda Evangelista and Kyle MacLachlan. The buzz was amazing."[8]

The models adored the exuberant Gianni, who treated them like princesses, flattering and joking with them backstage. While other designers paid little attention to their models, Gianni personally thanked each of them after a show. "*Sei bellissima!*" ("You are so beautiful!") he told one after another, pulling them over to join him while he gave television interviews. He surprised them with gifts for their birthdays and wrote them warm notes when they had personal problems. Donatella sent them to the boutique on Via Montenapoleone, where they giddily grabbed armfuls of free dresses. (Designers doled out so many free dresses to the models that most of them had racks of unworn clothes in their closets, the tags still hanging from them.)

"I understand them," Donatella said of her models after a 1995 party she threw in the Ritz discotheque to celebrate them. "Linda is the most difficult—she has to have her say on everything, from the light to the photographer. But with me, she's wonderful."[9]

Egged on by Donatella, Gianni paid the top models as much as fifty thousand dollars to appear exclusively on his catwalk, sending the total cost of an individual show to hundreds of thousands of dollars, including travel, hotels, and free clothes. Other designers complained bitterly that Gianni was driving the costs up for everyone. His shows were getting so much press that everyone had to play the same game. Armani, in particular, found Gianni's supermodel fixation vexing. He scrupulously chose anonymous models who would never eclipse his clothes. Years earlier, he had hired Iman, the splendid Somalian model, for one show, but he abruptly canceled her for a second show when he saw that the audience paid more attention to her than the Armani clothes she was wearing.[10] "I refuse to pay figures like that," Armani snapped to journalists in 1994. "It's an ethical question. There are people who live for an entire year on amounts like that."[11]

The models abetted the cost escalation. "Gianni had endless pots of money," said Carole White, Naomi's agent at the time. "The

Concorde became a status symbol. An agent would say to a designer, 'Well, Gianni is Concording her in. Why can't you?' These girls got anything they wanted."[12] In the end, most designers couldn't resist the frenzied press coverage that came with the supermodels. (After one Chanel show, Schiffer needed four bodyguards to fend off the paparazzi and reach her car.[13]) So a bidding war ensued.

"It got bigger and bigger because they were outbidding themselves," recalled Christy. "Every year I thought, I can't make more than this, but every year I almost doubled my income."[14]

The models' agents began demanding that magazines name the models in the photos, and they wanted approval over photographers, makeup artists, and hairdressers. In the September 1991 issue of *Vogue*, Linda alone had thirty pages and the cover. "We don't vogue—we are *Vogue*," she told a magazine that year. "We have this expression, Christy and I: We don't wake up for less than ten thousand dollars a day."

While that last remark brought down a rain of catcalls, for Gianni the glorification of the supermodel did more to entice the American public than millions of dollars in advertising could achieve.

"Before, it was, 'Who is this Versace guy?'" said celebrity stylist Wayne Scot Lukas. "They used to pronounce his name Ver-sayse. But then people knew him because those girls who wouldn't get up for less than ten thousand dollars a day chose his clothes. The lifestyle of these people made it something really fabulous.[15]

Of the original trinity, Gianni's favorite was Naomi Campbell. She became a muse for him. On her lithe five-foot-nine frame and pert thirty-four-inch bust, his show-stopping dresses looked fabulous. Her dance training helped her move like a natural star on Gianni's runway, her slinky walk beyond compare. "She's simply the greatest catwalk model ever," said one fashion editor. "When she's on the runway, you literally cannot take your eyes off her."[16]

But Naomi was notoriously difficult to deal with. Over the years, her tantrums were breathtaking in their vitriol and violence. Several personal assistants charged that she was violent and abusive with them. Court-ordered anger-management classes had little effect on the belligerent supermodel. Once, when yet another assistant sued her for assault, Naomi posed for paparazzi wearing a T-shirt emblazoned with "Naomi Hit Me" across the front.

After enduring her many demands, Naomi's agents lost their patience. When she decided to dump one agent, he blasted her publicly. "No amount of money or prestige could further justify the abuse that has been imposed on our staff and clients," he wrote in a press release. But the constant blaze of headlines about her latest dustup or new celebrity boyfriend—among them U2 bassist Adam Clayton, Sylvester Stallone, and Eric Clapton—only served to jack up her notoriety. And the more outlandish her behavior, the more she earned. Her burgeoning drug habit amplified her volatile personality. She first tried coke when she was twenty-four while attending a concert. "It made me feel invincible, like I could conquer the world," she once said. But in the 1990s, her habit would worsen.[17]

With Gianni, Naomi was different. She felt coddled and protected by Gianni and the Versace clan. He invited her to the villa in Como when he thought she needed some rest. He tended to her personally backstage before a show. Once, he hired the DJ from a hot Milan disco popular with the supermodels to come to Via Gesù to entertain Naomi and the others at home. In turn, she never turned up late for his shows and spared him her explosive temper.

"She trusted Gianni totally, which for Naomi was a big deal," said White. "She wants to be looked after and loved and he did that. He gave her the attention she craved."[18]

"Gianni was wonderful to us," Naomi recalled. "He fed us, he used to ask us if we felt okay, if we needed any help. He didn't treat us like cattle. He treated us like individuals. If something didn't fit or the shoes hurt, we could tell him. I used to get so nervous for his shows because I wanted to do my best for him."[19]

Naomi and Donatella were close. Naomi sent Donatella to her hairdresser in New York, who did weaves and extensions for such stars as Iman and Whitney Houston. Once, at about 2 a.m. the night before a Versace show, Naomi was coming back to the Four Seasons with Linda Evangelista when she bashed into a glass door and broke a tooth.

"When Linda saw me, she started to freak," Naomi recalled. "They wouldn't let me look in the mirror and kept telling me it was only chipped. But it was broken half off." The two women immediately called Gianni and Donatella.

"The next thing I knew, Gianni and Donatella were standing over me looking at my tooth," Naomi said. Even in the middle of the night, "Donatella was dressed immaculately in this patent leather trench coat."[20] Donatella promptly got her own dentist out of bed at dawn and insisted he see Naomi right away. At the dentist's office, Donatella, Naomi's agent, and a Versace bodyguard were sitting outside the examination room when they heard a ruckus inside. A nurse, clearly shaken up, emerged. "I think someone had better come in," she said. Donatella rushed in to find Naomi trying to wriggle out of the dentist's chair as the doctor approached with a large needle. "Help! Help!" she screamed. Donatella managed to calm Naomi down enough for the dentist to cap her tooth. Later that day, she looked perfect on the runway.[21]

In 1994, one lucky event showed just how powerful the mix of models, celebrity, and high fashion could be in Gianni's hands. That year, Gianni had an idea for a little black dress with daring slits, and he had his seamstresses cut one frock from under the arm down to the hip on each side. A seamstress used safety pins to hold the sides of the dress together on the mannequin while she worked. Gianni was struck by the effect. He had an assistant make oversized gilt safety pins with medusa heads stamped on the closures. He placed the pins along the sides of the dress and down the front of the deep décolleté. With the precariously placed safety pins and deep slashes, the dress was a coy, punk-inspired interpretation of the classic little black dress, a mix of high style and tough street fashion.

Versace PR people sent the collection to London to be photographed by the UK magazines. One day, Phyllis Walters, Versace's publicist in London, heard from a friend who worked in public relations and was trying to drum up publicity for the red-carpet premiere that evening of a small new film, *Four Weddings and a Funeral*. "There is this rather good-looking guy who is starring in the film," she told Phyllis. "His name is Hugh Grant. What do you think about dressing him tonight?"[22]

HOUSE OF VERSACE

Walters had Grant try on several Versace tuxedos, but none fit because the actor was quite thin at the time. But Grant had brought along his girlfriend, Elizabeth Hurley, a little-known model. "Is there anything here that I could wear tonight?" she asked, rummaging through the rack of clothes in Walters's office. She pulled out the safety pin dress and put it on. Walters and her assistants stopped to stare. Hurley looked stunning. The sample had been worn on the runway by Helena Christensen. Hurley, at five foot eight, had a similar figure, with an ample bust, flat stomach, and slim hips.

"We were all staring at her," Walters recalled. "She had no makeup on, her hair was tied back. She was in flat shoes. But she looked absolutely amazing." Walters immediately phoned two paparazzi photographers. "Listen, I know you're going to be looking for Hugh, but you need to focus on the girlfriend," she told them. "I promise you. You'll make a fortune."

The paps got the shot of Hurley, wearing an I-can't-believe-it smile, in the showstopping dress. Next to her, Grant peered down at her, appearing slightly baffled as to how she got into the gown. The photo made the front pages of newspapers around the world, turning an unexceptional film premiere into a memorable media event.

"When Gianni saw the photos, he said, 'Who on earth is this?'" Angelo Azzena remembered. "I thought he would be angry, but instead he was thrilled. Liz became famous. *We* made her famous."[23] The free publicity for Versace was priceless, and the safety-pin frock became one of the most famous little black dresses in fashion history. At Gianni's next show, Grant and Hurley sat in the front row, dressed head to toe in Versace.

❖ V ❖

By the time Hurley and Grant sat in Gianni's front row, Gianni's show was the undisputed high point of Milan's fashion week. He began staging them in the courtyard of Via Gesù, where he had an elaborate ten-meter-high iron-and-Plexiglas canopy mounted over a long runway. Gilt chairs with multicolored cushions were squeezed in tight. On each chair sat a slick catalog with photos from Versace ad shoots and celebrity pictures. The catalogs were so popular that fans waited after the show to beg guests for their copies.

Supermodels, Superstar

Outside, a pristine red carpet rolled like a tongue from the doors of the palazzo to the curb, with klieg lights mounted on either side. Beefy men in tight black T-shirts attempted to herd the waiting photographers into a secure formation, as one dark Mercedes after another pulled up, unloading the celebrity of the moment. Gianni could have had them arrive through the palazzo's back door, but he understood the PR value of having them run the gauntlet of photographers and gawkers. Gianni's show was often the week's finale, and guests could relax at Via Gesù after the grueling marathon. While Armani showed during the afternoon because his collection was heavy on day suits and dresses, Versace, with his abundance of cocktail dresses and evening gowns, always showed in the evening, adding to the festive air.

The buzz on the night of his shows was tremendous. Fans hoping for a glimpse of a supermodel or a celebrity ran up and down Via Gesù, from his headquarters to the neighboring Four Seasons Hotel, which, with its fifteenth-century frescoes and standing box at La Scala available to guests, was in such demand from the fashion crowd that the desk discreetly discouraged other travelers from booking that week. Bouquets of flowers overflowed from editors' and buyers' suites into the hallway outside. Row after row of embossed shopping bags of expensive gifts filled the lobby. Gianni often had a dress or a day suit waiting in the suite of an important guest, laid out with shoes and a bag, ready to wear to his show. Elton John sometimes thrilled guests by playing the black grand piano in the hotel's plush lobby. Since Gianni had to stage as many as three shows to meet demand, the supermodels, in full makeup and sexy evening gowns, sprawled on the deep easy chairs in the lobby between one show and another, drawing a crowd of admirers.

The era was ripe for an entrepreneur like Gianni Versace. The 1990s would be a feast for fashion, as the sudden wealth of the New Economy, globalization, and the explosion of international media combined to give the industry a sharp jolt of growth. While all boom times generate demand for baubles, the nouveaux riches of the 1990s were particularly young and demanded hipper, flashier symbols of their success. The spreading wealth of the Internet economy meant that even the middle class started to trade up to higher levels of quality and taste.

HOUSE OF VERSACE

At the same time, cheaper and cheaper airline tickets brought hordes of American and Japanese shoppers to Europe, where they got a close-up look at the easy élan of European clothes, shoes, and bags. The traveling shoppers spread the word back home, ratcheting up demand for European labels. American *Vogue,* which traditionally focused on American designers, began giving European houses much more coverage. By the middle of the decade, the global luxury goods sector was growing by as much as 30 percent annually.

Press coverage of fashion was also expanding enormously. By the early 1990s, there were fifteen hundred runway shows in the four fashion capitals—New York, Paris, Milan, and London—with hundreds of journalists covering each one.[24] The Internet, magazines, and new television programs focusing on fashion brought once-distant foreign names to the living rooms of shoppers around the world. Internet sites such as *Vogue*'s Style.com broadcast the runway shows in their entirety (along with shots of the after parties and celebrity guests) just hours after the lights went down. The media surge brought pictures of runway shows and fashionable baubles to countries such as South Korea, Russia, and Brazil just as their national incomes were soaring.

Gianni's embrace of fashion as high entertainment was perfect for the times. Media showmanship had become indispensable to fashion, and Gianni was a virtuoso performer. His appropriation of everything from fine art to rock music and dance—whipped up with a strong dash of celebrity—was a feast for the media and their voracious appetite for showy images. He would become the first true superstar designer, opening the door for the likes of Tom Ford, Stella McCartney, and John Galliano. (By the mid-1990s, Bernard Arnault, the billionaire owner of luxury goods giant LVMH, emulated Gianni by hiring John Galliano and Alexander McQueen—two technically brilliant designers with a flair for shocking the establishment—to shake up Christian Dior and Givenchy.)

"Versace knew that fashion could participate in the great *Gesamtkunstwerk*"—a great mixing of art forms—"of the end of the millennium that had recruited equal parts of rock, special effects, the cult of personality, and unadulterated eroticism," wrote fashion critic Richard Martin.[25]

Gianni primed it all with lavish spending on advertising. At its peak in the mid-1990s, Versace bought about three thousand pages of magazine advertising a year, often taking out nearly a dozen consecutive pages in a single issue. He once had a compact disc made of music from a runway show and paid for several magazines, including *Rolling Stone*, to carry it as an insert, along with a minicatalog of photos. In the late 1980s, Gianni had adopted a freewheeling approach to mixing advertising and editorial coverage in fashion magazines. He hired photographers that most publications (particularly those in Europe) couldn't dream of hiring and had them take scores of extra photos. Gianni then offered the shots to newspapers and magazines, who happily published them as editorial layouts. His press office pushed the magazines to run the images just before an ad campaign broke, creating a seamless stream of Versace propaganda. Editors often put a model wearing Versace on the cover just to persuade Gianni to buy ads.

As a result, a single edition of a glossy magazine was often brimming with Versace images, between the advertisements and editorial spreads, all projecting Gianni's chosen image or star of the season.

"Versace pioneered the whole 'I'll give you my ad campaign if you make it look like an editorial' thing, which the American press didn't buy but the European press went crazy for," said Patrick McCarthy, executive editor of *Women's Wear Daily* and *W Magazine*. "The London *Sunday Times* was running Avedon's pictures of Elton John in Versace on the cover, as editorial. You'd see a magazine with a Versace on the cover, and Versace would have given them the picture, taken the picture, paid for the picture."[26]

Gianni usually played the good cop, charming the top editors of the fashion magazines to convince them to use his clothes. In turn, Emanuela Schmeidler, his longtime head of public relations, played the bad cop if she thought Versace wasn't getting editorial coverage commensurate with the house's ad spending. By the mid-1990s, Schmeidler was a legend in fashion circles, infamous for her aggressive treatment of journalists. Lean, with catlike features, a fake-bake tan, and long auburn hair that was always freshly blown out, she dressed like a walking billboard for Versace.

HOUSE OF VERSACE

"When I was at *New York* magazine, I did this story on the communications directors at the various houses," Anna Wintour recalled. "I remember doing the girl at Versace and it was head-to-toe suede. That's what we started knowing Gianni for. It was full on, everything matched."[27]

As Gianni's shows became a must-see for journalists, Schmeidler wielded her power like a blunt ax. Once she assigned two top editors from a leading magazine to the same seat at a fashion show. When an associate protested, Schmeidler snorted. "They are very thin," she said in heavily accented English. "They will both fit."[28]

But Schmeidler was unstinting in the crucial game of lavishing attention on editors who might feature Gianni's clothes in their magazines. In 1994, when Vicki Woods, then editor of *Harpers & Queen*, admired a skinny slithery gold mesh dress that Schmeidler wore to a Versace event in London, Schmeidler asked immediately, "You like my dress? I send you one."

Woods laughed. "Emanuela, you don't have one big enough for me," she replied.

"Give me your size," Schmeidler shot back. When Woods told her, Schmeidler, who often marveled at the pear-shaped figures of many British editors, winced theatrically. Woods promptly forgot the exchange.

A few months later, a deliveryman arrived bearing two huge boxes. Inside, buried in layers of ribbons and crinkly tissue, lay a gold metal mesh skirt and matching top, a copy of Schmeidler's outfit, but cut much larger—or "eased," in fashion parlance—around the chest and thighs. In the other box was a black barathea dinner jacket with silk lapels and medusa-head buttons, cut long enough to cover an ample bottom. "With love, Gianni," read a little note. Such a couture outfit would sell for twenty thousand pounds, Woods reckoned. The editor stood before it agog.[29]

Gianni's campaign to remake fashion, and to capitalize on his creativity worldwide, was succeeding brilliantly. Thousands of pages of advertising, the models caught in bacchanalian poses, appeared every year in the top magazines, shot by the world's best photographers. The world's foremost celebrities such as Madonna, Prince, and

Sting filled his front rows, wore his camera-ready clothes to red-carpet events, appeared in his advertising, vacationed in his homes, and recorded music for his shows. The women on the catwalk were famous in a way that models would never be again. And Gianni had proved himself the superman of fashion.

ten

Diva

ONE SPRING AFTERNOON IN 1994, DONATELLA STOOD AT THE center of a huge loftlike photography set in downtown Manhattan. Next to her was Richard Avedon, the legendary fashion photographer, hunched behind a large camera under enormous umbrella lights. An array of assistants stood behind the pair, gaping at the spectacle unfolding before them. The subject of their attention was a male model, buck-naked and gyrating wildly to music blasting over the sound system. The man, who had an Atlas-like physique and curly dark hair, was in fact a stripper whom Donatella had spotted in a dance club in Miami. She thought he would be perfect for one of Gianni's ad campaigns and had flown him to New York.

As Donatella stared, the stripper turned the show up a notch and began sliding a silk Versace scarf between his legs. Next to her, Avedon, his face a mask of concentrated tension, clicked away. "Oh, my God!" Donatella said, laughing at the scene. "Gianni is going to love this!" The final photo showed the man with his head lolling back, an orgasmic look on his face.

By then, even as Gianni shirked much of the cosmopolitan, sexually charged lifestyle his clothes had come to represent, his sister was fully embracing the Versace mystique—and nowhere more so than on the Versace ad shoots. Indeed, as Gianni rose, so did Donatella. As the family business became an international success, she would be the lead player in the grand opera that was the Versace brand in the 1990s. By then, Donatella's natural theatricality served the company well, if expensively. Gianni had begun entrusting Donatella with the advertising campaigns in the 1980s, and a decade later, they were productions worthy of Hollywood films. Under Donatella's direction, Versace shoots had become notorious for their extravagance, their brazen sexiness, and their illicit fun.

From the birth of his house, Gianni had always demanded the most extravagant ads he could afford. When he launched his first ad campaign in 1978, he spent his entire budget to hire Richard Avedon, who since the 1940s had been the world's premier fashion photographer. Working with the top fashion magazines in the 1950s and 1960s, Avedon helped develop an image of women that reflected the times—freer and more flamboyant—with pictures full of drama and spontaneity. In 1955, for example, he shot Dovima at the Cirque d'Hiver in Paris. Avedon positioned the ephemeral American model in front of two elephants. It became one of the most famous fashion photographs of all time.

Avedon's collaboration with Versace would be nearly as iconic as his innovative early work. His theatrical style made Gianni's clothes come alive. But after initially working with Avedon in one campaign, Gianni had to deputize Donatella to deal with the famous photographer, because Avedon didn't want the pressure of having the star designer hovering over him. Donatella could channel Gianni's wishes with a lighter touch.

"Gianni came once, but he made such havoc," Donatella said.

HOUSE OF VERSACE

"It was hard for him to pull back from his clothes and see how a photographer interprets them. He used to say, 'No, you have to do it this way or that way.' Finally, Avedon said, 'You can't come anymore. Send your sister.'"[1]

Over the next twenty years, Avedon, a legendary perfectionist, staged elaborate shots of the Versace female models—for example, falling through the air or riding on the backs of naked men. For one shot showcasing Gianni's 1996 home furnishings line, Avedon had a dozen massive mattresses made, covered them in bright Versace prints, piled them high, and slid the models in between them, to create a huge princess-and-the-pea effect, with Naomi Campbell and Kristen McMenamy perched on top. In another shoot, he hired a choreographer from Twyla Tharp's dance troupe to give a jolt of drama and theater to the girls' movements.

The shoots, with Donatella orchestrating, involved dozens of people and lasted up to ten days. Avedon often photographed a large group of supermodels at a time, sprinkling in a couple of hunky men for the full sexual charge. The whole collection for the upcoming season hung on a battalion of clothing racks alongside long tables overflowing with shoes, bags, and jewelry. Some seasons, it took three assistants just to lay out the clothes. Avedon's own Manhattan studio was far too small to accommodate the shoots, so he sometimes rented Silvercup Studios, a sound set in Queens nearly the size of half a city block, where *The Sopranos* was later shot.

Donatella spent days assembling the outfits with several assistants, while seamstresses from the Manhattan Versace shop fitted the clothes. Each day of the shoot, hair and makeup artists spent at least six hours dolling up the girls in a mirror image of what was, in the late 1980s and early 1990s, Donatella's own look: strong eye makeup, ultratanned skin, and only a hint of beige lipstick, simulating the style of rich 1960s movie stars. Makeup assistants spent hours covering the models with full-body makeup, a gooey blend of several shades, before fixing it with a powder to keep it from rubbing off on the clothes. They put three or four pairs of false eyelashes on each woman. Donatella herself wore up to five pairs; to her delight, a makeup artist once found 1960s-era lashes made of real mink for her.

"She was a maximalist," said François Nars, a top makeup artist who worked on the Avedon shoots. "And the girls ended up looking like her. The more the better."[2]

During the long preparations, Donatella would float off the set to go shopping in New York, often coming back with gifts for the models and her assistants. One season she discovered a new skin cream made with animal placenta and brought back a jar for each one. Other times, she arrived with pricier baubles for herself.

"If she was thinking of buying a diamond and emerald ring, she would come in and show it to everyone," recalled Norma Stevens, Avedon's business partner. "She was wild, with that blond hair and the tight clothes and her figure."[3]

Donatella made sure the opulence and theater of the sets spilled over backstage. Gianni was using the same supermodels season after season, and the atmosphere was like a family reunion. Waiters refreshed buffet tables of food all day. (Once, on a Los Angeles beach set with another photographer, Donatella hired famed chef Nobu Matsuhisa to bring sushi for everyone.) She booked masseuses for the models and blasted music to keep the energy high. Sometimes the female models' boyfriends stopped by; one year, Johnny Depp hung out to watch his girlfriend Kate Moss be photographed. With all the high-drama clothes, gorgeous women and men, and creative frisson, the set was red hot.

After each carefully arranged shot, an assistant would hand Avedon an oversized photo, and he and Donatella would huddle over it. The photographer would mark up the shot with a black marker, pointing out where the line of the models' elbows or the flow of the dress broke the harmony. "My role was to tell him which outfits we wanted him to shoot and how," Donatella said. "He showed me these huge Polaroids and I would say yes or no. It was scary."[4]

Avedon was so exacting that he approved only one or two shots each day. (Today, with digital photos and computer retouching, photographers take scores of images daily, and shoots last no more than three days.) The shoots cost a fortune. "We had a so-called budget," Donatella said. "But Avedon used to work with the top models, the best set designers, the best hairdressers—all of whom cost a fortune. We just tallied it all up afterward."[5]

As the Versace mystique mounted, Donatella was leading a life of such operatic excess that one imagined she had hired an art director to conjure it all up. Her physical appearance morphed into a gilded Jan-from-the-Muppets look. She was rarely the most beautiful woman in the room—much to her chagrin—but she acquired a sort of mysterious charisma that made her the constant center of attention. Her high-voltage, Vegas-meets–St. Tropez style featured skin-tight, side-zipped tops in Crayola colors, neon orange nail varnish, chartreuse bikinis, and platform shoes with five-inch heels. She wore lots of sleeveless shift dresses in a variety of colors—but never red, which was Valentino's color—that showed off arms that were as thin as wands. She chucked her wardrobe at the end of each season and bought all new clothes.

In interviews with journalists, Donatella maintained her camp goddess persona, claiming to wear lace and silk lingerie around the house and diamonds to the gym. (When she answered questions, she blithely mangled the English language, often resorting to her favorite words, "modern" and "fabulous.") She knew which was her better side and insisted on being photographed standing up, lest she look thick in the waist. "I don't mind not being tall," she once told a *Vanity Fair* journalist defiantly. "I *think* tall."[6]

While Gianni took himself seriously, Donatella had a sense of irony and wry humor about herself and the grandiose life she and her siblings had created. Privately, she was utterly candid, frank, and hugely fun, possessing a comedian's sense of timing. "When I die, I want to be buried in a glass coffin like Snow White," she often quipped. In the atelier, her vampy image belied a more homey character. She traded diet tips with her female assistants and invited favored employees to eat lunch with her in the family kitchen. She listened to the personal travails of the people working with her, inquiring after their pets and babies with genuine interest. If the team had to work late, she ordered pizza for everyone and let the mothers on her staff bring their kids to do their homework in the atelier. She was unstintingly generous with loyal assistants. Once, she sent a stylist a bouquet of flowers the size of a coffee table—interlaced with chocolates and bananas, his diet during the long ad shoots they did together.

But as her brother grew more successful and celebrated, she gradually became the emperor's wife. For instance, at the Ritz in Paris, Gianni was enormously popular because he remembered hotel staff members' names and stopped to chat when he came down to raid the shop for newspapers and magazines. By contrast, Donatella breezed past when she came and went, wearing dark sunglasses and trailed by a couple of bodyguards. When she stayed at the Ritz, she often flew in her own florist from Milan, deeming the hotel's florist inadequate.

She outdid Gianni in her grandiosity. When the siblings stayed at the Ritz, Gianni opted for a normal suite, not one of the "name" accommodations, such as the Imperial Suite. Once, however, he asked to see one of the top suites. "Perhaps you would like to stay here instead?" the manager asked Gianni, after showing him the opulent rooms and telling him the price. "No, it's too expensive," he decreed. "Give it to my sister. She likes grand things."

Donatella spent money as if she were a spoiled teenager. She constantly overdrew her salary and the allowances Santo gave her, but her brothers always covered her debts.

"I'm so depressed today," she sometimes told an assistant, flopping in a chair. To cheer herself up, she went down to Cartier on Via Montenapoleone—her favorite jeweler, along with Harry Winston in New York—to pick up a new bracelet or ring. She traveled by Concorde or private jet and stayed in the best suites at the Dorchester Hotel in London, the Waldorf Towers in New York, and the bungalows at the Beverly Hills Hotel. She stayed so often at the Dorchester that they started to prep the room with a floral perfume that she loved. Once, she rented an enormous villa in St. Tropez that belonged to French rock star Johnny Hallyday. She loved the house—but not his furnishings, which ran to Native American taste. "Johnny, I love you, but I'm bringing my own furniture," she told the celebrity.[7]

In Milan, her apartment was a pleasure palace. The twenty-one-room home had two kitchens, always fully stocked so that she could throw impromptu dinner parties, and several dressing rooms, with vast closets. She had two stereo systems installed, on two different floors, with different music playing to suit her moods. Her bathroom—dubbed the eighth wonder of the world by one friend—contained python-covered chairs, intricate tile work depicting massive Magritte-like pink and red lips, and wide custom-made shelves holding a vast array of creams, potions, and bath salts. (Whenever she liked a product, she bought three bottles of it.) Every evening, she took a soak in a magnificent marble tub.[8]

With his enormous workload, Gianni typically went to bed early, leaving it to Donatella to create the high-life image that the Versace brand projected. Everyone in fashion and show business knew that, after Gianni went to bed, Donatella turned up the volume—supermodels, A-list celebrities, and über-hip photographers, all in a swirl of coke, champagne, and loud music. Donatella became Gianni's roving evangelist, spreading the gospel of Versace. With her partying, ad shoots, and celebrity friends, Donatella absorbed what was hot and new and, back in Milan, transmitted that to Gianni.

"I moved in this world that didn't really exist in Milan," said Donatella. "I was great friends with the models, the photographers. I hung out with rock stars and went to places he didn't go that often. I came back and gave him information he wouldn't have had if it weren't for my lifestyle. I would tell him how people are dressing or that a certain trend was over or that young people were looking for this. I was his eyes."[9]

❖ V ❖

During the week before a show, Gianni put enormous pressure on Donatella. She had to be at his side constantly. Yet Gianni did not make it easy for her. Most designers decide what looks they want to show and then have the samples made up, but Gianni did the opposite. He had a huge number of samples made, and then spent more than a week painstakingly mixing and matching until he distilled the looks he wanted. His color palette was far more vast than that of most designers, so he had skirts, jackets, leggings, and dresses made up in a rainbow of colors. He had as many as five hundred pairs of shoes

Even as Gianni's boyfriend, Antonio D'Amico, grieved at the funeral in Milan, his relationship with Donatella was disintegrating.

This little black dress not only shot Elizabeth Hurley to fame, but exemplified Gianni's newfound love affair with the stars.

The future of Gianni's house now sits on the shoulders of Allegra (shown with her father, Paul, who is separated from Donatella).

Together Santo and Donatella, with Allegra at her side, grieve their brother in Milan's magnificent Duomo. But the siblings would soon be at war over Gianni's legacy.

For Andrew Cunanan, Gianni Versace represented a deadly obsession.

The fierce rivalry between Giorgio Armani and Gianni Versace lit up the fashion world for two decades.

Gianni and Donatella put on a united front at a red-carpet event in London in 1995. But behind the scenes, tensions between the siblings were quickly rising.

Egged on by Donatella, Gianni created the 1990s supermodel phenomenon, making stars of women such as Naomi Campbell, Carla Bruni, and Christy Turlington.

Gianni with his niece Allegra at a ballet in Paris just months before his death. In one rash decision, he bestowed an enormous burden on his beloved *principessa*.

Elton John, comforted by his boyfriend, David Furnish, grieves Gianni's death with Princess Diana. It would be one of the princess's last public appearances before her death just a month later.

Donatella, Elton John, and Gianni arrive at a fashion awards gala in New York. Soon after, Elton would inform Gianni of Donatella's heavy drug use.

Donatella at a men's fashion show in 2008. Gianni's kid sister has prevailed over her drug habit and the near collapse of her brother's house only to face the worst recession to hit the fashion industry in decades.

Casa Casuarina, Gianni's fabulous Miami mansion, became a symbol of South Beach's 1990s decadence—and an exclamation point on Donatella's life of excess. But it also made Gianni the target of a killer.

Gianni spent millions renovating Casa Casuarina, sparking tensions with his brother, Santo. Gianni's extravagance would lead to a fight between the brothers that changed the fate of the house of Versace.

made, each in five sizes. Between the clothes and the accessories, there could be up to two thousand pieces for Gianni to choose from—and seek Donatella's advice about.

Because Gianni's shows were so complicated to stage, he held full dress rehearsals—after which he might reshuffle the models and even demand a new garment be made. The shows themselves were very long, lasting up to fifty minutes and featuring more than one hundred outfits. (Today, Versace shows last less than twenty minutes, with a third of the looks.)

Donatella was a living spark for Gianni's last-minute creativity. For instance, in 1990, Gianni made a dress that was a virtuoso display of his stagecraft and dressmaking skills. From the front, it was a prim black jersey dress, with a high neckline, long sleeves, and ankle-length skirt. But in the back it plunged to the base of the spine, while a slit ran all the way up the leg. The dress was held together precariously at the hip. Originally, Gianni had decided to show the dress with embroidered stockings and to have a black model wear it. But when Donatella saw it on the model, she understood that the tights and the woman drained the dress of its high drama. "Gianni, those stockings are going to kill it," she told him. "That dress will be nothing unless you show it without stockings."

Gianni refused. So in the backstage chaos before the show, Donatella instructed one of the dressers to put the dress on Christy Turlington—without stockings. "He's going to kill me when he sees this," she whispered to an assistant. As Christy made her way down the runway, the audience at first saw a prim black dress. But when the model made her turn at the end, showing the vertiginous gown on her long, bare legs, lean back, and perfect bottom, a roar went up from the audience.

"When she walked back up the runway, you sat there holding your breath because you thought you were going to see her backside at any moment," remembered Joan Kaner, fashion director of Neiman Marcus. "It was breathtaking."[10] Gianni was thrilled.

Later, in 1992, Gianni and Donatella were fitting Trudie Styler for the ornate dress she would wear for her wedding to Sting. Versace seamstresses had spent weeks embroidering the sleeves on the ensemble's gold jacket. In the atelier, Donatella paced furiously, looking at the gown, while Gianni stood nearby, his brow furrowed.

"What do you think?" he asked her in Italian, as Styler stood by, struggling to understand what they were saying.

"It's the sleeves," she said. "They're all wrong. They have to go." Gianni looked at her, glanced back at the dress, grabbed a pair of scissors, and snipped off the sleeves, leaving them to plop to the floor. The two seamstresses who had done the intricate work stood aghast. Styler's eyes widened in horror.

"*Brava*, Donatella! *Brava!*" Gianni told his sister, his eyes lighting up. "Now it's perfect." At Styler's wedding a few weeks later, she made a grand entrance on horseback, the train of the dress spread behind her.[11]

The strain of working closely with Gianni was tough on Donatella, who sought refuge from her brother's relentlessness in her long trips abroad. "He sucked her in," recalled an assistant. "He never let her in peace. He was always saying, 'Ask Donatella about this or that.' But Donatella wasn't as wholly devoted to work as Gianni was. She got up later. She had her hair appointments, her shopping, her children. So she escaped by traveling a lot." She frequently kept people waiting and made her assistants work late into the evening because her schedule ran hours behind. Gianni, so punctual and demanding of his team, often seethed at his sister's lax work habits.

Although Donatella inspired Gianni, she wasn't one to summon ideas on her own. Her role, while priceless, was a sideline to Gianni's talent. She was a catalyst or instigator, a brutally honest sounding board that pushed Gianni to distill his best work.

"The creative genius was Gianni," one assistant said. "Donatella was someone of whom you asked an opinion, but not ideas. She never came in saying, 'I've got this idea.' Their roles were very separate. Gianni needed advice on things like, 'Do we shorten it or lengthen it? Do we make it tighter or looser? Do we use more blue?'"

Donatella didn't have nearly the stamina or tremendous focus that Gianni had. Her attention span was like the beam from a lighthouse, shining on problems in short, sharp bursts before waning. "Donatella had the ability to take Gianni's designs to the extreme," said another longtime assistant. "If Gianni was the cake, she was the one who could put the icing and the cherry on it. But without him, there was no cake."

One day around 1994, Elton John told Gianni he needed to speak to him about something important. For some time, Elton had heard rumors about Donatella, but recently they had become embarrassing enough to push him to call his friend. "Listen, Gianni, people are laughing at Donatella in America," he told him over the telephone. "She goes to all of these parties and she's always running out of the room. When she comes back, everyone can see that she's stoned."[12]

Gianni was furious. Years earlier, Donatella had told him that she used cocaine, but he thought it was a youthful indulgence that had long ceased. In reality, Donatella had become a heavy user over the years. The first time she tried coke, she was unimpressed; she simply felt more awake. But during the 1980s, she became a hard partyer, running with an über-cool crowd of models, rock stars, celebrity hairdressers, and hot photographers. As a result, she found herself more and more often in clubs where people openly used drugs. At a party in New York, she was shocked to find people snorting cocaine on the dance floor.[13]

In a world of fragile, creative egos, many designers used cocaine to paper over their insecurities and cope with the relentless pressures of the fashion cycle. Some designers kept employees on their payroll because they had good drug connections. By the late 1980s, drugs had long since lost any scandalous sting backstage at fashion shows, with hairdressers and makeup artists especially avid users. Teenage fashion models, loath to drink alcohol because of the calories and seeking a boost to endure six weeks of dawn-to-midnight runway shows and rehearsals, snorted coke from "bullets" in the shape of lipstick holders stashed in their purses. Insiders knew that "Do I smell Chanel?" was code for "Is there any coke?"[14]

Initially, Donatella tried to confine her drug use to her long trips to the United States, far from the scrutiny of her two brothers. She used only cocaine and drank very little, with the exception of a flute of champagne. The photography shoots for Versace ads were a favorite escape for her. The ten-day events, with their high energy and sexed-up air, were heady fun, which Donatella upped with bumps of cocaine. She often drafted a friend or an assistant to join her, and they ducked into the nearest bathroom, the only private space on the sprawling sets.

"Donatella always had the best quality coke," recalled a friend who did it with her on the sets. "Donatella would pull it out and I would say, 'Oh, I really shouldn't.' She would just laugh. She used to do it almost every day, in the afternoon. It was like a cocktail."

Donatella would flip her long hair back over her shoulder and bend over, using whatever utensil she could find to scoop the powder into her nose. Afterward, she pulled back, with a satisfied, catlike look on her face. "We used to use the caps of Bic pens or rolled-up dollar bills," the friend recalled with a laugh. "We were like ghetto queens."

Once, Donatella was so high that she didn't even bother to turn up on the set. Normally, Gianni called her a dozen times a day when she was on a shoot. That particular day, as everyone looked for her, Gianni finally got her on the phone and asked, "How are the pictures?"

"Fabulous, Gianni," she replied. "Just fabulous."[15]

"I didn't regret at all not showing up at the shoot," she reflected years later. "I had so much fun. I had the best time of my life."[16]

When Elton called Gianni to tell him that people were sniggering about Donatella's drug use, Gianni, who had never touched drugs and barely drank, had no sympathy for his sister's habits. In part, he was worried that Donatella would damage her health. Moreover, he was afraid that Donatella's habit would cause problems for the company. He had indulged and spoiled his little sister their entire lives, but he couldn't fathom her fondness for drugs. He was also angry that Donatella's personal habits could make him—and his work—look bad.

"Gianni knew that, when you're on top, you're in everyone's sights, and you can't put a foot wrong," said Antonio D'Amico. "The idea that people were speaking badly about the company [because of Donatella's habit] hurt him."[17]

Gianni knew, however, that his sister wouldn't stop. Indeed, as he soon recognized, her drug use was interfering more and more often with her work in Milan. At Via Gesù, the seamstresses tittered when she ducked into their bathroom with an assistant, both giggling loudly before emerging with a glazed look on their faces. She didn't even refrain during fashion week, when Gianni, already a bag of nerves before a show, counted on her help the most. "Where the hell is my sister?" Gianni would scream, sending his team scrambling to look for her.

"You can imagine how hard that was, given her problem," said one assistant. "Every five minutes, she was running out, and we had to go find her."

On one occasion, she went too far. A group of friends had just flown into Milan for the show, and Donatella was restless to party. She and her friends stayed up all night, bingeing on cocaine. The next day, she slept until the afternoon, rolling up to Via Gesù feeling and looking awful. Gianni and his team had been waiting impatiently for her since the first thing that morning. When he saw her, he exploded. "It doesn't matter what you do, but you have to know how to do it and when to do it!" he screamed at her. Feeling guilty, she slunk away.[18]

As her drug habit deepened, Donatella became less predictable in the atelier, routinely turning up to work at noon. She kept associates waiting for hours, and her schedule ran late into the evening. Gianni demanded that his staff give him their all, and his sister's wayward habits drove him to distraction. "Gianni used to call her in the morning, and you could hear that she was still in this haze, with this croaky voice," Antonio said. "She wouldn't get to work until late, and when she did, she was in pieces."[19]

eleven

Spoiled by Success

ONE BALMY EVENING IN FALL 1993, WITH DONATELLA AND A host of celebrity friends at his side, Gianni threw open the doors to Casa Casuarina, the extravagant home in the heart of Miami's South Beach neighborhood that would lift him—and his brand—to new heights of fame. An invitation to his housewarming was the hot ticket of a Miami Beach social season that peaked on New Year's Eve and rollicked on until Easter. Champagne glasses in hand, guests streamed through the mansion and its luxurious garden, marveling at the frescoed walls, the antique furniture Gianni had re-upholstered in Versace fabrics, the elaborate marble bath-rooms, and most of all, the spectacular pool, tiled with thousands of tiny mosaics and illuminated with underwater lights.

By the time Gianni threw the party, the buzz around his new home was huge. "When Gianni came, it became such a media event," said Bruce Orosz, owner of a leading photography production company. "It went well beyond someone just renovating a house. The stories started to circulate about what he was spending, and it created this mystique around him and that house."[1]

Gianni had discovered the house that would become a symbol of his heady rise in the 1990s two years earlier. Just before Christmas 1991, he flew to Miami to attend the opening of a new boutique. During his last trip there five years before, he had found Miami cold and impersonal. But this time he was bewitched by the edgy frisson of the newly reinvigorated section of Miami Beach known as South Beach, with its population of drag queens, muscle boys, artists, and celebrities and its energetic embrace of sexual freedom and physical beauty. "Everything has changed so much here," Gianni told a journalist at the party for the shop opening. "At this moment, Miami to me is heaven. I want to stay forever."[2]

Over the next few years, South Beach became a slice of paradise for Gianni—as well as a pure distillation of the Versace world: decadent, guilt-free, and not a little bit vulgar. In the 1930s, developers had erected hundreds of low-rise Art Deco buildings in the area to provide cheap accommodations for northern snowbirds. Wedding cake details such as flowers and curlicues looked like sugar confections in the keystone used for the buildings' façades. After World War II, however, South Beach began a long, slow decline. By the 1970s, the neighborhood had become a decrepit place full of retirees, criminal flotsam, and poor Cuban refugees. At the same time, Miami's position as a byway in the decade's booming cocaine trade sent street crime in South Beach soaring.[3] Many of the Art Deco buildings became roach-infested crack houses, smelly retirement homes, or simply abandoned shells. But at the end of the decade, musicians, painters, and performance artists seeking cheap studio space had discovered Miami Beach. They began fixing up some of the buildings, opening a handful of funky restaurants, nightclubs, and boutiques amid the dollar stores and bodegas. The result was spectacular. The Art Deco buildings, originally painted in bland off-white or dirty beige, were repainted in a rainbow of Necco Wafer colors, such as lemon yellow and bubblegum pink, shades that pulsated under the tropical sun. Design magazines began producing spreads on the revival of the Art Deco district in South Beach.

The beach's bohemian atmosphere and sleek tropical design drew the so-called guppies, or gay yuppies, from New York. They brought along their friends from the fashion world, who discovered an ideal new backdrop for their ad campaigns. In 1985, fashion photographer Bruce Weber shot a Calvin Klein Obsession underwear ad on the roof of the Breakwater Hotel in South Beach. Photographers such as Annie Leibovitz and Patrick Demarchelier followed, and by the time Gianni arrived for Christmas 1991, South Beach was one lavish photo shoot. Models followed next. Within a few years, there were about twenty modeling agencies in the area, and Ocean Drive, the boardwalk that ran along the sea, became a real-life runway, with models in spandex hot pants and string-bikini tops inline skating to their next go-see with their portfolios tucked under their arms.

"There were so many gorgeous people here," remembered Merle Weiss, owner of a boutique that sold clothes to drag queens. "You went to Publix [supermarket] and you could just tear your heart out."[4] Designers such as Calvin Klein and Marc Jacobs began vacationing in South Beach, and on their heels came celebrities such as John F. Kennedy, Jr., Daryl Hannah, Jon Bon Jovi, Prince, and Elton John.

Gianni's clothes became the unofficial uniform in South Beach clubs, and his store there boomed. Pretty Latin girls went to the Versace shop, where a sound track of thumping dance music was always playing, to buy slinky metal-mesh cocktail dresses and head straight to the clubs. Hunky gay men wore his garish silk print shirts unbuttoned to the navel.

On that Christmas trip, Gianni came across Casa Casuarina, a 13,500-square-foot mansion that sat directly on Ocean Drive, at the corner of Eleventh Street. Casa Casuarina was originally built in 1930 by Alden Freeman, an eccentric philanthropist, as an homage to the Alcázar de Colón, a mansion built in 1510 in Santo Domingo that was home to Christopher Columbus's son Diego. (Freeman named the house after the casuarina tree, an Australian breed that was standing on the site when Freeman began building.) Diego had been viceroy of the Indies, and his wife was related to the Spanish monarchs, so the original Alcázar de Colón had Moorish, Spanish, and Byzantine influences. Freeman transposed many of those themes to Casa Casuarina, making for a gaudy confection of a residence.

By the time Gianni found Casa Casuarina, the building was a shadow of its former self. Previous owners had broken it up into thirty tiny apartments, and rented them out to a mix of down-and-out drug addicts, moribund old people, and edgy, penniless artists. Although developers had revived scores of Art Deco buildings, they were daunted by the cost of redoing Casa Casuarina.

"It was this mix of old Jews from New York dumped there by their kids and young artists who didn't have much money," Weiss recalled. "But it was very hip and funky. That's what Gianni liked about it."[5]

In 1992, Gianni spent nearly $8 million to buy both Casa Casuarina and a run-down hotel next door, which he razed to make space for a pool, guest wing, and garage. The entire compound covered half the block, and Casa Casuarina became the only private residence on Ocean Drive. It was an unusual choice for Gianni, given that his celebrity friends, such as Madonna and Sylvester Stallone, were buying homes—set far behind guarded gates—in mainland Miami on Brickell Avenue, known as Millionaire's Row. But Gianni loved the idea of remaking the eccentric mansion. The house, with its Moorish tiles, white stucco façade, slate roof, and wrought-iron balconies, was a complete break with the house's Art Deco neighbors. The main three-story building centers around an open-air courtyard enclosed on all four sides by balconies with wooden railings. On the roof is a large L-shaped terrace, covered in brightly colored Moroccan-style tiles. Next to the terrace is a domed observatory with a powerful telescope.

Gianni poured millions into renovating and furnishing Casa Casuarina, creating a flashy, mesmerizing style once described as "gay baroque." He built two concentric walls to close the compound off from the street. The ironwork on the walls and balconies—even the drains—were dotted with golden medusa heads. He spent ten thousand dollars apiece to ship in a certain type of palm tree from California because the ones native to Florida didn't have the right look.

His pool became legendary for its extravagance. He hired a Milanese craftsman, handed him one of his elaborate multicolored print scarves, and said, "Here, I want you to copy this." Fifty craftsmen worked for a year to create images of entwined dolphins, tridents, shells, and geometric designs, all in a blaze of red, blue, and gold. Working in Milan, they had to break slabs of marble by hand into hundreds of thousands of tiny tiles—and because he didn't want to wait months to receive them by boat, Gianni had them shipped by air, at an extra cost of $200,000. Between the pool area and the mosaic floors, ceilings, and walls inside the main house, they laid more than 21,500 square feet of tiles in all. The cost: $1.5 million.[6] Underwater lights made the pool a shimmering oasis at night. "That pool is probably the most expensive pool ever built," said the project manager for the house.[7]

Inside the mansion, Gianni was no more restrained. Carved wood panels, tiles, frescoes, and stained glass windows embellished the thirty-five rooms. In one room, a chandelier made of iron palm fronds hung from a ceiling that was, in turn, painted with trompe l'oeil palm fronds. In one bathroom, a golden seat sat on a marble toilet. Gianni's own suite, which looked out onto the ocean, covered eight hundred square feet and featured stained glass windows, beamed ceilings, and frescos of puffy clouds against a deep blue sky. He stuffed the house with a madcap array of furnishings—six hundred items in all. He had mahogany and gilt chairs reupholstered in red, blue, or gold Versace prints, creating a riot of colors and styles. He had silk lampshades made up in purple leopard print, and he covered plush sofas in deep yellow leopard-skin patterns.

The renovations cost a fortune—by one estimate, as much as $30 million—and Gianni's spending created tensions with Santo, who scrambled to pay the huge bills that arrived from art dealers, contractors, and craftsmen. After a heated call from Santo, Gianni railed against his brother. "I 'ate my brother!" Gianni screamed to the project manager. "I 'ate him! But you know what, darling? I'll show him." He then called his antiques dealers and bought something else.[8] The Miami house was Gianni's biggest splurge, and the tension it created between the brothers would persist for years to come.

From the very moment of the 1993 housewarming party, Casa Casuarina became the center of gravity on South Beach, and Gianni himself became a symbol of the area's 1990s zeitgeist like no other celebrity. His parties, usually organized by Donatella, were the envy of the beach. She would dispatch her assistants to organize the food and entertainment. "How much can we spend?" they asked her. "Whatever you want," she replied. "There's no budget." Drag queens, models, photographers, and muscle boys mixed with Elton John, Cindy Crawford, Jack Nicholson, and Alec Baldwin, all gaping at the extravagance of Casa Casuarina.

One year, Donatella and Gianni threw a birthday party for Madonna. The pop star had been a Miami habitué since around 1992, when she had shot part of her book *Sex* in a mansion in the city, which she subsequently bought. "She hung out with the top photographers at the time, which were the same ones I was working with," Donatella would say later. "We moved in the same circles and saw each other at parties. For a while, it was just *Ciao, ciao.* Then one day, she called me and said, 'We need to talk.' "[9]

Madonna was in the market for a new image. Donatella courted the star assiduously, sending diamond jewelry along with free couture dresses. Then, in 1995, Madonna agreed to appear in a Versace ad campaign, shot at Donald Trump's Mar al Lago estate in Palm Beach. For Versace, which had had more success in recruiting male stars, the ads featuring Madonna were a breakthrough, creating an association between Versace and celebrities that garnered endless press coverage. After Madonna, Donatella drafted one celebrity after another— Demi Moore, Courtney Love, Halle Berry—for her ad campaigns. (Madonna herself appeared twice more in Versace ads.) For Madonna's birthday, Donatella chose a cake so big that it had to be lowered into the turquoise pool of Casa Casuarina, where it drifted like a giant water-borne float. Men in Versace bikinis waded in to cut slices for the guests.

In 1992, Gianni dedicated a collection to South Beach that became a hit with club-goers there. It included pastel-colored silk shirts embellished with cartoonish images of 1950s-era Cadillacs, with "South Beach" spelled out on the back. He sent the entire collection—dozens of shirts, dresses, belts, and leggings—gratis to trendsetters on the beach.

"He must have sent me one hundred thousand dollars' worth of clothes," remembered Lee Schrager, then owner of Torpedo, a popular gay club. "There were twenty shirts, tons of belts. There were boxes and boxes of clothes."[10]

❖ V ❖

Once Gianni opened his house, he began flying to Miami Beach a half dozen times a year, usually taking the Concorde from Paris to New York and then hopping a flight down to Miami. (After Gianni's father died in 1992, Gianni celebrated Christmas in Miami rather than Como.) While Santo came only rarely—Cristiana preferred their family to vacation separately—Donatella was a devotee of South Beach. Before Gianni bought Casa Casuarina, she traveled there frequently, staying at the Fontainebleau Resort, a huge 1950s-era luxury hotel, with Paul and the children. After Gianni finished his house, she visited even more often.

With the whole clan there, even trips across Ocean Drive to the beach were done in high style. The staff blanketed a thirty-foot-square patch of sand with colorful Versace towels. Donatella would sit on a lounge chair, smoking and tanning, clad in a chartreuse bikini and colorful little wrap skirts, a huge Louis Vuitton tote full of suntan lotion and Marlboro Reds by her side.[11] (Sometimes, Donatella's fame in South Beach was too much. One transvestite, dolled up to resemble Donatella, often stood outside Casa Casuarina's gates. "Donatella, come out here!" she shouted. "I'm the original Donatella. You're just a fake!")

Gianni found his own temptation in the thriving gay scene on South Beach. He was a magnet for the buff young aspiring male models there. (He once shot a campaign at a park that was a popular cruising area for gays.) In turn, Gianni wasn't above using his superstar status in the gay world to have some fun. At Paragon, a gay club in South Beach, Gianni once homed in on a handsome go-go dancer there, beckoning to him—but the young guy, perhaps thinking the designer was just another older man on the make, ignored him. Finally, Gianni began gesturing to himself, mouthing what one local gossip columnist called "the magical word that will open any hustler's heart: Versace."[12]

Miami Beach's surfeit of ripe male flesh made for a thriving prostitution business, something Gianni and Antonio had indulged in from their first trips to South Beach in the early 1990s. Antonio and Gianni were largely faithful to each other, but each liked something on the side. In an interview with Miami police after Gianni's murder, Antonio stated that Gianni met an aspiring model named Jaime Cardona, who would discreetly provide him and Antonio with willing young men. Cardona also worked at the Warsaw Ballroom nightclub, Gianni's favorite haunt, where the entertainment was racy even by South Beach standards. There were amateur strip contests and drag queen shows, but the main attraction was Lady Hennessey Brown, whose show consisted of pulling objects, such as handkerchiefs and scarves, from her vagina. She could even make milk pour from her nipples.[13]

In the early days, Gianni went to the Warsaw with Antonio and a few Italian friends. Later, his entourage expanded to include the likes of Sting, Cindy Crawford, Elton John, and Ingrid Casares, a pretty Cuban who resembled Audrey Hepburn, with a short pixie haircut and dark Bambi eyes. (Casares, featured in Madonna's *Sex* book French-kissing the pop star, was reputed to be Madonna's lover for a time.)

"I remember Gianni would invite us over for tea, and it would be Elton John, Sting, Cindy Crawford, Madonna," said Casares. "We would all walk to the News Café and sit to organize our night out. Then we'd walk to Warsaw or wherever, and nobody bothered anybody. There was no paparazzi yet."[14]

At the Warsaw, Cardona got to know South Beach's hippest crowd, and he became a fixture in the Versace galaxy. Gianni had Cardona show him and Antonio around Miami Beach, taking them to the hottest clubs. He later did some modeling for Gianni. Gradually, Cardona became Gianni's informal social secretary, compiling the guest lists for the parties at Casa Casuarina.

"He would decide who was cool and who wasn't," said Louis Canales, a longtime publicist who did work for Gianni. "He had immense power."[15]

Cardona's help soon extended to more private encounters. According to statements provided to Miami Beach police by Cardona after Gianni's murder, Cardona sorted through the ads for male escorts and vetted the men at a bar near Casa Casuarina. He once found an escort who went by the name of Kyle and brought him to the back door of the mansion, instructing him to go straight up a private staircase that led to Gianni and Antonio's rooms. There, the three chatted briefly, and Kyle had sex with each man. Afterward, Antonio paid him. Kyle got the impression that such encounters were more for Antonio's benefit than for Gianni's. Sometimes, Gianni appeared disinterested or even left the room.[16]

Gianni moved blithely around South Beach, never worrying about his own personal safety. While Donatella often used bodyguards and sometimes pestered him to get his own security, Gianni didn't see the need. Despite Miami's reputation as a dangerous city—eight foreign tourists were killed there in less than a year in 1993—he was remarkably sanguine. Once, Andrea Tremolada, Versace's head of advertising, who had flown in from Milan, left the mansion one day with Gianni to go to lunch. When they swung open the gates on Ocean Drive, they found a large group of fans waiting with cameras on the sidewalk to snap a picture of Gianni. The intrusion unnerved Tremolada. "Signor Versace, aren't you afraid that someone could hurt you?" he asked.

"Why should I?" Gianni replied. "I've never hurt anyone, and I don't see why anyone would want to harm me."[17]

❖ V ❖

Once Gianni bought the mansion in South Beach, Miami became the exclamation point on the high life Donatella and Paul were enjoying. Drugs were as available as Good & Plenty candy in South Beach in the 1980s and 1990s, as Latin American drug cartels found a rich market in the anything-goes club scene there, selling everything from marijuana to a nasty mix of heroin, cocaine, and horse tranquilizer known as Special K.

Donatella became part of a tight celebrity pack that included Naomi Campbell, Gwyneth Paltrow, Kate Moss, Madonna, and Ingrid Casares. Before Donatella arrived in South Beach, the staff at Casa Casuarina called around to see which celebrities were in town and what parties were being planned. In 1994, she went to Madonna's thirty-sixth birthday party at her Brickell Avenue house. Organized by

Madonna's brother Christopher Ciccone, the party featured performances by drag queens and strippers, and culminated in Madonna baring her breasts to her guests and jumping into the pool fully dressed. Donatella danced most of the evening, clad in a gold dress covered with medusa heads.[18]

By the time her forty-first birthday rolled around in May 1996, Donatella's partying was hitting a new peak. That year, Casares threw a party for Donatella's birthday at Liquid, a club she owned. She invited about 150 guests to the private lounge downstairs from the main club, hired drag queens to make cotton candy and fresh popcorn for the guests, and brought in about a dozen male models, clad only in tight Versace underwear, to carry out a huge sheet cake, festooned with sparklers and emblazoned "Happy Birthday Donatella" in huge letters. One model dangled from a swing mounted from the ceiling and others danced on the bar. Paul and Allegra had come early in the evening, but Paul took the little girl home before the entertainment started.

Later that evening, Donatella and some friends went to an office upstairs in the club. She had someone there to fix her hair, brushing and touching up her blond extensions. While the hairdresser fussed, Donatella pulled out a slim hard case. She carefully unscrewed the top. Habitual users of cocaine often store their drugs in small containers slightly larger than cigarette lighters, which fit easily into pockets or small purses. Oftentimes, a tiny spoon, which is used to scoop out the cocaine, is attached to the side. When Donatella pulled out her case, her companions were amazed. She had come a long way from Bic pens and rolled-up dollar bills. Attached to the case was a tiny gold spoon with a finely wrought medusa on the handle. Donatella rolled her hair back over her shoulder in a practiced motion and leaned over, deftly scooping out some cocaine from her tiny case. After a while, the group went back downstairs to rejoin the other guests. Donatella arrived back at Casa Casuarina at around 4 a.m.[19] Despite the raucous evening, Donatella was always in control, even when she was high. "I never saw her out of control or messy," said Kevin Crawford, a friend who helped organize her birthday party.[20]

Gianni tried hard to ignore his sister's problem, rarely speaking of it even to his closest confidantes. "My sister is crazy," he often said, a veiled allusion to her hard-living lifestyle, his tone suggesting that it was a topic he didn't care to talk about. Despite his reputation as the wild man in fashion, he was a homebody, content to be in bed by 10 p.m. With his natural store of adrenaline, he had never felt the need to turn to drugs for a jolt. His sister's appetite for dope confounded and frustrated him, and her refusal to stop using cocaine was gradually helping to erode his bond with her.

But Gianni could hardly deny that Donatella's penchant for full-on excess was enormously useful to his empire. The more the rumors spread about the wild parties she threw—with the best-looking people, the best drugs, and the best music—the hotter his brand became. Gianni had long relied on her to add louche glamour to his image, with her blaze of diamonds, candy-gloss hair, and poured-on dresses. She had been his mascot and muse since he had dressed her back in Reggio. Now that her high-octane lifestyle was pushing his brand to a heady peak, he was castigating the very behavior that had helped him create the life he now enjoyed.

Not long after he bought Casa Casuarina, Gianni drafted Bruce Weber, a Versace favorite, to gin up a gauzy testimonial to family life à la Versace for all the world to see. Weber shot Allegra, then six, and Daniel, not yet two, playing on the beach with their buffed parents. Donatella's tiny black thong bikini showed off her trim and muscled legs and arms and her washboard stomach. In one shot Allegra holds a ballet pose while immersed in the water and in another she dances nude on the beach, her blond hair whipping in the wind while a guitarist plays nearby. In the book, titled *South Beach Stories*, the shots of the children were interspersed with pictures of drag queens, a male stripper, and male models wearing tight Versace bathing suits, bright silk shirts opened to the navel, and black-leather studded outfits.

By the time *South Beach Stories* came out in 1993, Gianni was increasingly channeling his familial devotion onto Allegra. From the time she was a toddler, Allegra was a precocious little girl. Blond with brown eyes, she had a seraphic, intelligent face and a sensitive character. She took up ballet early, and moved with a grace and poise unusual for children her age. Gianni fell madly in love with the little girl, even helping to choose her name. (Her brother, Daniel, who was born in December 1990, was named for the Elton John song.) Much more than just a doting uncle, he called her his *principessa* and showered her with gifts such as an antique tiara and a ruby necklace.

Allegra grew up a coddled, exceptional child in the red-hot core of Donatella and Gianni's celebrity world. Gianni took her to his runway shows and to the dinners afterward, where she chatted with models and celebrities as if they were ordinary family friends. Her uncle's supermodels, particularly Naomi, were like doting aunts. She hung out with the children of rock stars and world-famous actors. When Sting and his wife were guests, Allegra and their children made cookies together. She shared a desk with the son of Eric Clapton at her grammar school in Milan. For one birthday, Elton John sent her a grand piano, and when he visited he often serenaded the little girl. Donatella hired caretakers who treated Allegra like a fragile doll. She typically sent Allegra for visits to Calabria with an au pair, and on one visit, her old friends and family were horrified when the nanny refused to let them kiss the little girl and tested the temperature of the rooms Allegra stayed in to make sure they weren't too hot or cold.

Both mother and uncle happily employed Allegra and Daniel in the Versace promotional machine. The children quickly grew used to being photographed constantly, at Versace events, in glossy publicity photos of models and celebrities, and in advertisements. Allegra and Daniel would become the faces of Gianni's children's fragrance. By contrast, Santo scrupulously shielded his children from the public eye. Gianni cared far less for Santo's children, in part due to his antipathy for Cristiana.

While she reveled in the public image of glossy motherhood, Donatella was a restless parent. Anxious to escape Gianni's grip, she spent weeks at a time in the United States for ad campaigns, which were shot four times a year. She had long found Milan suffocating and tedious, while the high energy of New York suited her skittish, restless character—even as her travels separated her from her children. She doted affectionately on the pregnant women in the office, sending elaborate gifts when their children arrived and cooing over baby pictures. But for herself, the impulse to play the doting Italian *mamma* who clucked over every detail of her children's lives battled with the temptations that beckoned far away from home.

Donatella threw birthday parties for Allegra that were the envy of *la Milano bene*, the lofty circle of the city's richest families such as the Berlusconis. Organized by Gianni's top assistants, the party included some fifty children who would be invited for an afternoon at Via Gesù. Gianni often made a special party dress for Allegra. (Annoyed by the presence of other children, he didn't usually attend the party itself.) Each year, the children's mothers would receive a custom-made invitation, done in the theme Donatella had chosen for the party. One year the theme was Alice in Wonderland, featuring a full-blown show with live music and actors to entertain the kids. At the end of the party, each child (and his or her caretaker) could pick from a mountain of gifts piled on a table: Versace perfumes, T-shirts, or little purses. Other mothers—gray-flannel, bourgeois ladies who normally turned their nose up at the flashy Donatella—often tagged along with their nannies and the kids to see the spectacle for themselves.

Just as Donatella treated her daughter like a doll, so did Gianni dress her like one. He often made outfits for his niece that became the basis for some of the Versace children's collection. His seamstresses kept Allegra's measurements in the atelier, although her nanny often brought the little girl in for fittings when she visited Gianni. Donatella sometimes had the seamstresses make identical mother-daughter outfits.

But the glare of the Versace spotlight seared Allegra's innocence. While her friends were playing innocent dress-up games, Allegra was being dolled up like a miniature Versace model. She was often made up, complete with mascara and eyeliner, for the house's events. She wore smaller versions of adult fashion-forward clothes, such as flared pants and chain belts. For one Versace party, Donatella, wearing one of Gianni's elaborate sadomasochism gowns, dressed her six-year-old daughter in a dress made in leopard-skin print, which made for a jarring mother-daughter tableau. "My mom dressed me in silk to go to elementary school," Allegra told *Harper's Bazaar* years later. "In kindergarten, they sent me home because I couldn't do finger painting in my dress."[21]

Gianni's devotion to Allegra had little regard for the needs of a growing girl. He frequently had Donatella take her out of school so that she could accompany him on his trips to Miami and New York, where he took her to museum after museum.

"My children were his children," Donatella recalled years later. "Since she was nine years old only, she was going to see museums with him. She knew all the museums in America, in France, in England. She would sit with him and go through art books. . . . It was adorable."[22]

Meanwhile, Allegra was growing up in a household with contrasting messages regarding food. Donatella was enormously disciplined when it came to her own diet, ordering her chef to cook her own meals using low-fat ingredients, without salt and with very little oil. But while she followed a strict regimen, Donatella embraced the tradition of a country where so much hospitality revolves around eating. At her dinner parties, she was keenly involved in planning the menus and the presentation of the cuisine. She often had her chefs emulate trends she found in hip new restaurants, and guests were presented with their meals elaborately arranged on each plate. "Here, you have to eat!" she often encouraged her guests, pushing dishes at them.

At the same time, in Italy, *la bella figura*, or the imperative of looking perfectly turned out, extends to children, so that many Italian mothers dress and groom their kids as painstakingly as if they were adults.

"Donatella was very demanding with Allegra, about her clothes and how she looked," recalled an employee who worked for years with the family. "She wanted her to be this glamorous little girl."

Allegra was also growing up among the world's most beautiful women. When Allegra visited her uncle during the days before a show, he encouraged her to emulate the models. "Pretend you're Marpessa!" Gianni urged her as she cavorted on the runway, referring to a dark-haired beauty who was one of his favorite models.

By the time Allegra reached the cusp of adolescence, she was a sensitive girl who seemed oddly refined and mature for her age, an exacting perfectionist of a child, concentrating furiously when she drew and excelling in her studies. She took great care in how she dressed and looked, and moved with a self-conscious grace that often struck adults as overly mature. She was an obedient daughter, following Donatella's edicts without protest.

Her brother, Daniel, had an easier time of it, although his uncle had made himself a looming presence even before he was born. In 1990, when Donatella found out her second child would arrive around January 18 of the next year, Gianni squawked, "You must be nuts if you're thinking of having the baby during the men's shows or the couture shows," he told her. "I won't hear of it. The baby has to be born at the latest between Christmas and New Year's." So Donatella convinced her doctors to move the Cesarean birth to December 28.[23] Gianni loved Daniel, affectionately calling him his "Teddy-boy," but he grew into a normal little child, playing pickup soccer games with friends.

Both children had to reckon with the strikingly different parenting habits of their mother and father. Donatella tended to take the kids to five-star hotels and restaurants. Once, when she took Allegra ice skating at the posh Swiss resort of St. Moritz, Donatella wore a black catsuit, a gold ski jacket, and diamond bracelets, and was trailed by several beefy bodyguards.[24]

By contrast, Paul was a fun, down-to-earth parent, happy to play Mr. Mom. He had hankered for kids and used to dote on the children of Donatella's girlfriends. He took the kids to the beach or bike riding or tooling around Lake Como in his boat. When the kids were old enough, they attended an elite British school in Milan, where about half the students were children of foreign parents. (Allegra and Daniel both grew up bilingual in English and Italian.) He was an enthusiastic leader of Daniel's Boy Scout troop, happy to dress in the corny uniform of shorts and a yellow hat. He would pull up after school in his convertible to pick the kids up and take them for an ice cream, and he never missed Allegra's dance recitals.

"I remember how Allegra would light up when she saw her father in the audience," said another parent. "She was this little girl in this pink tutu. That dance teacher was quite a tough cookie, but it was clear that Allegra was among the best girls there. She loved it."

However, as Gianni's relationships with Santo and Donatella broke down, Allegra increasingly bore the weight of her uncle's high expectations. Those expectations would come to burden her almost unbearably in the years ahead.

While Gianni and Donatella reveled in their red-hot lifestyle and the rising notoriety of the Versace brand, Santo remained the grounded, paternal figure of the house, a mix of the down-to-earth parent who cleaned up after his offspring's grandiose habits and the charismatic leader who goaded his team to beat the previous year's sales figures. By the mid-1990s, as the Versace business grew, so did Santo's stature. By then, nearing fifty, he began to look the part of the elder statesman, with his distinguished gray hair and impeccable dark suits with a matching mock turtleneck underneath. But while he was one of Italy's best-known businessmen by then, Santo largely shunned the limelight except for the obligatory press interviews, happy to continue to play his life's role as the family's pragmatic fixer.

At home, Santo's personal life had none of the theater of his siblings' lives. He and Cristiana sent their children, Francesca and Antonio, to Milan's German-language school, believing the place would instill a Teutonic discipline in them. "If you can learn in German, everything else is easy," he told friends. Even though he was now a bigwig in Italian business circles, he was happy to walk to work each day from the comfortable rental apartment near the company headquarters that he and his family moved into early in his marriage. Because it was far less grand than Gianni's apartments in Via Gesù or Donatella's sprawling home, he virtually never held Versace events there. Aside from a passion for sports, he had few hobbies, preferring to spend weekends and evenings in the office.

Santo traveled constantly, monitoring the Versace shops. In the showroom in Milan, he ran his finger along the shelves to make sure they were immaculate. He was enormously popular with his staff—he was careful always to knock on a manager's door before entering his office—even as he pushed them to work long hours. "He used to say, '*Brava*, you did a good job, but now I want you to do this and that,'" recalled one longtime manager. "I used to wonder if I was ever going to get a break. But he was so excited by what was happening that he just pulled you along with him."

One winter, during a visit to Beijing for the opening of a new boutique, Santo and his team went to visit the Great Wall. While there, Santo spotted two French tourists clad in Versace jeans. He excitedly approached the pair to compliment them on their outfits, and promptly invited them to Gianni's next couture show back in Paris. Back in the office in Milan, he extended the paternalist role he played with his siblings to Versace employees. The staff, knowing he was a rabid sports fan, often asked him to procure tickets for soccer matches at Milan's giant San Siro Stadium. When employees brought their kids into the headquarters, he invited the children into his office, sitting them at a table near his desk so that they could draw.

Santo's exuberance and hyperkinetic energy waned little with age; he restlessly paced his office and spoke at such a rapid clip that guests had to strain to keep up with him. He had an extraordinary memory and grasp of even small details. Even as Gianni's label soared and became a global name, Santo remained the go-to person for the flood of new projects—boutique openings, licensing agreements, expanding factory space—that came in. He worked harder than ever, often eating dinner in the office and staying at his desk until nearly midnight.

During the first half of the 1990s, Santo embarked on a new strategy to ride Gianni's hot image and take the house to a new level. At the time, a new middle-class hunger for luxury goods was growing, creating a huge market for designers who found ways to sell little slices of the dream they served up in ad campaigns and on the runway. Companies such as Gucci, Prada, and Louis Vuitton began making millions not on couture dresses and ten-thousand-dollar traveling trunks but on nylon bags, leather wallets, and perfumes that cost hundreds.

Indeed, Santo knew that Gianni's one-of-a-kind couture dresses didn't make money. Couture in general had been losing millions for decades. (In 1993, Yves Saint Laurent's couture line was losing more than $5 million a year.[25]) But it hardly mattered to him. Couture had become a marketing vehicle to sell oodles of less pricey items, including everyday clothes. Indeed, unlike many designers who remain trapped in an ivory tower of designing for a few fashion-forward women, Gianni enthusiastically supported Santo's sales force. The day after a show, his team put together a large album of photos of the collection, and he tacked stickers on the outfits he wanted Santo's salespeople to sell the most of, along with sales targets. To Santo's delight, Gianni pushed his designers to update core items that always sold well—day suits, jackets, pants. His daywear was popular with women who wanted a more feminine uniform than Armani's androgynous suits. He updated Chanel's famous day suits by putting black leather straps down the front of a crisp white form-fitting wool suit. He made sure the pattern makers at the factory made them in sizes big enough to fit real women—up to a size twelve. "Loosen them up," he urged them. "Make it bigger. Not all women are runway models."[26]

"Of all the sexy things he made, what we used to sell were the suits," said Ron Frasch, chief executive of Neiman Marcus at the time. "They were great fitting and very structured. You didn't have to be a stick to wear them. It made a woman feel very strong."[27]

In the early 1990s, Santo pushed the Versace brand harder by adding a raft of new licenses for products that a bigger range of shoppers could afford, adding to the relatively small clutch of licenses he'd signed in the 1980s. For years, Gianni swore he would never design everyday items such as jeans or sportswear, but Santo gradually wore him down, pointing out how successful other brands, particularly Armani, had been with such products. It was a risky strategy, however, because licensees are always tempted to cut corners on the quality of the products in order to slash prices and sell more. Santo felt that, if he watched them carefully, licenses could boost Versace's growth. So he signed contracts for everything from jeans and perfumes for children to bathing suits, underwear, umbrellas, plus-sized clothes, and home furnishings. In 1989, he created Versus, a less expensive, edgier line aimed at twenty-something shoppers, as well as Versace Jeans Couture.

Santo's strategy worked. Gianni's image—fueled by his glitzy runway shows, his celebrity pals in South Beach, his spitfire sister—intrigued shoppers, who snapped up the more-affordable items. As a result, revenues from licensed products—led by the jeans—soon outstripped those of the house's main lines. In 1991, before Santo's most lucrative licensing deals, overall sales of Versace products were 770 billion lire (about $360 million), of which just less than half came from licensed products; most of the rest came from sales of the main men's and women's line.[28] In just five years, the picture changed dramatically. Overall sales had nearly doubled, to 1.52 billion lire (about $800 million). Two-thirds of that came from licenses, with the rest from the house's main lines.

But from the beginning, the licenses and extra lines were a source of worry for Santo. Shoppers didn't understand that some of the lines—such as Istante and Signatures, two toned-down variations on the main line—were produced by Versace. Some of the collections were too similar and would cannibalize one another's sales. Others, such as the plus-sized collection, detracted from the luster of the Versace image. Santo's salespeople pushed the franchisees hard to load up on licensed products, knowing that a percentage of sales flowed into the coffers of Via Gesù. But the franchisees often squawked, arguing that shoppers in their markets wouldn't buy all the goods. Years later, managers of rival fashion brands would cite Versace as an example of a company that overplayed its licensing strategy.

But in the 1990s, Santo pushed the licenses because he needed the extra money for a new business model that was gaining ground in fashion. It was the first rumblings of the luxury goods boom that would peak at the turn of the millennium, and the cornerstone of the new approach was fully owned boutiques. Around 1990, Louis Vuitton and Prada began spurning franchise contracts and instead started to open shops themselves. A franchise approach suits a company when it's just starting out, by sharing the burden and expense of opening new stores with boutique owners willing to take a risk on a new brand. However, when a brand begins to grow quickly, the franchisees pocket most of the gains. Santo saw that Versace could make far more money if it chucked the franchisees and opened more of its own shops.

The strategy of shunning the franchisees, however, cost a fortune. Prada, Vuitton, and later, Gucci were opening opulent stores that cost millions of dollars each. The booming economy sent rents on streets such as Fifth Avenue in New York and Bond Street in London soaring. The core of the model was the huge flagship store, complete with VIP rooms and ornate furnishings that were showcases for a house's full collection. The flagships often lost money, but their owners hardly cared. They were valuable marketing vehicles, rather than simple sales outlets. When a Japanese shopper came to Paris to buy a coveted Louis Vuitton bag at the boutique on the Avenue des Champs-Élysées, she wanted a dazzling experience. But the approach was very risky: When sales fell, the fixed costs of the shop—huge rents, large amounts of stock, and trained sales staff—were impossible to cut, throwing the stores quickly into the red.

In the early 1990s, when Gianni's collections were hot, the risks seemed slim to Santo, and he began buying back franchises. In turn, Gianni threw himself into planning a series of stunningly opulent flagships, designed by the best architects and with the highest quality materials. While other brands saved money by choosing a single image for all its shops and negotiating volume discounts for the renovations, Gianni treated the shops like his personal playthings, designing a different look for each big new boutique.

In 1991, Versace opened a twelve-thousand-square-foot store—his third in Paris—on the Rue du Faubourg Saint-Honoré complete with a large VIP room for couture clients. In Milan, the company opened a second shop on Via Montenapoleone, a three-story boutique with marble and mosaic floors, pillars, and trompe l'oeil paintings on the moldings of the arches. But the performance of the new shop was an ominous sign for the future: Sales of the two Via Montenapoleone stores remained the same. Adding a new shop had doubled costs but only cannibalized sales from the original boutique. Within just a few years, Santo's ambitious expansion strategy would come back to haunt him.

❖ V ❖

As Versace's growth soared, Gianni kept up a frenetic pace, fearful perhaps of letting the fruits of his extraordinary success slip through his fingers. He worked constantly, during vacations, holidays, and even during family events such as Allegra's baptism. By then, Via Gesù was the *casa-bottega* (house-and-shop) he'd always dreamed of, the atelier an extension of his own home. While his private apartments were richly furnished, the atelier on the upper floor was almost plain, workaday. Two cream-colored salons with floor-to-ceiling mirrors had plenty of space to hold fittings, receive suppliers, and lay out photos for ad campaigns. Along the corridors were shelves and shelves of books. He owned about twenty thousand volumes that served as inspiration for his collections, and he hired a librarian to manage them all.

As the company grew, his days became marathons, and at times he resented the unforgiving pace. "Are you trying to kill me?" he roared when he saw how many meetings his secretaries jammed into his schedule. The first one to arrive in the atelier in the morning, he left around 6:30 p.m. each evening, only to return many nights around 9, clad in one of his silk dressing gowns, to work as late as 3 a.m.

He was unstintingly generous with employees who met his high expectations. He bought a block of apartments in a building in the center of Milan so that his favorite associates could live rent-free. He adored a middle-aged couple, Lucia and Giovanni, who were his personal valets. When he learned that Giovanni, as a young man, hadn't been able to afford an engagement ring for Lucia, Gianni immediately sent an assistant down to his favorite jeweler to buy her one.

But in spite of his kindness, Gianni could also be a tyrant. If he felt disappointed with an employee's work, he seemed to take it personally, refusing to speak with that person for months at a time. He sometimes emerged from a meeting room after an argument with a supplier with his face red with rage and his hair flying around his head like Beethoven's. He engaged in a bitter war with the close friend who had bought half of Villa Fontanelle when Gianni himself hadn't had the money to buy it all. After a series of arguments over the renovation of the estate, Gianni turned petty and mean, cutting the electricity off in the friend's half of the property and even tossing her lounge chair into the lake in a fit of pique. His posturing could veer into prevarication and vanity. He blithely fed journalists lies that puffed up his image, claiming to have met Picasso when he was twenty-two (an age when he was still living in Calabria) and to have discovered the medusa logo in an ancient mosaic tile floor near his family home in Reggio, not on a door handle of Via Gesù.

In order to escape the pressure of the atelier, he and Antonio left for Villa Fontanelle every Thursday evening. Every Friday and Saturday, he had his silk suppliers bring him samples of his prints, and he happily pored over the color swaths laid out on large tables in the main salon. He brought guests to a restaurant on Isola Comacina, a tiny island, and took them for a tour of the lake afterward in his small boat. He and Antonio went for tea at nearby Villa D'Este, a five-star hotel with a plush gym where Antonio worked out every evening. Sometimes, Gianni joined his celebrity guests such as Sylvester Stallone or Madonna for a desultory session at the gym, but otherwise he mostly soaked in the sauna.

As he became more famous, he shunned the limelight. He had never liked appearing even in his own publicity photos, and he started wearing dark sunglasses more often. He and Antonio ate dinner mostly at home because he hated being stared at in restaurants. Once, he took Allegra to the opera in Miami, but left halfway through because so many people approached him for an autograph. He generally let his sister tend to the celebrities, his tastes running more toward art and theater. According to Ingrid Sischy, then editor of *Interview Magazine* and a close friend of Gianni's, at a dinner in New York, he once sat next to Madonna, Elton John, and the rapper Tupac Shakur, "but the person he left with at two a.m. was Philip Taaffe"—the prominent New York artist—"because he wanted to go to the studio. He wasn't running off with Madonna to a late-night cabaret. He had a lot of options that night. But what he wanted to do was look at this artist's studio."[29]

twelve

Conflict

*i*N AUGUST 1994, AFTER RETURNING FROM A TRIP TO THE United States, Gianni noticed his hearing in one ear had suddenly worsened. At first he thought it was a simple infection, but then his ear and his whole right cheek began to swell alarmingly. He began losing weight and grew worried. After a battery of tests, a doctor in Milan gave him the grim news: Gianni had a rare type of cancer of the inner ear, which had affected a nerve and caused the swelling. The doctor ruled out surgery because of the risk that touching the nerve could disfigure Gianni's face. Instead, he would have to undergo chemotherapy. Gianni was shocked. At forty-seven, he had long suffered from a type of anemia, which fatigued him at times. But otherwise, he had enjoyed excellent health.

The cancer diagnosis hit Gianni just when his company

had grown too big for him to manage as he had done for years—designing every line, checking every sample, deciding every advertising image. His days were so busy that in the evening his employees started giving his private valet briefcases of documents or photos he needed to review. Early the next morning, he would return the case with detailed comments or orders, having worked late into the night.

For more than a year, between August 1994 and October 1995, a nurse came regularly to Gianni's private apartments in Via Gesù to administer the chemotherapy. It was a relatively mild dose, sparing him the anguish of nausea and hair loss. However, the treatments left him feeling exhausted and frustrated, unable to sustain his normal frenetic pace. Rumors began to fly that Gianni was suffering from AIDS (despite his active sexual history, the regular blood tests required by his anemia had always showed him to be free of the virus). In the atelier, he never spoke of his cancer, but his face was drawn and tired, drained of color.

Gianni's illness brought to a head tensions with Donatella that had been building for several years. He went to bed earlier and sometimes had to nap after lunch to recover his energy. Often feeling tired and sick, he had little choice but to leave more and more responsibility to his sister. In turn, Donatella, nearing forty and beginning to chafe at the role of mascot and kid sister, was keen to emerge from Gianni's long shadow. According to friends, she felt that her big brothers too often dismissed her as a lightweight, treating her as the junior partner in the company.

As Gianni cut back his public appearances, Donatella soaked up the limelight. She presided at dinners and parties and courted more publicity. In years past, Donatella hadn't been a natural with the press, often seeming as nervous as an understudy with journalists. But with Gianni temporarily indisposed, Donatella triumphantly took center stage. Her outré look and prodigal lifestyle—her drug use was, by now, fashion's worst-kept secret—piqued press interest, and she, in turn, developed a candid, witty style that charmed journalists. She happily submitted to a slate of new requests for profiles. In June 1997, *Vanity Fair* ran a fawning ten-page spread entitled "La Bella Donatella," including a photo of her, nude except for a diamond

Gianni had given her, in a Plexiglas egg rising from the waves. It was a masterpiece of lighting, makeup, and retouching that succeeded in making her, if not beautiful, then extremely alluring. In another shot, Donatella sits at the breakfast table in a full-length evening gown, Daniel perched on her lap, with Allegra sitting next to her. A Wheaties box sits on the table, a cheeky prop in a family tableau that was otherwise anything but traditional.[1]

Her already fast-paced life rose another notch around then. One night in early 1997, after wrapping up a fashion shoot in Manhattan, Donatella asked a few members of its cast to join her for a night out—in high Versace style. A chauffeur-driven car shuttled them out to Teterboro Airport, an airstrip just outside Manhattan in New Jersey, where a private jet was idling. The group settled into their seats, and the luxury plane took off for the two-and-a-half-hour flight to Minneapolis. After the plane landed in the freezing city around 10 p.m., a car whisked Donatella's posse to the city's top five-star hotel, where a closetful of Versace party clothes hung in its best suite. Hair and makeup people were there to doll everyone up. The destination: a private concert by Prince at the pop star's palatial home. Donatella was a huge fan of Prince, inviting him often to the Versace house in Como. Gianni found the singer odd. "I saw very little of him," he told a journalist later. "I was quite shocked by the fact that he noticed the house was on a lake only after he'd been there for three days. He lives in the dark."[2]

To the consternation of the Versace entourage, when they arrived at Paisley Palace, Prince showed them the empty crib of his baby son, who had died of severe birth defects in the fall of 1996, a week after his birth. After mixing with other guests for a couple of hours, Prince finally climbed onstage for a dazzling two-hour concert. Afterward, Donatella, flushed from dancing, brought the group backstage, where they hung out with the diminutive pop star and his wife. After partying much of the night, they were ferried by car back to the airport, where the private jet waited to fly them back to New York. Donatella returned to her hotel suite around dawn.

"That's how Donatella rolled back then," said one participant in that evening's festivities. "It wasn't that she was a hanger-on. It wasn't like Armani or Gianni, who weren't really interested in that life. She was living a rock star's life. She was full on."

Since Gianni first beckoned Donatella to Milan in 1978, he had pushed her to do more, encouraging her to assume greater responsibility at the company and extolling her talent both in the atelier and in the press. But when he fell ill, things shifted. A man of prodigious energy, he was enormously frustrated at being ill, and it changed him. The pace of the past two decades had given him scant chance to reflect on his own mortality, absorbed as he was in his extraordinary success. Now, approaching his fiftieth birthday and facing the possibility of an early death, he began to ruminate on his family and the future of his label. He was feeling increasingly shunted aside by his siblings and was fearful that he would lose control of the atelier just as the company was soaring. While he signed off on press releases referring to Donatella as "codesigner" at Versace, privately he fumed at her showboating. He began to see her not as a kid sister but as a rival.

Since 1989, Gianni had let Donatella design Versus, the company's younger, edgier line. Donatella's role in Versus was nothing like that of Gianni's with the top line; she relied heavily on the talents of her design team, and the financial pressure on her was low, given that Versus made up little more than 3 percent of Versace's sales. But now the line became an increasing source of discord between the siblings. Donatella held some Versus shows in New York, partly to escape the full force of Gianni's scrutiny. She put off the moment that she showed Gianni the collection as much as possible, so that he couldn't interfere. Indeed, when Gianni checked his sister's work in the days before the runway show, he often didn't like it.

Changes in the fashion business only worsened the conflict between them. Just as Gianni fell ill, a shift was occurring, one that boded ill for the more-is-more vision that Versace championed so heartily. A new trend of spare, minimalist clothes was red hot, pushed principally by Miuccia Prada, a Milanese designer who had inherited her family's company, a blue-blood manufacturer of fine luggage. Prada shot to fame in the late 1980s when she used black nylon fabric to make small backpacks, a high-tech look that was an antidote to the decade's baroque fashions. The backpacks struck a chord with followers of so-called dog-whistle fashion, or items that were so high-concept that only an elect few got the message.

"The groovy people came into our Seventeenth Street store and inhaled those backpacks," recalled Simon Doonan, executive vice president of Barneys New York.[3]

Prada then launched a ready-to-wear line consisting of cerebral, pared-down clothes in muted colors that were the very antithesis of Versace's bold, statement pieces. The unassertive apparel and bags were popular because they looked like nothing. Miuccia Prada, with her dowdy skirts, granny shoes, and almost unkempt brown hair, was a walking refutation of Donatella's garish style. Women took to Prada because it let them feel beautiful without being perfect. Unlike Donatella, Prada and her husband, Patrizio Bertelli, shunned the beau monde of fashion, refusing to throw flashy postshow parties or court spoiled celebrities. In turn, magazine editors, stylists, and department store buyers considered anything Prada made a work of genius.

Minimalism was a foreign language to a man who viewed the world in bright, bold colors. Gianni wryly joked about his fashion friends' mania for Prada's designs. But privately, he found Prada's prim clothes, as well as similar collections at Jil Sander, Helmut Lang, and Calvin Klein, passionless and dull.

But Donatella understood the importance of the change. The models, photographers, and makeup artists she hung out with were crazy about minimalism. Donatella, ever sensitive to new vibes, was soon hooked herself. Her own dress style changed. She lost the colorful leggings, wild prints, and baroque jewelry and had Versace seamstresses whip up a series of pared-down Lycra sheaths for her. She embarked on a campaign to convince her brother to find a way to embrace the minimalist trend. Gianni obliged, in part. He came up with a collection of richly embroidered but simple sheaths, day suits, and dresses. But Donatella kept pushing him to go much further. She accused him of being infatuated with his own signature, glitzy style, which to her looked increasingly out of touch with how young, hip shoppers were dressing. "You're dressing old ladies now!" she shouted at him, leveling a charge she knew would wound him. "You're not modern. Your designs look old-fashioned. You have to move with the times!" Gianni fumed at her criticism, which made him feel even more defensive as he battled his illness.

Fashion houses had begun to bring in stylists, the highly hip freelance editors at fashion magazines, as consultants to help select the models, makeup, accessories, and music that would make for a hot, attention-grabbing runway show. Donatella flew in the biggest pushers of the new ascetic look from New York and London, hoping they could convince Gianni to change. But Gianni, resenting their interference, ignored them. He was the star designer and he felt that his instinct to resist the minimalist wave was the right one, no matter how many stylists Donatella brought in. With the stylists' encouragement, Donatella hired runway models that emulated the androgynous, slightly wasted look that the magazine editors now found cool. She understood that the strapping girls whom Gianni loved, with their tanned, oiled limbs and classic pinup sexiness, were as out of place now as the big hair and big shoulders of the previous decade. Unbeknownst to her chemotherapy-depleted brother, she cast a new crop of models who had a quirkiness that verged on ugliness—girls such as Erin O'Connor, with her beaklike nose and boy-short haircut, and Stella Tennant, with her wan complexion and pole-thin physique.

When he saw the girls, Gianni exploded, demanding that she change them. He resented Donatella's attempt to circumvent his wishes. "Let Prada use those models if they want!" he shouted at her. "I don't want them."

In 1995, Gianni planned a single men's show that would combine Versus with his signature line. As usual, he left the casting of the models to Donatella. During the dress rehearsal, he sat in the front row as the models began filing out. It was a full-on display of Donatella's favorite new look: pale, haggardly thin models with a punched-out look.

By the fifth model, Gianni was beside himself. *"Basta! Basta!"* he screamed, jumping up from his seat and waving his arms. He couldn't stand another moment of the spectacle. "These models are terrible! They don't even fill the clothes!" After a furious argument, he angrily let Donatella use the new models for Versus, but he made her find hunky guys with classic good looks for his own clothes.

HOUSE OF VERSACE

In years past, their clashes had brought out the best in Gianni. But now they deteriorated into bitter battles, as Gianni refused to listen to his sister. As the chemotherapy treatments took their toll, though, he had little choice but to let Donatella lead. One season, Donatella used the new girls—with uncombed hair, little makeup, and dark circles under their eyes—in the ad campaign. When Gianni saw the photos, he despaired. Around the same time, when Gianni was most ill, she came up with a couture collection almost entirely on her own, featuring dresses made of white plastic. Donatella hired Madonna to wear the clothes in ads that year. Gianni hated it.

Meanwhile, as the tensions rose between Donatella and Gianni, problems were also brewing with Santo. One day, after a couture show in Paris, Gianni and Antonio spent an afternoon trolling the antiques galleries in Paris for furnishings for the Miami house. Gianni had been a spendthrift since he was a kid, but now, with the company's fortunes soaring, he had become an almost compulsive shopper. That afternoon, he bought a Luigi XIV console and a boiserie with pink marble and gold embellishments, among other things. When the pair returned to their top-floor suites at the Ritz, Antonio gasped as he worked out that Gianni had spent 1.2 billion lire ($750,000) in just four hours.

"I've got to furnish my houses somehow!" Gianni said in response. "In any case, money is meant to be spent."[4]

Just as when they were children, it fell to Santo to keep his prodigal brother in check. "I never told Gianni what he could really spend," recalled Santo. "If I knew he could afford to spend one hundred, I told him he could spend ten. And then he would spend twenty." Gianni visited antiques dealers and art galleries, coming away with a long list of objects he'd picked out. Typically, his assistant then sent the list to Santo, who often tried to convince Gianni to drop some items. Gianni hated it when his big brother nagged him to pare back the orders he'd placed. "You're going to make me look bad!" he shouted, resentful that his brother should try to dictate what he could do.

But more and more frequently, Gianni spent so much that his

own dividends from the company didn't cover his bills, and Santo had to scramble to pay for his brother's works of art and opulent houses. As a result, he used the company's money to buy Gianni's toys so that the company—not Gianni personally—became the owner of the houses and art collection. Gianni's spending habits infuriated Santo. Gianni made no distinction between the company's money and his own wealth. The question of whether his siblings, who had large stakes in the house, agreed with how he spent the company's money didn't matter to him. Santo had always been scrupulous about keeping his own finances separate from the company's, while Donatella's and Gianni's homes, art work, and personal wealth were mostly on Versace's books.

But in Gianni's mind, the company was *his,* the fruit of his own sweat and tears. He felt his siblings had ridden the coattails of his success for years, and he resented it. He couldn't countenance Santo's recriminations about his spending. When they were kids, Santo used to give his little brother money when Gianni had spent all of his allowance; as adults, Gianni still expected Santo to clean up after him.

Antonio sometimes egged Gianni on in his resentments. "I don't understand why you are the one to do everything and then you have to split it all with your brother and sister, while they take care of themselves," he told him.

Gianni's spending increased a notch in 1994. As soon as he finished the lavish Miami villa, he set his sights on a grand new townhouse at Sixty-fourth Street near Fifth Avenue in New York. He spent $7.5 million to buy the eleven-thousand-square-foot spread, which was double the width of a normal brownstone and boasted a ballroom on one floor and a master bathroom that occupied nearly half of another floor. He then sank millions more into restoring it, adding two floors and a roof garden.

He decided the house would be a showcase for his new passion for contemporary art. His name was now famous around the globe, but he wanted to prove to the world that he had truly arrived. He began commissioning works from hot Manhattan artists such as Julian Schnabel and then went on a shopping spree, snapping up works by Andy Warhol, Jean-Michel Basquiat, and Roy Lichtenstein. But it was his fixation with Picasso that sparked a battle royal with Santo.

Gianni set out to assemble a world-class collection of the great artist's works, buying nearly twenty pieces, including *Fillette au Bateau,* a 1938 painting of the artist's daughter Maya, and *Femme Assise Sur Une Chaise,* a portrait of Dora Maar, one of Picasso's longtime lovers. Perhaps spurred by his brush with mortality, Gianni wanted to assemble a show-stopping collection that would demonstrate that he had reached a new level in terms of fame, wealth, and cultural taste. He could live his days literally surrounded by the work of one of the world's greatest artists. Meanwhile, some friends privately felt that Gianni was becoming something of a megalomaniac.

But Gianni's shopping spree cost him dearly at home. In 1996, when Santo saw the bill, he exploded. As Gianni's spending escalated, Santo, feeling heavy pressure to invest enough in the company to keep up with growing rivals, was losing his patience more and more often with his younger brother. The Picassos were the last straw. "You asked me for three million dollars for the house and then you present me with a bill for twenty-three million?" he shouted at his brother. "Do you know how many shops we could buy with that money?"

"The company is mine!" Gianni retorted. "I built it and I want to enjoy my money." Gianni knew that he had the last word in arguments over money because he was the driving force at the company, but his brother's harping bothered him enormously. In turn, Santo could do little except find small ways to exert control over Gianni. Around the same time, when the bank called Santo to say that Gianni had hit the limit on his credit cards, Santo refused to authorize an increase, leaving his brother without credit for the rest of the month. But Santo would take little satisfaction at his petty victory in cutting off Gianni's credit. Indeed, the battles with his brother over money would soon become the biggest regret of Santo's life.

❖ V ❖

In early 1996, Gianni's doctors found that his cancer had gone into remission, and his health was rapidly returning. The illness had changed him. "When, after the analyses, counteranalyses, CAT scans, and so on, I realized that it was possible that at not even fifty years old I could just . . . go, I said to myself, 'Well, every day that I live from now on—it's my party,' " he later told a journalist.[5]

He was determined to make some changes. Now that he was stronger than ever, the rising anger he felt toward his siblings boiled over, and he became more heavy-handed and aggressive with Donatella and Santo. He wanted to regain control of his company—starting with their respective stakes in the house.

Years earlier, Santo had engineered the divvying up of the shares, and Gianni, happy at the time to leave the financial side almost entirely to his older brother, had acceded. As a result, Gianni and Santo each had 40 percent of the company, with Donatella holding the remaining 20 percent. But after recovering his health, Gianni decided the division was unfair. The company had become what it was because of his talent, not that of his siblings. Technically, Santo and Donatella could join together to outvote him on big decisions. So he started pushing Santo into ceding some of his shares. Santo soon gave in. In June 1996, he sold 5 percent to Gianni, so that his own stake fell to 35 percent, while Gianni's rose to 45 percent.

By the following spring, after a series of discussions, Santo agreed to sell Gianni another 5 percent. As a result, Gianni finally controlled 50 percent of the company. He had always known that he had the last word when it came to critical decisions in the company and in disputes within the family, but now his control was unquestioned. It was a significant shift. Nearly twenty years after the birth of Versace, the house was for the first time firmly in his hands. Santo and Donatella were powerless to stop him from making whatever decisions he saw fit.

But before agreeing to the sale, Santo managed to extract an important promise from Gianni—one that someday could rebalance the power alignments within the family. He wanted his brother to change his will to leave the 5 percent to Santo's son, Antonio. Under heavy pressure from Santo, Gianni finally agreed. But it was a promise he wouldn't keep.

By then, Versace was growing fast—posting double-digit sales increases every year—but Gianni's spending on his houses, the art collection, and the flagship stores was growing even faster. The company's debt was rising, and it was destined to grow further, with Santo's plans to open more shops fully controlled by Versace. He needed a shot of new money to fuel the company's next stage of growth. But Gianni was dreaming of buying more art and setting up a foundation to show it off to the world. He'd also embarked on a new real estate venture that alarmed his brother: He was shopping for a grand new house in London. The city, in the midst of the "Cool Britannia" phase that was drawing in hipsters in media, advertising, and the art world, had an edgy buzz it hadn't enjoyed since the 1960s. Gianni had found a house he liked. "It wasn't a house—it was a castle," said one Versace executive. "I think he found it with Elton John. It was always dangerous when the two of them were together."

There was a problem: Santo wanted to take Versace public. It was a huge leap for the twenty-year-old house. For the first time, outside investors would scrutinize decisions taken by the three siblings, and they would surely object to Gianni's spending habits. But a stock market listing would give Versace the money to take a big step up in size and growth potential, and the time was clearly right. Santo watched as the stock of the Rome-based jewelry group Bulgari rose nearly fivefold in the two years after its July 1995 initial public offering, while Gucci's stock market listing gave the company the money it needed for a hugely successful turnaround. He understood that if they hoped to compete, fashion companies needed the sort of money that only the stock market could bring in.

After a series of arguments, Santo and Gianni came to an agreement. Rather than sinking most of the company's profits back into new shops or factories, they would pay out a larger dividend to the three siblings before they decided on taking the company public. In spring 1997, the company paid a dividend of 37 billion lire ($22 million), twice the previous year's amount. Half of the money went to Gianni. That way, he could spend his money as he pleased, without any interference from Santo.

By 1997, Versace products sold in three hundred boutiques around the world, as well as four thousand department stores. Total retail sales would top 1.7 trillion lire ($1 billion) in 1997, or about 950 billion lire ($550 million) earned directly by the company. Investment bankers reckoned that Versace was worth between $1.6 and $2 billion. The plan was to sell as much as 40 percent of the company to stock market investors, bringing $300 to $400 million to the company's coffers, and another $100 to $200 million to the three siblings personally. Half of that would end up in Gianni's pocket, to be spent as he liked.

But before giving the go-ahead, Santo got a call from an investment banker pitching a tantalizing idea: a merger with Gucci. Gucci's turnaround was one of the hottest business stories that year. Under the leadership of Domenico De Sole, an Italian-born lawyer, new management had taken a company laid low by family squabbles and made it the trendiest thing in fashion. But its success had also made it a juicy takeover target for a bigger company. De Sole was looking for a way to protect Gucci, and the banker had an idea: If Versace merged with Gucci, a core of shareholders, including the Versace family, could provide a bulwark against a hostile-takeover attempt.

Santo knew that a merger would make sense; Gucci was strong in Asia and in accessories such as handbags, while Versace's business was largely in clothes and was stronger in Europe. Santo dreamed of an Italian conglomerate big and powerful enough to compete with French fashion colossus LVMH. Giorgio Armani might even be persuaded to join, thought Santo. For months, bankers set up camp in Santo's offices, poring over the two groups' books. But in the spring of 1997, Gianni vetoed the idea. Since Gucci and Versace were roughly the same size, there was no way to engineer the deal and still keep full control. Gianni was unwilling to give up his baby. Versace, he declared, would go public on its own in the summer of 1998.

❖ V ❖

In August 1996, after the couture shows, a fully recovered Gianni took a short holiday in London. He was also planning a special treat for Zia Nora, who had never been to London. He loved to spoil Nora, flying her to the United States on the Concorde to join him for vacations in New York or Miami. He delighted in her amazement at his jet-set lifestyle, so different from her simple life in Calabria. In London, he put them up at the Dorchester and rented a Bentley, complete with a white-gloved chauffeur, to ferry the sixty-three-year-old Nora around to London's sights.

When Nora arrived at the luxury hotel, she found hanging in the closet a black evening gown, with a butterfly-shaped pin at the neck covered in diamonds.[6]

"What's this, Gianni?" she asked him in Calabrian dialect.

"You'll see," he said, smiling coyly. "I have a surprise for you this evening."

The Bentley carried Nora, Gianni, and Antonio out to Elton John's spread at Windsor, just outside London. Everyone was in good spirits, after a rare day of summery weather in London, with a bracing blue sky. Elton had planned a lavish dinner, with Hugh Grant, Elizabeth Hurley, and a surprise guest. At 8 p.m., a car pulled up. Princess Diana, who had driven herself, got out. Only days before, her divorce had been declared final with a decree absolute, and the newspapers were bulging with the news. Yet, Diana seemed happy and relaxed, and when she joined the group, the room lit up.

"Gianni, I have to apologize to you," Diana, who was dressed in a slim jacket and pantsuit, confided with a coy smile as soon as she entered the room. "I'm wearing Moschino this evening. I hope you'll forgive me!"

"Please, darling!" he replied. "Don't worry. You look wonderful." He then pulled out diamond-encrusted watches he had bought for Elton, Nora, and Princess Diana.

"What are you doing, Gianni?" Nora, who spoke no English, whispered to Gianni in dialect. "I don't need these things!" Gianni, in high spirits, laughed.

That evening, Elton John held court during dinner, entertaining the guests with jokes and the latest London gossip. *"Che bello!"* ("How beautiful!") Nora kept repeating, looking around the opulent room, understanding none of the dinner-table chatter. After the meal, everyone repaired to the living room for coffee, and the evening became more intimate and cozy. Diana sprawled on the floor with Elizabeth Hurley, confiding to the group her pain over the end of her marriage.

"How sad that such a sweet, beautiful woman like Diana feels so alone," Gianni remarked to Antonio afterward, as they went to their rooms.

The next day, Gianni, Nora, and Antonio were being driven back to London. Gianni, sitting next to his aunt, was silent for a long time. He had been mulling something since his illness, and he'd finally come to a decision.

He turned to Nora and announced that he was changing his will and would be leaving everything to Allegra. The clashes with both his siblings—the fights with Santo about money, the arguments with Donatella about the collections—had eaten away at him over the previous year. He had come to see Allegra as the future of Gianni Versace. Certainly, there was no doubt that he adored the young girl. But the decision to leave his entire fortune—including control of his business—to a child was clearly born of a fit of pique, one he must have known would hurt his siblings terribly. It showed just how deep Gianni's resentment of Donatella and Santo had become.

"What are you talking about, Gianni?" retorted Nora, clearly surprised. "Why would you leave everything to her? What about Santo?"

"Please! Santo has more money than I do!" Gianni snorted.

Two weeks later, in mid-September, Gianni went to his notary, unbeknownst to Donatella and Santo. Refusing the help of a lawyer, he sat before the notary and wrote out a two-page will in his own hand. When Gianni was done, the notary filed the document away for safekeeping. In one impulsive gesture, Gianni had changed the fate of his siblings and—most of all—the fate of his beloved niece forever, in ways that he couldn't have possibly imagined.

Later that year, Gianni stumbled badly in his relationship with Diana. With Elton's help, he convinced her to write the foreword to his latest coffee-table book, *Rock and Royalty*, with the promise that the proceeds would go to Elton's AIDS foundation. But when Gianni sent her a copy of the finished book, she was shocked to discover Gianni had interspersed photos of nude models with images of British royalty, including a shot of her own wedding. In another spread, Gianni had outdone himself: He placed a portrait of the three Versace siblings, shot by Lord Snowdon, former husband of Princess Margaret and an official royal photographer, across from a formal shot of Diana with her sons.

An official at the royal palace called a horrified Diana to register the displeasure of her former in-laws. Despite her cool relations with Charles's family, she was aghast at the idea of embarrassing them.

"Did you see what they did?" Diana lamented to a friend.

"Diana, you're naïve," he told her. "You know how Gianni is."[7]

Diana pulled out of the London party Gianni was planning to

launch the book. He was extremely upset, and immediately sent her three couture gowns as a peace gesture. To have had the princess, dressed in Versace, presenting a Versace book would have been a crowning achievement for him—and priceless publicity for his brand. After her withdrawal, he had little choice but to cancel the party. He was painfully aware that he had also caused a rift between Elton and Diana.

"I wrote her a stiff letter, and she wrote me a very stiff letter back," Elton said later. "We both sulked. . . . I phoned her, but she wouldn't take my calls."[8] The pair wouldn't speak until they met again in Milan the following summer.

❖ V ❖

On Sunday, July 6, 1997, the Ritz was buzzing. Under bright blue skies, a red carpet ran like a ribbon from the curb to a set of blue double doors just to the right of the hotel's grand main entrance, where two obelisks covered with roses sat like sentries. Red velvet ropes held back the crowd of gawkers and paparazzi who always turned up for Gianni's shows to catch a glimpse of a star or a supermodel. The stars, having stopped for a last-minute fitting at the shop on Rue du Faubourg Saint-Honoré, entered the hotel through its back entrance. Versace public relations people guided guests to their chairs in the hotel's pool area. The space held about 350 guests, but a few years earlier, Gianni's list had grown so large that the Ritz, concerned about fire regulations, insisted he hold a second show.

That year, a new generation of red-hot designers such as John Galliano and Alexander McQueen threatened to overshadow Gianni with their wild creativity and onstage antics. The previous season, Gianni's floaty bias-cut gowns seemed downright quaint compared to Galliano's Masai collars and McQueen's gilded bare breasts. Now, for the July show, the press was aflutter about what the British duo would come up with next.

During the preparation for the show, Donatella and Gianni had fought bitterly over the models, when Donatella pushed to use Karen Elson as the final model, the girl who wears the wedding dress. Gianni never liked her. "Why are you so pale?" he used to demand of

Elson, in Italian. The British girl looked blankly at him. "Why don't you go get some sun?"[9]

The night before the show, an odd incident occurred that would trouble Donatella later. She had invited Demi Moore to attend the show and threw a small dinner for her. Afterward, Moore insisted on reading Donatella's tarot cards. The two women huddled over the deck as Moore turned over each card. As she laid each card out, she saw an unsettling pattern. "I see two brothers," she told Donatella. "And I see death." Donatella laughed off the reading at the time.[10]

The next day, when the lights went up on the runway, Donatella's influence was clear. The girls wore Goth-type makeup on their pale faces, with fire-red lipstick and black eye shadow that extended up to the brow to create an angry, punched-out look. Wide black leather headbands pulled their hair from their faces. The music was ominous, switching between hard-driving house music and an eerie, chantlike dirge—none of the toe-tapping pop music of previous shows.

At twenty minutes, the show was half the length of those just five years earlier. About sixty of the eighty pieces were all black. It was Gianni's take on minimalism, with sharp, aggressive tailoring and a brooding air. Day suits had big, almost pointy shoulders and were paired with black patent leather boots. Near the end, he sent out a series of swinging baby-doll dresses in sparkling fabric. Naomi, her hair held back with a silver headband, emerged to close the show as the bride, in a short metal-mesh dress covered in crosses. A giant veil bearing a huge single cross fell to her waist, and she casually dangled a bouquet of white flowers.

Donatella pouted backstage. While she had succeeded in convincing Gianni to use mostly new girls, she hated the collection itself, finding the big shoulders and Byzantine references mired in the early 1990s. Moreover, she had been arguing in favor of dropping Naomi, that archsymbol of Versace's glamour-puss image, from Gianni's shows altogether. At the couture show, Donatella felt the supermodel looked wildly out of place amid the wan, flat-chested girls.

Gianni, however, was thrilled, singing and humming in delight. Wearing black tails over a black polo shirt, he kissed each of the girls, giving even Karen Elson a desultory peck on the cheek. His face was covered with smudges of red lipstick, but he looked tired and care-worn, with his three-day stubble and a rapidly retreating hairline. His health problems, the battles with his siblings, and the rising stress of managing his company had left him visibly aged. But despite that, Gianni was feeling stronger than he had in years, and reveled in the fact that he'd managed to regain both his health and control of his house.

After the show, Gianni and Donatella went to a private dinner with Demi Moore, Leonardo DiCaprio, and a few powerful editors and department store buyers. Ritz workers began dismantling the runway so that guests could use the pool the next morning. Much of his team, exhausted from the late nights and the stress of following Gianni, escaped, happy to crash in their hotel rooms. The next day, as usual, Gianni picked out several couture dresses to send to Diana, before going to the airport to catch the Concorde to New York—and from there to head to Miami.

thirteen

Murder

iT WAS A LITTLE AFTER 3 A.M. ON TUESDAY, JULY 15, 1997.
Gianni was wide awake. Outside, the tail end of a storm
blew away as late-night revelers made their way home from
the restaurants and clubs in the heart of South Beach. Gianni was exhausted, weary from the Paris show, but he
couldn't sleep.[1] After arriving in New York from Paris, he
and Antonio had spent several days at Gianni's new townhouse on Sixty-fourth Street near Fifth Avenue. While Gianni gave press interviews on the couture collection and met
with Richard Avedon about a new coffee-table book they
were working on together, Antonio went to the gym and saw
friends. On Thursday evening, they had flown to Miami.

Gianni, now fifty, was looking forward to two weeks of
rest at Casa Casuarina. After Miami, he and Antonio would

join Elton John at his new villa outside of Nice, in the south of France. Gianni had been pressing Donatella to let him take Allegra to Miami with him, but she had refused. He'd spent the previous couple of days working in the morning and relaxing with friends in the afternoon. After a dinner of rice salad and fruit, Gianni went to the media room, a large salon where he usually worked, and faxed sketches and instructions for the fall collection to his headquarters in Milan.[2] At 10 p.m., he was dozing in front of the TV. Antonio gently woke him.[3]

"Why don't you go to bed?" he said. "You're exhausted." Gianni assented and headed upstairs to his bedroom. It would be the last time Antonio would see Gianni.

By 3:30 a.m., Gianni had risen from his ultra-king-sized mahogany bed. On his nightstand was the June edition of *Vanity Fair*, carrying the long profile on Donatella. Gianni went downstairs to the media room to make calls to his office in Milan, where it was already 9 a.m. He spoke with Franco Lussana, a longtime friend who was in charge of sourcing fabrics for Gianni's clothes. Gianni asked him to find a type of jersey that he had in mind for his next collection. After about twenty minutes on the phone, he padded back upstairs to his bedroom for a few more hours' sleep.

But at 6 a.m., he was awake again. With the first light, he saw that it would be a hot, clear day, a welcome break from the overcast weather they'd had since arriving in Miami. He called Milan again to check that Lussana had found the fabric he was looking for.

"I haven't had time," Lussana told Gianni. "I'm running to get a flight to Rome. Donatella wants me to help with the show tonight."[4]

Gianni exploded. "Why are you bothering with that?" he said. "Why are you wasting time in Rome? My sister always has to be the princess!"

He immediately called Donatella, grilling her about the Rome show. He made some other calls and then phoned his sister again around 8:15 a.m. This time, Donatella didn't take the call. Gianni pulled on gray-and-white-checked shorts, a black T-shirt, and black Versace sport sandals, and grabbed his wallet, which held nearly $1,200 in cash as well as a yellowed picture of the Virgin of Medjugorje, and the large key to the tall wrought-iron front gates to the mansion.[5] The blind eye of a security camera that had never been turned on watched him as he stepped out onto Ocean Drive. Carlos, his groundskeeper, was coming back with the morning newspapers.

"Good morning, Mr. Versace," said Carlos, dressed in black shorts and a black shirt with buttons bearing the medusa logo. "I have the newspapers here. Do you want me to go get you something?"

"No, that's all right," Gianni replied. "I'll go myself. I'll be back in two minutes."[6]

Gianni walked south on Ocean Drive, its western side dotted with cafés and open-air restaurants, its seaward side a boardwalk with a grassy park that runs parallel to the beach. It was nearly deserted at that hour, as clubbers slept off the excesses of the night before. Gianni headed for the News Café. The News Café, open twenty-four hours a day, was a fixture on South Beach, its leafy sidewalk patio a popular spot from which to watch South Beach's beau monde skate by. Club kids and club kittens would meet there to plan a night out at the clubs, and circle back in the wee hours for a nightcap. Around dawn, the manager switched off the blaring rock music and put on softer pop for the early morning coffee-and-newspaper crowd. When he was in South Beach, Gianni stopped by nearly every morning to browse through the scores of American and international newspapers and magazines sold there.

When Gianni arrived, a handful of early birds were lingering over their breakfast. He bought a coffee and perused the racks of magazines. He quickly chose five: a *New Yorker* magazine with a cover article on gays working at Chrysler, a *People* magazine featuring Ivana Trump's divorce, and the latest editions of *Vogue*, *Entertainment Weekly*, and the Spanish-language *Newsweek*. The clerk slipped them into a brown paper bag. At 8:40 a.m., Gianni thanked her and headed back to the mansion.

❖ V ❖

Andrew Cunanan watched as Gianni made his way down Ocean Drive. Wearing dark knee-length shorts, a loose gray tank top that hung past his waist, and a black baseball hat pulled low on his face, he sat on a grassy rise on the boardwalk, just opposite Casa Casuarina. The area was virtually deserted except for two homeless men sleeping nearby. Cunanan, likely having monitored the Versace mansion, knew that Gianni typically took an early morning walk to buy newspapers alone.

The twenty-seven-year-old had arrived in South Beach on May 12, 1997, and checked into the Normandy Plaza Hotel, a thirty-six-dollars-a-night hotel on the wrong end of Miami Beach, at Collins Avenue and Sixty-ninth Street, four miles north of Casa Casuarina. It was a garish place with a hot-pink exterior, purple trim, and a sign out front advertising "Weekly Rates." Cunanan gave a false name—Kurt De Mars—and a fictitious home address in Paris. For two months, he had spent his days in a tiny room that contained a small television and a linoleum kitchenette, which he kept neat and tidy. He paid cash, and never bothered to have the phone turned on. He wouldn't be receiving any calls or visitors.

He had whiled away the days in his room, reading books such as *How the Irish Saved Civilization* and thick tomes on art history, and flipping through gay porn magazines such as *Ram, Urge, Hard,* and *XXX Showcase*.[7] He had also bought the June issue of *Vanity Fair*.[8] He declined the staff's offers of room service, venturing out instead for food at Miami Subs or McDonald's. Each night at about 10 p.m., Cunanan hit the gay clubs, including the Warsaw Ballroom, Gianni's favorite haunt, and would stay out until dawn.[9]

By early July, after two months in Miami Beach, Cunanan was running out of money. A week earlier, he had gone to the Casa de Oro Pawn Shop near the Normandy to pawn a $50 U.S. eagle gold coin. He showed the clerk his passport—with his real name—as identification and gave the Normandy as his address. The clerk handed him $190 in cash.

"You have three months to get the coin back," the clerk told Cunanan.

"Don't worry," Cunanan replied. "I'll be back before then."[10]

That weekend, Cunanan skipped out on his room at the Normandy. He would spend the next few days living out of a red pickup truck parked a few blocks from Gianni's home. On Friday evening, he went to Twist, a popular gay club that sat a couple of blocks west of Casa Casuarina. There, a bartender took note of Cunanan when he ordered only a glass of water and then bummed a cigarette—classic signs of a hustler or a prostitute.[11] After a while, Cunanan struck up a conversation with a young guy named Brad.

"What do you do for a living?" Brad asked.

"I'm a serial killer," Cunanan replied. When Brad gave him a strange look, Cunanan laughed, saying he was really in investment banking. Later when the two were dancing, Cunanan kept grabbing and rubbing up against Brad. The pair kissed, but then Cunanan broke away and disappeared into the crowd.[12]

On Tuesday morning, as the sun grew stronger and burned off the early morning haze, Cunanan waited patiently in front of Casa Casuarina, clutching a black backpack by his side. After he spotted Gianni on the other side of Ocean Drive, approaching the mansion, he got up suddenly, startling a man walking his dog, and pulled a .40-caliber Taurus handgun out of his backpack, holding it tightly by his right hip. He crossed the street quickly, keeping slightly behind Gianni so that he wouldn't be noticed. Gianni paused briefly to smile at a blond woman nearby who had clearly recognized him. As Gianni slipped his key into the lock on the iron gates, Cunanan climbed the five smooth marble steps behind him. His raised the gun, stretching his arm out taut until the tip of the barrel just about touched the back of Gianni's head.[13]

❖ V ❖

Andrew Cunanan grew up in Rancho Bernardo, California, a suburban community north of San Diego, the youngest of four children. His mother, MaryAnn, an intensely religious woman, stayed at home to raise Andrew and his siblings, while his father, Modesto Cunanan, a Philippine-born U.S. Navy veteran, worked as a stockbroker. Cunanan was a precocious, gifted child whose parents scrimped to send him to an elite prep school. As a teenager, Cunanan discovered that he was gay and came to terms with it without much evident angst. He developed a flamboyant personality, once turning up at a school event in a red leather jumpsuit, reportedly a gift from a much older man. He relished being the center of attention, tossing off witticisms and flattering friends. In 1987, his graduating high school class voted him "Least Likely to Be Forgotten." His yearbook quote was *"Après nous le deluge"* ("After us, the flood").[14]

HOUSE OF VERSACE

Cunanan enrolled in college in San Diego, but he grew bored and dropped out after his freshman year. He decided to follow his father to the Philippines, where Modesto had fled to escape allegations of embezzlement. But once he arrived there, Cunanan found his father living in squalid conditions. Disgusted, he immediately returned home. In separation papers filed soon afterward, MaryAnn Cunanan claimed Modesto had left the family destitute and homeless. In the early 1990s, Cunanan drifted to San Francisco and developed various smooth-talking personae that obscured his modest background. By his midtwenties, Cunanan had developed very expensive tastes, sporting luxury watches, Ferragamo shoes, and Armani suits. During one visit to Los Angeles, he spent nearly three thousand dollars to stay a few nights at the Chateau Marmont, a luxury hotel in West Hollywood frequented by celebrities. He carried around a thick wad of cash with him. He would eat only in the best restaurants, often treating friends to lavish sushi or French dinners that would cost more than a thousand dollars, including a generous tip. Once, at dinner with a group of friends, the waiter brought him a wine list and he waved him away, saying, "Just bring me the most expensive bottle you have."[15] In 1996, Cunanan had taken a long trip to Europe, staying in a string of luxury hotels, such as the Grand Hotel in Florence and the Gritti Palace Venice. He also made a stop in Milan, and while there is no evidence he encountered Gianni Versace there, he seemed the kind of man who would frequent the Versace shops worldwide.

Friends were puzzled about where Cunanan's money came from. His only job seems to have been as a manager of a Thrifty drugstore. Cunanan regaled his friends with wild stories to explain the money, claiming, for instance, that he came from a wealthy Philippine family that owned sugar plantations. He spun tales of a former wife and a child, his stories growing ever more far-fetched. He became an enigma, a blend of so many tall tales that his friends couldn't tell truth from fiction. The truth was that Cunanan, with handsome dark features and a slim body, had learned how to attract the attention of older men, manipulating them into buying him extravagant gifts and keeping him in high style. Even his mother would later describe him as a "high-class homosexual prostitute."

But early in 1997, Cunanan, usually jovial and outgoing, began to change. He gained about twenty pounds, started to drink heavily, and stopped looking after his appearance.[16] He withdrew from his social circle and became shaky and hyperactive. A few friends suspected he was using crystal meth, which was becoming popular in some urban gay circles.

On April 25, 1997, Cunanan flew on a one-way ticket from San Diego to Minneapolis to visit friends. He stayed with a former lover, thirty-three-year-old architect David Madson. A couple of evenings later, he arranged for twenty-eight-year-old Jeffrey Trail, a U.S. Naval Academy graduate whom Cunanan had befriended when Trail was stationed in San Diego several years earlier, to meet him at Madson's apartment. At about 9:30 p.m., neighbors heard loud voices coming from the apartment. "Get the fuck out!" someone shouted. The walls started shaking, and they heard thudding sounds. Two days later, police broke into the apartment and found Trail's body wrapped in a carpet. He had been beaten to death with a claw hammer. They also found a nylon gym bag with Cunanan's name on it, as well as an empty holster for a .40-caliber Taurus handgun that had been issued to Trail when he was a cadet at the California Highway Patrol Academy. Ten rounds of bullets were missing. The next week, police found Madson's body in a nearby marsh. He had been shot once in the head with a .40-caliber gun.

Cunanan stole Trail's car and started driving. On May 3, 1997, he arrived in Chicago, where he slipped into the suburban home of Lee Miglin, a wealthy older businessman. He tortured Miglin before slashing his throat with a saw blade and puncturing his chest repeatedly with pruning shears. He then bound the dead man's head in masking tape and wrapped his body in plastic. Cunanan stole Miglin's black 1994 Lexus and headed east. He left behind a half-eaten ham sandwich, a fake gun, and a razor with stubble on it.

Cunanan stopped in New York City for two days, where he found accommodations in a gay bathhouse. But on May 9, 1997, panicked that the police were tracking him via the car phone's transmitter in Miglin's Lexus, he left New York. Driving aimlessly, he arrived in a small town in New Jersey, where he shot William Reese, the caretaker of a cemetery, and stole his red 1995 Chevrolet pickup truck. Two days later, on May 12, he checked into the Normandy Hotel in

Miami Beach. Cunanan had killed four men in less than two weeks. As he settled in at the Normandy, the television program *America's Most Wanted* ran a piece on him. A few weeks later, on June 12, the FBI put him on their most-wanted list; on the same day, he parked the red pickup in a city garage a few blocks from Casa Casuarina.[17] Cunanan moved freely around Miami Beach, going largely unnoticed; his Latin appearance let him blend in easily. Moreover, he was scrawnier now than in the pictures on the posters.

At first, he paid for his room at the Normandy on a daily basis, but later he switched to monthly payments and asked for a better room. He carried a dark backpack everywhere he went. He wasn't talkative—the Normandy staff nicknamed him "The Hindu"—but was friendly when someone tried to engage him. His appearance was tidy; he kept his fingernails neatly manicured. On July 11, 1997, on one of his trips to a fast-food restaurant near the Normandy, an employee who had seen Cunanan's photo on *America's Most Wanted* recognized him. He called the police, but by the time they arrived, Cunanan was gone.[18]

❖ V ❖

Four days later, as Gianni Versace slipped the key into the lock of the gates of Casa Casuarina, Cunanan pulled the trigger. He first shot Gianni on the left side of his neck, just below his ear. The bullet severed Gianni's spinal cord and exited on the opposite side of his neck. Incredibly, it then ricocheted off the iron gate, and a fragment hit a mourning dove, which fell into the gutter in front of the house. As soon as Gianni hit the ground, crumpled on his left side, Cunanan shot him again, this time hitting him in the face, just to the right of his nose. This bullet lodged in his skull.

Antonio had gotten up just before 8:30 a.m. and gone downstairs for breakfast.

"Where's Mr. Versace?" he asked Thomas, the house manager.

"He's gone to get newspapers," Thomas replied.

As Antonio sat in the dining room eating breakfast, their close friend Lazaro Quintana arrived early for a 9 a.m. tennis date with Antonio. Quintana leaned over and stole a piece of pineapple from Antonio's plate, when they suddenly heard two loud bangs. Antonio ran to the window. He saw Gianni through the half-open gates, lying on the steps. "No! No!" Antonio screamed. The two men bolted out of the mansion, but Quintana reached Gianni first. He was slumped on his side, and blood was pouring from his head down the cream-colored steps to the sidewalk. Small bits of brain matter were scattered nearby. The paper bag with his magazines lay on the top step, near his black sunglasses.

Quintana checked to see if Gianni was breathing, but he couldn't tell. Antonio was right behind him. When he saw Gianni, he cried out, "*Non e' possibile!* It can't be!" He crumpled on the top step, sinking into a fetal position near Gianni's feet.[19] He clutched the gates, with his face turned away from Gianni, rocking and sobbing hysterically.

Quintana looked up at the blond woman who had recognized Gianni a few minutes before. "Did you see who did this?" he blurted. She nodded and pointed at Cunanan, who was only about a block north, walking away calmly with a splayed, ducklike gait.

"You bastard!" Quintana yelled at him. "Stop!"

Cunanan sped up, continuing another block before turning left onto Thirteenth Street, away from the ocean. Quintana chased him until Cunanan ducked into an alley. Quintana followed him, but when Cunanan turned to look back, Quintana could clearly see the black gun still in Cunanan's right hand. He remembered having seen a police car at a car accident nearby and ran to get a cop. He pointed at the alley where Cunanan had disappeared. As the cops pursued Cunanan, Quintana returned to the house.[20]

Meanwhile, a staff member in Casa Casuarina had called 911. Four minutes later, an ambulance arrived. The paramedics lowered Gianni carefully to the sidewalk. They found no vital signs, and his left pupil was fixed and dilated. His right eye had been destroyed by the bullet to his face. They wrapped a white brace around his neck and attached five electrodes to his chest, frantically pumping his chest as they loaded him into the ambulance. A man who had been walking his dog snapped Polaroid pictures of Gianni on the litter. Antonio tried to follow Gianni into the ambulance but the police wouldn't let him go, saying they needed his statement to get a description of the shooter.[21]

HOUSE OF VERSACE

Within fifteen minutes, Gianni arrived at Jackson Memorial Hospital. A local television cameraman was standing outside the hospital, waiting for a photo op of a Miami girl who was awaiting a kidney transplant. When he saw the paramedics quickly wheel in a man with his face covered in blood, he filmed it, figuring it was the latest victim of Miami's rampant gun crime.

At 9:20 a.m., doctors declared Gianni dead. Ninety minutes later, the hospital chaplain came to give him last rites. By that time, the footage of Gianni taken by the local cameraman was beaming around the world. [22]

❖ V ❖

Cunanan ran to the parking garage just two blocks from Casa Casuarina, shed his shorts and T-shirt, which were sweat-soaked and spattered with blood, and dropped them on the ground next to the pickup truck. He changed into fresh clothes and ran down a back stairwell, heading north. According to some, he had planned to escape in the truck but was spooked by a police car that happened to be in the parking garage just then, investigating an accident.

Within a half hour, police found the truck and, with it, a trove of clues about who had shot Gianni. There was Miglin's wallet, William Reese's identification, movie stubs from two movie theaters in New York, two passports—one in Cunanan's name—and several .40-caliber bullets.[23] It looked as if Cunanan had slept in the truck. There were clothes strewn all over the seats and floor, as well as a toiletry bag, a plastic bucket with taco chips, and Popsicle sticks.

Quintana and two staff members managed to get Antonio back into the house, virtually carrying him away from the bloody steps. Someone gave him a sedative to calm him. One staff member came back out to take Gianni's key out of the lock. A little later, another one got a hose to rinse the blood off the steps.

That afternoon, the police took Antonio to the station to answer questions and look at a lineup of photos. Still dressed in tennis shorts, Antonio was in a daze, shivering in the air-conditioned office as he responded to their queries until 10 p.m. Elton John called the mansion several times during the day from the south of France, nearly hysterical. As soon as he heard the news, he hired extra bodyguards for his villa there. "How could this happen?" he cried to the friend who was fielding the calls that were pouring in. "My two best friends—John Lennon and Gianni. I just don't get it. I just don't understand!"[24]

❖ V ❖

During the week between Gianni's murder and his funeral, the largest manhunt in U.S. history was launched. When it was discovered that Cunanan had been on the loose for nearly three months, local and federal authorities fielded a barrage of critical questions from the press and politicians. But the FBI and police departments in the three states where the first murders had occurred had struggled to coordinate their efforts, failing to exploit the publicity generated by Cunanan's previous crimes. By then, the killer was moving freely around Miami Beach, hustling as a prostitute and smoking crack with a junkie who had also taken up residence in the Normandy. Despite early tips that Cunanan might head south from Chicago, drawn to Miami's large and prominent gay community, the police there did remarkably little to find him. They posted just a few most-wanted flyers in public spots around Miami Beach and made little effort to elicit the help of local gay groups in watching for Cunanan at the city's clubs.

It took the death of an international celebrity to spark a massive response by the FBI, the Miami Beach police, and Florida state authorities, besieged as they were by enormous media coverage from around the world. More than two hundred agents in Florida joined the chase. They all struggled to sort through the thousands of tips flooding police hotlines, searching for real leads among the calls from psychics, devil-worshipping cults, and other crackpots.

In the hours after Gianni's death, police finally canvassed Miami Beach's gay scene, visiting bathhouses, video clubs, sex shops, and nightclubs, including the Warsaw, to distribute flyers and business cards. The day after the murder, they got a good tip when the owner of the pawnshop where Cunanan had sold the gold coin reported the transaction. Within hours, police were searching Room 205 at the Normandy, the address Cunanan had given the pawnshop, but they found no clues of his current whereabouts.

At the same time, police were grasping for a connection between Gianni and Cunanan. They interrogated Antonio for hours about Gianni's personal habits. Knowing that Cunanan had worked as a male prostitute, they pressed Antonio as to whether Gianni might have met his killer in the past. Highly distraught and under intense pressure from the police, Antonio finally admitted that he and Gianni had hired prostitutes in New York and Miami, but he claimed they had stopped the practice years earlier and had never encountered Cunanan.

The day after the murder, however, Maureen Orth, a writer for *Vanity Fair* who had already been preparing an article on Cunanan and his first four killings, gave a series of television interviews claiming she'd uncovered a possible connection. She said that in 1990 Cunanan had weaseled an invitation to a San Francisco reception thrown for Gianni, who had designed the costumes for a performance by the San Francisco Opera. According to accounts relayed by Cunanan's friends to Orth, Gianni surveyed the guests at the reception and quickly approached Cunanan.

"I know you," he said. "Lago di Como, no?"

"That's right," Cunanan responded, clearly thrilled. "Thank you for remembering, Signor Versace." Orth later reported Cunanan had never been to Italy, much less to Gianni's grand villa on Lake Como.[25] Cunanan, a celebrity hound, frequently boasted that he personally knew Gianni, but few of his friends, accustomed to Cunanan's wild lies, had ever believed him. For Cunanan, Gianni represented all that he would never be—a gay success story, glamorous, rich, and venerated around the world.

In 1996 and early 1997, as Cunanan's drug use apparently escalated and he became increasingly deranged, he began to rail against Gianni. Speaking with a friend on his way to the airport for his one-way flight from San Diego to Minneapolis, the site of his first murder, Cunanan called Gianni "the worst designer ever," adding that he was "pretentious, pompous and ostentatious."[26]

When Orth's claims hit the news, the family and Antonio vehemently denied that Gianni had ever crossed paths with Cunanan. Their denial, however, did little to rein in one of the most lurid rumors: that Gianni had been HIV-positive and had passed the virus to Cunanan, who murdered the designer out of revenge.

Santo and Donatella, as accustomed as they were to the limelight, were horrified by the media frenzy unfolding in the United States, where Cunanan's murder spree was attracting the sort of twenty-four-hour coverage attention hitherto afforded only to O. J. Simpson and JonBenét Ramsey. The tabloids published lurid details of Cunanan's alleged involvement in everything from violent S&M sex rings to private clubs of closeted gay millionaires. Newspapers and television programs offered thousands of dollars to even the most tenuous of Cunanan's friends in exchange for interviews or personal items belonging to the alleged murderer. The FBI put Cunanan's mother under protection to escape the media horde that surrounded her house. While Gianni was never implicated in Cunanan's sordid past, the dirt dug up by bottom-feeding television and tabloid journalists quickly soiled the reputations of both the designer and the gay world he had proudly represented.

For a week, Cunanan evaded the massive manhunt. Then, the day after Gianni's Milan funeral, Fernando Carreira, a seventy-one-year-old Portuguese immigrant who looked after properties for absentee owners, and his wife came to check on a baby-blue houseboat berthed on Indian Creek, the narrow strip of water that runs the length of Miami Beach. The houseboat sat at Fifty-second Street, about four miles north of the Versace mansion. It was owned by Torsten Reineck, a German businessman who managed a gay bathhouse in Las Vegas. According to local legend, the houseboat had in the past served as a hideaway for rich gay men who picked up hustlers at a cruising park nearby.

When Carreira entered the houseboat around midafternoon, he immediately sensed something was wrong. The lights were all on and the drapes, which he'd left open on his last visit, were drawn. Cushions from the sofa had been placed on the floor to make a bed, and a pair of sandals lay nearby. As Carreira pulled a handgun out of his waistband, he nervously whispered to his wife, "Somebody has been sleeping here. Someone is here right now."

As he began to move slowly through the house, a shot rang out from the master bedroom upstairs. Carreira and his wife scrambled to flee the boat and called the police. Within minutes, officers flooded the area, a swarm of media hard on their heels. TV helicopters hovered overhead, broadcasting the raid on the houseboat live. When the evening news went on the air shortly afterward, the newscasts cut between scenes of the houseboat raid and clips of Gianni's star-studded funeral in Milan the day before.

After a slow and careful entry, the SWAT team made its way upstairs to the houseboat's master bedroom. There they found Cunanan dead. Sporting several days' growth of beard and dressed in a red T-shirt and madras shorts, he was sprawled on the bed in a pool of blood with his eyes still open. He had shot himself through the mouth, sending blood flowing from his ears, nose, and mouth. In his hand lay the gun that he had stolen from his first victim, Jeff Trail, a single spent bullet casing lying on the floor nearby. It was the gun that had killed Gianni.

As the police searched the houseboat, it became clear that Cunanan had been hiding there for days. In the fridge sat a partially eaten plate of food, half a loaf of bread, and a bottle of orange soda. In the living room, *Vogue* magazines, rubbing alcohol, Q-tips, and a bottle of prescription medicine in the name of Torsten Reineck were strewn on the coffee table.

In Italy, Donatella and Santo stayed in constant phone contact with police in Miami most of the night, receiving updates on the raid on the houseboat. At 5 a.m. in Miami—11 a.m. in Italy—the police finally told them that a fingerprint analysis proved that the dead body on the boat was that of their brother's killer. The hunt was over.

But Cunanan's death did little to quash the increasingly wild rumors as to the true circumstances of Gianni's murder. The dead dove found next to Gianni was taken as a signature of a mafia hit, reviving talk that the Versaces had connections to Calabrian organized crime families. (An autopsy of the bird showed that it had indeed died after a fragment of one of the bullets that hit Gianni ricocheted off the mansion's iron gates and struck it in the head.) To Donatella and Santo's horror, the mafia stories were quickly gaining currency.

"Maybe this assassination will shed some light on Mr. Versace's business," Pierre Bergé, Yves Saint Laurent's business partner, remarked to journalists just hours after the murder. "I have never understood how there could be so many empty [Versace] stores. Perhaps

this event will lift a part of the mystery. In a way I am not surprised."[27]

Santo was furious at Bergé's remarks. Then, within days of the
murder, Frank Monte, an Australian private investigator, went to the
press with an extraordinary claim: In a furtive predawn meeting
the year before in Central Park, Gianni had hired him for protection
against mafia threats. To prove it, Monte brandished a note from Gianni on Versace corporate letterhead.

Monte claimed that Gianni feared for his life because a former
Versace employee—known in the underworld as Guglielmo Gat-
torini or Johnny the Cat—had stolen company books showing the
family was laundering money for the Calabrian mafia, and he was
trying to extort money from Gianni for their return. Monte's claims
were near-comical. He later went so far as to allege that Gianni's siblings might have been involved with the murder and that Cunanan
had actually been killed before Gianni, his body frozen and then
moved to the houseboat in an elaborate ruse. Despite the outrageousness of his story, the media—hungry for a new angle in the Miami
murder—leaped on it. Monte soon had book and film deals.

Later, conspiracy theorists would declare as suspect the family's
rush to cremate Gianni's body and their successful appeal to have the
state of Florida seal Gianni's autopsy—reviving the question as to
whether Gianni had been HIV-positive. When in a book on Cunanan,
Orth quoted a Miami Beach police officer as claiming that the autopsy showed Gianni to be HIV-positive, the family released a letter
from Gianni's doctor in Milan denying it.[28] Antonio D'Amico also denied that Gianni had the virus. (Cunanan's autopsy revealed that he
was actually HIV-negative, bursting the theory that he killed Gianni
because the designer had infected him.)

But it was a series of shady characters associated with the houseboat that most troubled investigators. Inside the boat they had found a
fake driver's license and passport from Sealand, a tiny island off the
coast of Britain. Both were in the name of Matthias Ruehl. The police
then discovered that Reineck was wanted in Germany for tax fraud. A
few days after Cunanan's death, Reineck told authorities that he wasn't,
in fact, the owner of the houseboat, claiming he'd sold it to Ruehl
in early June. Authorities became suspicious and began looking in to

the two Germans, but before they could discover much, both Reineck and Ruehl fled to Germany.

In early August, an Italian named Enrico Forti came to the Miami Beach police claiming he was in fact the real owner of the houseboat and producing papers to prove it. Around the same time, FBI officers in Las Vegas received vague reports that Cunanan had frequented the gay bathhouse Reineck owned there, but they never fully substantiated the connection. Soon afterward, Forti was arrested and later convicted in the murder of a wealthy hotelier in Spain. As they dug further, some of the investigators on the case came to suspect that Cunanan had known of the existence of the houseboat through some connection with Forti, Reineck, or Ruehl.

But they were never able to connect Cunanan to Gianni or to the putative owners of the houseboat, despite more than a thousand interviews conducted during their investigation of Cunanan's crimes. Burned by criticism of their Keystone Kops–like chase for Cunanan, both the FBI and local police were determined to close the case. When the final report came out in December 1997, it concluded that Cunanan's murder of Gianni was the desperate final act of an unbalanced man. The police found no evidence of a connection to organized crime. In January 1998, the city of Miami Beach ordered the houseboat demolished, happy to be rid of what had become a macabre tourist attraction.

Over the next several years, the Versace family would spend 2.2 billion lire (more than $1 million) in lawyers' fees to convince a court to quash the book by Monte, the alleged private investigator. (The film—low-budget and little-noticed—was later made.) They also successfully sued at least one major UK newspaper that repeated the claims of mafia connections. But such verdicts were small victories for Santo and Donatella despite a massive police investigation that put to rest the allegations. Though the rumors were unfounded, they could never entirely erase the taint of alleged organized crime connections from the Versace image no matter how many high-priced lawyers they hired.

Given the lack of apparent motive, pop criminal psychologists have long speculated about why Cunanan targeted Gianni. Some claimed he was motivated by a desire to finally become famous, driven by a deranged narcissism that had been building since the first murder in April. After killing three more people, perhaps Cunanan knew he was trapped and decided to go out in a blaze of glory, taking with him a man whom he both idolized and loathed. By the time the caretaker arrived at the door of the blue houseboat, Cunanan had only four bullets left in his gun and must have known from news reports that Miami was swarming with police searching for him. He had little chance at escape.

But in the end, Santo and Donatella would never have the closure of knowing exactly why Cunanan had targeted their brother. Gianni's killer would take the motivation for the murder to his grave.

fourteen

Underststudy on the Stage

*a*s THE LAST ORGAN PEALS OF THE MEMORIAL SERVICE FADED and the final fashion luminaries and celebrities left the Duomo di Milano to head for the airport, the enormity of their loss washed over Donatella and Santo like a cold wave. Their adult lives had been built around their brother, defined entirely by his talent, fame, and ambition. Ironically, Gianni, Donatella, and Santo had always avoided flying in airplanes together in the belief that the company would be lost if deprived of the trio. But the truth was that Gianni was the only one who counted. His was the last word in family disputes; his opinion was the one that trumped all others in big decisions. The fierce family ties that bound the three actually relied on the force of his outsized personality, with Donatella and Santo dutifully playing the supporting roles assigned them. The company, in turn, was little more than an extension of their family dynamic.

Gianni's sudden absence left a chasm that would quickly overwhelm his siblings, still reeling from the pain and shock of their brother's violent death. Santo immediately grasped the gravity of Gianni's loss, both for the family's integrity and the company's fortunes. But the ever-capable elder brother who took care of everything was now facing a problem that even he couldn't fix.

For Donatella, Gianni's death meant a brutal end to an extended adolescence. In the last years of Gianni's life, she'd been agitating for her brother to treat her as an equal instead of like a spoiled kid sister or blithe company mascot. Little did she realize how much Gianni's personality and talent had shielded her from her own personal defects and demons. As the world's attention fell on her in the wake of Gianni's death, Donatella felt like an actress in a film, forced to play the role of the dignified, responsible adult, even as she felt utterly alone and lost.

❖ V ❖

In the midst of mourning Gianni, Donatella and Santo had to quickly show Versace employees, retailers, and rivals that they were in control of their brother's company. In the days between Gianni's death and the Mass at the Duomo, Santo and Donatella briefly considered hiring an outside designer to replace their brother; they even drew up a short list of names that included Karl Lagerfeld. Very quickly, however, they agreed that Donatella would step into Gianni's shoes. But even as Versace's spokeswoman drafted the communiqué announcing the decision, Donatella felt like a fraud.

Donatella realized the immensity of her task the very night of the memorial service. After the Mass, she retreated to her office in Via Gesù with Julie Mannion, an executive at Keeble Cavaco & Duka, Inc., a prominent New York PR firm that for years helped stage the Versace runway shows. Mannion, a veteran who worked with a slate of top houses, helped write out a calendar for each of Versace's upcoming collections, from the purchase of the fabrics to the ordering of final runway samples.

The calendars drove home to Donatella just how much Gianni

had done, even during his illness. A classic control freak, Gianni had checked every press release, every licensed product, and every order for new fabric. Other fashion companies might have split responsibilities into clear divisions and departments, but Gianni had still tried to run Versace as a scrappy one-man show. He liked having a small, tightly knit design team who could come up with shopwindows one day and a new skirt the next. He was the one to decide which ad images to run in the United States or France to coincide with the delivery of a dress or suit he wanted to push that season. He had carried so many details around in his head that his sudden absence created a thousand loose ends Donatella had to tie together—and quickly.

To manage everything, she needed a far larger group than Gianni had relied on. Together she and Mannion made plans to assemble separate teams for the couture, men's, and women's lines, as well as for Versus and the other brands. She shied away from using her brother's designers, perhaps aware that she could never live up to Gianni in their minds, and branded them passé and out of touch. "We need young blood here!" she told an assistant. "I want to work with young people, not all these old fogies." Many of Gianni's assistants, already grieving for their charismatic boss and indeed doubtful of his sister's abilities, were hurt and stung by her words.

Soon after the funeral, Donatella, Paul, and their children fled the ongoing media barrage and flew to Necker Island, the seventy-four-acre private island in the British Virgin Islands owned by UK magnate Richard Branson. The island, which accommodated only twenty-four people at a time at a cost of at least twelve thousand dollars per day, was a popular hideaway among the Versaces' celebrity friends, including Sting and Princess Diana. Guests slept in Indonesian-style bedrooms under white canopies of mosquito netting. (Meanwhile, Santo retreated with his family to an island in Greece.)

But the sybaritic setting offered Donatella little rest. Throughout the month, Donatella fielded résumés of design candidates and conducted phone interviews. The next runway show, the spring-summer collection, was scheduled for October 9, 1997. Before leaving for Miami, Gianni had worked up some rough sketches and ordered the fabrics—he was going to revisit the Prince of Wales fabrics he'd revolutionized in the 1980s—but most of the collection still had to be completed. Donatella had to have her team in place by the end of August if she hoped to have the collection finished in time for the show.

With a free hand, Donatella could now push Versace in the direction she had fruitlessly championed in battles with Gianni, starting with the hiring of a new team. She filled the atelier with young foreign designers fresh out of such prestigious fashion schools as Central Saint Martins College of Art and Design in London. These edgy young Brits and Americans, many in their early twenties, venerated the now-reigning minimalist look: Prada's prim dresses, the eccentric clothes by new Belgian designers such as Olivier Theyskens, and the sharply tailored, ultraslim men's suits by Dior's new designer Hedi Slimane. For them, Gianni's designs looked baroque. Very few of them had ever worn his clothes.

Donatella then drafted stylists who were the leading champions of the minimalist wave, ones who had helped stage Prada's and Jil Sander's runway shows and had set the same tone in the ad campaigns and editorial shoots they put together for influential magazines such as *Vogue* and *Harper's Bazaar*. She summoned the group to Milan to start work the last Saturday of August. Some of her new assistants turned up in the atelier in the slouchy fashion uniform of the moment—cargo pants, tennis shoes, and quirky T-shirts. Donatella had hired them to co-opt their funky design sense, but she drew a line on their wardrobe choices. "You can't dress like that here!" she barked at one startled new hire. "Go down to Prada or wherever you want, but get some proper clothes. Don't come back if you're not in heels."

Early that Sunday, Donatella and her new designers arrived in the office to the news that Princess Diana had died during the night in a grisly car crash in Paris, as she was being chased by a pack of paparazzi. The group spent the day huddled around the television watching updates from France and the United Kingdom. On stands in the atelier lay the couture dresses that Gianni had put aside for Diana just six weeks earlier. Versace seamstresses had been applying the finishing touches in order to send them to the princess after her summer holiday. Donatella, badly shaken by the news, faxed Prince Charles a personal note of condolence and made plans to fly to London for the funeral the next weekend. Gianni and Diana, two of the early masters—and targets—of the new media age, had died just weeks apart; the voracious interest in their deaths marked a turning point in the sort of nonstop tabloid television coverage that would soon become routine.

As soon as Donatella's new group got back to work, the first problems emerged. She and a prominent stylist she had hired were scanning a large board that held stapled swatches of the Prince of Wales fabric that Gianni had chosen. The British stylist twisted his face at Gianni's choice. "How sad!" he commented wryly. He then took a pair of scissors and began slashing at a sample dress to create a frayed, edgy look.

"But Gianni's woman is a sexy woman!" Donatella protested. Members of Gianni's old team, aghast at the stylist's work, watched as the two debated intensely in English. Later, when one of them cautiously questioned Donatella about whether to follow the stylist's direction, she said, "Just go ahead and let him do this for the time being. I'll fix it later."

But it was already clear that Donatella was wholly unprepared to step into the role of leader of a badly shaken company. In her brother's house, she had always played the role of the friend, the carefree muse, the accessorizer, the office confidante. Now she had to become the boss, commanding respect and exuding confidence in her decisions. She was painfully aware that everyone—her brother's loyalists inside the company, the fashion world, Versace's competitors—was watching her, skeptical that the kid sister could step into her brother's shoes. At meetings with her designers in the atelier, she looked like a tiny, frightened bird. She spoke in a quiet voice that her team struggled to hear and was so nervous that she trembled at times. Some members of her team had to resist the urge to scoop her up in a hug to comfort her. "She was like a little baby," recalled one longtime associate. "You just wanted to hug her right there."[1]

She struggled to remember what her brother had taught her during his illness, but she was too overwhelmed to think straight. Moreover, she felt trapped. If she fell back on Gianni's well-worn themes, critics would blast her for resting on her brother's laurels. Her instinct told her to strike out in a new modern path that would set her apart from Gianni, but she lacked a clear, compelling vision, and if she strayed too far from the classic Gianni look, those same critics would blast her for denying her brother's legacy. She had excelled as a brilliant sounding board and editor for her brother's ideas, but she lacked the creativity and ingenuity to conjure up her own ideas from scratch.

As the weeks before her first solo show slipped by, Donatella's moods varied wildly. Some days she was calm and determined to master her new role, cutting through the myriad decisions before her as if felling a line of trees. Other days, she sobbed in the atelier in full view of her staff. In the weeks after Gianni's death, she'd grown even thinner and her face was drawn and tired.

"At least Gianni had me to help him," she lamented often. "But who do I have? I don't have anyone!"

❖ V ❖

While struggling to gain control of the atelier, Donatella received another serious blow—this one from her late brother. In early September, Luciano Severini, the notary who had drawn up Gianni's will just a year before, sent letters to Donatella, Santo, and Antonio convening them to his offices near the Duomo. Along with Paul, the trio settled into their seats opposite Severini's imposing desk. He pulled a brief, handwritten document from a file and began to slowly read it out loud.

"On this date, September 16, 1996, I, Gianni Versace, revoke my last will dated May 11, 1990. I hereby name my niece Allegra my sole heir. I leave to Antonio D'Amico a payment of 50 million lire each month, to be adjusted by inflation after my death. I also leave to Antonio D'Amico the right to live in any of my properties: Via Gesù 12 in Milan, Miami, New York and the house in Via Porta Nuova in Milan, currently owned by Gianni Versace SpA. I leave my art collection to my nephew Daniel Paul Beck."

When the notary finished reading the brief document, a stunned silence hung in the air. Each of the four looked at one another in shock, struggling for a moment to digest the significance of what Gianni had done. Donatella's eyes bulged as she speechlessly turned to Paul. Next to her Santo was slack-jawed, fighting for a moment to regain his composure.

Gianni had left absolutely nothing to his siblings—not a single share in the company, no personal token of affection. He had not even mentioned them. Moreover, he had entirely ignored Santo's children, betraying an indifference to Francesca and Antonio that stung his brother badly. The year before, Santo had agreed to sell Gianni a 5 percent stake in the company on the condition that Gianni would leave the holding to Santo's son, Antonio, in his will. But at a family lunch a few weeks before Gianni left for Miami, Santo was furious to hear that his younger brother still hadn't made the change to his will.

"Gianni, what are you waiting for?" Santo demanded. "Just get it done!"

"I know, I know," Gianni replied. "I promise to do it as soon as I get back from Miami. Don't worry."[2]

His brother flew to Miami with the 1996 will still in place. His siblings would always wonder what else he might have changed had he fixed the appointment with the notary before that tragic trip. Instead, his rash decision to leave half of an empire worth as much as $2 billion to a delicate eleven-year-old girl still stood. In that moment of anger at his siblings, he had convinced himself that he was protecting his company by bestowing his stake on Allegra. He never considered the impact his decision would have on the people who had worked for him for so long, on his two siblings, or on Allegra herself. He could hardly have imagined that a single, handwritten document, scribbled in anger, would set his company and his family on a path to near destruction.

Santo was the first to break the silence in the notary's office. While he was the quickest of the four to grasp the significance of what Gianni had done, he put a brave face on the news, determined as ever to maintain family unity. "If these were Gianni's wishes, we'll respect them," he said in a somber tone.[3]

Donatella, recovering her composure, abruptly asked Severini for a copy of her own will and left the room without a word to the others. She was still reeling from the news that Gianni had snubbed her entirely—but had left virtually his entire fortune and control of his company to her young daughter.

Antonio stood up slowly, still absorbing Gianni's generous effort to take care of him after his death with the use of his magnificent houses and a monthly stipend that would keep him in comfort. But Donatella's brusque exit reminded Antonio that without Gianni there to protect him, he would have to bear the full brunt of Donatella's animus toward him. In the weeks after Gianni's death, she had virtually ignored him, leaving Antonio with the feeling that Gianni's family held him responsible in some way for their brother's violent death. After fifteen years of vacations, birthday parties, and Christmases together, he realized that his days as a member of the Versace clan were over.

Santo confirmed that feeling. "I think you had better find yourself a lawyer," he told Antonio in a clipped tone, before walking briskly away.

❖ V ❖

On a gray, overcast afternoon in early September 1997, a parade of celebrities, most of them scrupulously dressed in Versace, ascended the grand marble staircase of the Metropolitan Museum of Art in New York. The day before, museum workers had mounted a white awning with side flaps over the entire staircase to shield the notables from the phalanx of reporters and photographers that would gather out front on Fifth Avenue. New York City police officers stood by to keep the media at bay. Since the death of Princess Diana the week before, paparazzi had become the bane of celebrities, and some of these famous people had attended her funeral the previous weekend.

Inside the museum's Temple of Dendur, the soaring glassed-in atrium that was a favorite setting for the city's glitziest parties, a memorial service for Gianni was getting under way. Robert Isabell, Manhattan's premier party planner, had decked the space out with masses of white flowers. In a press release, Versace's PR office declared the event off-limits to the media, saying it was a private memorial for just "family and friends." But privacy was an alien concept at the house of Versace. Donatella's PR chief admitted a journalist from Condé Nast's ever-compliant *Women's Wear Daily*, who could be trusted to write a flattering account of the service and duly drop names of Versace's A-list "friends": Whitney Houston, Jon Bon Jovi, Ralph Lauren, Tom Ford, Donald Trump, Courtney Love, and Woody Allen.

One celebrity after another stood to pay tribute to Gianni. Madonna read a poem she had composed herself. Anna Wintour, famous for her chilly reserve, choked up as she recalled the monthly faxes Gianni sent her with punctilious comments on each issue of *Vogue*.

"It's hard for me to believe that I'll never talk to him on the phone again," Elton John told the group. The singer then sat down at a piano to sing "Live Like Horses," one of Gianni's favorite songs.

Then Donatella stood to make her first public appearance since the funeral in Milan. It was her official debut as the face of Versace. Her short speech moved many guests to tears. "Each time Gianni asked me to do what back then seemed like these impossible things, I'd tell him I couldn't do it," she recalled, speaking nervously in her thick Italian accent. "I'd tell him I couldn't do it, and he'd tell me I could. I did it. He was always the most exciting person I knew. He was my best friend."

After the memorial, Donatella invited a clutch of stars back to Gianni's townhouse. The New York home had been Gianni's final toy. The previous October, when the renovations were finally complete, Gianni threw the party of the season, gathering A-listers such as John Kennedy, Jr., Richard Gere, and Hugh Grant to inaugurate his new home. Gianni happily played tour guide of the house, which showcased an art collection that included a portrait of Gianni by Andy Warhol and important works by Roy Lichtenstein and Jean-Michel Basquiat. But those paled in comparison to Gianni's stunning new collection of twenty-five Picassos, which glowed in the light of dozens of candles. It was the collection that had sparked the brutal argument with Santo just a year before.

That carefree October evening, during which Donatella had played the witty consort to Gianni's glittering court, seemed a distant memory. Now a small circle of guests, including Madonna, her brother Christopher Ciccone, Lisa Marie Presley, Luciano Pavarotti, and Courtney Love, gathered with Donatella in the townhouse's secluded garden. She changed out of the black outfit she'd worn for her speech and into tight white jeans and a matching T-shirt and made subdued small talk with her celebrity friends.

Just after 10 p.m., Madonna, who prefers to be in bed by 11 p.m., left the townhouse. As soon as she was gone, her brother Christopher Ciccone and Love went into one of Gianni's guest bedrooms—where Love pulled out a large packet of coke. They expertly cut the powder into neat lines and began snorting it. Madonna, who hated drugs, frequently berated her brother for his cocaine habit, but Ciccone and Donatella often shared hits together while out clubbing in Miami Beach. Shortly afterward, Donatella came upon the scene and beckoned Ciccone and Love into a sitting room nearby, where she joined in. But the coke hardly seemed to lift her mood.

"Chreestopher, Chreestopher, play 'Candle in the Wind' for me," she pleaded. He got up and slipped a CD into the expensive stereo system. That week, the song had soared to the top of the charts after Elton John reworked his classic ballad to honor Princess Diana at her funeral. For Donatella, the sad song, originally a paean to Marilyn Monroe and her early death, might have been a fitting tribute to her brother. When the song ended, she begged Christopher to play it again and again.[4]

❖ V ❖

When Donatella returned to Milan, just a month remained before the show. Feeling entirely adrift, she told herself over and over that even Versace's fiercest detractors wouldn't have the heart to trash her debut collection—yet she couldn't shake the pressure of having the world's eyes on her. "You have to hold on," she told herself every morning. "You can't fall apart."[5]

The show, as usual, would be staged in the courtyard of Via Gesù. Ever since Gianni's death, Donatella had become fixated on security and told her assistants to ensure that guards had completely secured the building. Afraid of being overwhelmed by the crush of well-wishers after the show, she ordered her press office to limit the number of backstage passes they issued; she personally vetted the list of the guests who received them.

On the day of the dress rehearsal, an unseasonable heat settled on Milan, which compounded the fatigue the team felt after weeks of marathon days. Donatella had taken particular care in choosing the models, falling back on the role that she felt most comfortable with. She assembled a mix of new girls such as Stella Tennant and Karen Elson—the mannequin Gianni had so disliked at the July couture show—and traditional Versace models such as Naomi Campbell and Linda Evangelista. As Donatella oversaw the last-minute run-through, a white butterfly floated among her team. It seemed to linger, refusing to go away.

"That's my brother," Donatella repeated, as if she could conjure up his presence by wishing it. "That's Gianni. It's his spirit."

On the day of the show, Donatella presided over the standard press conference that walked the fashion journalists through the themes of the collection they would see that evening. Clad in black, she lit one cigarette after another as she nervously reeled off her inspiration.

"These are clothes for a woman who is sweet and tough at the same time, someone who can survive life's catastrophes with dignity and stand on her own two feet," she said as if reciting from a script. She then took a slow drag on her cigarette and her voice nearly broke as she continued. "I'm terrified," she admitted to the clutch of journalists, many of whom had known her brother for years. "Gianni is irreplaceable. I would like to be judged for what *I* am doing, not compared to him. If you compare me to him, I can only fall short."[6]

That evening, under a giant tent set up in the courtyard at Via Gesù, the lights dimmed briefly and the music surged, signaling the audience to take their seats. Gianni's old rivals had all turned out to support his little sister, although the effect was only to ratchet up the pressure on Donatella. Giorgio Armani, Donna Karan, Karl Lagerfeld, and Miuccia Prada took their places in the front row, ready to scrutinize Gianni's little sister's work. Demi Moore, Peter Gabriel, Cher, Boy George, and Rupert Everett sat nearby.

Laser lights burst from the screen and "Candy Perfume Girl," a new, unreleased single by Madonna, boomed over the speakers. Neon squiggles in white, green, and blue shot along the runway. Naomi and Kate Moss sauntered out first, a bright spotlight following them down the length of the runway. The first dresses were funky variations on the traditional Prince of Wales fabric. Donatella had used the gray check pattern in halter dresses, silk chiffon camisoles, and as ribbons running through silk evening gowns. Then followed a mish-mash of themes and ideas, from bright red pantsuits to a bold blue dress with a galaxy motif drawn in pink to rubberized silk dresses that looked as if they'd been poured onto the models. Girls in bright green bikinis followed others clad in tiny pink hot pants.

While some individual pieces clicked, the collection as a whole fell woefully short of Gianni's work. It was scattershot and confused, a muddle of references to Gianni's winning themes and the street-inspired look Donatella had pushed at Versus. Donatella was groping for a way to update her brother's label, to make it more hip and relevant. She had brought in the new young designers and the powerful stylists to help her find a fresh look—without losing the Versace DNA. But without a clear vision of her own, she was buffeted by the jumble of ideas her team pitched her while feeling pressure from legacy Versace employees to stick to Gianni's familiar tracks.

At the end of the twenty-minute parade, Donatella came out for her bow. She wore a simple black sheath with a deep slit up the left side. She had on very little makeup and her ironed hair looked slightly rough, her extensions imperfectly done. The audience jumped to their feet as she made her way to the end of the runway with the reluctance of a pirate walking a plank. She kept her eyes fixed on the ground, ignoring the models around her, her face contorted as she struggled to control herself. After a rushed bow, she retreated back up the runway, her face buried in her hands.

Once safely backstage, she nearly collapsed, sobbing in the arms of her assistants. For fifteen minutes, she stood visibly shaking as her assistants and thirty seamstresses formed a circle around her, clapping and stomping their congratulations. The VIP guests began streaming in. Armani, accompanied personally by a grim-faced Santo, was among the first to break through the crowd, hugging Donatella and kissing her wet cheeks. "I miss my brother so much," she told him. "I've never felt so overwhelmed in all my life."

House music continued to pound over the sound system as the television cameras jostled hard for a shot of Donatella and Santo with the VIPs. Reporters scrambled to extract a verdict on the show from the rival designers. "Very interesting, very interesting," Lagerfeld murmured cryptically as he pulled away from the reporters.

"It looked very good," said Miuccia Prada encouragingly. "Donatella must and can improve, but you can see how hard she worked."[7]

Gianni loomed in absence. Both brother and sister recognized it that day.

"My phone doesn't ring like it used to," Donatella told the journalists. "Gianni used to call me for anything, even to describe to me the color of the roses that had bloomed in his garden that morning."

Santo stood nearby, pale and drawn. "How I miss Gianni's phone calls," he told one reporter. "I even miss our fights about whether he could buy another Picasso. We were side by side for fifty years. And now he is gone."[8]

fifteen

Inheritance and Loss

*e*VEN AS THE PRESSURES IN THE ATELIER MOUNTED, A FAR more serious situation was emerging for Donatella at home that fall of 1997. Ever since the reading of the will, she worried about how the news of Gianni's bequeathal would affect Allegra. The little girl was already distraught by the loss of her doting uncle. The news that she was now the controlling shareholder of Gianni's company was confusing and upsetting to the sensitive eleven-year-old.

When classes resumed in September at the expensive British school she attended in Milan, Allegra became the object of intense gossip after newspapers broke the story of Gianni's will. She couldn't help picking up on the curious chatter, and any semblance of a normal life vanished for her as Donatella, fixated with security, hired bodyguards to accompany Allegra to school every day. The beefy men spent the entire day stationed outside the school in a hulking SUV, drawing curious stares from classmates and their parents. Visits to the homes of family and friends now required advanced planning. Not long after Gianni's death, Paul took Allegra to Reggio to visit Zia Nora, and he decided to take his daughter to see the city's renowned archaeological museum. Even though the museum was a short walk from Nora's home, Allegra's security guards refused to let her go by foot. Instead, they got permission from the museum to park their car right in front of the door so that the girl could go straight inside.[1]

The strain on Allegra began to manifest itself more seriously just weeks after Gianni's death. Soon after, just as Donatella was preparing her debut runway show, Allegra simply stopped eating. As the fall wore on, the girl grew alarmingly thin.

Anorexia nervosa is considered one of the most insidious psychological disorders. The term "anorexia" literally means "loss of appetite," but the label is misleading. People with the disease still feel hungry but are so terrified by the idea of gaining weight that they become obsessed with food, eating, and counting calories. They measure their value as a person by the number they see on the scale. Sufferers of anorexia virtually starve themselves, fast for days, and overexercise. They think of little else but food and begin to behave in ways that often create enormous stress for family members. They lie about what they have eaten, avoid dining with others, and develop obsessive habits such as cutting their food into tiny pieces or eating dishes that are extremely hot in temperature.

Since it staves off the onset of the physical signs of adolescence, it often strikes girls in their teenage years who dread the idea of becoming women. Teenaged girls with anorexia have so little body fat that they often don't develop breasts or hips. By starving themselves, they avoid the typical adolescent growth spurt, leaving them with undersized, childlike bodies. Anorexic teenagers oftentimes never get their periods, a comfort for girls who are struggling with their bodies' physical changes.

The illness is notoriously difficult to treat. Eating disorders are insidious because, unlike alcoholism or drug addiction, they may not have an obvious impact on work or family life. Moreover, anorexics'

perception of themselves becomes so distorted that even in an ema-
ciated state, they see a fat person when they look in the mirror. Their
drive for perfection—that is, the lowest weight their bodies can
stand—is insatiable. Plus, unlike other compulsions, anorexia inspires
envy. Early on, a woman suffering from anorexia may thrive on compliments she might receive for being so thin, which sometimes eggs her
on to lose more weight. The social acceptability of thinness has even
encouraged some anorexics to argue that the condition is not a disease,
but a lifestyle choice. Nonetheless, a significant number of people with
anorexia—estimates range from 5 percent to 20 percent—die from the
condition, either from suicide or the myriad physical problems stem-
ming from chronic malnourishment. According to some studies, fewer
than half of anorexics fully recover.

An acrimonious debate has raged for years as to whether the
media and fashion world contribute to the spread of anorexia. Without a doubt, fashion propagates a virtually impossible standard of
beauty and thinness. Models often go to great lengths to reach an
ethereally slim state. They smoke like long-haul truckers, in no small
part because nicotine suppresses the appetite. Some also go beyond
the usual laxatives and diuretics that purge their meals, resorting to
prescription drugs such as Clenbuterol, a steroid that athletes and
horse trainers employ to reduce body fat. By the time of Gianni's
death, the ascendant image in magazines and billboards was even
more extreme.

The crop of new models that Donatella and other designers venerated were hauntingly thin, far skinnier than the likes of Naomi
Campbell or Cindy Crawford. Gianni's supermodels were undoubtedly lean, but they had breasts and bottoms that gave them a healthy,
womanly look. The minimalist wave ushered in a new type of girl—
beanpole thin, flat-chested, and hollow-cheeked. By the mid-1990s,
newly open countries in the former Soviet bloc became the biggest
suppliers of these wraiths. Girls from countries such as Ukraine,
Poland, and Lithuania were often so desperate to escape poverty that
they were willing to starve themselves to achieve the rickety frames
that designers in Milan, Paris, and New York sought.

While experts are still debating the exact causes of anorexia,
they have a rough idea of patterns that contribute to the disease. In

retrospect, Allegra was a classic case, even if she was somewhat younger than the norm. Anorexics often set themselves standards that are impossible to achieve, leaving them with a sense of constant inadequacy. Moreover, Allegra was raised among the most beautiful women in the world, establishing in her mind an impossible physical standard for a sensitive preteen girl.

Then, Gianni's death—along with the news of her inheritance—arrived just as Allegra was on the brink of puberty, a delicate moment for any young girl. Anorexia is considered a disease of control. The enormous stress the family came under after Gianni's murder could easily have triggered in Allegra a search for a way to exert control over a situation that must have felt overwhelming. The amount of time and energy an anorexic devotes to food and weight loss can crowd out other emotions, providing a protective barrier against the sort of external problems that Allegra was then facing.

So when Christmas arrived, Donatella was feeling desperate. Her daughter was alarmingly ill, her marriage was falling apart, and she was struggling in the atelier. She had rallied for that first show in October, but the prospect of carrying the burden season after season was overwhelming. Fashion critics had been gentle with her debut collection, but she knew she was coming up short. Her new hires hadn't gelled into an effective team with a clear, winning style. She had to create a men's collection for the first time ever (when Gianni was alive, she had taken little interest in menswear). In December, she decided to cancel the haute couture show in January, marking Versace's first absence from the Paris calendar since Gianni launched the collection in 1990. Over the Christmas holidays, the first without Gianni, Donatella felt so low that she considered quitting it all. But the idea of failing Gianni haunted her too much. She decided to stick it out.

❖ V ❖

During the preparations for the October show, Antonio D'Amico understood that his days at Gianni's company were numbered. In August, he had retreated with Elton John and his boyfriend, David Furnish, to the star's sprawling home in the south of France, where they grieved together for Gianni. Elton and David would be Antonio's main source of support over the years as he recovered from his loss. Elton called Antonio frequently—as many as three times a day—gave him a cocker spaniel puppy to keep him company, and invited him for holidays, birthdays, and concerts.

Returning to Via Gesù, Antonio soon became persona non grata. He was still responsible for putting together the house's Istante collection, a lower-priced variant on Versace's signature line, and that September, he started work on Istante's October presentation. His team worked in close quarters with Donatella and her group, but she ignored Antonio entirely. With Gianni gone, she had no need to keep up the pretense of civility.

"Donatella completely erased me from the picture," Antonio said later. "I tried to speak with her to explain what I was doing with Istante, but she just ignored me."[2]

Gianni's wish that Antonio have use of the palazzo in Via Gesù, the townhouse in New York, and the villa in Miami also proved to be an enormous point of tension. Donatella wouldn't countenance the idea of finding Antonio in the Versace homes. Santo was more civil with Antonio that fall, but he, too, found the continued presence of his brother's boyfriend uncomfortable.

"You've become a source of embarrassment for the family," Antonio's lawyer told him after meeting with Versace legal advisers one day. Antonio was a daily reminder of Gianni's death, and some friends felt Santo and Donatella held him responsible in some way for letting their brother expose himself to danger in Miami.

Moreover, Gianni's ham-handed plan to see that Antonio was taken care of began falling apart as soon as the will was read. Gianni, having scribbled out his will without the benefit of legal advice, hadn't considered the fact that the houses were the property of the company. As a result, his edict giving Antonio use of the houses had no legal standing. The company—along with the houses—now belonged to Donatella, Santo, and Allegra.

The fact that gay partnerships were not legally recognized in Italy meant that Antonio had no spousal claim to Gianni's estate. As a result, the moment that Gianni died, Antonio was just another Versace employee, one for whom Gianni had provided in his will. Antonio's lawyers advised him to reach a settlement with the family to end his employment at the house and vacate the large apartment he'd shared with Gianni in Via Gesù. In January 1998, the lawyers for both sides came to an agreement whereby Antonio received a lump-sum payment as well as a company-owned apartment elsewhere in Milan.

At the end of that month, Antonio was escorted out of the atelier by a Versace security guard, without a word from Santo or Donatella.[3] He asked the family to return some personal items, such as several watches, that Gianni had given him over the years, but they refused.[4] Later, when he tried to enter the villa on Lake Como to pay his respects to Gianni's ashes, which were interred in a grotto there, security guards chased him away.

❖ V ❖

After her debut show, Donatella had little time to catch her breath. Although months had passed since Gianni's sensational death, the public's fascination with the Versace family—in particular Donatella—hardly waned. The Metropolitan Museum, riding the wave of interest in Gianni's work, decided to dedicate the annual grand gala its Costume Institute held each December to Versace. The event was a high-water mark in the social tide of Manhattan's swanky set, drawing a mix of New York socialites, corporate grandees, and celebrities, all pimped out in Oscar-worthy couture. The $2,000 tickets to the bash sold out just days after the Met put them on sale in September, raising an easy $2.3 million.

That evening, nearly thirty thousand twinkling blue and violet lights adorned a giant tree in the center of the museum's Great Hall. Centerpieces made of huge bunches of pink peonies sat on tables draped with tablecloths edged in chain mail, a homage to one of Gianni's great design innovations. Sting staged a miniconcert before an audience that included *New York Times* publisher Arthur Sulzberger, the photographer David LaChapelle, and actresses Gwyneth Paltrow and Salma Hayek.

After the gala, Donatella gathered with Kate Moss, Marianne Faithfull, Cher, and other friends at Gianni's townhouse. The group was sipping champagne in one of the mansion's grand salons when Kate decided they should stage a sort of Irish wake, each guest singing a tribute to Gianni. Marianne Faithfull went first, warbling an old Irish folk song. When she finished, Kate prodded Cher to go next.

Cher stood up. Despite a lifetime of notorious plastic surgery, the singer looked mesmerizing, her long, slim figure sheathed in a leather Versace evening gown. She took a breath and began to sing "Danny Boy," the somber ballad that is often sung at Irish funerals, in a ringing, poignant voice. By the time she had finished, the entire group, including Donatella, was sobbing.[5]

❖ V ❖

For Santo, the months after Gianni's death were no less painful than they were for his sister. The shock of his younger brother's death subsided little even as the autumn wore on. He returned from the August holidays a changed man, his tailored Versace suits and lightweight turtleneck sweaters hanging looser on his frame. He looked drawn and tired, suddenly older than his fifty-two years. He struggled to find a way to come to terms with Gianni's death, but he felt overwhelmed by the grief and pain. Santo knew that the shaken company needed his leadership more than it ever had before—thanks not only to the murder of its founder and creative source but also because radical changes in the fashion business threatened to overwhelm the company. But he couldn't seem to find his old energy or enthusiasm.

For two decades, Santo had been an energizing force in the Versace headquarters. Like his brother, Santo used to roam into his associates' offices, cheerfully dropping new projects onto their desks or offering words of praise. During the selling season, he swept through the showroom, turning on the Italian charm with buyers from the big American department stores and owners of Versace franchise shops from Europe and Asia.

After Gianni's death, he continued to put in long days, arriving well before much of his team in the morning, offering what support he could to grief-stricken and unnerved Versace employees. "*Corraggio!* Everything will be fine," he told them often. "We just have to keep on working." But his heart wasn't in it. He appeared distant during meetings and struggled to focus on his work, his usual charisma and high energy drained away. He smiled little and was uncharacteristically withdrawn with even his closest colleagues. A chronic back problem flared up more often now. He delegated more and more work to other Versace executives, asking them to make the trips for store openings and business meetings that he had always handled personally.

Worse still, Santo's relationship with his sister was shifting ominously—thanks in part to Gianni's stinging decision to exclude Santo's children and elevate Donatella's daughter as the company's heir. In public, he put on a brave face about the inheritance. "I have much more than I'll ever need," he told journalists. "Besides, Allegra was like a daughter to Gianni—even though he loved his other niece and nephews very much." But privately, the will opened a wound in Donatella and Santo's relationship that would fester steadily for years, eventually threatening to consume both the family and the company.

Santo and Donatella had each been devoted to Gianni, but without him their own rapport was far more tenuous. In the past, if either Santo or Donatella had an issue with the other, each turned to Gianni. Gianni had been able to relate to each of his siblings in different ways. He and his sister shared an extravagant, Technicolor view of life; driving ambition and a prodigious capacity for work united Gianni with his older brother. But Santo and Donatella had little to bring them together. Their ten-year age difference created a sort of generation gap. Santo was more homey, even provincial, in his outlook and personal habits. He kept a strong attachment to Calabria, disdained the limelight, and spoke only Italian, given that his attempts to learn English had been largely a bust. He liked to come to the office by foot each morning, often after walking his children to school and chatting with the other parents on his way from the spacious but hardly grand apartment he and Cristiana had shared for years. He remembered the names of the café owners and shopkeepers he frequented. He relished his role as the provider for his family, diligently socking away the dividends and salary he'd earned at the company over the decades. His children, Antonio and Francesca, venerated their father in true southern Italian style; he, in turn, adored them. When they became teenagers and received cell phones, he would speak with them several times a day.

If Santo lived in a sober world of black and white, Donatella's life was incandescent. She felt more at home in Manhattan than Milan and virtually never set foot in Reggio. She spoke English at home with Paul and with her celebrity friends. And as her brother's fame had grown, so did her streak of megalomania. Her personal car and driver ferried her and her family for even the shortest of distances. She burned through her dividends and salary at a stunning rate, spending huge amounts on hairdressers, clothes, and furnishings for her lavish apartment. But she was also the most generous of the three siblings to close friends and employees.

After the shock of the will had worn off, Donatella found herself privately satisfied by Gianni's decision. Gianni had left nothing to Donatella, believing that he was safeguarding his company by bequeathing his 50 percent stake to his niece. Instead, he had unwittingly handed over control to his little sister. For another seven years—until Allegra turned eighteen—Donatella would control her daughter's share in the company. With Allegra's 50 percent stake and her own 20 percent share, she could easily outvote Santo at shareholder meetings. Hers would be the last word on management appointments, the company's strategy, and investment decisions. Santo, with just a 30 percent share, had gone from being the authoritative eldest brother to his kid sister's minion.

Meanwhile, Gianni's decision to leave his art collection to Daniel was later quashed in court. The art collection had been bought by the company, not by Gianni personally, and since it was not part of his own estate, Gianni couldn't bequeath it to his nephew. Instead, the works of art went to Santo, Donatella, and Allegra as the three principals of the Versace company. Daniel inherited nothing in the end.

In the immediate aftermath of the murder, Donatella and Santo had put up a united public front against media inquiries into their family and their company. In interviews, Donatella was careful to emphasize that all decisions would be made in concert with Santo. The siblings initially pulled together in their grief, partly because they felt besieged by the media barrage and relentless speculation swirling around Gianni's death. Within hours after Gianni's murder, a large U.S. publishing house announced a deal for a racy book on Versace to be written by a freelance journalist who had barely met Gianni. (The book was later canceled.) Reporters in Europe and the

United States continued to propagate Frank Monte's spurious claims about a connection between Gianni and the Calabrian mafia. Santo was especially furious with the media reports. "These people aren't professionals!" he told friends. "They don't deserve to clean toilets, much less work as reporters!" Donatella, equally upset, backed Santo in deciding to sue some publications that repeated the mafia claims.

In turn, Santo extolled his sister to friends and Versace executives, singing her praises as a designer worthy of stepping into Gianni's shoes. His cheerleading sprang in part from wishful thinking, knowing that the company's fate was entirely in Donatella's hands. More important, it grew from Santo's unshakable belief that, in true southern Italian style, the family was sacred, never more so than when under attack. The memories of his fights with his brother over money—in particular the bitter arguments that drove Gianni to change his will—were painfully fresh in Santo's mind. "If I had ever known that Gianni was going to die, I would have let him buy all the works of art he wanted," he lamented to friends. He wasn't about to do battle with his little sister.

A surge in sales in the autumn soothed some of Santo's worries. The murder had raised Versace's profile and profits to new heights. Indeed, Gianni became even more famous in death than in life, his sensational murder—along with the mafia speculation—making him a household name around the world. Shoppers suddenly wanted anything associated with Gianni, and sales of Versace products—particularly cheaper items such as jeans and perfumes—swelled. The company's 1997 sales rose 10 percent to 940 billion lire ($540 million). The balance sheet also got a boost from the 35 billion lire ($20 million) the company pocketed from a payout on Gianni's life insurance policy.

But while the fashion press treated Donatella's first runway show gently, department store buyers and Versace shop owners were privately unimpressed. They understood immediately that she was no substitute for Gianni. They'd also heard the stories over the years of Donatella's heavy drug use and her wild personal life, and they were wary of committing their buying budgets or valuable selling space to the designs of such a volatile personality. They could also see that Santo was struggling, delegating more of the crucial care and feeding of retailers to his team. In short order, most of the buyers would abandon the aggrieved house.

Despite the fog of grief and pain that enveloped him, Santo was all too aware that the fashion business was hurtling into a period of enormous change that would rewrite the rules of engagement. The luxury goods industry was entering the richest, frothiest market it would ever see. Strong, well-managed companies with deep pockets, pitch-perfect products, and a discipline hitherto rare in the fashion world would reap bonanza profits. But weak companies would struggle mightily to compete in the new high-stakes game.

At the frontier of this new territory was LVMH and its owner, Bernard Arnault, a Frenchman determined to change the way fashion did business. He was among the first to recognize that luxury goods didn't have to be stuffy and old and that the yen for stylish, high-quality goods had grown well beyond the traditional audience of the truly rich and was now inspiring middle-class consumers. He saw a fortune to be made if he could leverage the heritage and mystique of European luxury brands while making them modern and fun enough for a mass audience.

Arnault had gotten his start in 1984 when he bought the then bankrupt Christian Dior. But it was his 1990 acquisition of Louis Vuitton that created an entirely new approach to fashion. The company, which started making traveling trunks for the French bourgeoisie in 1854, still enjoyed a reputation for high-quality leather goods, but it had become overly dependent on its signature chocolate-brown travel bags emblazoned with the gold "LV" logo. To transform Vuitton, Arnault pursued a new strategy of controlling every inch of the business, from the factories that made the bags to the shops that sold them. His approach challenged other brands, which often relied on contracts with third-party craftsmen to make their goods and sold them through franchise shops owned by local entrepreneurs. Instead, LVMH controlled each one of Vuitton's stores. (The company owned some stores and held long-term leases on the rest.) To support the stores, Arnault found myriad ways to goose Vuitton's sales, launching a whole raft of products with the classic LV monogram and inventing a slate of new lines. In the mid-1990s, Vuitton proved that accessories could be a gold mine for a fashion brand. Leather bags offered women the instant gratification of feeling fashionable, without the anxiety of trying to squeeze into—or afford—a designer dress or skirt. They also offered millions of women around the world their first chance at owning a bit of European elegance.

Other fashion brands jumped on the accessories bandwagon. They came up with sticky, easy-to-remember names and then spun them off into different versions—a baby one priced at a few hundred dollars for twenty-somethings and larger bags in precious materials such as lizard or ostrich costing thousands of dollars for wealthier shoppers. The brand owners placed their bags of the season prominently in shopwindows, sent them down the runway over and over again, and devoted millions to advertising them. All the hype worked. Women who would normally have owned just one handbag now bought a whole collection to match every mood, occasion, and outfit.

The profits in leather goods were huge because they cost relatively little to make but sold for thousands of dollars each. Unlike clothes, they didn't come in sizes, and so there was far less unsold stock. Louis Vuitton's performance showed just how lucrative the accessories business could be. Between 1990 and 1996, its sales doubled to hit eight billion francs ($1.4 billion), and that figure doubled again within five years. Arnault used rich profits to open scores of impeccable new shops worldwide that became heady shopping meccas for fashionistas. Women lined up for hours just to get inside Vuitton's flagship boutique on the Avenue des Champs-Élysées in Paris. By the late 1990s, its cavernous Tokyo store was drawing four thousand customers a day.

Similarly, Gucci was finding that leather bags, wallets, and belts would prove to be a desperately needed lifeline. Laid low by years of family squabbles, Gucci was practically bust when Domenico De Sole and Tom Ford took over in 1994. The pair made an odd couple. De Sole was born in a tiny town in Calabria to a peripatetic military family but immigrated in his twenties to the United States, where he earned a law degree at Harvard University. Ford was the son of a real estate developer in Santa Fe, New Mexico, who went into design after an early career as a commercial actor foundered.

Backed by De Sole's business acumen, Ford proved a master at channeling the 1990s zeitgeist. His first collection of velvet hip-huggers, fringed and beaded jackets, and slinky gowns evoked the 1970s jet set. More important, he had an uncanny knack for designing the purse that would be the season's "it" bag. In 1997, not long before Gianni's death, Ford designed a $300 G-string held together by a metal Gucci logo. It was pure marketing genius. Costing virtually nothing to make, the garment was all profit. Moreover, it conjured up enormous hype that boosted sales of more conventional items. By 1998, Gucci's sales were $1 billion, five times the level of 1994, when Ford and De Sole—by then dubbed the "Dom-Tom Bomb"—took over the company.

Ford understood the power of personality in the new media-driven era. With an actor's sense of presence, he exploited his smoldering good looks to the hilt. Before a show, he went to a tanning salon and shaved with an electric razor set to leave a stylish two-day stubble. On the runway, he cut a striking figure in his black suit, open-collar shirt, and longish sideburns. Journalists came away from interviews feeling slightly starstruck. For modern women who found European designers of yore self-important and intimidating, Ford offered a bracing, refreshingly wicked new presence.

"When the customer puts on a pair of pants, she doesn't care what the original inspiration was," he once told a journalist. "She cares about whether her butt looks good."

The boom in fashion was transforming shopping thoroughfares in the world's capitals. In Milan, luxury powerhouses swept the city's old-line shops off Via Montenapoleone. Rents rose by double digits each year, and the big brands began offering as much as 15 million euros in "key money" to convince the street's traditional shopkeepers to break their long leases. Marketing budgets were also soaring as the big brands battled for the attention of shoppers. By the end of the 1990s, when the biggest issues of *Vogue* included more than seven hundred pages (and weighed more than four pounds), nothing less than a high-production, ten-page advertising spread would do. Ad campaigns also had to be global as the brands opened shop after shop in new cities.

At the same time, Versace's rivals were taking the celebrity game that Donatella and Gianni had pioneered to new heights. When Gianni was still alive, it was enough for Donatella to buttonhole a celebrity friend and send her assistant out to Los Angeles with a dress for the requisite red-carpet event. The stars were flattered just to be wearing Versace couture. But just around the time of Gianni's death, the game changed entirely, as stylists elbowed their way between the stars and the designers. Given the massive increase in media coverage of celebrities and the huge money at stake for their films, the stars couldn't risk looking frumpy, whether on a red carpet or on the playground with their kids. They hired stylists from the magazine or retail world to give them advice on hair, makeup, and clothes. In turn, the stylists quickly leveraged their clients' star power with the fashion houses. They wheedled racks of freebie designer clothes—including couture dresses costing thousands of dollars each—for their celebrity clients, often demanding outfits for their entourages as well. The houses complied, knowing that reams of press coverage awaited the brands that managed to dress the A-list stars. In the end, the top actresses received dozens of free designer gowns just for the Oscars. Some celebrities called in multiple dresses only to decide at the very last minute which one to wear, making it difficult for the house's public relations team to disseminate the news to the press. It also meant that a house's best evening gowns might never see the outside of a star's closet. Exasperated designers finally resorted to simply paying the stars. Fashion houses began shelling out six-figure fees to convince top stars to sit in the front row of their runway shows, in addition to the requisite private jets, five-star hotels, and free clothes. Donatella and Gianni had helped create an expensive, greedy monster.

Fashion's new business model required deep pockets and deft managers. Naturally, the companies that could tap the riches proffered by the decade's bull run in the stock market would have a huge edge. An IPO not only brought in a wave of fresh money, but a company's stock options were juicy bait in recruiting talented executives. Companies such as Bulgari and Gucci had seen their stock prices soar since going public in the mid-1990s, and they succeeded in attracting some of the best managers in the business. In 1997, 30 percent of luxury products were made by publicly traded companies. Within two years, that figure would double.

Just as Versace's rivals were hitting the accelerator, however, Santo was putting on the brakes. He was the first to understand that his plans to take Versace public went up in smoke the moment Andrew Cunanan shot Gianni. With 50 percent of the company in the hands of an eleven-year-old girl, an IPO would be virtually out of the question. While Donatella was free to vote Allegra's share in routine shareholder meetings, any major decisions affecting the girl's patrimony—including the sale of a piece of the company to outside investors—had to win the blessing of an Italian court that protected the interests of minors. And even if a judge approved an IPO, stock market investors would be reluctant to buy shares until they felt sure the company could thrive without Gianni.

Santo had another worry. In bequeathing his fortune to Allegra, Gianni also left her with an enormous tax bill. Had Gianni consulted the company's lawyers before scribbling out his will, they might have found a way to shield Allegra from at least part of the enormous inheritance taxes the Italian state levied. Instead, Allegra had to come up with as much as 70 billion lire ($36 million). To find the cash, she would have to draw very large dividends from the company—draining the house of money that could have been invested in the brand—or sell part of her stake. Versace lawyers quickly appealed the estimate produced by Italian tax authorities, hoping to scale the figure back. In the meantime, the tax bill hung like a sword over the house.

Donatella's second show in March 1998 did little to allay Santo's concerns. It was a mishmash of looks: pinstriped skirts, Goth-inspired dresses, romantic flower-print skirts, and pastel halter-top dresses. While Gianni had always been careful to update the suits, jackets, and pants that made up the bulk of the house's sales, Donatella sent out just a few lackluster day clothes. She had little patience for everyday outfits. She wanted glitzy, red-carpet clothes. Santo sat in the audience, solemnly watching his sister take her bow. While Donatella was far more at ease than she had been at her debut show, the audience was clearly underwhelmed, mustering a weak round of applause as the models filed out.

In the weeks that followed, the semiannual reports from Versace's sales team—detailing what sold and what didn't, along with feedback from the stores—landed on Santo's desk. They made for difficult reading. Many of the big American stores sliced their orders in half—a drastic move for such a prominent brand. Some, reluctant to remove Versace entirely from their sales floor, cherry-picked just a handful of classic pieces, often in neutral black. But a few retailers had lost all confidence in Donatella's designs. Neiman Marcus, which had bought about $20 million of Versace clothes the year before Gianni's death, didn't purchase a stitch from Donatella's March collection.

At the same time, Santo's boom-time business decisions were coming back to haunt him: Versace's company-owned boutiques were struggling. The cavernous flagships that Gianni had opened over the previous few years were the first to crumble. Even in the best of times it had been a stretch to make a profit from the shops. Leather goods brands such as Gucci, Prada, and Louis Vuitton could afford to open flagships because the profits on accessories were so high. The margins on clothing brands were lower, and accessories made up less than 5 percent of Versace sales. Furthermore, Gianni's clothing designs, with their bold patterns and close cuts, required extra help from well-trained saleswomen, so the number of staff at Versace boutiques was often higher.

As a result, stores such as the huge Fifth Avenue boutique in New York began to lose money almost as soon as sales fell. The Fifth Avenue store was an extraordinarily expensive shop, with its staff of about fifty salespeople, seamstresses, and security guards. Worse still, it competed with an older Versace store a few blocks away on Madison Avenue. With Gianni alive and the company thriving, Santo could afford to bet that two boutiques so close together would add up to more sales. Instead, like the two shops on Via Montenapoleone in Milan, they only cannibalized each other while doubling costs. Santo had overplayed his hand elsewhere in Italy as well. Versace had forty shops there, and many—particularly in conservative cities such as Turin, where shoppers turned their noses up at Versace's outré style—had struggled even when Gianni was alive.

More dismaying news came in June 1998. Prada had bought 10 percent of Gucci, making it the fashion house's largest shareholder. By the end of the year, Prada would flip the holding to Bernard Arnault, who had been eyeing a takeover of Gucci for months and began build-ing up his stake further. De Sole and Ford aggressively resisted LVMH's hostile-takeover attempt, thus laying the groundwork for one of the longest and most bitter corporate battles Europe had ever seen.

The news was an enormous blow for Santo. Less than a year ear-lier, he had contemplated a Versace-Gucci merger that might have created a multibrand luxury conglomerate strong enough to compete with LVMH. Now he could do little but sit on the sidelines and watch the drama unfold, the outcome of which would reshape the global fashion business.

sixteen

Siblings at War

*i*N July 1998, with the news of the attempted takeover of Gucci still ricocheting in the press, Santo and Donatella traveled to Paris for her first haute couture show. The memory of Gianni's final show at the Ritz, almost exactly a year before, haunted them. Some fashionistas were surprised that Donatella had decided to go ahead with a couture collection at all. A designer takes on haute couture at the peak of his or her skills, after years of work in the atelier. Donatella was going up against the likes of Karl Lagerfeld and Valentino, two masters who had learned how to craft handmade dresses during the golden years of couture in the 1950s.

By the time he flew to Paris, Santo was despairing over his sister's collections. To be sure, Donatella faced a daunting challenge. If Gianni had found it vexing to adapt his de trop style to the new minimalist era, it would surely be an immense challenge for Donatella. Other houses that had lost their founders had survived—even thrived. But brands such as Chanel or Dior had a signature style that was instantly identifiable, whereas Gianni had dipped into so many different themes and references over twenty years that Donatella was left without a single clear path to follow. But when Santo saw his sister's couture collection in the pool area at the Ritz, the very room where Gianni had staged his final show, he was horrified.

Donatella wanted to make Versace couture modern and hip, but her stab at innovation was so gimmicky that it resembled something conjured up by a fashion student for an experimental show. The clothes had neither the refinement of old-line couture nor the brilliant creativity that John Galliano and Alexander McQueen could conjure. Prodded by her new team of callow, iconoclastic Brits and Americans fresh out of fashion school, she based the collection on new fabrics: tulle mixed with copper fibers, aluminum knit into lace and cashmere, metal wires crocheted with glass beads. Versace seamstresses struggled to work with the odd new materials.

As they raced in the final days before the show to finish the collection, Donatella became more and more frightened at the prospect of facing a couture audience. She was also feeling overwhelmed by the approach of the first anniversary of Gianni's death, just days away. She numbed the pain and fear with a three-day cocaine binge, finding an enthusiastic partner once again in Christopher Ciccone, who was trailing her around the Ritz with a camera crew for a documentary about the new face of Versace. (It was never completed.)[1]

Finally, just hours before the show, Gianni's seamstresses finished the designs Donatella had ordered up: dresses with lopped-off hemlines and frayed edges that made for a tough, heavy-metal look. On the day of the show, Donatella rallied enough to play hostess to the celebrities—Robin Williams, Matt Dillon, Jon Bon Jovi, and Isabella Rossellini—whom she'd flown in for the event.

The following day, Donatella utterly crashed, holed up in her suite. The reviews were scathing. Fashion's most influential critics had cut Gianni's kid sister a break for almost a year, but now the gloves were off. The *New York Times* wrote that the show "exposed the gulf that lay between Ms. Versace's esthetic and her brother's," the frayed clothes betraying "a hint of madness."[2] Sales of Versace couture plummeted immediately.

As the year wore on, Donatella appeared blithely unaware of the fact that Versace was starting to founder under her watch. Instead of curtailing expenses, she spent the company's money with abandon. When Lilly Tartikoff, the widow of television producer Brandon Tartikoff, asked Versace to sponsor a fashion show for her annual Fire & Ice cancer benefit in December, Donatella immediately said yes. The dinner was the hottest event of the season in Los Angeles, and the socialite outdid herself each year with a more and more elaborate spectacle. This time, the ball would be held on a soundstage at Universal Studios and hosted by comedian Jerry Seinfeld. Tables went for up to fifty thousand dollars each. The Versace name, hotter than ever after Gianni's murder, was a huge draw. Eighteen months after the murder in Miami, Fire & Ice would be a sort of coming-out for Donatella as the new public face of Versace.

The house had agreed to cover most of the cost of the fashion show, and the bill quickly ran to hundreds of thousands of dollars. The company flew a dozen seamstresses to L.A. to fit more than one hundred models in everything from couture gowns to rhinestone bikinis. About fifteen dresses were new creations, and a number of frocks were to be donated for auction that evening. Donatella hired the house's signature supermodels for the evening, including Naomi Campbell, Amber Valletta, and Stephanie Seymour. Tens of thousands of Swarovski crystals were embedded in a runway that snaked in between the tables. On the evening of the gala, the models strolled amid an audience of 1,500, including Dennis Hopper, Dustin Hoffman, Carolyn Bessette Kennedy, and Goldie Hawn. The guests ate off colorful Versace plates.

At one point during the party, Donatella slipped away to a private room with some other friends. When they were alone, she pulled out a bag of cocaine and a key. Seasoned users do "key bumps"— inhaling a bit of the powder off the tip of a key—when they don't want to indulge in a full line. A friend took the key from Donatella and dipped it into the bag, snorting it quickly. Donatella followed him, savoring her evening with the stars.[5]

At the start of 1999, Versace's troubles worsened, driven in no small part by a destructive turn in Donatella's personality. As long as Gianni was alive, everyone laughed off Donatella's excesses. Her own sense of irony about her grandiose lifestyle tempered the friction that such prodigal habits might have created with someone else, and her wild personal habits could hardly do the company much harm. But after Gianni's death, Donatella developed the lethal mix of egomania and self-loathing that is so common in addicts, which the stress of her situation only exacerbated. For years, she had badly wanted to be respected for her own ability, to be more than just a helpmeet to her virtuosic big brother. Now that she had the chance to prove herself, she was failing miserably.

Her family life was unraveling quickly. After years of deterioration, her marriage to Paul finally crumbled. In June 1999, the day before Allegra's thirteenth birthday, the couple officially separated.

Donatella got little relief in the atelier, where the atmosphere was increasingly chaotic. There had been a steady exodus of longtime Versace employees who couldn't adapt to Donatella's style. She had always been chronically tardy, but her schedule now ran hours behind. She rarely turned up much before noon and often called meetings late in the evening. The large turnover of people, combined with Donatella's lackadaisical management style, left her group working marathon days.

The team she'd put together only made things worse. Painfully aware of her own shortcomings as a designer, she relied heavily on the taste of the young people she'd hired. But much of the group was horribly out of place at Versace. One of her main assistants, who came from the punk scene in London, had spiky bleached-blond hair and brought a skull-and-crossbones aesthetic to Versace. Others made sly jokes about the traditional Versace look, rolling their eyes when they had to wear the designs to company events. Longtime Versace employees viewed the newcomers as disrespectful young Turks and resisted working with them.

HOUSE OF VERSACE

Donatella added to the confusion by hiring outside stylists to help her lead the group, hoping they could serve up the vision she lacked. Instead, they only seeded confusion. They clashed with Donatella's top assistants over how the collection should be put together. They also reinforced Donatella's own inclination to favor flash over substance. As a result, the collections emphasized elaborate evening gowns but neglected more marketable day clothes. The stylists also ignored the feedback from the sales executives about what department store buyers wanted. While Gianni had been able to cherry-pick fresh ideas his assistants came up with and meld them into a coherent collection, Donatella was paralyzed. She carried the key to the gate of the Miami mansion—the last thing that Gianni had touched—everywhere she went, fingering it as if it could conjure up Gianni's spirit to help her.

Unsurprisingly, the reviews got worse and worse. When Donatella stuffed her front row with eight A-list stars for one show in 1999, the *New York Times* pilloried her for "stocking the show with celebrities, like a trout farm in the Catskills. It's bogus, it's bush league, but mainly, it's just old." The collection of screen-printed T-shirts slashed open in the back, white denim skirts, and Lolita-like tops "looked as if [it] had been designed by a lecherous old groupie on break from a Grateful Dead tour."[4] Editors at powerful magazines such as *Vogue* and *Harper's Bazaar* used Versace clothes in their editorial spreads less and less often. Complaints from the Versace press office on the drop in coverage were politely ignored.

The reviews stung Donatella badly, and the strain she felt began to poison the atmosphere at Via Gesù. The atelier was starting to resemble an alcoholic home where the children constantly try to anticipate the humors and vagaries of a drinking parent. Donatella was moody, coldly ignoring one longtime employee one day only to warmly embrace him the next. She insulated herself within a tight inner circle of assistants that became her enablers, catering to her whims and reinforcing her feelings of being under siege.

In the presence of her posse, she was the old Donatella. She threw five-course dinners in her apartment for friends and close assistants, and took the leftover desserts to Via Gesù the next day for all to enjoy. When she discovered that one employee loved lasagna, she had her cook prepare a pan of it whenever they traveled together. She lavished her favorite employees with gifts. When an assistant admired a delicate diamond necklace a jeweler had brought for a photo shoot, Donatella flicked her hand dismissively. "Oh please, darling," she quipped, as if the item were costume jewelry. "If you like it, just take it."[5] On good days in the atelier, she exuded her former irony and wittiness. She joked that she wanted actress Charlize Theron to play her should a film ever be made about Versace. Happy to forget her own personal problems, she delved into her assistants' private lives with relish, doling out tough-love advice whether they asked for it or not.

But more and more, the heavy drug use, the personal stress, and her growing fame combined to create a destructive diva. Her self-restraint was slipping away. She snorted cocaine openly in front of Versace staff. Just hours before one runway show in 1999, she did a line in the courtyard of Via Gesù in full sight of the workers who were finishing mounting the set. At after-parties in her apartment, she disappeared to her bathroom, a bodyguard standing sentry outside while she got high.

As the company's downward spiral accelerated, she became defiantly extravagant and started spending the house's money with stunning abandon. In the atelier, Donatella mimicked Gianni's over-the-top habits, justifying huge expenditures in the name of creative freedom. She ordered far more samples than her team would ever use on the runway and demanded as many as two hundred pairs of shoes just days before a show, despite the enormous cost involved in such a rush job. Her reliance on stylists was another huge expense. They charged up to five thousand dollars a day plus accommodations and business-class travel, and spent at least ten days most months in the atelier in Milan. For the runway, Donatella not only hired the most expensive models but gave favorites such as Naomi and Kate Moss diamond bracelets or rings backstage after the show.

Her personal spending was rocketing. She used only private jets for herself and her family, even for ninety-minute flights to Paris. Bodyguards followed her everywhere, sitting in the reception area of Via Gesù as she worked. While chatting with guests at parties, she often raised one hand with two fingers flipped open into a "V." It was a sign for the nearest bodyguard to whip out a Marlboro Red and slip it between her fingers, ready to be lit with her rhinestone-encrusted lighter. When she was depressed, she sent one of them down to a jeweler near Via Gesù to buy her a new bauble. It was all on the company's dime.

Donatella, now nearing forty-five, also became enormously obsessed with her physical appearance. A hairstylist and a makeup person trailed her everywhere, brushing invisible specks from her clothes and dabbing her face with fresh foundation. She flew a top hairdresser who specialized in extensions from New York to wherever she was at the time. Harsh color treatments and daily styling with hot irons had burned Donatella's natural hair to a crisp. To attach extensions, her hairdresser had to braid Donatella's real hair into tiny cornrows running horizontally around her head. She then took thick wefts of real human hair—costing more than $1,000 altogether because that shade of blond is so rare—and painstakingly sewed them into the cornrows with a curved needle and thread. While most women go as long as four months before replacing their extensions, Donatella redid hers every six to eight weeks. The cost: more than $150,000 each year.

❖ V ❖

As Donatella morphed into a prima donna, any lingering solidarity between her and Santo melted away. Publicly, Santo was still unflagging in his support of his sister. When close friends urged him to find a way to replace her, he rose in her defense. "You don't understand!" he often replied. "Donatella is the right person. She just needs some time." In the office, no one had the courage to challenge Donatella about her increasingly extravagant behavior, so they asked Santo to intervene when they had problems with her. Santo urged them to be patient and then tried to resolve the problem himself, usually in vain. If one of Santo's team members openly criticized her, he sharply reprimanded him.

But privately, Santo was galled to see the changes in Donatella and believed that her newfound fame had gone to her head. While he had agreed that Donatella would take over the role of creative chief of Versace after Gianni's death, he felt she had come to view herself as an equal to their late brother. Donatella had even ordered the house's brand name to be changed from "Gianni Versace" to "Versace." The labels on the clothes and signs on many of the shops were changed. Santo was horrified.

He and Donatella were also at loggerheads over the creative direction the company should take. Santo argued futilely that the house should hew closely to the style of Gianni's glory days. Santo was, by nature, more conservative, so he fell back on what had worked in the past. Sometimes he tried to circumvent his sister. He would surreptitiously bring Donatella's assistants bestselling items from Gianni's collections, such as trench coats or men's shirts, urging them to create new versions and slip them into the collection. But the design team, taking their cue from Donatella, snubbed him.

Once, the head of the factory that produced Versace clothes asked Santo if he could make a minicollection of men's colorful printed shirts, which had been wildly popular before Gianni's death. Donatella lacked the technical skill and sharp eye required to make printed shirts, dresses, and scarves, and she had cut them from Versace's lineup. Santo had long pressed Donatella to revive Versace's prints and gave the okay for the factory to whip up some shirts. When Donatella saw them in the showroom, she exploded. "What is this?" she demanded of an assistant. "These things don't have any part in the Versace style now! There's a new designer around here now. Get rid of these things!"

In June 1999, the tensions between the siblings erupted into a violent argument. Santo and Donatella had flown to London for the opening of a new boutique. That evening, Donatella was to stage a charity runway-show-cum-dinner in partnership with South African diamond giant De Beers. Before an eclectic audience that included Prince Charles, Pierce Brosnan, Ivana Trump, and the Backstreet Boys, a parade of models, each dripping with diamond jewelry, showed a selection of silver lamé and semitransparent couture dresses, followed by a series of tiny bikinis. One girl's breast popped out of an ill-fitting dress. Donatella herself wore a 103 karat solitaire diamond necklace.[6]

Sitting among the VIPs, Santo felt more and more agitated as he watched the models saunter out in his sister's creations. After the party, he confronted his sister in a fury. "*Che schifo!* Those clothes are disgusting!" he screamed at her. "I can't even look at them. They are simply ugly. Even I could do better than that!"

The bitter quarrel degenerated into an angry stalemate. By then, Santo understood that it mattered little what he thought of his sister's collections. He was powerless. Any pretense of their working together had long disintegrated into a loop of bitter recriminations. The company had split into two warring camps—Santo's team of managers in the offices at Via Manzoni and Donatella's creative group in Via Gesù. But every employee at Versace understood that Via Gesù was the center of power now. At Versace parties, Donatella's guests even had precedence on the list over Santo's. The house of Versace was firmly in Donatella's hands.

❖ V ❖

The torrent of news coming from Versace's rivals in 1999 only deepened Santo's distress. In March, Domenico De Sole, grasping for a way to keep Gucci from falling into the clutches of Bernard Arnault's LVMH, found his white knight: François Pinault. Pinault was Arnault's nemesis, a rival French billionaire who had built a powerful retail conglomerate. Pinault wrote a check for $3 billion, buying a 42 percent slice in Gucci and leaving LVMH with a useless minority stake.

In unsuccessfully going after Gucci, Arnault had unwittingly created a monster. The Pinault deal gave Gucci a $3 billion war chest and a mandate to scoop up other brands into a new fashion conglomerate—the first real competition Arnault had ever seen. He suddenly found himself in a billion-dollar arms race with Gucci in buying up other houses. Fueled by the deep personal animosity between Pinault and Arnault as well as the wave of money created by the Internet boom, LVMH and Gucci sent the price of corporate acquisitions to head-spinning levels. Just months after the deal with Pinault, De Sole paid $1 billion to snatch up Yves Saint Laurent.

Over the next few years, LVMH and Gucci would sweep up a raft of independent fashion houses, which were only too happy to cash out at peak prices. Gucci bought luxury shoe maker Sergio Rossi, jeweler Boucheron, and French couturier Balenciaga. LVMH spent nearly $3 billion in 1999 alone, adding Thomas Pink, Donna Karan, and Pucci to its stable. Prada also got into the act, buying seven labels in quick succession, including Jil Sander, Helmut Lang, and Church's, maker of fine men's shoes. Stock market investors joined the fray, and luxury stocks rose 144 percent in 1999.[7]

But it was the Fendi acquisition that marked the giddy peak of the handbag wars. Before the boom of the late 1990s, Fendi had been a sleepy Roman fashion house run by five tight-knit sisters and was best known for stylish furs designed by Karl Lagerfeld. All that changed in 1998, when one of the sisters came up with a new bag she dubbed the Baguette, a small, soft purse that fit neatly under the arm and came in an array of bright colors and baroque designs. To their great surprise, the sisters soon had a megahit on their hands, selling more than half a million bags for prices of up to $5,000. Fendi soon found itself in the sights of LVMH, Prada, and Gucci, who embarked on a bidding war for the house. Finally, Prada joined forces with LVMH to beat out Gucci by offering more than $1 billion for a label that had been virtually unknown outside of Italy two years earlier. It was a mind-boggling amount for a house that had just $150 million in sales and $10 million in profit.

With their size and heft, LVMH, Gucci, and Prada raised the bar immensely for smaller independent fashion houses such as Versace. For instance, the fashion company troika demanded deep discounts from the fashion magazines by negotiating advertisement placements across all of their brands. In 2000, LVMH owned forty different brands and spent 650 million euros a year for communications. By negotiating in bulk for all of its brands, it enjoyed a 20 percent discount on ad rates, giving it an enormous edge over smaller competitors such as Versace.

The rivals also spent huge sums to kit out a series of ostentatious new boutiques. Gucci poured $70 million into revamping its Madison Avenue flagship, while LVMH plunked down $150 million to buy the Warner Bros. store on Fifth Avenue for a new Louis Vuitton shop. Between 1999 and 2002, the top brands would spend a whopping $4.2 billion to open 1,400 new shops around the world.

Versace was being outclassed on every front. The house's boutiques looked tatty and dated next to other brands' shiny new shops. Versace franchisees saw a sharp drop in sales after Gianni's death, and worried about the future of the house, they stopped spending to refurbish the shops. While most fashion houses revamp their boutiques every three to five years, some Versace boutiques hadn't been remodeled in nearly a decade.

As their shoppers disappeared, the franchise owners put pressure on Santo to cut the royalties the house collected from the boutiques, and he had little choice but to cave. When sales deteriorated further, they then pressured Santo to cancel their contracts with Versace altogether. They knew that Santo had little choice but to follow the new industry trend of shunning franchise boutiques in favor of fully controlled shops, so it was an easy game. Many of them threatened to sue Versace if the company resisted. Santo couldn't bear to see his brand disappear from important cities such as San Francisco, Brussels, and Berlin, unraveling two decades' worth of work, so he spent huge sums to buy out the remaining years on the franchisees' contracts. The company then had to spend additional millions to refurbish shop after shop, while at the same time open expensive new boutiques in hot new markets such as Russia and China, where rivals were planting their flags.

Santo's early 1990s drive to bump profits by signing a jumble of licenses was now also backfiring badly. Versace had nineteen licenses when Gianni died, for everything from plus-sized clothes to underwear, bathing suits, and children's clothes, as well as several different women's lines. All of the licenses confused shoppers and tarnished the Versace brand. Santo had to start closing them.

As the new millennium drew near, Versace looked increasingly puny next to fashion's new multibrand behemoths; it was missing out on the global bonanza in luxury goods. By 1999, Versace sales were just 404 million euros, down 11 percent from the year before. By contrast, LVMH had 8.5 billion euros in sales that year—twenty times as much as Versace—and was growing by double digits. Prada and Gucci, both smaller than Versace before Gianni's death, raced past their old rival, fueled by the boom in sales of leather goods as well as their voracious corporate shopping sprees. Prada's sales soared from 40 million euros in 1990 to 1.6 billion euros ten years later. Gucci's sales topped $2 billion.

The question of the tax on Allegra's inheritance also weighed on the company. While Versace lawyers pursued an appeal to lower the amount the little girl owed, Italian law required that the company set aside a large portion of that figure. The money had to come from the house's profits, which meant Donatella and Santo had to approve an extra-large dividend of 58 billion lire ($30 million) to be paid to all three shareholders. It was money that Santo could have sunk into new shops, advertising, or factory space.

Meanwhile, Donatella's spending continued virtually unchecked. In 1999, she spent 9.6 million euros on runway shows, more than twice the amount Gianni spent the year before he died. The care and feeding of celebrities was also costing more and more as stars became more demanding. Donatella spent 2.7 million euros on free clothes, travel, accommodations, and gifts for celebrities, 40 percent more than the year before Gianni died. She also used the company as if it were her own personal bank account, spending the house's money to cover personal expenditures, from private planes to the villa she rented for the month of August in St. Tropez. As a result, Versace's 1999 net profit was less than 13 million euros, one-sixth the figure in 1996. Santo harped on his sister to cut her spending and had his finance managers come up with a plan to cut the company's costs. Donatella ignored it.

Santo began looking for ways to raise fresh cash to cover the house's growing costs. In 1999, retail executives from LVMH came calling with an offer to pay Versace 15 million euros to vacate the shop that the company rented at Via Montenapoleone 2. The location was the best one on the street, tucked just inside a majestic courtyard with porticos on three sides. When Gianni first opened it eight years earlier, the boutique, with its etched glass windows, yellow and burnt orange marble, and trompe l'oeil ceilings, had been a glittering showplace on an otherwise prim street. But the shop had become a daily reminder of the company's sagging fortunes. Santo had little choice but to accept LVMH's rich offer. It pained him to stand by while workers pulled up the inlaid mosaic medusa heads from the floor of his brother's store. The new boutique that opened a few months later was a key piece of LVMH's plan to plant Vuitton shops in the best locations on the best streets around the world. For Santo and for Versace, the loss of the Via Montenapoleone shop would be the first step in the dismantling of the empire Gianni had built.

That summer, Santo made a decision that would profoundly

affect the company's fate years later. He signed the papers to launch a bond for 100 million euros to be repaid in July 2004. Bonds usually require a borrower to maintain a healthy balance sheet for the life of the loan. If the borrower's financial health declines, the bondholders can demand their money back anytime. In Versace's case, the house pledged to keep its operating profit above net financial payments, or the cost of servicing its debt. When Santo agreed to the bond, he never suspected that the company would have trouble meeting the requirements; in twenty years, Versace had never had trouble paying off its debt. In signing the deal for the bond, Santo was trying to bring some order to the company's financial situation by consolidating its debt. He could hardly have imagined that by agreeing to the bond, he was hanging a stone around the company's neck.

Donatella decided to see off the 1990s—a decade that had brought her the greatest highs of her life along with the most unimaginable lows—in grand style. During the summer, she and Santo put Casa Casuarina up for sale, anxious to free themselves of the constant reminder of the moment their world came crashing down. But before bidding farewell to Miami Beach, Donatella wanted to throw one last son et lumière bash.

For her final New Year's Eve in Casa Casuarina, Donatella assembled the sort of guest list that only a Versace party could draw. Even the most jaded celebrity couldn't resist the idea of ringing in the new millennium at the infamous Versace mansion. In deference to her brother, Donatella had the staff hang a sign on the front gate with an arrow directing guests to an entrance around the back. Inside the high walls, music thumped over the elaborate stereo system, with a group of live musicians drumming on bongos to hype the beat. Jennifer Lopez arrived on the arm of her new manager, Benny Medina, while Gwyneth Paltrow and Madonna huddled together in the garden over flutes of champagne. Trailing behind Madonna was her new British boyfriend, Guy Ritchie. Underwater lights in the pool, with its riot of colorful mosaic tiles, gave off a sensual glow.

The glittering crowd and picture-perfect setting once would

have sent Donatella's adrenaline surging. But tonight, she simply couldn't conjure up the blithe delight that South Beach had always brought her before Gianni's death. That jet-set whirl of dinners, discos, and divertissement was forever over. Languid vacations spent lounging by the pool with her brother, as Allegra and Daniel splashed happily beside them, seemed almost beyond the grasp of memory, erased by two and a half years of near-constant woe. Hopeful gate-crashers used to gather outside Gianni's front gate, straining for a glimpse of the star designer or one of his celebrity friends. Now, the spot had become a macabre tourist attraction, as dough-faced vacationers snapped one another's picture on the marble steps where Gianni had lay dying.

Miami Beach had also changed. Gianni's presence had helped make South Beach a symbol of a roaring decade. His killing brought the decade-long party to an abrupt halt. Six years after Gianni first threw open the doors to his grandiose house, his baby sister's bash was a farewell party. Soon after, Madonna would put her own house up for sale as well, ending her disco days, with its drag queens and cone-shaped bras, and migrating to London to join Ritchie for a new life as a wannabe European sophisticate.

Wearing a glittery silver dress and clutching her pack of Marlboro Reds, Donatella was ever the practiced host, ushering friends into Gianni's elaborately tiled garden and leaning in close to divulge tidbits of juicy gossip. She orbited from one constellation of guests to another, bussing each one Italian-style on both cheeks and squealing over new designer dresses. The crowd of beautiful people danced and gawked and drank under the watchful eyes of a flank of security guards.

But behind the veil of ebullience, Donatella was deeply weary. She had little to celebrate this New Year's Eve. The fights with Santo, the searing reviews, and the precarious health of her daughter had all taken a heavy toll that year. "I'm so depressed," she confided somberly to Rupert Everett, one of her closest celebrity friends, pausing a moment before putting her party face back on to greet a new guest.[8]

As the garden filled with revelers, Donatella and Everett

closeted themselves in a bathroom, a Versace bodyguard posted outside as they got stoned together. They emerged briefly to join Donatella's guests for the countdown to midnight before disappearing again.[9] The day after the party, Donatella left Casa Casuarina, never to return.

seventeen

Toward Ruin

*f*OR GIORGIO ARMANI, OCTOBER 18, 2000, WAS AN ENCHANTED evening. The Guggenheim Museum in New York was launching a retrospective of his work and for one night, the Italian designer was the toast of Manhattan. The opening party for the show featured a roll call of famous Armani devotees. Lauren Bacall, Robert De Niro, Michelle Pfeiffer, Glenn Close, Richard Gere, and others served up gushing comments for waiting reporters, testifying to how Armani had rescued them from fashion ignominy. The parade of A-list celebrities climbed the museum's famous rotunda, amid scores of Armani's signature designs hanging on walls.

The Guggenheim party was the high point of a year that had been one long victory lap for Armani. At sixty-six, he was celebrating the twenty-fifth anniversary of his brand,

and the fashion world was only too happy to toast him again and again. Publication after publication—*Vanity Fair*, *Vogue*, the *New Yorker*, *InStyle*—ran sunny articles about Armani, complete with ruminative interviews with the master himself.

The cloying coverage neglected to report that many department store buyers and magazine editors privately thought that Armani's collections had long lost much of their freshness. Next to the pyrotechnics of John Galliano or the sex-on-a-stick collections that Tom Ford served up twice a year, Armani's designs verged on dowdy. Many whispered that Armani had more money than ideas, and there was some truth to the charge. Sensing this, Armani railed against the hot new talent in interviews with the press, branding them little more than slick marketers who had cheapened fashion.

But the millions of shoppers who wanted a bit of Italian chic, yet felt intimidated by the groovy young designers, trusted Armani. In turn, he had deftly slapped his name on a range of mass-market products—from underwear to jeans to home furnishings—without debasing his brand. As a result, his company had prospered enormously in the 1990s. By 2000, his annual sales were 1 billion euros, more than enough to let him indulge in some vanity projects: a new $30 million corporate headquarters in Milan and a huge $73 million, three-floor flagship store near Via Montenapoleone.

Halfway through his seventh decade, Armani was hardly slowing down. The sharp planes of his face that had made him a heart-throb in his youth had softened into the mellowed look of a distinguished, Continental gentleman. Daily sessions with a personal trainer left him as trim and fit as a man twenty years his junior. Posing next to fresh-faced celebrities less than half his age, he played the part of the smooth elder statesman, with his snow-white hair and cobalt blue eyes.

But even as he griped about the changes in the fashion world, he couldn't entirely ignore them. His executives urged him to think about how to safeguard the company's future after his retirement or death. Avid investment bankers lined up to court him, each regaling him with the mouthwatering valuations he could command if he sold. Some reckoned that if a damp squib such as Fendi could fetch $1 billion, the house of Armani could possibly demand at least four times that. He could finally relax, they told him, and enjoy his island vacation home in Pantelleria.

LVMH and Gucci were the only two houses rich enough to afford Armani, and both courted the designer intently. For many months in 2000, Bernard Arnault pressed for an audience with the designer, eventually securing an afternoon cup of tea and a front-row seat to an Armani runway show. Armani reveled in the attention. For much of the year, he very publicly dithered about whether to accept the offers dangling before him. He also considered listing the house on the stock market in an IPO, just as Santo Versace had planned to do several years earlier.

For Santo, the incessant coverage of Armani's year-long anniversary bash and the stratospheric valuations bandied about for his old rival were painful reminders of what Versace could have become. He watched as Armani and other houses took advantage of the boom years. Across town, Prada was planning its own stock market listing, with talk of valuations for the house of up to $8 billion. Meanwhile, Versace was mired in family intrigue, watching the richest luxury goods market the business had ever seen go by. Santo's vision of seeing Versace listed on the stock market was a distant dream.

In January 2001, as the coverage of his silver anniversary finally ebbed, Armani made his choice. He was put off by the commercial culture of Tom Ford's Gucci but feared his house would become just a cog in the wheel at LVMH. Even billions of dollars in cash didn't sway him. He already had more money than he could spend, he told friends. Unable to imagine life without his work, he decided to turn down both De Sole and Arnault.

Nine months later, on a perfect autumn day in New York, fashion week was just gearing up. Armani was in town for a series of publicity events, as was Tom Ford, who was putting the final touches on plans for a party the following evening to open a redesigned Yves Saint Laurent flagship store on Madison Avenue. The bash, coming less than a year after Ford's debut collection for the French couture house, was the week's hot ticket.

But on the morning of September 11, 2001, the fashion week

reverie was shattered when terrorists plunged two airliners into the towers at the World Trade Center. With the city seized by fear and chaos, the organizers of fashion week abruptly called off the shows. New York City police commandeered the runway spaces to set up makeshift morgues. Coltish young models fled Manhattan by bus and by train without bothering to contact their agents.

The shock to a business that thrives on frivolity and fun came fast and hard. Retailers halved their buying budgets and powerful department stores such as Neiman Marcus and Bergdorf Goodman even canceled orders for fall fashions that had already been shipped from Europe. In some U.S. cities, Gucci took down billboard ads featuring an out-all-night party girl with her hand provocatively plunged down the front of her pants. Much of London's fashion week, which follows right after New York's, was scotched. Milan and Paris decided to go ahead with their shows, but few retailers were willing to make the trip. Celebrities who had been booked for the shows months earlier also refused to board planes.

For those who did make the trip, the shows in Milan had a funereal air. Fashionistas had to run their designer leather bags through metal detectors to get into the shows. The marble lobby of the Four Seasons was conspicuously empty of the designer swag the houses usually delivered for their best guests. Even the catwalk photographers, normally full of whistles and catcalls for the prettiest models, were quiet.

But Donatella wasn't going to let the gloom and doom ruin her fashion week. Although other houses canceled virtually all parties until Christmas, she was going ahead with a huge bash she had been planning for months—a celebration of the recent marriage of Jennifer Lopez to Cris Judd, a former dancer who had directed one of her music videos. Even by Donatella's standards, the party was breathtaking. She'd originally planned to hold it at Via Gesù, but after the terrorist attacks she moved it all to the Versace villa on Lake Como because it was easier to secure. After Donatella's runway show, which closed the somber fashion week, a fleet of cars ferried more than 150 fashion editors, models, and local socialites—virtually none of whom knew J.Lo personally—out to the lake. About a hundred security guards watched over the guests as they filled the house and gardens.

Villa Fontanelle was a sumptuous sight that evening. More than three thousand yellow roses and one thousand white candles lined the length of the driveway and spilled into the mansion and throughout the gardens. Workers had erected a three-story-high glass enclosure over the terrace. Floodlights beamed over the lake to foil any paparazzi hoping to get an unauthorized photo of the golden couple by shooting from a boat. Violinists wearing black, hedonistic masks sat on marble plinths, serenading guests who sipped Cristal champagne and loaded their plates with caviar, butter-soft prosciutto, and potato gnocchi.

Just before 11 p.m., Lopez, wearing a jade silk plunge-neck jumpsuit and an enormous diamond ring, arrived with her new husband, trailed by Donatella, clad in a floor-length leopard-print dress. Under a full moon, the newlyweds obligingly cut into a giant cake, elaborately decorated with white, green, and yellow icing, and fed each other small slices as photographers snapped away. They settled on a plush red sofa and canoodled some more for the benefit of the cameras.

"During hard times, it's important to continue celebrating life's beautiful moments," Donatella told reporters who queried her on why she didn't cancel the party. "Nothing is more beautiful or full of promise than a marriage."[1] Eight months later, Jennifer Lopez filed for divorce.

If the terrorist attacks were a serious trial for the most self-confident designers, they were nearly Donatella's undoing. Her ongoing psychodrama both titillated and horrified the fashion world. Rivals had once happily trafficked in gossip about her outrageousness, swapping stories about her spending, her celebrity friends, and her parties. But as her predicament visibly worsened, they simply felt sorry for Gianni's kid sister. No one wanted to see a storied brand such as Versace simply wither away.

The atelier was descending into chaos. Donatella began sleeping until lunchtime and often didn't turn up at Via Gesù until midafternoon. Her secretary learned not to schedule appointments before 2 p.m., but even then Donatella often canceled at the last minute. She withdrew more and more, leaving her personal assistants to run interference with staff members, journalists, and friends. When she did turn up in the atelier, she was extremely moody, foul-tempered one day and sunny the next.

Oftentimes, she was so befuddled that members of her team who spoke no Italian couldn't make sense of her garbled English. During long meetings with Versace executives, she escaped to the bathroom halfway through. When she returned, she was so confused that the managers had to start the meetings virtually from scratch. The atmosphere in the atelier became increasingly strained, her group afraid to provoke her whenever she turned up. Their respect for her deteriorated as her behavior grew more erratic. She phoned one employee in the middle of the night raving about something she wanted them to do. Wild stories about how many grams of cocaine Donatella snorted each day flew through Via Gesù.

Her design team, stretched woefully thin, was working all hours. With Donatella absent for long stretches, they came to rely more and more on the hired stylists to make decisions on how to put together the collections—only to have their boss swoop back in at the last minute, change her mind, and demand wholesale alterations just days before a show.

Sensing that she was losing control of the atelier, Donatella grew increasingly paranoid. She grilled her assistants to find out what the design team was saying about her. In Los Angeles, she once suddenly decided she had to see her team's work. Two assistants flew out the next day from Milan to show her the boards—the sketches of the designs the team was working on. After an eleven-hour flight, the pair arrived at the thousand-dollar-a-night Beverly Hills Hotel on Sunset Boulevard where Donatella always stayed. But when they called over to her villa, Donatella's personal assistant answered the phone. "She's not feeling well," he told them. "She can't see you. I think you should just go back to Milan." The next day, the designers packed up and flew home.

The stress and heavy drug use sent her sense of style veering wildly off course. At one point, one of her assistants came up with a new logo consisting of her initials, DV, written in forbidding Goth lettering. The rest of her team and the Versace sales managers were horrified, but Donatella loved it. It soon turned up on men's clothing and some women's bags. She had slipcovers made with the logo to cover the health warnings on her packages of Marlboros and had "I Love DV" emblazoned on T-shirts. Versace's medusa logo was also mushrooming. "Make it more Versace!" she told her team when they showed her a sample. At a loss, the overworked group piled medusa heads willy-nilly onto clothes and bags, slapping them on everything from belts to the rivets on purses to the bridge of platform shoes.

Without a strong hand to guide them, the various lines took off in different directions. The women's collection was alternatively sweet and romantic or hard-edged. The men's line had largely fallen apart as the team put studs, zips, and the Goth DV logo on the clothes in a clumsy effort to appeal to a younger crowd. Elsewhere, the Versus team was making teenybopper clothes that looked cheap and fit terribly. And with virtually no one watching in the Milan atelier, the companies that made other licensed products such as jeans and sportswear churned out whatever they liked.

Meanwhile, Donatella's personal life was hardly less fraught. She found little solace in men and rarely dated, preferring to be alone. To be sure, her heavy drug use, the stress of Allegra's illness, and the troubles in the atelier were hardly ideal ingredients for a healthy relationship. She joked wryly about her single status with friends and associates. "What I need is someone like Prince," she quipped. "He would be the perfect man for me!"

❖ V ❖

Donatella's problems were mounting just when the company could least afford them. The post–September 11, 2001, malaise spread like an oil slick through the luxury goods market. Shopping suddenly felt crass and tasteless. In the weeks after the attacks, the sales at many houses fell by half. In the following months, the globe-traveling shoppers who accounted for about a third of luxury goods sales stayed home. Stores in tourist destinations such as Louis Vuitton's flagship in Hawaii, which had pulled in more than $100 million in sales the year before, were deserted. Luxury goods groups learned a harsh lesson on September 11. While the very rich would always be able to afford the $6,000 Dior gown or the $5,000 Hermès Birkin bag, the companies' fortunes had soared by hawking $150 Louis Vuitton key chains and $500 Prada bags to the middle classes. After the terrorist attacks, these consumers traded down as quickly as they had traded up. They turned away from the logo-heavy status symbols that had felt so good in the 1990s but which now seemed completely wrong.

Prada was the quickest to fall. The house canceled plans for an IPO and, $1.2 billion in debt, was too strapped to invest much in its new brands. At the end of 2001, it also whipped up a public relations storm with its opening of an extravagant $40 million shop in New York's Soho neighborhood. Just a mile north of the World Trade Center site, the store's avant-garde design and high-tech gimmicks were wildly out of sync with an area where shoppers could still inhale the burning debris of Ground Zero. The mighty LVMH was also hit hard. Arnault had doubled the group's sales with his late-1990s shopping spree, but few of the brands in his stable were making money, leaving him to rely on Louis Vuitton to make most of LVMH's profit. Meanwhile, Gucci's sales slowed for the first time since its 1990s comeback.

While the megacompanies could count on the rich profit margins of their marquee brands to keep them afloat, the downturn devastated houses that had struggled to keep pace even in the fat times. Bulgari abruptly broke off talks to acquire the Rome couture house Valentino, which had been limping along for years. In the United States, falling sales forced Tommy Hilfiger to close most of his retail stores and reorganize the company.

But virtually no fashion house was as ill-prepared to cope with the blow of September 11, 2001, as Versace. Until that day, Santo could still hope to find a way out of the mess the house had sunk into over the previous four years. But after the terrorist attacks, the problems that had been mounting since Gianni's death began to pile up like a spectacular car crash.

At the heart of it was the desperate state of Santo and Donatella's relationship. In October 2002, the siblings flew to London to celebrate the opening of a retrospective of Gianni's work at the Victoria & Albert Museum. The show was a high point of the city's cultural calendar that year and was the largest exhibit that the V&A—renowned for a costume collection dating back four hundred years—had ever devoted to a single designer.

Before the evening's festivities, Santo made a private visit to the museum, walking through rooms that were as quiet as a church, where Gianni's best work hung on sleek black, gold, and silver mannequins. There were more than 130 of Gianni's designs, with separate rooms showcasing his magnificent prints, innovative metal mesh fabrics, embroidered couture gowns, and costumes for the ballet and theater. There was the eggshell and blue dress worn by Diana to great acclaim, as well as Elizabeth Hurley's safety pin dress. Just six of the designs were by Donatella. Seeing Gianni's life work gathered in one of the world's great museums, Santo fought back tears. "Just look at these clothes! Look how beautiful they are!" he told the Versace executive who had helped organize the show. "Gianni was a genius."

By the time of the V&A celebration, Donatella and Santo made little effort to present a united front to the world. In Milan, they had retreated into two hostile camps. The business side regarded Donatella as an out-of-control diva who was steadily running the house into the ground. To Donatella's merry band of designers, hairstylists, and personal assistants, Santo's managers were a bunch of bean counters who harped endlessly about budgets and schedules and thwarted their creativity. Knowing that Donatella had the last word only egged them on. Each camp included provocateurs who fed to each of the Versace siblings unflattering items about the other side. While their offices were a five-minute walk apart, the siblings rarely met, instead using emissaries to do their business.

The animosity between brother and sister was rippling throughout the business. Successful fashion houses find a balance between the creative side—which often sees fashion as an artistic expression—and the business side, which simply wants clothes that sell. In well-run houses, the creative team uses feedback on trends and sales reports from the business side to make clothes that are fresh and forward looking but will still appeal to shoppers. A disciplined atelier then follows a tight schedule in designing and making the samples to be shown on the runway. Tightly run houses such as Gucci and Armani will only show samples on the runway that they actually plan to produce. But at Versace, Donatella ignored the sales reports that landed on her desk and waved away pleas from the business side to stick to a strict design schedule. She took so long to decide which samples to show on the runway that production managers were hopelessly late in ordering fabrics, buttons, and zippers, delaying the rest of the process. In turn, the samples often had embellishments and details that were impossible to replicate in the factory. As a result, many of the outfits shown on the runway were never produced—an enormous waste of money.

The delays in the atelier meant that deliveries were chronically late. And when the clothes did arrive, they were a mess; a crate of jackets might arrive without any skirts or pants. Complete, on-time deliveries are crucial in retailing, particularly in the dog-eat-dog U.S. market. Stores typically have only about eight weeks to sell clothes at full price, before the pressure mounts to start discounting. Stores began slashing prices aggressively after September 11, 2001, and on-time deliveries meant the difference between profit and loss.

Moreover, while European women tend to buy their clothes in a few large shopping trips at the start of a season, American women are grazers, looking for something new year-round. U.S. department stores encourage them to keep coming back by pressing the fashion houses to deliver new stock as often as every two months. (Later in the decade, the best fashion houses would even move to monthly deliveries.) For Versace, that sort of pace was impossible; it was struggling to deliver even semiannual collections on time. When Versace sales executives relayed buyers' complaints about the delays to Donatella, she retorted that the fault lay with the factory, not her team.

The chaos in the atelier created further domino effects. When buyers visited the Versace showroom, they found a collection that seemed afflicted with attention deficit disorder. The atelier was coming up with a jumble of different styles, materials, and colors. When the clothes did arrive on the sales floor of the stores, there were still other problems. Gianni's designs had been famous for their exquisite, flattering fit. Donatella's dresses, skirts, and pants fit poorly. She preferred to design for smaller sizes such as American twos and fours and neglected the larger sizes that most women, particularly in the United States, could fit into. Indeed, while other houses cut a different pattern to accommodate American women's typical pear-shaped figures, Versace stuck to the slim, unforgiving fit used for European women.

Department store buyers still sat in the front row of Donatella's shows, but fewer and fewer bothered to view the collections in the showroom. They turned instead to Roberto Cavalli, a crass Florence-based designer who had been designing since the early 1970s without ever really breaking through. When Gianni was still alive, few buyers bothered to visit Cavalli's showroom, finding his designs to be tacky takeoffs on Versace's sultry sophistication. But after Gianni's death, Cavalli found salvation. He rushed to fill the gap left by Donatella's disastrous collections, making form-fitting gowns in bold animal prints and jersey dresses in brightly colored patterns that were reminiscent of Versace's greatest hits. Department stores began placing large orders and magazine editors who might have used Versace pieces to inject a sexy charge into an editorial spread instead called in Cavalli dresses.

With department stores abandoning the brand, Santo had to rely on the company's own shops to pick up the slack. He had tripled the number of Versace-controlled stores since Gianni's death, but the strategy, particularly in the wake of September 11, 2001, flopped badly. Santo was trying to run with the pack of top-notch brands such as Chanel and Louis Vuitton, but Versace was no longer in that league. It was a costly mistake, perhaps born from a refusal to accept that his sister's work would never sell well enough to support such a grand store network.

The palatial Versace flagship on Fifth Avenue in New York was the most painful failure. Inside the store, Donatella's eveningwear had pride of place, but the top line was hardly enough to fill the huge space. A confused array of cheap licensed products such as jeans and sportswear clashed with the boutique's grandeur and rich finishings. The collapse in management at the top of the company had trickled down to the store, where poorly trained shop assistants spent their days socializing and snapping gum, with little idea about how to handle the few shoppers who walked in the door. Both the Fifth Avenue boutique and its lonely sibling on Madison Avenue were hemorrhaging money.

In the weeks after September 11, 2001, sales in Versace shops fell by as much as a quarter worldwide. But while other brands eventually rebounded, Versace's sales never came back. Some boutiques became a dumping ground for the unsold stock that was piling up in Versace warehouses, as franchisees forced Santo to buy back clothes they couldn't get rid of. Santo finally began cutting stores, closing about a fifth of the shops within a couple of years.

Yet Donatella's spending went unchecked. She spent $2 million on a huge new diamond ring and sent the bill to the company, without a word to Santo. When the invoice landed on Santo's desk, he exploded. But there was little he could do. Her parties also betrayed little sign of the house's strained finances. The Versace events team flew flowers, candles, and complete sets of the house's china to parties around the world. Hot DJs from New York and London traveled to Milan for galas at the company's expense. For an invitation to one bash in New York, the house sent each guest a Versace china plate, the details of the evening printed on the ribbon wrapping the box it came in.[2] Donatella continued to fly in consultants, celebrities, and staff from the United States to Europe on the Concorde or in private jets. The house catered to the increasingly outrageous demands of spoiled stars without a quibble. For instance, some celebrities would fly to Italy only if the private jet was of a certain size.

Sales of red-carpet attire had collapsed since Donatella's first collection in Paris in 1998. The time-consuming handmade dresses monopolized the atelier for weeks. Donatella sometimes slowed down the seamstresses' work further by asking them to whip up an elaborate gown for her to wear to an event with just days' notice. Moreover, the cost of staging the shows was high. One year, Donatella sent her personal florist from Milan to lay eighteen thousand roses—carefully chosen to match the fuchsia, cream, and blush pink in the collection—under a glass runway. Five assistants spent two days planting the flowers into moist sponges under the glass. The effect was mesmerizing; on the night of the show, lights illuminated the bed of roses from below, creating a soft pastel haze.[3] But the expense was enormous for a collection that represented less than 2 percent of the house's sales.

Santo lobbied hard for her to shutter the couture line, but like a little girl playing dress-up, Donatella was enamored of the glamour and adrenaline of the red carpet, which provided an escape from the tedium of everyday business. It was her link to the celebrity world that she adored. She loved conjuring up extravagant gowns for the actresses and singers she counted as friends. Closing the line would be tantamount to admitting she lacked the skills for couture. For a long time, she argued that the PR value of the glitzy, one-of-a-kind clothes made up for the losses the line racked up. For instance, when Jennifer Lopez wore a spectacular jungle print dress cut down to her navel to the Grammy Awards in 2000, the outfit won heavy coverage from daily newspapers and fashion magazines alike.

But in the end, Santo scored a rare victory in his war with Donatella and convinced her to scale back on the line. In 2000, Versace quit the Ritz and staged the show in the Rue du Faubourg Saint-Honoré boutique, showing just a few dozen pieces. In January 2003, the house scrapped the couture runway show altogether, replacing it with a small showroom presentation featuring just two models and a roster of fiberglass mannequins.

Otherwise, however, Santo largely failed in his attempts to contain Donatella's spending. He even tried to protect his little sister. He had the house's finance team find ways to tuck Donatella's enormous expenses into Versace's balance sheet, even though most of the outlays would never have passed as corporate costs in a more professional company. The free clothes she gave to her celebrity friends, her personal travel in private jets, and the cost of entertaining her entourage—who happily lapped up Versace largesse—were classified generically as image-building costs (known as *spese di rappresentanza* in Italian). In 2001, this figure was about $2.5 million. That was on top of $53 million for advertising and promotion and another $9 million for runway shows and parties.

Her spending hit new heights with the remodeling of her vast apartment. Since the company owned the flat, she was obliged to pay Versace rent to live there. But after Gianni's death, she simply stopped paying. In 2001, she embarked on a wholesale renovation of the place—again on the company's dime. When the work got under way, she decamped to the royal suite at the Principe Di Savoia, the grand 1920s-era building that is one of Milan's top luxury hotels, along with her children and personal staff. She stayed for nearly a year, the immense bill paid for by Versace. Even for a hotel accustomed to hosting celebrities, Arab princes, and corporate magnates, Donatella's sojourn there became the stuff of legend.

❖ V ❖

Meanwhile, Santo tried to plug the holes in the company balance sheet by putting on the block the expensive toys that Gianni had collected. Versace was once again a fixture on the auction circuit, but now it was a seller. The sale of the Miami house by Sotheby's in autumn 2000 brought in $19 million, and an auction of the villa's contents brought another $10 million the following spring. The sale in London of Gianni's beloved collection of twenty-five Picassos netted 11 million pounds ($18 million). Santo even got rid of part of Via della Spiga 25, the original Versace headquarters where Gianni and his hungry young team tasted the first fruits of the brand's success twenty years earlier.

But Santo soon believed that Versace needed far greater support than asset sales could provide. In the first years after Gianni's death, the company had considered selling a stake in the house to an outside investor to raise the money for Allegra to pay her huge inheritance tax bill. Ultimately, the Italian government largely abolished inheritance taxes and she had to pay far less, but Santo kept the idea of selling a stake alive. He felt a sale could resolve two problems at once: It could loosen Donatella's grip on the company and it would give him the chunk of fresh money he needed to fix the brand's myriad problems once and for all.

He had another reason to look for a shot of cash. The house's 2002 results were going to be a disaster. Sales were falling, and the company was headed for a loss. At the end of the year, the interest Versace had to pay on its debt would likely be higher than its operating profit, thus violating the terms of its 100-million-euro bond. If Versace defaulted, investors who held the bond could demand the amount be paid in full immediately. Since the house couldn't possibly pay, it could find itself facing bankruptcy. Versace's creditors, concerned about the company's precarious situation and sensitive to the gossip about the dire state of Santo and Donatella's relationship, prodded him toward seeking an outside investor. In 2002, Santo gave a mandate to an investment bank to search for an investor willing to buy a stake in the house.

But the move set off a firestorm of opposition from Donatella.

She still believed she was the best leader for the company; she wouldn't hear of letting go of her own holding or her daughter's. Her drug use had dimmed her judgment enormously. The fights between the siblings grew so bitter that Donatella instructed her lawyers to deliver a stark message to her older brother: If he crossed her, she would kick him out of Versace.

Many wondered why Santo didn't simply abandon the company as it spun out of control. After five years of grieving, he had finally overcome the acute sense of loss at his brother's death, only to find himself in a battle royal with his sister. In moments of pique and despondency, he threatened to sell his stake and be done with her. But his commitment to the company that Gianni had built—and to the idea of family, however riven by conflict—was too strong for him to jump ship.

In any event, the search for an outside investor ended in a whimper. As Versace's situation deteriorated, the company's bankers struggled to put together a coherent version of the so-called book, the document that laid out a company's financial situation and future strategic plans for potential investors. Moreover, they couldn't entertain offers from rival companies such as Gucci and LVMH; the family would consider only offers to buy a minority stake of 20 percent to 30 percent from financial investors such as private equity funds. Once the house's fortunes turned up, the investor would have to sell its stake as part of a future stock market listing.

But potential investors were extremely leery. The few funds that made tentative offers demanded the power to sweep out the current management—especially Donatella. Furthermore, they were willing to sink very little money into such a troubled situation. Santo felt the house was worth about 500 million euros. The offers by the investment funds, however, valued it at about 100 million euros—virtually nothing. Before Gianni's death, investment bankers had expected an IPO to value the house at as much as $2 billion. Now, it was worth less than a tenth of that. In the end, neither Donatella nor Santo even met with potential investors. Donatella would never agree to step aside, and Santo eventually acknowledged that selling just a small stake in the company wouldn't raise the sort of money needed to bail the company out. As 2002 drew to a close, it became evident that

HOUSE OF VERSACE

Versace was going to violate the covenants of the bond if it didn't find some fresh cash quickly.

An unlikely savior came in the form of a man named Leonardo Del Vecchio. The founder of the eyeglasses manufacturer Luxottica, Del Vecchio boasted a Dickensian story that was rare in Italy. Raised in an orphanage, he never finished high school, instead going to work as an apprentice to a craftsman at fourteen. Ten years later, in 1961, he founded his own company, originally a small manufacturer of simple eyeglass frames, which rode the wave of consumer interest in designer eyewear and ultimately bought the LensCrafters and Sunglass Hut chains. Del Vecchio spotted an opportunity in Versace's troubles. In fall 2002, he lost his license to make Giorgio Armani–brand eyeglasses and thought Versace could be an ideal replacement. If Santo agreed to sign a ten-year contract to license its eyewear to him, Luxottica would pay 25 million euros up front for the renewal of the deal for a further ten years. Santo and Del Vecchio reached an agreement right around Christmas, saving Versace from default with just days to spare. It hardly solved Santo's problems, but it bought him a little more time to stop his family company's slide toward disaster.

eighteen

Breaking Down

*i*N JANUARY OF EVERY YEAR FROM 1960 UNTIL HIS DEATH IN 2008, Richard Blackwell published a list of the worst-dressed celebrities. The list, laced with bitchy put-downs and high-camp commentary, mercilessly skewered the great and the good. The style guru once dubbed Barbra Streisand as "the masculine bride of Frankenstein." The media, looking for an antidote to so much fawning celebrity coverage, gave Blackwell's acid-tipped list ample play each year. In January 2003, Donatella Versace landed on Blackwell's list, alongside Anna Nicole Smith and Princess Anne. Donatella, he wrote, "resembles a flash-fried Venus, stuck in a Miami strip mall. Time to toss the peroxide once and for all." To the dismay of Versace's press office, newspapers and magazines eagerly picked up the withering description. It was hardly the image that Donatella wanted to project for herself or for her business.

As a young woman, Donatella had had an alluring prettiness, but by the time she landed on Blackwell's list, sunlight had leathered her beautiful alabaster skin and plastic surgery had ruined her features, leaving her with an appearance so cartoonish it made her the butt of jokes. The heavy makeup she'd always worn to create a vampish image now looked like a painted mask. With her frozen face, odd-shaped nose, and lips collagen-injected into a "trout pout," Donatella at forty-seven had become an outlandish camp goddess. Her legendary discipline at the dinner table was also crumbling. Instead of the sculpted physique she'd maintained in her thirties and early forties, rolls of fat now spilled over her waistband. She stopped sporting the ultra-miniskirts she'd worn for thirty years. She doubled up her efforts to lose weight, trying to subsist some days on just Diet Coke, strong espressos, and dozens of Marlboro Reds, stubbing them out distractedly in ashtrays the staff scattered for her throughout Via Gesù. But it didn't work. When she emerged for her bow at the end of shows, looking dumpy next to a willowy model half her age, her forced smile was an expression of painful self-consciousness.

Ironically, her shocking appearance increased her fame even more. But instead of projecting cool, Donatella was becoming a caricature representing the extremes of the fashion world. Her physical appearance and hard-living style had become so notorious that *Saturday Night Live* turned it into a recurring spoof. One of the television show's lead comediennes, Maya Rudolph, played Donatella as a foot-stomping diva, cigarette and glass in hand. Following her everywhere was a clutch of hunky male assistants clad in leather trousers and stripped to the waist, gyrating flamboyantly. "I am Donatella Versace. Welcome to my show where I smoke and look good," says Rudolph to open the sketch. The real Donatella was a remarkably good sport about Rudolph's impersonation. She appeared with the comedienne at Radio City Music Hall for the VH1/*Vogue* fashion awards, walking onto the stage and deadpanning, "What are you all doing in my bathroom?"

❖ **V** ❖

Donatella's appearance on Blackwell's list kicked off a year in which she and the company would career from crisis to crisis. Her life was going off the rails, but she didn't have the courage to admit it. Inside her cocoon, she could blame everyone but herself for the chaos around her. As her failures piled up for all the world to see, she fell into a vicious cycle. The more things spun out of control, the faster she ran from her problems. Swinging from fits of self-hatred to stubborn displays of megalomania, she was at a loss about how to escape the painful loop. It took bigger and bigger hits of cocaine to maintain this state of denial. But time was running out.

By the spring of 2003, the management of the company was breaking down completely. Executives were tired of fighting with her about her spending and watching the house lurch forward without a strategy for recovery. In short order, the house's chief operating officer, chief financial officer, and two board members all quit. Versace was rudderless. As a result, it missed the rare opportunities for rescue that came along.

At Versace's show that March, Ron Frasch, the chief executive of Bergdorf Goodman, was pleasantly surprised with the collection, particularly a series of corsetlike evening dresses that tied up the back and came in soft pastel shades of green and pink. Bergdorf had long stopped carrying Versace, but the store was selling oodles of sexy designs by Cavalli and Dolce & Gabbana. Frasch thought Versace could provide a similar shot of excitement. Given the perilous state of the house, it was an enormous leap of faith on his part. He decided to stage a trunk show, a private viewing of a designer's collection for a store's regular clients. If the trunk show did well, Bergdorf would carve out a space for Versace on its selling floor. The store put Versace designs in its windows and featured them in full-page ads in the *New York Times* under the headline "Very Bergdorf." At the trunk show, Bergdorf clients snapped up the corset dresses, as well as white moleskin coats, leather bags, and black leather jackets. In all, the store sold $620,000 worth of goods—far less than the $5 million the store pocketed for a Chanel trunk show around the same time, but enough to green-light a permanent space.[1]

HOUSE OF VERSACE

But by then the management vacuum in Milan had paralyzed Versace. When Bergdorf asked for help in designing the space, it couldn't wrench a decision—or money—out of the house, so it built a simple white box. Requests to Donatella to schedule personal appearances in the store went unanswered. Disastrously, the store received very few of the pieces it ordered. Within a few months, Frasch filled the space with other brands.[2] Other retailers took note, and faith in the house sank to a new low.

In June 2003, Versace published the disastrous 2002 accounts. Sales were falling, net debt had risen from 100 million euros in 2001 to 130 million euros a year later, and the house posted a loss of 5.5 million euros. (The payment from Luxottica pushed the operating profit into the black, thus preventing Versace from defaulting on the bond, but it still had a net loss for the year.)

But more embarrassingly, the company's auditors finally called Donatella on her habit of using the house as a personal bank machine. Corporate auditors are independent watchdogs who have the responsibility of making sure the balance sheet conforms with accounting standards. For several years, they had stayed silent as Donatella's expenditures grew. But in 2003, they finally objected to a series of costs on the company's books that were clearly unjustified. They slapped a stern statement on the annual report demanding that Donatella reimburse Versace for her personal expenditures and warning that the house's soaring costs threatened to destroy the company. Santo had battled with the auditors for weeks, trying to convince them not to attach the note, but the problems were too big for them to ignore. The warning was a serious blow to Versace's corporate credibility. But Donatella still refused to reimburse the house for the expenditures.

Versace's creditors were also growing alarmed. In just a year's time—in July 2004—Versace would have to pay back the 100-million-euro bond, but its finances were clearly falling apart. The search for an outside investor had been fruitless. The management vacancies at the top of the company were hard to fill; fashion's best executives refused to risk going to work there. When the bond came due, Versace would need to convince its bankers to refinance the loan, but if the company remained in its current state, they would hardly agree. If the banks cut off new financing, Versace could go bankrupt.

Another deadline began to loom as well: Allegra's eighteenth birthday. The young woman would finally come into her controlling stake on June 30, 2004, just days before the bond came due. Since Gianni's death, Allegra had been a shadowy presence that haunted the house. She virtually never turned up in the Versace offices, although she did occasionally appear in the front row of her mother's runway shows. Once, she was seated next to Mariah Carey, whose ample bust spilled voluptuously over the top of a Versace gown, making Allegra appear shockingly thin in contrast. She looked tiny and frail next to the hulking bodyguards who trailed her everywhere she went.

During her rare public appearances, she seemed painfully uncomfortable. She rarely smiled, often wearing a wary, slightly wounded look when photographers jostled for a picture of her. Hawk-eyed PR people kept curious journalists from even approaching the girl at the shows. Allegra's anorexia was an open secret—just a glimpse of her rickety frame said it all—but the Versace press office convinced the media to refrain from writing about the young heiress as long as she was a minor.

But despite her illness, Allegra was growing into that rare creature—a celebrity child who wears her wealth and extravagant upbringing lightly. She was raised among the offspring of the world's most prominent celebrities, spending birthdays and holidays with the children of Madonna, Demi Moore, Sting, Eric Clapton, and Anna Wintour. As Donatella's daughter and Gianni's heir, she had lifelong membership in the rarefied world of the truly rich and famous. She traveled in private jets, learned to swim in the pool of the Beverly Hills Hotel, and spoke several languages; she seemed as comfortable in the celebrity hothouse of Los Angeles as in the Eurotrash circles of Milan or London. When she spoke English, she pronounced her words with a light British lilt that was a product of the expensive expatriate school she attended in Milan.

As a child, there had been something special about Allegra, a poise and self-possession that made adults want to engage her. As she approached adulthood, she still had an aura that generated a great deal of fascination, fed in no small part by her reclusiveness. She could easily have been one of those heirs who grow into spoiled, petulant monsters and wind up in the tabloid gossip columns for their antics. Instead, she was growing into a remarkably unassuming, down-to-earth young woman, the trials of her family life and her illness having matured her beyond her years. She was more diligent than her mother in calling Zia Nora in Reggio, much to the delight of the old lady. With friends, who called her "Allie," she never sought to be the center of attention or tried to exploit her status. She inherited her mother's dry wit and sense of irony but not her grandeur or megalomania, and she was the first to joke about her surreal upbringing.

Like Donatella, Allegra wasn't a classic beauty but possessed a mysterious physical allure. Growing up amid people who spent much of their waking hours critiquing clothes and appearances, she was extremely fashion conscious but not ostentatious. While other girls her age struggled with grooming, makeup, and hairstyles, Allegra had a preternaturally mature sense of how to put herself together. She loved girly, colorful clothes, mixing H&M pieces with Miss Sixty denim or Versace slip skirts. But, despite her good looks—she had pretty, shoulder-length brown hair and dark brown eyes—she shied away from dating even as her peers began to break off into couples. In high school, she became interested in acting, perhaps as an escape from the tensions at home. She had a regal sense of presence that came from growing up in the limelight and being the constant center of attention. Years of dance training made her more graceful and refined in the way she moved, her extreme thinness adding an arresting sense of fragility.

As she headed into her senior year, she applied and was accepted to Brown University, the Ivy League college in Providence, Rhode Island. It was a good fit for Allegra. Brown is a popular destination for celebrity children, from the scions of Hollywood stars such as Susan Sarandon to the likes of John F. Kennedy, Jr., and Amy Carter. The college is the most easygoing of the Ivy Leagues, with few core requirements and the option of taking classes on a pass/fail basis, and the school's strong performing arts program is a big draw for artistically inclined students such as Allegra.

Until 2003, Allegra's youth, long absences, and precarious health left Donatella free to exercise her daughter's share. But as her eighteenth birthday approached, Allegra took more interest, beginning to prepare for the day that she would control her uncle's company. She started attending shareholder meetings, although she still said little. The enormous damage wrought to Allegra's inheritance by devaluation of the company became steadily more evident. When Gianni died, the child was worth as much as $1 billion. When she was finally primed to take possession of her inheritance, it had shriveled to a fraction of that amount. The money gleaned from the sale of the Picassos, the Miami mansion, and other of Gianni's assets had gone up in smoke.

At the same time, Donatella's spiraling drug use was shredding her relationship with Allegra as well as with Daniel, then thirteen. Her mood swings—laughing one minute, sobbing the next—were terrifying to the children. Other times she screamed at them, and if they tried to reason with her, she refused to listen.[3]

The confluence of the deadline for the bond and Allegra's coming of age piled the pressure on Donatella. Allegra would effectively become her boss when the girl became an adult, free to challenge both Donatella's and Santo's decisions. How Allegra would exercise her power was a wild card—for Donatella and for the company.

❖ V ❖

During the spring of 2003, Santo and a clutch of Versace executives made a last-ditch effort to salvage the company and soothe its bankers. They brought in Fabio Massimo Cacciatori, a consultant with an expertise in restructuring, as CEO, to see how the house of Versace might be cleaned up.

When Cacciatori arrived, the company was halfway through the calendar year but its 2003 budget had yet to be completed. From the start, Cacciatori was a misfit at Versace, a company long driven more by the whims of the controlling family than by good management practices. He was the classic consultant called in to conduct a dry-eyed analysis of a troubled business. His approach was de rigueur in other businesses—measuring performance against competitors, looking for areas to cut waste, setting specific budgets for each department—but they were downright bizarre in the fashion world, where the suits are considered second-class citizens. At Versace, no one had ever taken a really close look at how the business was—or should be—run.

HOUSE OF VERSACE

Twelve consultants from Cacciatori's firm set up camp inside the Versace headquarters that summer, sifting through the company's contracts with suppliers and sales reports for the stores. They interviewed bemused employees on the workings of every department, filling out so-called activity efficiency worksheets that measured the performance of each one. Santo stopped in daily to greet the group and scan the thick reports they were compiling. Cacciatori presented Donatella and Santo with a twenty-page analysis that laid bare just how badly off the company was. The amount of unsold goods was rising alarmingly. Versace's costs had been increasing 10 percent to 15 percent a year without a clear plan, even as sales fell. Business managers had very loose budgets—if they had any at all. The comparison of Versace's performance to its best-run rivals was abysmal. The house had a huge staff but very small sales. Companies such as Gucci and Prada had three times the sales per employee that Versace did. Versace's own shops were money pits; its rivals' boutiques made *seven* times as much in sales per square foot of selling space as Versace's. Within a couple of months, Cacciatori found five million euros' worth of potential cost cutting.

Cacciatori, with the reluctant assent of Santo and Donatella, fired hundreds of employees, closed the boutique in San Francisco, and shuttered part of Versace's U.S. headquarters. He saved hundreds of thousands of euros by striking new deals with Versace suppliers, some of whom had taken advantage of the chaos in the company over the years to overcharge them. But the bigger problem was Donatella's spending. Cacciatori imposed a limit of one hundred thousand euros on any expense that Donatella or Santo could authorize autonomously. If they wanted to spend more—on the runway shows or to remodel a boutique—they needed his okay.

For a while, Donatella, chastened somewhat by the public uproar over the auditors' note on her spending that spring, fell in line. She gave up the private jets and ran the costs of her runway shows by Cacciatori. But the delicate détente lasted only until the October runway show. Within weeks, their relationship had crumbled. Donatella's contempt for Cacciatori had grown steadily over his tenure there, as he barged through the company with his passel of consultants in tow. Donatella's profligate ways were an enormous problem for the house, but her frustration was justified; Cacciatori was the wrong man to correct her course. He came from a world of Excel spreadsheets, financial analysis, and management techniques gleaned from business school case studies. He had no feel for the creative process at a fashion house. He applied cold cost-benefit analysis to the business as if it were a widget maker, failing to understand that designers have to shoot a lot of arrows before they hit the target with a blockbuster bag or dress. Cacciatori saw only the cost of the arrows.

Worse still, Donatella associated Cacciatori's efforts with Santo and their bitter arguments over her spending. The bean counter's intrusion in the house only widened the gulf between Via Gesù and the business offices on Via Manzoni. Donatella's own clique, perhaps worried that the Versace gravy train would grind to a halt, became a Greek chorus that egged her on, feeding her tidbits about Santo's meetings with Cacciatori and his team. By November, a battle of wills between Donatella and Cacciatori was shaping up, and the CEO could only lose. Donatella resisted his demands to cut back on the samples she ordered for the runway show or to buy cheaper fabric for her samples. "If I want three hundred pairs of shoes for the runway shows, then I'll have them!" she screamed at him during one heated meeting in the fall. "You can't stop me."

A few weeks later, not long before Christmas, Cacciatori went before the board with a plan for further cuts and changes in the strategy for 2004. He proposed cutting Donatella's and Santo's salaries— even as he charged Versace three thousand euros a day for his own services—and wanted to sell Via Gesù in order to lighten the company's debt load. But by then Donatella had had enough.

"What exactly have you accomplished here?" she demanded. "We're paying you all of this money but I don't see what it's for!" She accused him of seeking only to enrich himself at Versace's expense. A few days later, Donatella fired him. The next day, security guards escorted Cacciatori and his team out of the building.

❖ V ❖

The year 2004 promised to be an annus horribilis for Versace, the worst of the seven that had passed since Gianni's death. Donatella was in a free fall. Over the years, she had tried at times to rein in her cocaine use without giving it up entirely, limiting herself to just two or three lines at a time—which was nothing for her.[4] But by the start of 2004, her appetite for drugs had deepened along with the company's troubles. She began mixing cocaine with sedatives such as Halcion, Valium, Ativan, and Rohypnol. She downed handfuls of Excedrin to fight chronic headaches. Cocaine braced her for the marathon hours before a show, but afterward Donatella crashed, sitting on her couch for four or five days, hating herself. She began going on premeditated binges, retreating to her apartment for several days and telling her associates she wasn't well.[5] When she did turn up in the atelier, she was virtually paralyzed. Her team had grown to dread her arrival. She was jittery and restless, fidgeting with her jeweled cigarette case as if it were a worry bead and constantly wiping her nose. When she spoke, she was virtually incomprehensible.

At the end of shows, when Donatella teetered out on her five-inch stilettos for her bow, the audience was rapt, waiting to see if she would make it down the runway. Backstage, she hid in a separate dressing room, her handlers parrying visitors and the media. When she emerged to grant the obligatory round of press interviews on her collection, she wore the pained look of an injured animal. Television journalists struggled to get even a coherent ten-second sound bite out of her, and her makeup artists had to stop the cameras repeatedly to retouch her heavy foundation, which melted with her constantly running nose. After a while, many journalists simply stopped asking to interview her. Employees and friends watched in horror, fearing Donatella was on course for a deadly overdose.

❖ V ❖

In the midst of the meltdown came an offer that promised to pull the company out of its death spiral. Tom Ford and Domenico De Sole came calling. The pair had recently fallen out with François Pinault, the French billionaire who had saved Gucci from the LVMH takeover bid, and they were leaving the house after an extraordinary ten-year run. Their turnaround of Gucci had earned them each tens of millions of dollars over the years, and they wanted to invest it in another fashion brand. Right away, the new parlor game in the fashion world became guessing what the Dom-Tom Bomb would do next. Would they somehow buy Yves Saint Laurent back from Pinault? Or would they launch a new fashion line under Tom's name?

But instead they were interested in Versace. At Gucci, Ford and De Sole had gained experience in turning around a fashion house that had been nearly destroyed by the founding family. De Sole's enormous credibility with retailers around the world could help convince stores to start selling Versace collections again. Ford, with his satyr sensibility and commercial nous, could repair Versace's tattered image.

Santo was excited about the prospect, seeing the offer as a way to restore Versace to its former glory. He also knew that this was the company's last chance before the banks closed in. The clock was ticking on the bond, but Versace's creditors were willing to see how the talks with De Sole and Ford turned out. They preferred to have the company in the hands of new owners rather than stepping in themselves. Donatella, exhausted and seriously depressed, was willing to consider an offer for the first time. She was put off by the idea of sharing the limelight with a designer as famous and successful as Ford but relieved at the idea of handing some of the creative responsibilities over to someone else.

De Sole spent days going through Versace's catastrophic financial situation, coming up with a rough plan to close foundering stores, fix its sputtering production facilities, and launch an accessories line. But his help would come at a price. He and Ford were willing to take on Versace, but they wouldn't shell out a dime for a stake in the company. They wanted a share that guaranteed them control of the house, but their equity would come in exchange for their management expertise and reputation in the fashion sector. Santo was furious that De Sole could expect to walk into Versace for free, yet he had little choice but to entertain their offer on their terms. If the duo restored Versace to profitability, he would benefit as well. Much of Santo's wealth was tied up in his stake in the company; if Versace recovered, his holding—now practically worthless—would increase in value.

But there was a bigger problem. De Sole and Ford agreed that, for their plan to work, Donatella had to go. At her runway show in February 2004, Donatella was a mess. Over the winter she began hearing things and had grown even more paranoid. She was throwing fits in the atelier, accusing her team of sniping about her behind her back;

her tantrums left the young designers in tears.[6] The collection reflected the chaos in the atelier, a jumble of designs ranging from ladylike twinsets paired with huge Jackie-O sunglasses to black evening dresses with awkward slits. *Women's Wear Daily*'s verdict: "The evening clothes, well, let's just say, oops." Elizabeth Hurley, who had written Donatella a letter pleading with her to get help for her cocaine habit, sat in the front row with her new fiancé, distraught. After the last models filed backstage, Donatella teetered out. With a woozy smile, she gave a strange thumbs-up to someone in the audience. After that show, Donatella began using cocaine every day, a first for her.[7]

The night before, Ford had sent his last Gucci collection down the runway in Milan to what would be rave reviews. For months, the fashion press had been churning out glowing retrospectives of his revival of Gucci. He was leaving the brand at the top of his game. On a snowy day in February, De Sole, Ford, and Donatella finally met. Donatella listened as Ford and De Sole explained their plan to raise Versace from the ashes. Afterward, Ford stood up. He launched into a long, emotional monologue about how he had revived Gucci virtually single-handedly. "I *am* Gucci," he told Donatella. He then declared he would take on Versace only if he had full control of the brand—with absolutely no interference from Donatella, he told her. He would be the sole head designer.

Donatella was shocked at Ford's arrogance. She felt disrespected and discarded. Before his speech, she had been willing to consider a scenario where she would let go of some of her responsibilities, but she never dreamed that Ford would banish her entirely. She would be relegated to making anodyne personal appearances in department stores and signing perfume bottles. If Ford had approached her with more tact and sensitivity, she might have considered their offer. But instead he had humiliated her. "Absolutely not!" she said, struggling to remain calm. "Versace is my life. There's no way I could step aside." In a fury, she got up and left the room. All contact between the parties was cut off.*

In rejecting the offer from De Sole and Ford, Donatella unwit-

*This account, based on several sources, is disputed by Donatella Versace, who maintains that her role in the company was not an issue in the discussions but that Ford's offer was turned down because it was not an attractive offer financially.

tingly set in motion a chain of events that would finally pry her brother's house from her grasp. By the spring, the company was as out of control as she was. Staff spent more time gossiping and swapping rumors about the operatic drama unfolding in the family than actually working. Many had been excited at the idea of a takeover by De Sole and Ford and were sorely disappointed when word spread of the disastrous meeting with Donatella. The media's speculation about what would happen after Allegra's impending birthday only compounded the intrigue.

After the failure of the De Sole–Ford talks, Santo was deflated and disappointed. His team began searching for a new chief executive, contacting current and former heads of rival fashion houses. But no one would touch the job. They even reached out to Rose Marie Bravo, the former president of Saks who had gained fame for her turnaround of British brand Burberry. She refused to take the call.

Finally, Versace's creditors came calling. With a heavy heart, Santo sat down with Banca Intesa, Italy's largest financial institution and the house's longtime bankers. Intesa owned about 10 million euros of the bond, making it one of the largest holders, and would take the lead in working out what to do with the troubled house. Versace needed to find a way to repay the bond by the July 6, 2004, deadline, but any deal would clearly come at a heavy price. Racing to find a solution, Santo twice delayed the publication of the company's 2003 accounts—the board normally approved them in April—because he knew Versace was in default. And indeed, the 2003 results were catastrophic: The house would lose 97 million euros for the year. Moreover, the auditors were preparing another note, warning that Donatella owed the company nearly 5 million euros.

While Santo was meeting with bankers, the simmering questions as to what would happen when Allegra turned eighteen were rapidly coming to a head. Given her delicate health, would she choose not to exercise her share? Would she instead allow her mother to continue to manage the holding? Would the tensions that already existed between Allegra and Donatella—then in the grip of severe depression and a debilitating drug habit—rise further over the question of how to manage the teenager's stake? Versace employees feared that Allegra's health meant that Donatella would continue to control her daughter's stake even after Allegra turned eighteen. But little did they know that Allegra had a surprise in store.

At the men's collection debut in June 2004, Donatella finally hit bottom. Often for her shows, she hired a celebrity band to perform a miniconcert next to the runway. That year, she had chosen Prodigy, a hardcore group that had cut its teeth in the illegal rave scene in the United Kingdom. Prodigy's lead singer was Keith Flint, a Johnny Rotten–like character with a spiky Mohawk hairstyle and a serious drug habit.

As crews put the last touches on the runway in the courtyard of Via Gesù, Flint stood on the stage for the dress rehearsal while Donatella sat on a sofa nearby, so dazed that her bodyguards had to sit on either side of her to prop her up. Flint, appearing stoned, started singing and dancing wildly. As he danced, he began to strip his clothes off. He then lost his balance and toppled off the stage, bucknaked. He gashed his leg so badly that Versace staff had to call in a doctor to patch him up.

Donatella sat through the spectacle unfazed. At a press conference afterward, she gave rambling, incoherent answers to journalists' questions. By then, she was barely eating, her stomach in knots from anxiety, and she had grown very thin. When the journalists asked about her weight loss, she parried their questions with a blithe response. "I've been on this amazing diet and have been killing myself in the gym, in honor of the Duchess of Windsor's belief that one can never be too rich or too thin," she said.[8] One longtime Versace executive who witnessed the spectacle tendered his resignation soon afterward.

The runway show the next day was a disaster, a Technicolor display of Versace's catastrophic situation. Models walked the runway wearing T-shirts bearing the "DV" logo scrawled in neon letters or emblazoned with slogans such as "Why don't you fuck yourself?" The audience covered their ears to block out Prodigy's screeching music. Then, Flint suddenly jumped off the stage and began accosting the audience. He ground his pelvis close to one man's face and licked another woman, before climbing over the shocked attendees, dripping with sweat. The crowd of journalists and department store buyers shouted and tried to wriggle away as he approached.[9]

Donatella's conspicuous problems fed the voracious interest in Allegra's impending eighteenth birthday. Around the time of the men's show, Donatella and her daughter granted the media a photo op, hoping to sate the Italian newspapers' appetite for news about the heiress, whose eating problem was starkly obvious. Allegra posed for the paparazzi in a short polka-dot Versace skirt and a dark T-shirt, looking uncomfortable and heartbreakingly thin as she held hands with her mother, both women's faces portraits of pain.

A week later, Donatella threw Allegra a lavish, public birthday bash at Alcatraz, a cavernous disco that was Milan's most popular nightspot. The club was decked out in purple and pink, with huge flower bouquets, gilt chairs, and a pyramid of champagne glasses with expensive bubbly rippling down the sides. There was a massive buffet dinner of lobster, an open bar, and gurgling chocolate fountains. Donatella had flown Pharrell Williams, an American hip-hop sensation, over to Milan in a private jet to perform. She had model agencies hold castings to stock the party with male and female models, all outfitted in glitzy Versace clothes. Few of the models even knew Allegra. At midnight, Williams serenaded Allegra with a sassy version of "Happy Birthday" as the caterers rolled out a giant cake with sparklers. Donatella, dressed in a gold gown and heavy jewelry, stumbled to the stage with a flute of champagne and gave a rambling toast to her daughter.

A few days later, Donatella made a trip to Reggio that would change everything. Elton John was giving a concert in her native city. The singer had tried to support Donatella after Gianni's death, but she started avoiding him when her drug addiction spiraled because she knew he was one of the few people who would call her on her behavior. Ironically, when Elton had decided to get clean many years earlier, Gianni and Donatella had supported him; after rehab, he went straight to Donatella's vacation home in St. Tropez.[10] He then became a crusader, with a mission to help other celebrities kick their drug habits. He famously "kidnapped" Robbie Williams and took him to a rehab clinic in the 1990s and helped Robert Downey, Jr., kick a notorious drug habit.

But even Elton couldn't bear to watch Donatella self-destruct, and for a time he preferred to avoid her as well.[11] After much dithering, Donatella decided to attend Elton's concert in her hometown. She landed in Calabria on a balmy summer night and headed for her childhood home, where Zia Nora still lived. She hadn't been to Reggio in years. Entering the familiar house where she had spent so many happy years with her parents and her brothers brought back a rush of memories. The pain of returning home in such a desperate state was overwhelming. When she saw the woman who had been like a mother to her, she broke down, sobbing in Nora's arms.

After a while, she pulled herself together and headed for Reggio's soccer stadium, where Elton was due to sing. Crews had built a large, simple stage on the field, flanked by two huge screens and covered in the dark gray carpet that Elton demanded for his shows. Two dressing rooms complete with Versace furnishings had been kitted out, one for Elton and one for Donatella. Before the show, the duo gamely posed for photos backstage, the exhaustion etched clearly on Donatella's face despite her heavy makeup. A shimmery gold catsuit highlighted her sunken stomach and thin arms.

Elton stepped onto the stage and sat at a black grand piano. He would be singing solo, without any backup band. In his right ear, he wore a quarter-sized gold earring engraved with an image of a medusa head. He opened with "Your Song," Gianni's favorite. "I want to dedicate this whole show to my good friend Gianni Versace," he said, after finishing the tune. The crowd cheered.

Donatella stood in the wings, sobbing and shaking. Elton looked at her and realized that she was ready for a change in her life. He felt he had to take action. As soon as he got back to London, he called Donatella's top assistant and exploded. "You people are doing nothing but enabling Donatella by protecting her!" he said. "She's going to die if we don't do something." He decided he would go to Milan to confront Donatella himself. He told the assistant that he had only one day free in the next six weeks: June 30, 2004, Allegra's birthday.

In the meantime, Allegra turned to her father for help. Even after separating from Donatella, Paul often shuttled between New York and Milan to be with both kids, following their schoolwork and taking them on vacations. But when it came to Allegra's stake in Versace, he let Donatella take command.

As her birthday approached, Allegra decided it was time to take up her rightful role in the company. It was an immensely difficult decision for a high school senior to make. She had always been the quintessential good little girl who submitted to her mother's wishes. But she was also smart enough to have realized that her inheritance had withered to a fraction of what it was when Gianni left it to her. She understood that it was time for her to step in. But first she needed an adviser, someone independent of both her mother and Santo, who could help her untangle the mess.

She asked Paul for help in finding the right person. Through a Versace associate, her father gathered a short list of white-shoe lawyers in Milan who were renowned both for their business acumen and their discretion in dealing with the intricacies of family-controlled businesses. One of them, Michele Carpinelli, was a leading lawyer in Italian corporate circles, who was well-regarded by top executives at Banca Intesa, having worked with the bank on a number of deals. Carpinelli could very well be the right person to help Allegra take command of her company.

Not long before Allegra's birthday, Donatella had set up a time to sit down with her daughter to discuss the management of her stake after she turned eighteen. By then Allegra was a determined young woman, not a meek girl. Allegra announced that she intended to begin exercising control of her stake in the house. She would manage the share herself from now on and would hire an adviser to help.

When the news spread that Allegra had engaged Carpinelli, Versace employees and friends of the family, enormously surprised at the young woman's gumption, were immensely relieved. They recognized that if Donatella continued to call the shots, the company risked ending up bankrupt or being sold to a rival. They admired the teenager's courage in asserting her role in the company. With Allegra in charge, there was a glimmer of hope.

❖ V ❖

On the evening of June 30, 2004, two dozen close friends and family members, including Santo, Paul, Daniel, and Donatella, gathered at Via Gesù for a private dinner party to celebrate Allegra's birthday.

HOUSE OF VERSACE

Two of Gianni's best friends, Ingrid Sischy, the editor in chief of *Interview Magazine,* and her girlfriend, Sandy Brant, CEO of the magazine, were also there. Once everyone was gathered, Donatella made a move to slip away, headed to the bathroom for a line of cocaine to brace herself for the evening ahead.

Just then, Elton John walked into the room. Some guests were delighted, thinking it a surprise visit for Allegra, but Donatella was shocked; she knew she hadn't invited him. On cue, Elton, Santo, Paul, Allegra, and a couple of close friends led Donatella to another room in the magnificent palazzo, while assistants quietly asked the other guests to leave.

Elton took the lead. He confronted Donatella with her behavior, telling her that she would destroy everything if she didn't make a change and get clean. "Donatella, we're not forcing you, but you need to to rehab," he told her. "There's a plane waiting for you." Late into the night, her friends and family—Allegra in particular—pressed Donatella, recounting how much damage her addiction was causing to the company, her children, and her friends. Overwhelmed, she finally gave in. She changed out of her evening gown, took off her jewelry, and put on a jogging suit. Then she headed to the airport, where she boarded a private plane headed for Arizona.[12] For much of the long trip, she sobbed.

❖ V ❖

At first glance, the Meadows rehab clinic in Wickenburg, Arizona, hardly seems a destination for the rich and famous. Sitting about sixty miles northwest of Phoenix, it is nestled in a picture-perfect southwestern setting on the edge of the Sonoran Desert. Wickenburg, population 6,500, is a proverbial one-horse town, bereft of luxury hotels or fashionable restaurants. With its giant cacti and cottonwood trees, it once claimed itself the "Dude Ranch Capital of the World." Dry and hot by day, it often enjoys a cool breeze at night, under a sky dotted with countless twinkling stars.

The Meadows was the project of a woman named Pia Mellody, who, in the late 1970s, established an intense treatment plan based on twelve-step programs such as Alcoholics Anonymous. By 2004, the Meadows was offering an array of treatment programs for addictions to drugs, alcohol, sex, and gambling, charging about $35,000 for the typical five-week stint. While Los Angeles and New York claim countless rehab facilities, celebrities looking for privacy chose the Meadows for its remote locale and reputation for discretion. Stars could fly into Phoenix, far from paparazzi, and disappear. The clinic's staff was trained to be on guard for journalists, with a book holding the details of attempts by media to wheedle information about VIPs. Guards patrolled the compound twenty-four hours a day.

For Donatella, the Meadows was a universe away from her usual five-star standards. The compound consisted of a half-dozen low-rise buildings of brown stucco, surrounded by a high fence. There was a pool, closed in by a high tan-colored railing. Rooms were spartan, a functional cross between a hospital and a dorm room, with narrow single beds, tiny closets, and plain white bathrooms with Dixie-cup dispensers. Flagstone paths edged with low gray and beige stone walls connected the buildings. From the compound, the only view was of stretches of reddish brown desert.

Donatella arrived at the Meadows thinking the doctors would console her about her myriad troubles, but during her intake, she saw that the treatment plan was very different.[13] At their arrival, patients had to sign "suicide contracts" pledging not to harm themselves, and nurses collected urine samples to do a drug screen. The staff searched luggage for contraband such as drugs, razors, or sexually explicit literature. Because the clinic has a large sex-addiction treatment program, women weren't allowed to wear any tight or skimpy clothing, open-toed shoes, or even makeup. Donatella traded in her usual garb of skintight tops and pants for baggy T-shirts with round necks and shapeless pants. Swimming times at the pools were strictly segregated, and if she wanted to swim, she would have to wear a one-piece bathing suit. Versace's skimpy bikinis were taboo.

New patients received a tote bag of required reading, including several books on codependency by Pia Mellody and John Bradshaw, a therapist who has appeared on Oprah Winfrey's and Geraldo Rivera's talk shows. She received a name tag with her photo and her name—simply "Donatella V."—written in block letters next to her intake number. The badges were color-coded so that the staff would immediately recognize which addiction the patient was suffering from.

Patients had to wear the badges around their necks at all times and had to carry pagers so that the staff could reach them wherever they went on campus. After her intake, a nurse led Donatella to her room, which she would share with two other patients. On her chart was her diagnosis: severe depression.

She ate her meals in a communal cafeteria, where patients often stood up to shout slogans they'd learned in therapy, such as "I'm a codependent in recovery." The pronouncements sparked rounds of applause from fellow patients, who followed with their own slogans. Meals were bland but nutritious, and sugar and caffeine were banned—a hardship for someone used to downing a dozen espressos a day. Patients could smoke only outdoors, under the scorching summer sun, in one of the designated smoking "pits," which were segregated by sex to discourage fraternizing.

Donatella's contact with the outside world was minimal. Cell phones were banned. Patients bought calling cards and stood in line to make short calls home on pay phones. Timers on the phones cut off calls after the time allocated, and calls were noted in a log that the doctors would later examine. At night, the nurses checked on patients with small flashlights.

Every day, a nurse asked Donatella to identify her feelings from a printed list. For three weeks, her answer was the same: guilt and shame.[14] Every day, Donatella woke at 5:30 a.m., ate breakfast at 5:45 a.m., and started on group therapy. Her schedule was full: several hours of intensive group therapy sessions a day, plus twelve-step meetings, spirituality counseling, art therapy, lectures, and sessions with a psychiatrist. After the meetings, Donatella had to do such "homework" assignments as writing an autobiographical time line recounting her life from birth to the age of nineteen.

At first, Donatella balked at having to air her dirty laundry in front of strangers in group therapy. "Can't I tell my story in private?" she asked her counselor.[15] But the Meadows made no exceptions, not even for VIPs. The other patients, who recognized Donatella in spite of—or because of—her coy, twelve-step-style name tag, sat rapt while she recounted her story.

She went through a therapy boot camp dubbed "Survivors Week," in which she picked through her life for evidence of the trauma and neglect that were the sources of her problems. During Survivors Week, patients were encouraged to act out their rage; for instance, to beat on chairs that represented their mothers. On the fifth day, other members of the group kissed and hugged one another when they "graduated" from the weeklong intensive therapy.

Around a month after her arrival came Family Week. The staff asked Donatella for her children's phone numbers. "No, no, no!" she said, recoiling, horrified that her children should see her in such condition. "I don't want to involve my children." The staff insisted. Family sessions were a critical part of healing the damage created by years of drug abuse. When Donatella told her children she was against their coming to the Meadows, they were upset. Why don't you want us to come? they asked her. Why don't you want to have anything to do with us?[16]

Donatella relented. A few days later, Allegra and Daniel arrived in Arizona. Allegra had to follow the same dress code as her mother—no revealing clothes, such as shorts or tank tops. She and Daniel were given name tags, and they ate together with Donatella in the communal cafeteria. It was agonizing for their mother, yet she sobbed when they left, happy to end years of hiding her problems from her children.

After several weeks in the facility, Donatella started feeling better. She earned some privileges, and she could indulge a bit—she had a manicurist come in from a salon in town to do her nails. In mid-August, after five weeks in Arizona, a clean and sober Donatella flew to the Caribbean for a vacation with Daniel and Allegra. She left armed with phone numbers for twelve-steps groups that catered to celebrities as well as contact information for other patients—known in Meadows jargon as "peers"—whom she had befriended at the clinic.

Her focus now was on repairing her tattered relationship with her children, particularly Allegra. After their Caribbean vacation, Allegra was due to move to the United States to join the freshman class at Brown. Just as Donatella was determined to heal her relationship with her daughter, Allegra was leaving the nest.

nineteen

Recovery

*W*HILE DONATELLA CONFRONTED HER DEMONS IN THE ARI-
zona desert, business executive Giancarlo Di Risio was
wrestling with his own dilemma back in Italy. During the
summer of 2004, an emissary from Versace's creditors had
approached him: Was he interested in becoming chief executive of the house?

Di Risio, forty-nine, was tempted. His professional
background and distinctive temperament might suit the job
of wrangling such a messy company back into shape. First,
Di Risio shared the Versaces' southern heritage. He was born
the eldest son in a well-to-do family from Molise, a poor region northwest of Naples. His father had a passion for fast
cars and had owned one of the largest car dealerships in
Italy, selling luxury Italian brands such as Alfa Romeo and

Lancia during the peak of the country's economic boom in the 1950s and 1960s. As a teenager in the early 1970s, Di Risio was the envy of his high school friends, tooling around in sports cars he was allowed to borrow from his father's fleet. His father had also become an avid race-car driver, and both Di Risio and his younger brother, Massimo, joined him in his avocation, racing often in multistage rallies that lasted for days.

After an extended adolescence, a young Di Risio enrolled at the University of Bologna to study political science but dropped out to join the sales team at Lamborghini, the storied Italian carmaker that also produced high-powered motors for race boats as well as more mundane products such as tractors. Then, in the mid-1980s, he met Tonino Perna, a Molise entrepreneur. Perna, a graduate of Naples's fine arts academy, had launched Jesus Jeans with his brother in the early 1970s. The line became a short-lived hot seller after kicking up a scandal for a risqué advertising campaign featuring a closeup shot of a woman's denim-clad bottom and a headline reading "Those Who Love Me Will Follow Me." In 1986, Perna set out to establish his own company, founding Ittierre in Pettoranello di Molise, an industrial area two hours southwest of Rome. Di Risio met Perna when the businessman sponsored a race he was competing in. Impressed by the young man, Perna soon convinced Di Risio to help him get his new venture off the ground.

At Ittierre, the thirty-year-old Di Risio found his calling. At first glance, he had little of the back-slapping charisma or bonhomie typical of Italian executives. He cut a sober figure, with wire-rimmed glasses, a conservative taste for clothes, and an intense, slightly dogged style of speaking, as if he were reciting a PowerPoint presentation. He had the plain look of an accounting professor: slightly skinny, with brown hair and a pale complexion.

Yet, Di Risio proved himself to be one of those rare executives with both a far-reaching vision and the stamina to carry it out. He had an extraordinary capacity to work, keeping a grueling eighteen-hours-a-day schedule and often going as long as forty-eight hours without eating, subsisting on a stream of strong cappuccinos. He and Perna had spotted a new, rich market. Young people who had snapped up the stylish jeans launched in the early 1980s by Calvin Klein and

HOUSE OF VERSACE

Armani had started to look for more than just trendy dungarees. Hanging out around local high schools and universities, Di Risio saw the potential for creating a full range of designer clothes that were stylish but casual and cheap enough for people in their twenties. Armed with market research, including interviews with sociologists, Di Risio doggedly canvassed star Italian designers with proposals to create secondary lines together. He scored a big win in 1989 when, after two years of pressing, he convinced Gianni and Santo to launch a pair of casual lines—Versus and Versace Jeans Couture. Other designers, such as Dolce & Gabbana and Roberto Cavalli, soon followed.

Di Risio built Ittierre into an epitome of efficiency, making it a precursor to the "fast-fashion" giants such as Zara and H&M that would erupt around the turn of the millennium. Each brand had its own staff housed in individual two-story buildings on a campuslike headquarters, churning out offbeat collections of clothes, jackets, shoes, bags, and belts in coordination with the brands' own design teams. A fully automated factory produced eighty thousand pieces a day. When a new product became a hot seller, the teams produced flash collections, delivering them in days. Ittierre opened shops for the brands' secondary lines, handled advertising, and designed the window displays. By the time of Gianni's death, Ittierre had opened sixty Versus and ten Versace Jeans Couture shops for Versace. In 2001, its sales topped $500 million.

Even though he was the chief executive of one of Italy's most successful companies, Di Risio was remarkably low-key. He dressed in well-cut but conservative suits and classic silk Hermès ties. Extremely reserved, he shunned the sort of showboating that so many top executives revel in. In interviews with the press, he studiously evaded any questions about his personal life. He often called early morning or late-night meetings with his managers—unheard of in a country where the workday starts as late as 10 a.m. His was closer to the American style of management than the Italians' unruly, makeshift approach. On the rare weekends when he didn't work, he liked to make jam with his wife and two children in their home in the countryside outside Rome. Cars were a rare extravagance; he collected a fleet of antique autos, including a pair of sleek Aston Martins.

In the early 2000s, Di Risio, then forty-five, wanted a change. At the time, LVMH was looking for someone to fix Fendi, its problem child. In November 2001, LVMH bought out Prada's stake and took control of the Roman house. Fendi was a wreck, bleeding money and heavily in debt. The house, whose extraordinary sale price had marked the peak of fashion's aquisition frenzy, had turned out to be a one-trick pony. Sales of the Baguette bag had gone stone-cold. Deliveries were chronically late, and exasperated retailers were canceling orders. The quarrelsome Fendi clan, who still owned 49 percent of the company, had established a series of fiefdoms and ignored LVMH's efforts to clean up a tangle of cheap licenses, unprofitable lines, and sky-high costs. Bernard Arnault thought the situation required an Italian executive schooled in the ways of family-run companies. In January 2002, Di Risio became Fendi's chief executive officer.

Over the course of a year, Di Risio managed to ease out most of the family members, persuading them to sell their stakes to LVMH. (The French giant would spend more than $1 billion in all to acquire the small house.) He cut costs and replaced the Fendi family with professional managers, but the company continued to bleed money. At the same time, Di Risio clashed with Karl Lagerfeld, who had designed Fendi's fur and clothing collections for three decades; the two butted heads over cost cutting and the fact that Fendi was a sideline to the star designer's main act at Chanel. Lagerfeld threatened to quit.[1] Wary of alienating Lagerfeld and impatient with the house's red ink, in May 2003 Arnault gave responsibility for Fendi's strategy to a star LVMH executive who had brought Christian Dior back to profitability. That fall, Di Risio resigned.

When Versace came calling the following summer, Di Risio, happily unemployed, was reluctant to take on the leadership of another troubled house. He had worked closely with the company on Versus and the jeans line for nearly two decades and knew the family's vagaries all too well. Moreover, after the collapse of the talks with De Sole and Ford, Versace's creditors had arrived in force. While Donatella was in Arizona, Santo negotiated a deal to pay off the bond, but the banks exacted a heavy price, effectively taking control of the company. They extended 120 million euros in new loans to pay off the bond, but demanded Versace's prize assets as collateral, including the Via Gesù palazzo and the townhouse in Manhattan. A new seven-person board would include four outside directors answerable to the banks. Santo had to step aside, clearing the way for new management. Donatella could stay, but a new chief executive would have full control of budgets and would carefully monitor her atelier. The new CEO had until Christmas to prove that Versace could survive. If not, the banks would sell everything.

Versace was a potential hand grenade for any executive, and indeed the company had failed to lure a star manager from one of the best-run fashion houses. But Di Risio decided to risk it, perhaps anxious to redeem his reputation after his bumpy tenure at Fendi. Allegra's decision to exercise her stake with the help of an outside lawyer who had the trust of Versace's creditors would make his task immensely easier. But the banks' patience wouldn't last long. And even though Donatella was now a minority shareholder, she was still a wild card. If the rehab program failed and she slipped back into her old ways, she could still cause chaos.

Soon after returning from an August holiday in the Caribbean with her mother, Allegra, with Carpinelli by her side, voted to approve both the new board and Di Risio's nomination as CEO. Donatella also gave her assent. Santo, who had quietly lobbied for Di Risio for months, voted in favor as well. Santo remained president but was now powerless. Nearly thirty years after joining Gianni in Milan and after seven years of woe, Santo was set adrift. Allegra had effectively voted her uncle out of a job and put her mother on a very short leash.

When the staff returned from their summer holidays, they held their breath. They had read news reports about Donatella's rehab stint and the deal with the banks. Many doubted whether the latest coup de théâtre could really mean the end of years of drama and intrigue. The next runway show, just a month away, would be decisive.

❖ V ❖

Donatella returned to Milan a changed woman. She had always been a black-or-white personality, someone drawn to the extremes. So just as she had hit bottom with a decisive thump, she bounced back just as resolutely. Many addicts take several stabs at rehab before they manage to stay clean, but Donatella was ready to embrace the program that promised to help her regain control of her life. When she came back to Italy, she was chastened by the damage caused during her wilderness years and wanted to finally make amends. She would never touch drugs again.

On her return to the office, she warily took the measure of her new CEO. She knew Di Risio somewhat through their dealings over the Versus line, but she had never worked closely with him. Without the haze of drugs, she could size up her situation with the brutal pragmatism that had once given her the courage to tell Gianni when he was being wrong or pig-headed. The banks and her daughter were in control of the house, and they had invested Di Risio with full power. He held all the cards. If she wanted to remain creative chief of Versace, she had to find a way to work with the man.

Within weeks, it became clear that Di Risio could be an ideal antidote to what ailed Versace. To be sure, his strengths lay in the nuts and bolts of logistics, distribution, and factory organization that had made Ittierre run like a well-oiled machine, and he lacked some of the depth of a manager of international caliber. His sparse English was also a problem. But since he knew Versace well, he wouldn't face the steep learning curve that would leave other executives vulnerable to palace intrigue. He had also learned how to deal with capricious families during his stint at Fendi.

Even his somewhat peculiar personality was reassuring to the traumatized company. Di Risio would be happy to leave the limelight to Donatella. His southern heritage was a plus in a company still proud of its Calabrian roots. More important, his ascetic style helped leech the emotion and personal drama out of a house where work-life boundaries were almost nonexistent. Unlike Donatella, he never got involved with his associates' personal lives. And unlike Gianni or Santo, he wasn't the convivial boss who wandered amiably into managers' offices to check on their work. Instead, he had his secretary summon associates to his office when he needed something. There they noticed that Di Risio's desk was bereft of photos of his family, and even top Versace executives never met his wife or children. He rarely smiled and scrupulously used the formal *lei* with even the closest colleagues. Donatella insisted he address her with the informal *tu*. He assented, but it clearly made him uncomfortable. His detachment was a relief to the staff.

Donatella quickly pegged Di Risio as someone who lacked creativity, which was a black mark in her book. He had a level-headed approach that came from his low-key personality and the knowledge that he was in control. But he was unfailingly polite and diplomatic with her, careful not to turn their relationship into a battle of wills. While he summoned other executives to his office, he made a point of going to Donatella's when they needed to speak. Undoubtedly, he had little of the verve she admired in other people, but he gave her the respect that she craved. In her battered state, that meant a great deal.

Moreover, he was willing to make the changes that she knew were needed but lacked the courage to carry out. Di Risio arrived to find a traumatized staff. Even the palazzo on Via Gesù looked like a battleground, with litter strewn in the glorious gardens and broken mirrors and furniture going unrepaired. More than 1.4 million euros of unsold clothes, bags, and shoes were piled up in warehouses.[2] The only marketable asset Versace had left was its name. With a mixture of relief and regret, Donatella decided to trust him.

Working from 7:30 a.m. until midnight, Di Risio tackled problems that had been festering for years. He began dismissing people who had been entwined in Donatella's personal life but whom she lacked the courage to fire. He hired a new menswear designer and told him to get rid of the DV logo and replace it with a sophisticated gold and black label. He cut ties with the outside stylists who had led Donatella astray by pushing for controversy on the runway rather than sales in the stores. He then moved Donatella and her design team from Via Gesù into the business headquarters on Via Manzoni so they would meet regularly with his new sales team. Donatella could no longer ignore the bean counters.

The first test of their relationship came as Donatella and her team prepared the collection for the October 2004 runway show. Donatella's own staff watched her skeptically, looking for signs of a slip. For years, they had dreaded the weeks before a show, when they became lightning rods for all her frustration and paranoia. Moreover, their new chief executive was clearly determined to have a say in the atelier. Soon after his arrival, he upset Donatella by telling her the house could no longer stage couture shows. Donatella still harbored a dream of putting the couture collection back on the runway, but Di Risio refused to sink any more money into the loss-making business. The atelier could still make red-carpet gowns, but it would display them in private showings with clients.

Di Risio gave Donatella and her team clear directives for the October 2004 show. He wanted a cleaner, more sophisticated collection. The team could use the medusa head only sparingly and tastefully in order to restore the logo's prestige. They had to pay closer attention to the fit of the clothes and include more wearable, basic items—not just eveningwear made for willowy models—and follow a strict design calendar so that the factory had time to make the clothes. But Di Risio sugared the pill by giving Donatella a generous budget to buy fabrics, make up samples, and stage the show. He called an end to lavishing clothes on celebrities willy-nilly but signed off on using Madonna in the advertisements for the collection. And as long as Donatella followed the guidelines he laid down for the collection, she was free to come up with whatever designs she wanted.

The atelier staff wondered if she was going to buck. But she didn't. Even if it was painful, she was finally ready to trust someone. In meetings with her team, she was clear and calm, turning up at work punctually at 10 a.m. and methodically running through the myriad preshow decisions. At meetings, her closest assistants turned to one another, eyebrows raised in amazement.

In the early days of the new regime, Donatella's priority was to safeguard her recovery and repair her relationship with her kids. She spoke often with Elton John, and had her assistants budget time in her schedule for regular phone calls to her recovery peers abroad. Italy has little in the way of Narcotics Anonymous meetings, but when she traveled overseas, she attended twelve-step gatherings. She spent all of her spare time with her son. Daniel, then thirteen, was growing into an exuberant teenager, crazy about soccer and rock music. Donatella pushed for business meetings to end on time so that she could curl up on the sofa at home to watch a soccer game with him or listen to him play in his high school band Nucleus.

Despite Donatella's newfound equanimity, the show in October was the hardest thing she had done since her first solo presentation after Gianni's death. It was her first one ever without the crutch of drugs. There were none of the celebrities the house often used to distract attention away from the trashy clothes. As the models filed out onto a clean, simple runway, Donatella stood backstage shaking, clutching the hand of a close assistant. Despite the nerves, her more peaceful state of mind shone through. She showed draped silk jersey dresses with flirty fishtail skirts, white trouser suits, halter-neck dresses in pastels, and a luscious lemon-yellow draped gown. The medusa medallion subtly punctuated the base of the spine on a short white dress that dripped with crystals. For daytime, there were safari-like jackets and satiny chemise dresses.

After the last model filed backstage, Donatella stepped onto the runway. She glowed with health, beaming a heartfelt smile as the audience jumped to its feet. Despite all its cattiness, the fashion world was rooting for Donatella and the revival of Gianni's house. Santo stood in the audience, applauding warmly. When she was safely backstage, Donatella burst into tears. Afterward, she held an intimate dinner for forty in her own apartment rather than the usual postshow megafete in Via Gesù.

The successful show gave fresh momentum to Di Risio's race to revive the house before the banks' end-of-year deadline. Donatella and Santo stood by while Di Risio dismantled cherished bits of Versace history. He put the New York townhouse on the block for $30 million and sold the licenses for Versace perfumes and watches to outsiders. The rest of Gianni's contemporary art collection—including works by Roy Lichtenstein, Jean-Michel Basquiat, Henri Matisse, and Marc Chagall—would go to auction in the new year. The last bit of Gianni's original headquarters on Via della Spiga was sold. Finally, Di Risio wrote off millions of euros' worth of goods that sat unsold in warehouses and boutiques.

By casting off the dross, Di Risio could home in on the more promising nuggets: the core men's and women's lines. If he could restore the prestige of the top collections, the house might win back its luxury cred with retailers and high-end shoppers. Then it might add the sort of less-expensive lines that swelled the coffers of Prada, Armani, and Louis Vuitton. But first he shrank the business drastically.

Sales for 2004 would be just 328 million euros, down 20 percent from 2003 and a third less than when Gianni died. That year, Armani was four times the size of Versace, and the Gucci group nearly five times. Despite its famous name, Versace was now little more than a niche player.

Just days before Christmas 2004, Di Risio sat down with Versace's creditors. Without the asset sales, Versace would have lost nearly 100 million euros that year and been technically insolvent. By hawking the licenses and the real estate, the house instead turned a profit of 104 million euros. More important, the debt fell from about 120 million euros when he arrived to 84 million euros. To his relief, the banks approved. With the emergency phase over, Di Risio could begin rebuilding the house, brick by brick.

❖ V ❖

Providence, a gritty smokestack city in Rhode Island, is as unlikely a destination for a European heiress as one could find. With its blue-collar populace and high unemployment rate, it is one of the grimmest metropolitan areas in the northeast. Brown University sits on a hill in the heart of the city, its stately buildings a world away from the industrial neighborhoods surrounding the campus. The privileged kids who descend on Brown each year are as different from the locals as chalk from cheese.

In September 2004, as Donatella and Di Risio hammered out their relationship in Milan, Allegra arrived in the New England city to join the incoming class of 2008. Eager to try to be a normal American college student, she had decided before leaving Milan not to join the board at Versace, preferring to entrust the company to her lawyer and the new board. She dreamed of escaping the strife of her life in Italy and becoming an actress. Donatella had agreed to let her pursue her dream until she turned twenty-four. If she didn't succeed by then, she would go to work at Versace.

❖ V ❖

As Allegra grappled with a new life, her mother was steadily finding her feet in a sober world. Donatella was remarkably open about her past, publicly and privately admitting her mistakes. In press interviews, she surprised journalists with frank answers about her drug habit, recounting private details of her stay in Arizona and admitting the fallout her addiction had had on her children. Her no-excuses approach went far to deflate the prurient curiosity about her drug use and wildness. Free of the haze of drugs, the witty, generous Donatella of old came through. In the atelier, she coddled the staff who had stuck close by her. In 2004, when the photo shoot in London for the Madonna ad campaign fell during Thanksgiving week, as a treat for the Americans on the team who had to miss the holiday, she organized a full Thanksgiving dinner in her suite at Claridge's hotel, including turkey-themed decorations and Indian headdresses. Over time, she softened her look, wearing her long hair in loose waves or ringlets and lightening her makeup. She adopted a polished uniform of close-cut tailored pants, topped with a T-shirt and a jacket in the summer or a fitted coat in the winter. She got back into shape, working with a personal trainer in her apartment each morning, blasting rock or pop music at full volume and singing at the top of her lungs as she walked on a treadmill.

In the atelier, she displayed a new confidence in her own instincts, and she stopped the anguished second-guessing that had paralyzed her for so long. Her team had her full attention for the first time in years. Taking clear leadership of the meetings, she could finally tap her sixth sense of what was hot, homing in quickly on ideas that would work. She got rid of three elements that had characterized Gianni's style: bright colors, very revealing clothes, and a great deal of embellishment. Times had changed. The conspicuous consumption that Gianni celebrated was passé in the 2000s, when stealth wealth—perfectly cut clothes, luxurious fabrics, subtle finishings— marked the new sensibility. Dress rehearsals that once dragged on until 3 a.m. or 4 a.m. as a frustrated Donatella demanded more and more changes now finished in as little as thirty minutes. The collections grew stronger each season, finding a balance between Versace's signature sexiness and polished, pulled-together sophistication. She focused more on monochrome tailored clothing. One season, she showed an assortment of navy outfits that had leather piping that formed stylish V's. In another, she did a collection largely in white.

In May 2005, for her fiftieth birthday, two close assistants threw a surprise party for her at Mr. Chow's, a Chinese restaurant in Manhattan popular with celebrities. She was just the age Gianni had been when he was killed, and she was hardly anxious to celebrate the milestone. But when she walked into Mr. Chow's, she found two dozen friends who represented the happiest time of her life, including Mario Testino, Helena Christensen, Linda Evangelista, the hairdresser Oribe, and makeup artist Pat McGrath. Allegra, Daniel, and Paul were also there. It was Donatella's first sober birthday celebration in years, and she felt overwhelmed. Trying to break the tension of being the object of attention, she hammed it up, making the rounds of the tables and quipping, "Hello, I will be your server tonight. Can I take your order?"

❖ V ❖

Having won a reprieve from the banks before Christmas, Di Risio dug in in 2005, year zero for Versace. Early each morning, he walked to work from a pied-à-terre not far from the Versace headquarters. By then, he was dressing head to toe in Versace, wearing conservative suits from the house's top menswear line. He traded his Hermès ties and fine Swiss watches in for Versace versions. Di Risio's straightforward, no-drama approach gradually set the tone in the house, and the intrigue-ridden atmosphere melted away. His measured presence belied the deep changes he was making. He replaced every single senior executive, from the public relations chief to the head of sales, freeing his management ranks of the baggage of Versace's messy past. (Many of the new arrivals faced pointed questions from friends and colleagues who viewed Versace as a surefire career buster.)

Di Risio reined in Donatella's spending, cutting the private jets and holidays paid for by the company. (As befit her VIP status, Donatella still flew first class—preferably Air France—and always sat in a window seat to shield her from other passengers' prying eyes.) Managers got bonuses if they came in under the tight new budgets he imposed. The house's travel spending fell by half, and the cost of runway shows dropped by 40 percent.

The new team then did a detailed analysis of the performance of each shop, a first for the house. The results showed disaster. The top-priced collections were too thin to fill the huge shops, so sales managers were padding them with a hodgepodge of cheaper licensed items and secondary lines. Many boutiques still sported the overwrought look of Gianni's era, heavy on baroque finishings that now looked kitsch and gaudy. Window displays were often tatty and differed from shop to shop.

Early in 2005, the new management began rolling out a fresh design in all Versace shops. Black marble, leather furnishings, enamel ceilings, and crystal bead curtains replaced the medusa logos and garish embellishments. A new layout left ample space for eyeglasses, perfumes, and leather bags near the entrance, and a fresh window display went up in all the shops. Sales in the revamped boutiques immediately surged 25 percent. Other stores that were too big or that underperformed—including the huge boutique on Madison Avenue that Santo had long protected despite heavy losses—were shuttered.

Meanwhile, Donatella's collections were finally winning plaudits from her harshest critics. Early on, the reviews had been cautiously positive, but by the end of 2005, she'd garnered three seasons in a row of kudos. In October, she felt confident enough of her own reputation to dare an ironic take on Gianni's era, opening the show with five Amazonian models striding down the runway in beige outfits, a coy reference to Armani's signature color. Her personal appearances and preshow press conferences were smooth and polished, sending a reassuring message to retailers that her wilderness days were over.

The house seemed to be on the mend. The debt dropped to 20 million euros and the sales were stabilized. The year 2006 was about selling the new Versace to the outside world. Di Risio and his sales executives began to court the powerful department stores in the United States. The American buyers sat in the front rows of Donatella's shows and came for private viewings of the collection in the showroom. But the memory of Versace's travails was too fresh for them to risk their budgets on the house. Versace executives continued to press their case. They brought buyers to see the improvements in the house's own boutiques, including the new range of plush leather bags designed by a new accessories design team. The ready-to-wear collection had plenty of stylish basics such as pantsuits, pencil skirts, day dresses, and sheaths. The house proved it was serious about rejoining the ranks of deluxe brands such as Chanel and Christian Dior by dropping the cheap licensed stuff, thus forgoing rich royalty payments. A modern new warehouse packaged a store's entire order—from dresses to leather belts—in a single crate and delivered it on time.

In the fall of 2006, Versace announced it had broken even for the first six months, well ahead of Di Risio's schedule. The austerity campaign had worked, but it came at a heavy price. The debt was close to zero, but the elimination of unprofitable lines such as swimwear, underwear, and children's clothing shrank the house drastically. The staff was half the size it had been when Di Risio arrived. For 2006, Versace sales were just 288 million euros—a fifth the size of Armani's—and its profit was 19 million euros, a tiny fraction of those of bigger houses. Versace was off life support, but it was still a shadow of its former self.

❖ V ❖

In February 2007, Di Risio, Donatella, and Santo flew to Los Angeles on a rare trip together. Donatella and her late brother were to receive the Rodeo Drive Walk of Style award. With three successful years to her credit, Donatella was finally receiving the acclaim of her peers. The evening would be a celebration of one of the industry's great comeback stories.

Donatella stayed in Bungalow 1A of the Beverly Hills Hotel. A salon-style chair had been moved into one bedroom. Her assistant, Bruce, a handsome Frenchman, hovered with a Bluetooth headset wedged into his ear, while Donatella's hairdresser and makeup artist fussed over her incessantly. She even hired a hairdresser for some of the journalists attending the party that evening.[3]

In the days before the award ceremony, Donatella smoothly ran through a parade of interviews. Asked about Gianni, she deliberately played down the comparison with her brother. "I don't feel I am good enough for an award," she said. A chauffeured car bearing license plate "DIVA 11" ferried her to an appearance on *Access Hollywood*. The anchor asked about the infamous honeymoon party Donatella threw for Jennifer Lopez soon after September 11, 2001. Donatella impatiently waved for the cameras to stop. "That was two husbands ago," she said protectively. "We can't talk about that."[4]

HOUSE OF VERSACE

On the evening of the award ceremony, an eye-popping crowd of superstars, including Jennifer Lopez, Eva Longoria, Tyra Banks, Prince, Demi Moore, Drew Barrymore, and Stevie Wonder, lounged on white Versace leather couches in a roped-in mosh pit under an enormous tent. The 1990s-era supermodels, clad in Versace couture gowns, turned out in force. Donatella, wearing a mermaid-style gown, expertly held court, bussing each celebrity guest on both cheeks and patiently butting up against star after star for the waiting photographers. On giant screens, images of Gianni and his spectacular runway shows played over and over again. But in truth, it was Donatella's night. Santo and his daughter, Francesca, sat alone at a table off to the side. Di Risio hovered anonymously nearby.

Sharon Stone ran the auction, lacing her patter with a profanity-laced Donatella impersonation. About one Versace-designed Lamborghini, she cracked, "I love it so much my boobies stay right up." In a show of good sportsmanship, Donatella chose *Saturday Night Live* star Maya Rudolph to introduce her. When the designer finally took the stage, she dedicated the award to her children.[5] Elton John wiped away a tear as he sang Gianni's favorite songs. Guns N' Roses sang "Knockin' on Heaven's Door," while Donatella danced, her eyes closed and her arms swaying above her head, lost in the music.

A few weeks later in Milan, Donatella sent one of her best collections yet onto the runway, with exaggerated A-line coats, gowns in white silk, and silver shift dresses. "Ms. Versace's collection was a real testament to her brother's genius," wrote Cathy Horyn in the *New York Times*, labeling the collection "outstanding."[6] The morning after the show, Patrick Guadagno, the head of Versace's American business, received a message on his cell phone. It was the head of Bergdorf Goodman. "Congratulations on a truly beautiful show," he said. "We're ready to move forward. Let's schedule a meeting as soon as possible."[7]

Nearly three years after hitting bottom, it was all coming together. Donatella's image had been rehabilitated. A larger design team was churning out fresh, sharp collections that were beefy enough to fill the boutiques, and deliveries were arriving on time. One by one, American department stores placed new orders. Bergdorf even put Versace on the cover of its catalog. Not long after the Milan runway show, Saks scheduled a personal appearance with Donatella for the launch of a new perfume, holding it in the center of its main floor on Fifth Avenue. For some personal appearances, the department store has to stock the line with staff because too few customers turn up. But Donatella was like a rock star, signing autographs and graciously posing for pictures for two hours. The store sold $35,000 worth of perfume.[8]

The house's new approach to celebrity dressing was also paying off. Given its limited budget, Versace had to be selective in targeting a small number of stars. At the Oscars ceremony that February, Penelope Cruz wore a spectacular rose-colored gown with a sweeping feathered train that was featured over and over again on the best-dressed lists.

❖ V ❖

Even as Donatella celebrated the house's bull run, she worried about Allegra. By then, Allegra had dropped out of Brown and was settled in Los Angeles, riding her bike on Venice Beach on the weekends and socializing with a tight circle of close friends. She was invited to the hot parties thrown by her mother's celebrity friends, but she shied away from them. On the rare occasions she went clubbing in Hollywood, she avoided the celebrity-brat set and virtually never appeared in the gossip columns. Journalists frequently asked for interviews, hoping for a profile of the reclusive Versace heiress, but with the exception of an anodyne article for one fashion magazine, she turned them all down.

Donatella flew to Los Angeles for monthly visits with her daughter, taking her shopping for clothes and CDs and trying to coax her into an occasional dinner at Matsuhisa, a hot sushi spot. When Donatella was in town, Allegra scouted out movies beforehand to see whether her mother would like something enough to sit for two hours without smoking. Even as Allegra approached her twenty-first birthday, Donatella still hovered, keeping close track of what she was doing and whom she was hanging out with. She even forbade Allegra from driving a car. "Why should she have to park?" she told a journalist once. "Who wants to deal with that?"[9]

Allegra had been conspicuously absent from the February 2007 Walk of Style celebrations. Around the same time, rumors regarding her health began circulating on the Internet. One site claimed she was "barely hanging on to life" and weighed less than eighty pounds. In recent years, Allegra had become an icon worthy of worship on so-called thinspo or pro-ana sites, where anorexics posted photos of superthin celebrities such as Mary-Kate Olsen and Kate Bosworth as inspiration to starve themselves.

By the spring of 2007, Donatella and Paul could no longer ignore the speculation. For the first time, they confirmed publicly that Allegra suffered from anorexia, but they denied her life was in danger and said she was receiving help. Their statement got huge coverage in the press, coming as it did in the wake of the death of two models from anorexia and a heated public debate about whether the ultrathin mannequins on the catwalks contributed to the disease.

Allegra remained out of the public eye until July 2007, when a commemoration of the tenth anniversary of Gianni's death was planned at La Scala opera house in Milan. Most of the women in the celebrity crowd wore revealing low-cut Versace gowns. But despite the suffocating heat, Allegra was covered from head to toe. She wore a loose, black bell-shaped dress with long sleeves and a hem falling to her calves. Thick black tights covered her legs. Donatella stuck close by Allegra's side the whole time, flanked by a bodyguard also dressed in black. Allegra dutifully posed for the waiting photographers, but refused to smile.

The evening was also marred by a contretemps with Antonio D'Amico. Gianni's boyfriend had struggled for years after the murder, trying his hand at launching his own fashion line and later opening a restaurant in the Italian countryside. He had even attempted suicide before finally coming to terms with the loss of Gianni. He and Donatella had scrupulously avoided each other over the years. When Elton John married his longtime boyfriend in the United Kingdom in 2005, the singer invited them both. But Antonio declined to go, unwilling to see Donatella. When the La Scala celebration rolled around, the family claimed to have invited him. "That's a lie and they know it," he retorted to the Italian press. "I wasn't invited. Gianni wouldn't be happy if he knew that I wasn't there."

twenty

A New Beginning

*m*ORE THAN TEN YEARS HAD PASSED SINCE GIANNI'S death, and Donatella continued to think of him every day. When she was nervous, she fingered that iron key to the gate of the Miami mansion. Despite the improvement in the collections, she batted away comparisons with her virtuosic brother, still keenly aware of her limits as a designer.

Nonetheless, the anniversary marked a new beginning for Donatella. Santo often reveled in the past, happy to recount war stories from Gianni's glory days. Donatella was more chastened but had made a certain peace with her failures and achievements. By 2007, the narrative of the renewed Versace, of a battered house rising from the ashes, had taken root. Journalists were gentle with Donatella, dutifully noting her lost years, but they spared her too many uncomfortable questions. She submitted to interviews with practiced patience, parrying the same questions over and over again with grace and good manners, flipping her Barbie doll hair as she served up the telling quip. She exhibited far less of the verve and flamboyance that she had showed in the past. She often spoke soberly about her own mothering skills, opening a window into the guilt she felt about how little time she'd had for Daniel and Allegra over the years. At times, she seemed almost fragile, her hands shaking slightly as she sipped an espresso from a Versace bone china cup, and she still became endearingly nervous during television appearances.

The fashion business, with its bottomless hunger for something new, had become a treadmill for designers who must churn out frequent flash collections in between their semiannual runway shows. Donatella worked hard, going months at a time without a day off. Long-haul airplane trips became a rare escape, when she was unreachable for hours. She rarely dated and she admitted a certain loneliness, but she had long grown fatalistic about relationships.

She still visited the limestone grotto on the grounds of the villa in Como that housed the gilt box containing Gianni's ashes, next to a framed photograph and a silver crucifix. On the day of the tenth anniversary, Donatella had sent to Villa Fontanelle five dozen red roses—Gianni would have been sixty that year—along with a single gardenia slipped in at the request of Allegra. But otherwise, Santo and Donatella rarely went to the Lake Como retreat.

For months at a time, the house that had sheltered the family's best private and public moments—Allegra's baptism, Donatella's wedding, lazy visits with celebrity friends, a garden full of toys and children's laughter, and many dazzling parties—was an empty shell. The large salon where a huge Christmas tree used to stand each year was barren, the maids dusting off Gianni's beloved books and the desk where he sketched for hours. In the garden, the gliding swing under a magnolia tree where Gianni and Donatella often sat together was empty. In the living room, the speed dial on the phone was like a clock that stopped the moment Gianni died: New York Casa, Miami Casa, A. Wintour, Avedon Studio.[1] The villa was a reminder of what life might have been had Gianni not been murdered that awful summer. Donatella and Santo had long stopped celebrating holidays together there.

Indeed, Santo went there less and less often as he considered a new career in Italian politics, and his children left to attend college in New York and London. (In spring 2008, Santo was elected a member of parliament, representing Silvio Berlusconi's center-right party.)

Ten years after Gianni's murder, Santo and Donatella decided it was time to sell Villa Fontanelle. In early 2008, a Russian millionaire bought it for 35 million euros. Before handing over the villa, the siblings moved their brother's ashes to a small mausoleum deep inside the gardens of Via Gesù.

❖ V ❖

Versace's success remained uncertain in the years that followed. The violent economic downturn in the fall of 2008 hit the luxury sector hard. That holiday season was the worst in memory. By Thanksgiving weekend, department stores such as Saks had slashed the prices of its fall clothing, bags, and shoes by as much as 70 percent. Global sales of luxury goods dropped by one-fourth that month. Bulgari canceled virtually all of its planned new store openings, while Prada wallets turned up in the discount bins of Walmart. Yet the rebirth of Versace left it on far more solid ground to face the dire economic situation than would have been the case several years earlier. Back then, a recession of that magnitude would doubtlessly have swept away the company. Instead, Versace's sales even rose slightly for 2008 to 336 million euros. But its profit was tiny at just nine million euros, boosted largely by the sale of Villa Fontanelle.

Giancarlo Di Risio hoped his strategy of pushing Versace into the priciest products would safeguard the house, betting that ultra-rich shoppers would hardly feel the downturn. Versace began designing the interiors of Lamborghinis, including one half-million-dollar model, as well as yachts, private jets, and helicopters: five million dollars would buy a bird complete with gold handles, plasma TVs, and plush leather Versace seats embellished with a Greek frieze motif, one of the house's signature designs. The house was also working on designing a seven-star hotel in Dubai, complete with an underground system to cool the sand. Donatella's collections continued to win kudos with the fashion press, although some pieces look so toned-down and genteel that they seem to have little Versace soul. Her team was churning out six collections a year that sold at stores such as Neiman Marcus, Saks, Barneys, and Nordstrom. The accessories business had grown from nothing in 2004 to 40 percent of sales, and Versace bags often had pride of place near Chanel in American department stores.

But as the recession deepened in 2009, there were signs that Versace was struggling. The men's line limped along, struggling to find a clientele. Stronger houses such as Chanel began staging elaborate runway shows even for their winter cruise collection, while Versace could afford no more than a private showing with clients. For catwalk shows in Milan, modeling agencies favored houses such as Dolce & Gabbana over Versace, which hired far fewer girls. Indeed, the March 2009 season in Milan represented a sort of role reversal for Versace. The house had conspicuously few celebrities, planting just a couple of Italian soccer stars in the front row. A few blocks away, Dolce & Gabbana's show resembled one of Gianni's spectacles from his heyday, with Eva Mendes, Kate Hudson, Scarlett Johansson, Naomi Watts, and Lauren Hutton in the front row, along with Eva Herzigova and Claudia Schiffer, both former Versace models.

Versace's lost years still dog the company, making it virtually impossible to close the gap with its rivals. Louis Vuitton's shop on Avenue des Champs-Élysées in Paris makes as much as 90 million euros a year alone, more than a quarter of Versace's entire revenue. And as in so many businesses, the new frontier lies in markets such as China, India, and Russia, which are all churning out thousands of new millionaires every year. The challenge is to sink millions into new shops and new advertising in these markets, while still keeping up in traditional regions in Europe and the United States. Versace has opened fifteen shops in China so far, but that pales in comparison to Armani's fifty-five.

❖ V ❖

In the spring of 2009, a bombshell landed. After five years at the helm of the house, Giancarlo Di Risio announced his resignation. For months, he and Donatella had been at loggerheads over how the brand should react to the deep crisis.

For a number of years after her stint in rehab, Donatella had been happy to step back and let Di Risio have the upper hand in the house. The pressure of running the house after Gianni's death was still fresh in Donatella's mind, and she was relieved to be free of much of the burden for a time. Newly sober and feeling well for the first time in years, she was glad to have the space and freedom to tend to herself, as well as to Allegra, visiting the young woman frequently in the United States. Indeed, as Donatella celebrated one year after another of sobriety, the relationship between mother and daughter appeared to improve. Donatella and Allegra attended dinners and parties more frequently together, and Allegra began acting as a virtual cohost at Versace events, schmoozing a bit with retail executives, celebrities, and fashion editors. Meanwhile, Allegra herself became somewhat less reclusive, even turning up occasionally at nightclubs, once making the rounds of the hot spots of London with Kate Moss.

As Donatella felt more sure of herself, and Allegra seemed more settled, she grew increasingly impatient with deferring to Di Risio. Di Risio had set up large teams of designers for the accessories business and homeware products that reported straight to him, not to Donatella, who sometimes didn't see the items until they were virtually ready to go on the market. For several years, she also quietly assented when Di Risio asked for changes in her ready-to-wear line.

However, by the start of 2009, the crisis began to weigh more heavily on Versace. In the first three months of the year, sales fell by 13 percent—hit in part by the bankruptcy of ITR, which stopped paying Versace royalties on its jeans line. Versace was still profitable in the first quarter and sales picked up in the spring, but by then, Donatella was convinced that the house needed a new leader—one who would *take* orders from the family, instead of giving them. With several years of solid collections and steady management of the atelier under her belt, Donatella felt more confident than ever. By then, she and Santo agreed that a slate of decisions made by Di Risio—for example, large investments in the accessories business and his plan to open new franchises—were the wrong responses to such a serious crisis. Di Risio argued that he was cutting costs quickly in reaction to the fall in sales, while the new stores, particularly in China, were important for future growth. But the family felt that didn't go far enough, and now that they were free of the pressure from the banks—the debt was well under control—the family could reassert itself for the first time in five years.

Since coming into her stake, Allegra had been a largely passive presence in the house, hewing closely to the advice of her lawyer, Michele Carpinelli, and Marco Salomoni, a Versace board member with long experience in the fashion business. She diligently read the reports that Di Risio sent her on the developments at her company, but she virtually never attended board meetings. By early 2009, Allegra began spending a bit more time in Milan and in her mother's atelier, although by then New York had become home, where she continued her studies. As the sales figures for the first months of the year reached her, she began to agree with her mother and uncle that it was time for fresh blood. While the pressure of such a change might have driven the family apart in the past, it now united Santo, Allegra, and Donatella. At the end of March, the family decided to hire Bain & Co., a leading consulting firm, to come up with a new plan to address the dire market. At that point, Di Risio understood that it was time to leave. He tendered his resignation in early June. A week later, the house hired Gian Giacomo Ferraris, the fifty-one-year-old chief executive of Jil Sander.

Even with a new chief executive, at some point, the Versace family will face difficult choices about what kind of future will best ensure the company's enduring success and preserve its legacy. It can remain a niche player, running the risk of becoming irrelevant as other houses gradually crowd it out. It is too small to go public, so if it wants to grow, the family will have to consider selling out to a bigger rival such as LVMH or Gucci or to a deep-pocketed investor such as a private equity fund. Either way, the family would have little choice but to give up control. During the 2007 boom, when houses such as Roberto Cavalli had considered going public, investment banks had again proposed selling a piece of Versace to private equity or hedge-fund investors. But the family had declined. Indeed, as 2009 unfolded, Versace's weakness became dangerously evident. In autumn, Ferraris announced he expected the house to lose 30 million euros for the year, while sales were likely to fall by nearly 20 percent, the lowest level the brand has ever seen. To stanch the red ink, the new CEO laid off a quarter of Versace's employees and shut its stores in Japan, one of the world's biggest luxury markets.

As a result, in 2009, Versace finds itself once again at the mercy of its founding family's dynamics. And, as before, much hangs on the choices that Allegra will make in the coming years. Her health remains a private challenge and a corporate uncertainty. In early 2009, Allegra began spending more time in Milan and took up a desk in her mother's atelier.

Once, when Allegra was very young, she was perched on the desk of her beloved uncle as he gave an interview to a journalist. The reporter, charmed by the sunny child, asked her, "Do you want to be a model when you grow up?"

"No, I want to be a designer!" Allegra retorted immediately, much to the delight of Gianni. But now Allegra is a sober twenty-three-year-old woman, and her wishes for her uncle's company—and her own future—remain a mystery. She could choose to sell the house, freeing herself of an enormous emotional and business burden, in order to strike a path of her own. But that would surely leave her mother, at fifty-four, without a job. Alternatively, Allegra could maintain the status quo, hoping the house will catch a new wave of growth and collecting the meager dividends in the meantime.

The Versace story, in its drama and pathos, almost defies belief, a fairy tale that dissolved into a long, protracted horror story with the firing of two inexplicable gunshots. A hard-fought recovery has partly redeemed the years of woe and grief. But no matter what Allegra decides, the house will always be tinged with the sad knowledge that things will never be the same. Gianni Versace changed fashion forever. More than ten years after his death, one wonders whether his creation—for all its precarious recovery—is destined to become a relic of the past or a force for the future in fashion. The fate of the storied house rests as heavily as ever on the thin shoulders of Gianni's beloved *principessa*.

Acknowledgments

I am indebted to scores of people who helped make this book possible, generously granting me their time and sharing with me their memories of an extraordinary man and the legacy he left. While I never had the privilege of meeting Gianni Versace, he became a growing source of inspiration over the course of this project as I learned more of his uncommon talent, determination, and humanity.

This book is based primarily on my firsthand reporting, consisting of 220 interviews with friends, family, former lovers, co-workers, rivals, and business partners of the Versaces, as well as on my review of three decades of financial documents, historical footage of runway shows, police reports, and public records in Milan, New York, Calabria, and Miami.

My greatest debt of gratitude surely goes to Santo and Donatella Versace. This is the first book to enjoy the help of the Versace family. In a world that depends on spinning a dream, fashion houses are fiercer than most businesses in protecting their images, and the Versaces are no exception. The drama and pathos of the Versaces' personal and professional lives have made them understandably reticent to cooperate with authors in the past, wary of how their story would be treated. Yet, once they agreed to help, they answered my many questions with grace and patience, reliving not just the good times, but recounting for me a long terrible period they would just as soon forget. Their devotion and deep affection for their brother and his memory came through clearly in every one of my long interviews with them.

Donatella is all too often caricatured in the media, but the picture that friends, colleagues, and family painted for me is of a warm, loving, if at times troubled woman. She has wrestled with her demons and is admirably open about her shortcomings. I hope this book offers the world a more nuanced portrait that goes beyond the spitfire blonde in the Versace evening dress.

Over the course of many hours of interviews, Santo offered me a treasure trove of memories, facts, and details that enormously enriched my portrait of the business side of the story, in particular the early days when he and his brother ventured north to Milan to set up shop. Santo has now moved on to a career in Italian politics, but his passion for his brother's house is evident even today. I hope I have done justice to his story.

Antonio D'Amico, Gianni's longtime partner, deserves a special thanks for graciously answering hours of questions, some delving into the most painful moments of his life. His insights into Gianni's life and personality were invaluable in writing this book.

Virtually the only person who declined to speak with me was Allegra Versace, despite my repeated pleas. I regret that she chose not to participate in this book, as her voice would have further enriched the complicated story of her family and the company that she now controls. It might also have gone far toward chasing away the speculation that continues to swirl around the delicate young woman.

I owe a special thanks to Isabelle Harvie Watt and Deirdre McCready, as well as to Cristina Crolli and Lisa Hellman in the Versace press office for putting up with nearly two years of pestering for interviews, invitations to fashion shows, historical material, and insight into the company and the family. They most certainly must have tired of my incessant requests, but nonetheless met each one of them with good humor. Stefania Alberti, Santo's loyal assistant, cheerfully helped me navigate her boss's busy schedule.

Giancarlo Di Risio took time out of his busy schedule to sit for several interviews, recounting in detail his work in restoring Versace's health.

Santo and Donatella opened the door to a large number of friends and family who were instrumental in understanding the roots of this storied clan. Childhood friends in Calabria lovingly described the happy early family life of the siblings and their remarkable parents, in particular their mother. I would first thank Nora Macheda, the woman who helped raise the Versace siblings and who welcomed me into the family home to entrust me with her recollections of the clan. Enzo Crupi, Donatella's high school sweetheart, played my personal tour guide to Reggio. Anna Candela, a dear friend of Gianni's, offered me valuable insight into his childhood and teenage years. Other family and friends who helped include Tita Versace, Carlo Casile, Bruno De Robertis, Antonella Freno, Donatella Benedetto, and Anna Camerata.

This book would not have been possible without the unstinting cooperation of many people with firsthand knowledge of the House of Versace since its birth. Many people reached back in time to recall details of the early days of working with Gianni. I would like to thank particularly Franca Biagini, Gianni's beloved *premiere*, who welcomed me into her home and fed me a wonderful Tuscan meal while she shared fond memories of her years at Versace. Patrizia Cucco, Gianni's devoted personal assistant, lived up to her reputation as the house's living historian. Franco Lussana, a dear family friend and one of Versace's first employees, recalled the very first days when a fresh-faced Gianni landed in Milan. Wanda Galtrucco, a dear friend of Gianni, painted a fond picture of the designer. Donatella Girombelli recalled the period when she and her husband gave Gianni one of his big breaks. David Brown offered me priceless recollections of the supermodel era.

Other current and former longtime Versace employees answered my many questions about the history of the house, including Nunzio Palamara, Angelo Azzena, Paola Marletta, Anna Cernuschi, Stefano Guerriero, Bruno Gianesi, Brian Atwood, Jurgen Oeltjenbruns, Luca Callegari, Jason Weisenfeld,

Acknowledgments

Andrea Tremolada, Enrico Genevois, Anna Caputo, Patrick Guadagno, Emanuela Schmeidler, and Loredana Nastro.

Other business associates filled out the history of the house: Mario Mangano, Walter Ragazzi, Giuseppe Menta, Riccardo Guy, Roberto Devorik, Nando Miglio, Dawn Mello, Carole White, Ellin Saltzman, Barbara Vitti, Donato De Santis, Anne Marie Paltsou, Mario Boselli, Ron Frasch, Gio Moretti, Wallace Tutt, Julie Mannion, Sergio Salerni, Andrea Gottleib Vizcarrondo, Paolo Tomei, Carolyn Mahboubi, Agostino Guardamagna, Enrico Fantini, Donatella Ratti, Renato Molteni, Paola Terenghi, Joan Kaner, Nicoletta Santoro, Joe McKenna, Brana Wolf, Lori Goldstein, Norma Stevens, Phyllis Walters, Alan Rohwer, and Francois Nars.

In Miami, I would like to thank Larry Rivero, Irene Marie, Rick Moeser, Tara Solomon, Merle Weiss, Tom Austin, Bruce Orosz, Lee Schrager, Louis Canales, Frank Scottolini, and the press office of Casa Casuarina. A very warm thanks goes to Denise Burne Fein, who offered her valuable insights into the workings of the Meadows. Paola Bottelli, the doyenne of the fashion business at Italian newspaper *Il Sole 24 Ore*, was enormously generous with her insights into the Milan fashion scene. I would also like to thank Fran Curtis, Elton John's publicist.

The press offices of the FBI and the Miami Beach Police Department helped me pull together the extensive files on Gianni's murder, which consisted of nearly a thousand pages. Antonella Barberis and Pietro Marzo at Milan's Chamber of Commerce pulled three decades of Versace balance sheets for me.

I would also like to extend a special thanks to Anna Wintour and Naomi Campbell, who entrusted me with their recollections of Gianni and his siblings.

I would also like to thank Lucia Mari, Patrick Jephson, Pietro Jovane Scott, Vincenzo Finizzola, Rita Airaghi, Stefano Dominella, Beppe Modenese, Logan Bentley, Rosemary Ferrari, Bob Kreiger, Noris Morano, Concetta Lanciaux, Vicki Woods, Wayne Scot Lukas, Jonathan Sidhu, Stu Woo, Albert Reed, Kevin Crawford, Ellin Levar, Claudia Buccellati, Giuseppe Mondani, Mary Lou Luther, Robert Burke, Ruggero Pegna, Patrick O'Connell, Arne Glimcher, Carla Ling, Dickie Arbiter, Gianfranco Manfredi, Pino Bertone, Michela Bertone, Gisella Borioli, and the Diocese of Milan.

Dozens of other people, fearful of offending the Versace family, chose to speak with me on a non-for-attribution basis. I wish to thank them for the time and trust they invested in me and this book.

A heartfelt appreciation goes to a number of people at the *Wall Street Journal*, my professional home for the last twelve years. This book simply would not have been possible had it not been for the extraordinary training that the *Wall Street Journal* provides its journalists. I have had the great good fortune to work with a group of talented editors and fellow reporters who, in the face of enormous challenges, remain committed to a level of excellence that is increasingly rare in today's media world.

I would especially like to thank Michael Williams, Emily Nelson, and Nik

Acknowledgments

Deogun, for graciously supporting this project, including granting me an extensive leave to complete it. Rose Ellen D'Angelo, the *Journal*'s books-projects editor, has been supportive of this book from the moment of its inception. Steve Stecklow offered valuable feedback on the book's early chapters. I would also like to thank Alan Murray, Alix Freedman, Karen Pensiero, and Robert Thomson.

I owe a special word for Teri Agins, a dear friend and the most selfless colleague one could ever hope for. Teri is rightfully a legend in the fashion world for her smart, sassy, and incisive coverage of a business that often eludes serious scrutiny. *The End of Fashion*, her landmark book on the fashion business, was an inspiration and guide well before I embarked on this adventure. From her sharp editing of my initial proposal to her unstinting support during the grueling process of reporting and writing this book, Teri bucked me up countless times when I felt overwhelmed with what I'd taken on.

I owe a special thanks to the team at Crown—John Mahaney, Tina Constable, and Jo Rodgers—who ferried this long project to completion. I would also like to express my gratitude to Milena Vercellino, a talented young Italian journalist who transcribed a number of interviews, helped me with valuable legwork during the early stages of the reporting and did a thorough fact-checking at the end that saved me from more than one embarrassing error. I am also indebted to David Groff for his elegant edit of my manuscript. He smoothed out many bumpy passages and fixed sections where I got lost in the weeds.

My agent, Jane Dystel, has done more hand-holding in the last three years than she probably ever bargained for. Her deep experience in the industry as well as her unstinting support of this project helped me navigate more than one harrowing moment. Her business partner, Miriam Goderich, was invaluable in guiding this first-time author in crafting the initial proposal.

Finally, I owe special appreciation to my family and friends, who have borne a disproportionate share of the burden of this book. Friends in Boston, Milan, New York, and London have generously indulged my self-absorption with this project for many, many months. My mother, my three brothers, their families and our dear friend Pam McLeod endured my setting up camp—with my laptop and an endless load of notes piled high on the kitchen table—during family vacations and holidays.

Most of all, I wish to thank my husband, Fabrizio Mucci, who supported me through two long years of distractions, frustrations, complaints, and frequent absences. He lived literally surrounded by this project for far too long. He read my first proposal, patiently helped me sift through thirty years of Versace balance sheets and caught more than one error on Italian history and business. I will do my best to repay his patience in the days and years to come.

Milan, October 26, 2009

Notes

one *"They've Shot Gianni"*

[1] Interview with Rita Airaghi, February 20, 2008.

[2] Maer Roshan, "Surviving at the Top," *New York*, December 15, 1997, p. 40.

[3] Rody Mirri, *It's Your Song: Gianni Versace e Antonio D'Amico*. Quindici Anni di Vita Insieme (Gussago: Societa' Editrice Vannini, 2007), p. 111.

[4] Minnie Gastel, *Il mito Versace: Una biografia* (Milan: Baldini Castoldi Dalai, 2007), p. 247.

[5] Interview with Donato De Santis, May 20, 2008.

[6] Renata Molho, *Essere Armani: Una biografia* (Milan: Baldini Castoldi Dalai, 2006), p. 168.

[7] Andrea Lee, "The Emperor of Dreams," *New Yorker*, July 28, 1997, p. 46.

[8] Ibid., p. 42.

two *The Black Sheep*

[1] Interview with Tita Versace, March 18, 2008.

[2] Interview with Santo Versace, February 13, 2008.

[3] Interview with Tita Versace, July 2008.

[4] Luciano Gulli, "L'Utopia," *Il Giornale*, February 8, 2008.

[5] Interview with Santo Versace, February 13, 2008.

[6] Mario Guarino, *Versace Versus Versace: La Biographia di Gianni Versace* (Rome: Edizioni Libreria Croce di Fabio Croce, 2003), p. 15.

[7] Interview with Gianni Versace, *La Stampa*, July 29, 1994.

[8] Gastel *Il mito Versace*, p. 18.

[9] Interview with Anna Candela, September 16, 2008.

[10] Lorella Capparucci, "Due rose rosse appoggiate accanto alle pozze di sangue," *Gazzetta del Sud*, July 16, 1997.

[11] Interview with Nora Macheda, March 18, 2008.

[12] *Secret Lives: Versace*, original broadcast on December 23, 1997, NBC.

Notes

[13] Interview with Donatella Benedetto, September 18, 2008.

[14] Ingrid Sischy, "Style Is Not a Pain in the Neck," *Interview*, June 1, 1995. p. 58.

[15] Capparucci, "Due rose rosse appoggiate."

[16] "La Tragica Notizia di Miami," *Gente*, July 1997, p. 30.

[17] Interview with Anna Candela, September 16, 2008.

[18] Roberto Alessi, V*ersace: Eleganza di vita* (Milan: Rusconi, 1990), p. 35.

[19] *Secret Lives: Versace.*

[20] Ibid.

[21] Interview with Tita Versace, September 17, 2008.

[22] Donatella Versace, speech at the memorial for Gianni Versace at the Metropolitan Museum of Art, September 8, 1997.

[23] Daniela Fedi, "Basta Pettegolezzi, Noi Non Molliamo," *Il Giornale*, June 27, 2004.

[24] Lee, "The Emperor of Dreams."

[25] Interview with Donatella Versace, April 7, 2008.

three *Breaking Free*

[1] Teri Agins, *The End of Fashion: How Marketing Changed the Clothing Business Forever* (New York: HarperCollins, 1999), p. 27.

[2] Nicola White, *Reconstructing Italian Fashion: America and the Development of the Italian Fashion Industry* (New York: Berg, 2000), p. 82.

[3] Marya Mannes, "Italian Fashion," *Vogue*, January 1, 1947, p. 119.

[4] Samantha Conti, "Fifty Years of Fashion: They Arrived Late to Fashion's Table, but Have Been Feasting Ever Since," *Women's Wear Daily*, February 22, 2000.

[5] White, *Reconstructing Italian Fashion*, p. 69.

[6] Ibid., p. 40.

[7] Agins, *End of Fashion*, p. 23.

[8] Interview with Franco Lussana, March 4, 2008.

[9] Interview with Santo Versace, June 28, 2008.

[10] "La Tragica Notizia di Miami," p. 28.

[11] "Modenese: Che Ansia, Voleva Case in Ogni Angolo del Mondo," *Corriere della Sera*, July 17, 1997.

[12] Interview with Santo Versace, February 13, 2008.

[13] Guarino, p. 52.

[14] Interview with Santo Versace, June 28, 2008.

[15] Michael Gross, *Model: The Ugly Business of Beautiful Women* (New York: Warner Books, 1996), p. 250.

[16] Interview with Giuseppe Menta, May 16, 2008.

[17] Gastel, *Il mito Versace*, p. 29.

[18] Interview with Donatella Girombelli, *La Stampa*, July 16, 1997.

[19] Gastel, *Il mito Versace*, p. 25.

[20] Interview with Franco Lussana, February 20, 2008.

[21] Lee, "The Emperor of Dreams," p. 44.

[22] Gigi Monti, interviewed in *Secret Lives: Versace.*

[23] Interview with Franco Lussana, February 20, 2008.

[24] Interview with Donatella Girombelli, *La Stampa*, July 16, 1997.

four *Sister, Playmate, Confidante*

[1] Fashion Week Daily e-newsletter, May 2008.

[2] Daniela Fedi, "Basta Pettegolezzi, Noi Non Molliamo. Donatella Parla Del Futuro dell'Azienda," *Il Giornale*, June 27, 2004.

[3] Interview with Donatella Versace, April 7, 2008.

[4] Interview with Nora Macheda, March 18, 2008.

[5] Interview with Donatella Versace, April 7, 2008.

[6] Lee, "The Emperor of Dreams," pp. 51–52.

[7] Interview with Donatella Versace, April 7, 2008.

[8] Lauren Collins, "Mondo Donatella," *New Yorker*, p. 158.

[9] Ariel Levy, "Summer for the Sun Queen," *New York*, August 20, 2006, p. 48.

[10] Interview with Donatella Versace, April 7, 2008.

[11] Ibid.

[12] Interview with Santo Versace, June 28, 2008.

[13] Enno Lagana, "Forse un Giorno Tornerò a Spiare il Sole," *Gazzetta del Sud*, July 16, 1997.

[14] Interview with Tita Versace, September 17, 2008.

five *A New Era*

[1] Interview with Santo Versace, June 28, 2008.

[2] Ibid.

[3] Ibid.

Notes

[4] Ibid.

[5] Interview with Roberto Devorik, April 18, 2008.

[6] Interview with Santo Versace, January 26, 2009.

[7] Interview with Anne Marie Paltsou, October 7, 2008.

[8] Overall sales are a total of all the sales of Versace items made by the franchisees, department stores, and other outlets. Net sales include only the slice that retailers and licensees pay directly to the brand owner. Net sales is considered a more accurate measure of a house's growth. Versace only began reporting consolidated net revenues in 1988.

[9] Interview with Anna Cernuschi, April 2, 2008.

[10] Interview with Donatella Versace, April 7, 2008.

six: *Rivals and Lovers*

[1] Interview with Sergio Salerni, March 7, 2008.

[2] Interview with Anna Zegna, December 11, 2007.

[3] Molho, *Essere Armani*, p. 30.

[4] Richard Buckley, "Since Dawn of Armani, Italian Tailoring a Touchstone for Quality," *International Herald Tribune*, March 17, 1997.

[5] Agins, *End of Fashion*, p. 132.

[6] Interview with Ellin Saltzman, October 30, 2008.

[7] Bridget Foley, "Master Armani," *W Magazine*, October 2000, p. 385.

[8] Molho, *Essere Armani*, p. 131.

[9] Judy Bachrach, "Armani in Full," *Vanity Fair*, October 2000, p. 190.

[10] Lee, "The Emperor of Dreams," *New Yorker*, p. 53.

[11] Mirri, *It's Your Song*, pp. 47–50.

[12] Ibid., p. 104.

[13] Interview with Antonio D'Amico, June 23, 2008.

[14] Mirri, *It's Your Song*, p. 76.

[15] Interview with Antonio D'Amico, June 23, 2008.

seven: *Inspiration and Muse*

[1] Interview with Angelo Azzena, April 8, 2008.

[2] *Secret Lives: Versace.*

[3] Interview with Donatella Versace, April 7, 2008.

[4] Interview with Angelo Azzena, April 8, 2008.

[5] Cathy Horyn, "La Bella Donatella," *Vanity Fair*, June 1997, p. 162.

[6] Ibid.

[7] Interview with Andrea Gottleib, April 24, 2008.

[8] Interview with Donatella Versace, April 7, 2008.

[9] Interview with Enrico Genevois, March 27, 2008.

[10] Interview with Franco Lussana, February 20, 2008.

[11] Giusy Ferrè, "Sprazzi di Vita Meravigliosa," *Omaggio a Gianni Versace, Operare*, March 22, 2001, p. 27.

[12] Ibid.

[13] Patrizia Cucco, "Avanti, Senza Sosta," *Omaggio a Gianni Versace, Operare*, March 22, 2001, p. 41.

[14] Interview with Carolyn Mahboubi, March 6, 2008.

[15] Interview with Patrizia Cucco, March 12, 2008.

[16] Interview with Nunzio Palamara, July 1, 2008.

[17] Interview with Franco Lussana, February 20, 2008.

[18] Interview with Dawn Mello, April 25, 2008.

[19] Interview with Roberto Devorik, April 18, 2008.

[20] *Fashion Victim: The Killing of Gianni Versace,* first broadcast on November 20, 2001.

[21] Interview with Jurgen Oeltjenbruns, February 29, 2009.

[22] Interview with Patrizia Cucco, March 12, 2008.

[23] Interview with Carlo Casile, September 17, 2008.

eight *Rock and Royalty*

[1] Gastel, *Il mito Versace*, p. 99.

[2] Philip Norman, *Sir Elton: The Definitive Biography of Elton John* (London: Pan Books, 2001), p. 7.

[3] Graydon Carter, "Starface," *Vogue*, October 1989, p. 419.

[4] Bronwyn Cosgrave, *Made for Each Other: Fashion and the Academy Awards* (New York: Bloomsbury USA, 2006), p. 184.

[5] Gastel, *Il mito Versace*. p. 145.

[6] Ginia Bellafante, "La Dolce Vita: Gianni Versace Sold the World a Fantasy of Unrestrained Opulence," *Time*, July 28, 1997, p. 36.

[7] Interview with Giuseppe Menta, May 16, 2008.

[8] *Fashion Victim.*

[9] James Servin, "Chic or Cruel?" *New York Times*, November 1, 1992.

[10] Interview with Anna Wintour, October 22, 2008.

Notes

11 Ibid.

12 Ibid.

13 Interview with Donatella Versace, April 7, 2008.

14 Cathy Horyn, "The Murder on Ocean Drive," *New York Times,* July 19, 2007.

15 Interview with Angelo Azzena, April 8, 2008.

16 Interview with Roberto Devorik, April 18, 2008.

17 *Fashion Victim.*

18 Interview with Franca Biagini, March 13, 2008.

19 Interview with Wayne Scot Lukas, April 25, 2008.

20 Victoria Beckham, *That Extra Half an Inch* (London: Michael Joseph Ltd, 2006), p. 125.

21 Interview with Donatella Versace, December 15, 2008.

22 Samantha Conti, "The Versace VIP: Celebrities Are an Integral Part of the Weave at the House of Donatella," *Women's Wear Daily,* February 7, 2003.

nine: *Supermodels, Superstar*

1 Gross, *Model,* p. 15.

2 Ibid., p. 479.

3 Ibid., p. 491.

4 Interview with Donatella Versace, April 7, 2008.

5 Interview with David Brown, November 22, 2007.

6 Interview with Nunzio Palamara, July 1, 2008.

7 Interview with Angelo Azzena, April 8, 2008.

8 Conti, "Versace VIP."

9 Gastel, *Il mito Versace,* p. 207.

10 Interview with Riccardo Gay, May 29, 2007.

11 Gastel, *Il mito Versace,* p. 202.

12 Interview with Carole White, January 14, 2009.

13 Liz Jones, "Monsters . . . But," *Daily Mail,* September 5, 2007.

14 Gross, *Model,* p. 492.

15 Interview with Wayne Scot Lukas, April 25, 2008.

16 Polly Vernon, "Naomi Campbell: Catwoman," *Observer,* August 7, 2005.

17 Rachel Porter, "Naomi Campbell: After All the Tantrums, Drink and Drugs, I've Finally Grown Up," *Daily Express,* March 3, 2007.

[18] Interview with Carole White, January 14, 2009.

[19] Interview with Naomi Campbell, February 8, 2009.

[20] Ibid.

[21] Natasha Bita, "Model Citizen," *Australian Magazine*, April 22, 2006, p. 16.

[22] Interview with Phyllis Walters, September 10, 2008.

[23] Interview with Angelo Azzena, April 8, 2008.

[24] Agins, *End of Fashion*, p. 37.

[25] Richard Martin, *Gianni Versace* (New York: The Metropolitan Museum of Art. 1997), p. 14.

[26] Andrea Lee, "The Emperor of Dreams," p. 46.

[27] Interview with Anna Wintour, October 22, 2008.

[28] Interview with Phyllis Walters, September 10, 2008.

[29] Interview with Vicki Woods, September 15, 2008.

ten *Diva*

[1] Interview with Donatella Versace, April 7, 2008.

[2] Interview with François Nars, October 28, 2008.

[3] Interview with Norma Stevens, April 18, 2008.

[4] Interview with Donatella Versace, April 7, 2008.

[5] Interview with Donatella Versace, April 7, 2008.

[6] Horyn, "La Bella Donatella," p. 158.

[7] Collins, "Mondo Donatella," p. 161.

[8] Ibid., p. 161.

[9] Interview with Donatella Versace, April 7, 2008.

[10] Interview with Joan Kaner, January 14, 2008.

[11] Horyn, "La Bella Donatella," p. 186.

[12] Interview with Antonio D'Amico, June 23, 2008.

[13] Sally Singer, "Coming Clean," *Vogue*, May 2005, p. 256.

[14] Guy Trebay, "Taking the Fall for Fashion," *New York Times*, September 29, 2005.

[15] Singer, "Coming Clean," p. 256.

[16] Ibid., p. 256.

[17] Interview with Antonio D'Amico, June 23, 2008.

Notes

[18] Singer, "Coming Clean," p. 256.

[19] Interview with Antonio D'Amico, June 23, 2008.

eleven: *Spoiled by Success*

[1] Interview with Bruce Orosz, May 8, 2008.

[2] Tom Austin, "Swelter," *Ocean Drive Magazine*, January 8, 1992.

[3] Bill Wisser, *South Beach: America's Riviera, Miami Beach, Florida* (New York: Arcade Publishing, 1995), pp. 16–22.

[4] Interview with Merle Weiss, May 7, 2008.

[5] Ibid.

[6] Interview with Enrico Fantini, January 10, 2008.

[7] Interview with J. Wallace Tutt III, May 11, 2008.

[8] Interview with J. Wallace Tutt III, January 2, 2008.

[9] Interview with Donatella Versace, December 15, 2008.

[10] Interview with Lee Schrager, May 10, 2008.

[11] Horyn, "La Bella Donatella," p. 188.

[12] Austin, "Swelter."

[13] Interview with Kevin Crawford, May 21, 2008.

[14] Lydia Martin, "In Two Decades, Miami Beach's Southernmost Square Mile Has Become a Big Draw with Art, Cuisine, Architecture and Nightlife," *Miami Herald*, July 15, 2007.

[15] Interview with Louis Canales, May 11, 2008.

[16] Miami Beach Police Department report, police interview, July 17, 1997.

[17] Gastel, *Il mito Versace*, p. 245.

[18] Interview with Kevin Crawford, May 21, 2008.

[19] Ibid.

[20] Ibid.

[21] Merle Ginsberg, "Donatella & Allegra," *Harper's Bazaar*, March 2007, p. 456.

[22] Levy, "Summer for the Sun Queen," p. 48.

[23] Daniela Fedi, "Basta Pettegolezzi, Noi Non Molliamo."

[24] Lee, "The Emperor of Dreams," p. 51.

[25] Agins, *End of Fashion*, p. 35.

[26] Interview with Franca Biagini, March 13, 2008.

[27] Interview with Ron Frasch, April 23, 2008.

[28] Overall sales figures include the sales rung up by franchisees, only a portion of which flowed directly to the house. In 1991, Versace's net sales were 270 billion lire ($150 million).

[29] Amy M. Spindler, "Gianni Versace, 50, the Designer Who Infused Fashion with Life and Art," *New York Times*, July 16, 1997.

Twelve *Conflict*

[1] Gastel, *Il mito Versace*, p. 191.

[2] Ibid., p. 140

[3] Teri Agins, "How Fallen Gucci Got Its Glamour Back," *Wall Street Journal*, January 27, 1999.

[4] Mirri, *It's Your Song*, p. 94.

[5] Lee, "The Emperor of Dreams," p. 42.

[6] Interview with Nora Macheda, March 18, 2008.

[7] Interview with Roberto Devorik, April 18, 2008.

[8] Roshan, "Surviving at the Top," p. 40.

[9] Interview with Angelo Azzena, April 8, 2008.

[10] Interview with Donatella Versace, December 15, 2008.

Thirteen *Murder*

[1] Interview with Franco Lussana, March 4, 2008.

[2] Mirri, *It's Your Song*, pp. 109–10.

[3] Gian Luigi Paracchini, "Faro' Lo Stilista Senza Copiare Gianni. Era Unico," *Corriere della Sera*, June 21, 1998.

[4] Interview with Franco Lussana, March 4, 2008.

[5] Maureen Orth, *Vulgar Favors: Andrew Cunanan, Gianni Versace, and the Largest Failed Manhunt in U.S. History* (New York: Dell, 1999), p. 416.

[6] Miami Beach Police Department report, case No. 97–24687. Statement given to police by Carlos Silva on July 15, 1997.

[7] Miami Beach Police Department report. Evidence/Inventory Log, 6979 Collins Ave, room 322, p. 5.

[8] Horyn, "The Murder on Ocean Drive."

[9] Pat Jordan, "Versace's Paradise: In a World of Pleasure, Murder Can Be the Most Powerful Memory," *Playboy*, December 1, 1997, p. 90.

[10] Miami Beach Police Department report. Statement given to police by Vivan C. Oliva on July 16, 1997.

[11] Interview with Frank Scottolini, May 14, 2008.

Notes

[12] Miami Beach Police Department report. Statement given by Brad (no last name given) to police on July 16, 1997, via MBPD's Crimestoppers tips phone line.

[13] Miami Beach Police Department report. Statement given by Mersiha Colakovic on July 24, 1997.

[14] Todd S. Purdum, "Stark Images of a Suspect Who Lived Fast and Loose," *New York Times*, July 17, 1997.

[15] Ibid.

[16] Ibid.

[17] Ibid.

[18] Mireya Navarro, "At End of Cunanan Manhunt, Suicide and Mystery," *New York Times*, July 25, 1997.

[19] Miami Beach Police Department report. Statement given by Mirian Hernandez on July 18, 1997.

[20] Miami Beach Police Department report. Statement given by Lazaro Quintana on July 15, 1997.

[21] Gastel, *Il mito Versace*, p. 246.

[22] Austin, "Swelter," *Ocean Drive Magazine*.

[23] Lizette Alvarez with Don Van Natta, Jr., "In the End, Cunanan Proved Neither Cunning Nor Brazen," *New York Times*, July 27, 1997.

[24] Interview with J. Wallace Tutt III, January 2, 2008.

[25] Orth, *Vulgar Favors*, p. 80.

[26] Ibid., p. 216.

[27] "An Industry Grieves," *Women's Wear Daily*, July 16, 1997, p. 7.

[28] Orth, *Vulgar Favors*, p. 468.

fourteen: *Understudy on the Stage*

[1] Interview with Brian Atwood, January 30, 2009.

[2] Interview with Santo Versace, February 12, 2009.

[3] Interview with Antonio D'Amico, February 9, 2009.

[4] Christopher Ciccone, *Life with My Sister Madonna* (London: Simon & Schuster, 2008), pp. 254–57.

[5] Chiara Di Beria, "Senza Gianni Ho Paura, Lui E' Insostituibile," *La Stampa*, October 1, 1997.

[6] Ibid.

[7] "Il Tributo degli altri Re alla Nuova Regina," *Corriere della Sera*, October 10, 1997.

[8] Di Beria, "Senza Gianni."

fifteen: *Inheritance and Loss*

[1] Interview with Anna Candela, September 16, 2008.

[2] Interview with Antonio D'Amico, February 9, 2009.

[3] Ibid.

[4] Mirri, *It's Your Song*, pp. 132–33.

[5] Naomi McElroy, "Kate Gives Versace Mourners a Wake-Up Call," *Sunday Mirror*, October 14, 2007.

sixteen: *Siblings at War*

[1] Ciccone, *Life with My Sister Madonna*, pp. 262–64.

[2] Amy M. Spindler, "In Paris Couture, the Spectacle's the Thing," *New York Times*, July 21, 1998.

[3] Ciccone, *Life with My Sister Madonna*, p. 265.

[4] Cathy Horyn, "Boatloads of Stars, but Ideas Are Elsewhere," *New York Times*, September 14, 1999.

[5] Interview with Lori Goldstein, April 23, 2008.

[6] Fabio Galvano, "Abiti, diamanti e tanti VIP alla grade festa organizzata per beneficenza da Donatella e Santo," *La Stampa*, June 11, 1999.

[7] Dana Thomas, *Deluxe: How Luxury Lost Its Luster* (London: Penguin, 2007), p. 9.

[8] Rupert Everett, *Red Carpets and Other Banana Skins* (London: Little, Brown, 2006), pp. 328–29.

[9] Ibid., p. 331.

seventeen: *Toward Ruin*

[1] "Lo and Behold," *Women's Wear Daily*, October 4, 2001, p. 7.

[2] Interview with Alan Rohwer, September 24, 2008.

[3] Ibid.

eighteen: *Breaking Down*

[1] Anamaria Wilson, "Versace Drums Up $620,000 at Bergdorf," *Women's Wear Daily*, April 16, 2003, p. 15.

[2] Interview with Ron Frasch, April 23, 2008.

[3] Singer, "Coming Clean," p. 275.

[4] Ibid., p. 257.

[5] Ibid., p. 257.

[6] Ibid., p. 275.

Notes

7 Ibid., p. 257.

8 Daniela Fedi, "Cocaina, Donatella Versace in Clinica. La Stilista E' Ricoverata per Disintossicarsi," *Il Giornale*, July 29, 2004.

9 Gian Marco Ansaloni, "Vicious Versace Sfila Lo Stile Savile Rock," *Milano Finanza*, June 29, 2004.

10 Singer, "Coming Clean," p. 257.

11 Maria Corbi, "Da Lady Diana e Donatella Versace alla new entry Afef, il principe gay del pop e tutte le sue donne," *La Stampa*, March 27, 2007.

12 Collins, "Mondo Donatella," p. 159.

13 Singer, "Coming Clean," p. 275.

14 Ibid., p. 275.

15 Ibid.

16 Levy, "Summer for the Sun Queen."

nineteen: *Recovery*

1 Amanda Kaiser, "Fendi's Next Phase: Scent, More Stores and the Great Wall," *Women's Wear Daily*, May 1, 2007, p. 4.

2 Interview with Giancarlo Di Risio, March 12, 2009.

3 Peter Howarth, "Prima Donna," *Observer Magazine*, March 11, 2007, p. 14.

4 Collins, "Mondo Donatella," p. 161.

5 Jenny Peters, "The Big Party: Gianni and Donatella Versace Honored with Rodeo Drive Walk of Style Award," www.FashionWireDaily.com, February 9, 2007.

6 Cathy Horyn, "At Versace, a Testament to Genius," *New York Times*, February 26, 2007.

7 Interview with Patrick Guadagno, April 1, 2009.

8 Interview with Ron Frasch, April 23, 2008.

9 Ginsberg, "Donatella & Allegra," p. 455.

twenty: *A New Beginning*

1 Collins, "Mondo Donatella," p. 163.

INDEX

Index

Index

Index

Index

About the Author

A native of Boston, Deborah Ball has been a business journalist in Europe for more than fifteen years. For twelve years, she has been a reporter for the *Wall Street Journal* in Milan, London, and Zurich, covering a wide variety of business, finance, and political topics. Between 1999 and 2002, she covered the European luxury-goods sector for the *Journal*. Ms. Ball currently lives between Italy and Switzerland with her husband, Fabrizio Mucci.

Printed in the United States
by Baker & Taylor Publisher Services